What
About E

The Ultimate Power
Lessons from a Near-Death Experience
How to Unlock Your Mind-Body-Soul Potential

"Wow – what a great book. If you are ready to turn on your Ultimate Power, read Ken's brilliant and illuminating book."
— Mark Victor Hansen, co-author,
Chicken Soup for the Soul series, New York Times #1 Bestseller

"Ken Vegotsky has written a GREAT book. A heroic book. He is the Viktor Frankl of our day. You will want to purchase many copies to give to those you love, those who are discouraged, those who need to rise again from adversity. Magnificent!"
— Dottie Walters, Walters International Speakers Bureau,
author of *Speak and Grow Rich*

"The Ultimate Power will be an inspiration to anyone who reads it. It is the story of turning challenges into opportunities to grow, and it is filled with a sense of humor to make it digestible."
— Cavett Roberts, Chairman Emeritus,
National Speakers Association.

Natural Remedies and Supplements
The All-in-One Guide to™

"...is a veritable naturopathic Bible." – The Post, newspaper

"...this book is a steal, and given the rising tide of consumer interest in the role of natural remedies and supplements to enhance well-being, it deserves its place in your library."
— Pat Young, reprinted from *Vitality* Magazine

The Tea Tree Oil Bible
Your Essential Guide for Health and Home Uses
Your First Aid Kit in a Bottle

"The Tea Tree Oil Bible is the definitive book on this essential oil."
— Michael Dean, President, Thursday Plantation,
Premier #1 grower and producer of tea tree oil world-wide.

the ALL-IN-ONE GUIDE to™ ADD & HYPER-ACTIVITY

Attention Deficit Disorder & Attention Deficit Hyperactivity Disorder

Dr. Elvis Ali, David Garshowitz,
Fred Hui, M.D., Harold N. Levinson, M.D.,
Michael Lyon, M.D., Dorothy Marshall

— plus a host of others including —

Stefan Ball, Kyle Brownell, Chip Dopson, Pam Floener,
Naomi Gold, Dr. George Grant, Marla Hauer, Jane Hersey,
Dr. Richard Lord, Nancy L. Morse, Selim Nakla, M.D.,
Aleks Radojcic, Michael Rae, Dr. Paul Richard Saunders,
Laurie Simmons, Michael O. Smith, M.D.,
Daniel Tamin, Dr. Lynda Thompson, Ken Vegotsky...

AGES Publications™
Niagara Falls, New York

ADD & Hyperactivity

The All-In-One Guide to™ Series
The Love Living & Live Loving® Series
The Love Living & Live Loving Health™ Series

Library of Congress Cataloging-in-Publication Data

The all-in-one guide to ADD & hyperactivity / Elvis Ali ... [et al].
    p. cm. — (The all-in-one guide to series) (The love living & live loving series ; v. 2)
Includes bibliographical references and index.
ISBN 1-886508-29-1
1. Attention-deficit hyperactivity disorder. 2. Attention-deficit hyperactivity disorder—
Alternative treatment. 3. Attention-deficit-disorder children. I. Title: All in one guide to
ADD & hyperactivity II. Ali, Elvis A. III. Series. IV. Series: The love living & live loving
series ; v. 2
    RJ506.H9 A584 2001
    616.85'89—dc21   00-048476
                                       CIP

Book Design by Inside Bestsellers Design Group™ 1 800 595-1955
http://www.800line.com/

Quantity discounted orders available for groups. Please make enquiries to
Bulk Sales Department: 1 888 545-0053, or E-Mail: ages@800line.com

Printing history 05 04 03 02 :** * 9 8 7 – first printing
Printed in Canada. Simultaneously released in the U.S.A. and Canada.

We dedicate this book...

To you, the reader.

To those who are seeking gentle and safe natural alternatives for health, healing and well-being.

To those women and men who are using the psychological transformational path outlined in *The Ultimate Power* for study groups, to enhance and change their lives. You are making a difference, each and every day.

To those who have discovered the powerful natural remedy in *The Tea Tree Oil Bible* and *The All-in-One Guide to™ Tea Tree Oil*.

To those who have used *Natural Remedies and Supplements: The All-in-One Guide to™* book, to discover the awesome power of self-health care, using the tools of naturally inclined healers, to enhance their lives and those of their loved ones, family and friends.

To Stephanie and Alan, the children who inspired this book.

"We vow each and every day, to share with you the miracles we have found in this greatest of gifts called life. Our mission is not to change the world but fine tune it for our children--- for all children."

– Elvis Ali, Stefan Ball, Kyle Brownell, Chip Dopson, Pam Floener, David Garshowitz, George Grant, Naomi Gold, Marla Hauer, Jane Hersey, Harold N. Levinson, Richard Lord, Michael Lyon, Dorothy Marshall, Nancy L. Morse, Selim Nakla, Aleks Radojcic, Michael Rae, Paul Richard Saunders, Laurie Simmons, Michael O. Smith, Daniel Tamin, Lynda Thompson, Ken Vegotsky

We acknowledge with thanks:

The medical, health care and numerous other professionals who made this book possible.

The permission to reprint the DSM IV from the *Diagnostic and Statistical Manual of Mental Disorders,* Fourth Edition, Copyright © 1994, American Psychiatric Association, and permission to reprint Chapter 25, Meditation of Cognitive Competencies for Students in Need: The Fuerstein Method, with acknowledgement of Presseisen, Barbara (editor), *Teaching for Intelligence: A Collection of Articles,* pp 305-318, Skylight Training and Publishing Inc., Arlington Heights, IL, 1999.

The principle editors, Naomi Gold and Ken Vegotsky, and all the authors involved who verified and checked the information in the book, plus those whose comments and help were critical to this project.

Alicia Agard and Aleksandra Trajkovio for their invaluable contribution to the chapter on drugs and interactions,

Celina Klee and Nancy Brown of the Upledger Institute for their help with compiling a list of complementary health care practitioners.

Aloe, John Latimer, Al Daniels, and the incredible design team at Inside BestSellers Design Group™.

Louis Alaimo, a friend and the best paver with integrity on this side of the world, whose support in so many ways made this and all the other books in the series possible.

Raymond Aaron and Sue Lacher of the Raymond Aaron Group, who are making a difference! Raymond et al. are also co-authors of 2 *Chicken Soup for the Soul* books.

The alternative and traditional print, radio and TV media, who support our efforts to make this a better world. We are forever thankful to these fine folks who started the ball rolling. Tony, Chris and Charlette of KSON, Deborah Ray and Tom Connolly of the Nationally Syndicated show *Here's To Your Health,* Jana & Ted Bart and Karlin Evins of the show *Beyond Reason* on the Bart Evins Broadcasting Co. Network, Greg Lanning and Dr. Joseph Michelli, of the *Wishing You Well Show* on the Business Radio Network, Kim Mason of *The Nightside Show* on 1010 AM, Willa and Bob McLean of *McLean & Company, Canada AM* and *Eye On Toronto, Concepts Magazine,* Tony Ricciuto of *The Niagara Falls Review,* Julia Woodford and Pat Young of *Vitality Magazines,* Susan Schwartz of *The Gazette,* Casey Korstanje of *The Spectator,* Tess Kalinowski of *The London Free Press,* Len Butcher & Dr. David Saul of *The Tribune,* Joanne Tedesco of *The Arizona Networking News,* Joe Mazza & Sabastion the Wonderdog of *The Joe Mazza Show* on Talk America. The support of Mark Victor Hansen, New York Times #1 co-author of the *Chicken Soup for the Soul series,* Brian Tracy author *Maximum Achievement,* Jerry Jenkins of *Independent Publisher Magazine and The Jenkins Group,* Barry Seltzer, Lawyer and author, Dr. Jonathon Siegel, Psychologist, Cavett Robert, Chairman Emeritus of the *National Speakers Association,* Hennie Bekker, *Juno Award Nominee,* Dr. Michael Greenwood, M.B.,B. Chir., Dip. Acup., C.C.F.P., F.R.S.A., co-author *Paradox and Healing,* Dottie Walters, President of Walters Speakers Bureaus International and author of *Speak & Grow Rich* and Victoria Sutherland of *Foreword Magazine.*

Dave, Nancy and Ian Christie, Mike Van Meter, Bill Hushion, Gretchen Edwards, Debbie Elvald, Robert Butt, Jules Beauregard, Lynne Ford, Lora Tamburri, Ed Deren, Joanne Micciola, Mark Field, Marilyn and Tom Ross, Jerry Jenkins, Barbara Cooper-Haas, Sam Siegel, Joe Schlue, Baye Taff, Rita Wilson, Roger Willbanks, Cheri Hutchison...

...along with a host of others, too numerous to list.

Preface

The All-In-One Guide to™ ADD and Hyperactivity takes your health and that of the children and adults with these conditions as seriously as you do. We share your interest in identifying the best products and methods for dealing with ADD and hyperactivity. We share your interest in safety and purity. We respect the power of an informed consumer, and this book works to create informed consumers. We are making a long-term commitment to natural health care in the twenty-first century. Use *The All-In-One Guide to™ Natural Remedies and Supplements'* list of Do's and Do not's for self-health care:

- Do talk to your pharmacist or health care provider about any supplement that may help you. If they do not respect and honor your right to know, then find professionals who do.

- Do read all labels carefully. Pay attention to warnings, side effects and contraindications.

- Do follow dosage instructions precisely, unless instructed to do so differently by your pharmacist or health care provider.

- Do listen to your body for signs of positive and negative effects, or the absence of effects, to a diet change, drug or supplement.

- Do consult your pharmacist or health care provider if you have any concerns or questions.

- Do not take natural remedies, supplements or drugs, in larger quantities than recommended, unless directed to do so by your pharmacist or health care provider.

- Do not take supplements or drugs for longer than directed.

- Do not assume natural remedies or supplements are substitutes for medications your health care provider has prescribed.

Be patient when using natural remedies, supplements, psychological and other complementary choices for health and healing. There is a difference between alleviating symptoms and healing—healing takes time. Alleviating symptoms may offer short-term relief, but result in the long-term use of medications to deal with the symptom or underlying problem.

The choices shared in this book nourish the body so that the body can function at an optimal level. When necessary, these remedies cause the appropriate healing response(s) in the body. The focus shifts toward long-term solutions that deal with the underlying cause of the conditions, and helps the body with effective and safer choices than are traditionally used by our society. It is said, "Today's wisdom becomes tomorrow's common sense."

The need for long-term solutions surrounds us every day. Increasing numbers of children and adults are being afflicted with attention deficit disorder, hyperactivity, autism, and other health-related problems that greatly affect our quality of life: polluted water and air; foods grown in soils depleted of the very substances—trace minerals and other ingredients—needed for sound bodies and minds; excessive stress, due to chemical, environmental, social and emotional pressures; and other factors too numerous to mention. These factors slowly erode and overwhelm our bodies' natural abilities to cope.

Ask an honest medical internist, and he or she will tell you the greatest health secret, generally unknown to the public, is that the body heals itself. Use the information provided in this book to tap into your body's wisdom to heal itself using the choices shared in this book today!

Publisher's Notes

The co-authors of this book have chosen to include the writings of lead-ing authorities in their areas of expertise. The principle contributor of a sec-tion or chapter is usually listed, along with his or her accreditations. Each chapter was reviewed by at least 3 of the co-authors to ensure high stan-dards and the integrity of the information being provided. In many cases, the co-authors have edited, added to or enhanced other contributors' efforts, yet have chosen not to point this out, giving credit where credit is due to that section's or chapter's principle author.

While some of these contributors are not listed on the cover or title page of the book, we honor them and their contributions where and when possi-ble throughout the book. A work of this nature required the direct and indi-rect contributions of hundreds of people worldwide. The Acknowledge-ments page is the usual place in which such people are noted, but we cannot stress enough how deeply their help was appreciated.

Our books are what we call, *Living Books*™, which means that as new and pertinent information becomes available, it will be included in future editions of *The All-in-One Guide to*™ series of books. This is the case with all books in *The All-in-One Guide to*™ series and *The Love Living and Live Loving*® series. It is said that "Today's philosophy or wisdom becomes tomorrow's common sense." For this reason, we exclude highly speculative information until sufficient data and/or studies are produced. This ensures we maintain the high level and quality of information contained in our books.

The drug, natural remedy and supplement information in this book is based on information from numerous resources. Please refer to the appendices and bibliography. While extensive effort was taken and due dili-gence was made to ensure the accuracy of this information, every action, interaction, adverse reaction, and precaution is not listed in this book. The information is given without any guarantees by the authors, contributors, consultants, and publisher, who all disclaim any liability, error or omission in connection with the use of this book.

The intention of *The All-in-One Guide to™ ADD and Hyperactivity* is for your use as a reference in the mutually beneficial and ongoing relationship between physician, patient and/or care giver in the vigilant and watchful management of the recipient's or patient's health care. It is not a replacement for a physician's professional decisions and judgment.

Use your copy of *The All-in-One Guide to™ ADD and Hyperactivity* as a reminder for any questions, concerns or matters that require discussion with your health-care provider. All readers are recommended to consult with their doctor, psychiatrist, naturally-oriented health-care provider, naturopath, pharmacist and/or medical professional before starting or ending the use of any drug, natural remedy, or supplement, or starting any form of self-health care treatment.

Generic and brand names listed herein represent the most frequently used products and may not be the only available products, since new developments and old options are constantly being created or reintroduced as our level of knowledge and awareness expands. Inclusion of a brand or generic name is not an endorsement of the item and/or product. If a name or product is not included in the text of this book, it does not signify a rejection or criticism of the name or product.

The publisher does not advocate, warrant or guarantee any product described in this book.

The publisher has not done any independent analysis in reference to the product information in the book.

Table of Contents

Antidepressants: Generic and (Brand) name(s)
- Bupropion (Wellbutrin, Wellbutrin SR, Zyban)
- Desipramine (Norpramin)
- Fluoxetine (Prozac)
- Imipramine (Tofranil, Tofranil-PM)
- Nortriptyline (Aventyl, Aventyl Pulvules, Pamelor)
- Paroxetine (Paxil)
- A discontinued safe option, Deaner

At-A-Glance Quick Reference™ Interaction Chart

Section Six
In Closing: The Law, Your Rights, and
How to Use This Book

Appendicies

Prologue
Our Purpose

This book is a labor of love. A journey that began over ten years ago.

It is the vision of a man who in his own words says, "My wondrous beautiful four year old daughter became learning disabled, seemingly overnight. This friendly creative child who taught me that love is in the air, and who loved people, suddenly lost all her friends. She struggled with the changes within, not understanding what was happening, becoming frustrated and then angry. Stubbornly she tried to exert control over the world around her, as if this would calm her world within.

School just worsened the situation, forcing conformity, not celebrating her uniqueness. It labeled and thereby invalidated her. This meant that the school no longer had to see themselves as a part of the problem, but could hold themselves apart from the problem. The system was no longer accountable in any way for the child's behavioral problems, which were a manifestation of deeper underlying problems. And yet this child still survived, her creativity grew, her spiritual growth accelerated, and she started blossoming in many ways.

The issue here is a society and world that devalues human life for the sake of power, control and money. By investing its energy and life force in money and business, the top priority—our children—ends up going to the bottom of the list. The teachers, who are on the front lines, desperately trying to deal with the devaluation of their jobs, are also relegated to the bottom of the pile.

The priority is and always should be the children. The only way our priorities will change is if we can give voice to the voiceless. Each individual can choose to take an active, caring and loving role toward fixing what is not working in the best interests of all who are being victimized by the upside down priorities many are buying into. Blame is not the issue here. Outcomes are the key. And you can make a difference, but first you must be given the information so you are empowered. This book is your wake-up call."

As Nietzsche once wrote, "That which does not kill me, makes me stronger."

And so it was and is with this man's child, who is now blossoming into a beautiful woman, well on the path to adulthood. This learning disabled child has become learning enabled. His vision, which was sparked by her pain, and which caused him to begin the long journey toward finding out answers, is now a success story – one we share with you now.

The purpose of this book is to build bridges by tearing down the walls between children, adults, health care providers, and those in society with vested interests in the labels and wealth that are to the detriment of optimal health and healing. These labels have been misused. Labels should not be used as an excuse to absolve ourselves of responsibility.

> "The journey
> of a thousand miles
> begins with the first step."
> — Ancient Chinese proverb.
>
> Congratulations,
> you have begun your journey.
> You are now on a path
> to success."
> — Ken Vegotsky,
> *The Ultimate Power*

You, the reader, are being given the information and tools necessary to heal and help others heal.

Today in America, over half of all bankruptcies are due to health-care expenses. In Canada, health-care costs are rarely the reason for bankruptcy, but vested interests control the flow of funds, thereby preventing those who want to choose freely the opportunity of doing so. Significant resources and money are used by school boards in America and Canada trying desperately to deal with the problem of learning disabilities. In both countries, there are those whose vested interests put wealth, power and control before the health and well-being of the children.

It is said, "The truth shall set you free." There is a price to pay for this truth—giving up the illusions you have, and moving from illusions of pain and fear to the reality of pleasure, peace, and eventually, serenity and freedom.

Many publishers simplify their books to a grade seven level of reading comprehension, (called "dumming down" in the book trade). We choose to give you the information in the way many health-care professionals require. You can use the safer and more effective choices before resorting to drugs and other methods which only offer temporary relief without safe long-term results. Included are methodologies health-care professionals require to help the attention deficit disordered (ADD), hyperactive, learning-disabled child or adult heal.

As surely as these words are being written, we can tell you that certain chapters in this book should qualify their authors for a Nobel Prize in medicine. But before that can happen, you will discover truths usually hidden from the public.

The first one is the greatest secret generally not known by the public: it is that all healing occurs from within. Just ask any honest medical internist. Wholesome food, health care products and empowering health-care providers nourish and honor this process by facilitating it. Some attempt to control the symptoms and do not deal with the underlying cause or causes. This book brings that out into the open, to help you in your search for superior self-health care options, thereby enabling you to be the guide in your learning disabled child's or adult's healing path.

There are those who take away your power by using catch-all phrases like, "It hasn't been scientifically proven," or "Maybe you did not read enough to your child." Sometimes this is deliberately done to manipulate people into steering clear of safer and gentler options or setting them up for further manipulation by using emotions such as guilt. By bringing this out into the open, we are giving you back your power.

We bring this into your conscious awareness so that you will not fall prey to these inappropriate methods of control. These methods, combined with the subtle blame games, serve to divert attention away from the real underlying cause or causes of the problem. The problems are not usually resolved with one quick fix, such as a drug which masks the symptoms, but by a series of small baby steps, leading to a successful outcome.

"The level of thinking needed to solve a problem, must be higher than that which created the problem."

— Albert Einstein

The answers are deceptively simple. Even if you do not fully understand them, give a copy of this book to your doctor, complementary health-care provider, teacher, and those you love who can benefit from it. Just as this man's journey began in pain, so shall it end in the pleasure of your success, which is your just reward. As the man who began this journey with his vision as an outgrowth of love, this book is here for one reason and one reason alone, "So all may be healed."

Section One

Overviews of
Leading Specialists' Successes
plus
Methods of Treatment
and
Complementary Choices

Physicians are not your healers:
they are but guides on your healing path.
The poor one manages illness.
The common one cures your impending illness.

The desirable healer is a listener who hears your
body's cry, your mind's cry, your spirit's cry
before you hear it, and so prevents illness.

When in crisis due to accident or uncommon acts of nature,
the best healer hears your heart- and soul-song, and
guides you upon your healing path and
through any crisis you may face.

For they know a truth, and it is The Truth
that all healing comes from within.

— Bahir Ben Ken, *The Prophet Revisited* by Ken Vegotsky

Thirty-Five Years and 35,000 Patients Later

Harold N. Levinson, M.D.

Groundbreaking work on ADD/ADHD and
Related Learning and Anxiety Disorders

Their Inner-Ear/Cerebellar-Vestibular Origins,
Understanding, and Treatment

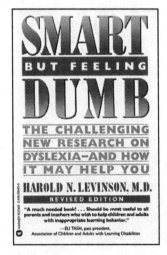

*Two roads diverged in the woods, and
I —, I took the one less traveled by,
and that has made all the difference.*

— Robert Frost

Introduction

Most readers will probably have heard of the terms ADD/ADHD as well as about the therapeutic effects of stimulant medications such as Ritalin. However, few, if any, may have come across the unique inner-ear and related cerebellar-vestibular (CV) insights into this syndrome as initially provided in *Total Concentration* (1990), as well as my follow-up research. As a result, the primary aim of this chapter is to summarize my three and a half decades of clinical research with ADHD and its related learning, mood, anxiety, and coordination disorders.

Utilizing two representative case presentations and commonsense reasoning, I will attempt to develop a comprehensive clinically-determined theory fully capable of explaining *all* the many and diverse symptoms and diagnostic/therapeutic facts characterizing this heretofore puzzling and complex appearing disorder. Indeed, I suspect that you all will then wonder: "How could such a clear and 'obvious' understanding have escaped recognition by all others—considering the many decades of combined efforts by scores of gifted researchers?" Indeed, you may paradoxically also be forced to wonder: "If indeed ADD/ADHD is a complex multifaceted and multidimensional learning, mood/anxiety, and balance/coordination/rhythmic syndrome, how could it have been traditionally viewed and defined as if it were only a pure and simple attention/activity impairment?"

Hopefully, the following pages will enable you to fully recognize the complex portrait of ADD/ADHD as well as the explanatory benefits provided by my inner-ear/cerebellar concepts. Only by listening carefully to the following clinical descriptions of "typical" ADD/ADHD cases, as well as countless others, will you begin to understand how this unique theory can completely explain all the symptoms, therapies, and diverse data found characterizing this previously puzzling disorder.

Understanding ADD/ADHD

To meaningfully understand ADD/ADHD, one must follow a road less traveled: Listen carefully to *all* the varied symptoms reported by many, many patients—and then attempt to find hidden common denominators and determining mechanisms. Only by doing so will the hidden face of this complex disorder materialize. This is not only the best way to understand ADD/ADHD—it's the only way. As a result, I will now introduce two cases of mine—typical of thousands and thousands of others. Pay careful attention to *all* their symptoms—not only those you and I were taught to expect. In other words, follow Huxley's ingeniously simple directive:

> *"Sit down before fact as a little child, be prepared to give up every preconceived notion, follow humbly wherever and to whatever abyss nature leads, or you shall learn nothing."*

To date, most researchers took another well traveled road—and so learned nothing significantly new for their enormous and dedicated efforts. They merely recognized only those symptoms previously believed to be part of ADD/ADHD, and then mistakenly attempted to define this rather complex disorder in an overly simplistic manner via a highly biased, tunnel vision perspective. In other words, most traditionalist experts saw only what they were looking for and then tried to define the total seen and "unseen" disorder with only 6 of the 14 parts they mistakenly believed to represent the complete portrait. Needless to say, this approach raised more questions and created more riddles than it solved.

By presenting you with typical cases, I hope to provide the vital data needed by readers to independently judge the value and validity of all my stated insights. In this way you can more objectively compare my inner-ear/CV concepts versus those espoused by other clinicians and theorists.

Two ADD Presentations — Laurel and Joey

In the two cases that follow, I have taken the liberty of italicizing all the so-called "atypical" and previously "non-recognized" symptoms of ADD/ADHD so that they might more readily be seen and eventually integrated into the total portrait of this disorder—a portrait never before clearly understood by those following the road most traveled.

Laurel

Laurel's mother describes her daughter's ADHD symptoms as follows:

"Laurel, now age seven, has always been a very active, restless, and fidgety child. She never liked or needed much sleep, even as a newborn infant. Naps were out of the question. Many nights we succeeded in lulling her to sleep only by rocking her in a swing. However, if we then tried to place her in a crib, she would invariably awaken and we'd be back to square one. Strange! But it seemed she needed motion to relax sufficiently enough to sleep. As she grew slightly older, it didn't matter how early we put her to bed, or how many stories we read to her. She wouldn't or couldn't fall asleep until nine or ten at night. At times, she even rocked herself to sleep, but it was always very, very late. It's like she tried to fall asleep and just couldn't. It's not like she wouldn't, as many tried to tell us.

"No matter how late she fell asleep, Laurel was up and ready to run by seven o'clock on weekdays. So it was never a case of staying up late and sleeping in late. This pattern has continued until the present day. Only recently has she begun to sleep in a little later on weekends. And that's only until around eight.

"She's never still. Even when she's asleep, some part of her body is always moving. I've questioned her pediatrician about this. All he said was, 'she is just a restless sleeper.' However, watching her sleeping in motion, it seems impossible for her to be getting any rest.

"Laurel has boundless energy. As a result, she has to be involved in numerous events throughout the day. Even after a major activity which leaves her peers worn out, she wants to know (and is ready for) 'What's next?' A good word to describe her is 'scattered.' She goes from one thing to the next thing at lightning speeds. But Laurel can't stick with anything long enough to complete it. As a result, many things she does remain incomplete, disorganized, and messy. Either she is forced to race through everything, leaving her no time to finish, and/or she gets too distracted and forgets what she was just doing or thinking a moment before.

"Laurel began to show signs of unpredictable behavior as an infant.

Rapidly changing mood swings emerged which included tantrums and severe acting-out behaviors. She's always been a very demanding child and requires constant attention. Were it not for our continuous supervision, Laurel and things around her—including her siblings—would rapidly deteriorate into bedlam and chaos.

"When I explained Laurel's mood swings to Dr. K., a clinical psychologist, she recommended a referral to a pediatric neurologist. Interestingly, she noted none of the mood swings that I had reported but did observe a definite restlessness about her that suggested a mild hyperactivity. The neurologist felt she probably had ADD, but not severely enough to warrant medication. However, Laurel needs something to calm her down—and to help her concentrate! Besides, she was a lot calmer in his presence than in mine or even the teacher's. In fact, when I now think logically about all his comments, Laurel's functioning was minimal and her disorder was severe. In addition, the neurologist also noted a *delay in her fine-motor coordination*. But he didn't feel this was medically significant at this time, either. It may not have been significant to him, but *it certainly affected the way Laurel read and wrote. For example, whenever she tried to read, she kept losing her place and needed a finger or a marker. And her writing was completely atrocious—unrecognizable. It's as if she had no control over the pencil or the angles and directions her writing was supposed to go. She was also accident-prone.* Not only because she was active and impulsive, but because *she was really, really, klutzy.* When I think back over her development, it appears very easy to understand that her *poor coordination corresponded with difficulties that she had with buttoning and zippering and even attempting to hold a pencil in a normal way, rather than the awkward grasp she still maintains.* In any event, the neurologist suggested a sleep EEG. This turned out to be an awake EEG because the fifty milligrams of *Benadryl* given her did not put her to sleep. Her EEG results were normal. However, *the medication calmed her down significantly and she was more alert and less distracted than ever before.*

"Shortly thereafter, we took Laurel to an optometrist for vision therapy. *He also noted a definite eye/hand fine-motor coordination problem* as well as *difficulty distinguishing right from left.*

"Since Laurel started school, I have noticed definite and increasing *problems with reading, writing, spelling, and organizational skills.* These problems led me to read up on *learning disabilities.* And when I discussed all these many problems with Laurel's school psychologist, she agreed with me that *Laurel was dyslexic,* but did not feel the case was severe enough to be overly concerned. But I am! When I finally realized and understood the nature of all of Laurel's symptoms as well as her response to Benadryl, I decided to consult with you!

"In the meantime, we even had her fitted with *colored lenses. She*

*claimed to see the letters and words more clearly, and some decrease in rever-
sals and word movement occurred."*

Some Interesting Questions

Is Laurel's ADD/ADHD atypical in that it is mixed or compounded
with typical dyslexic/LD symptoms affecting reading, writing, spelling,
direction, as well as balance/coordination/organization signs? Is it an accident that Benadryl, an antihistamine with inner-ear-enhancing potency,
calmed Laurel down while enhancing her alertness and minimizing her distractibility—an effect often expected from stimulants?

Joey

Perhaps the description of another "obvious" child with ADHD named
Joey might help clarify both the expected and unexpected symptoms characterizing this disorder. As you will soon understand, any valid and reliable
definition of ADHD must include all of its symptoms—the typically recognized as well as the typically unrecognized. As before, I will italicize and thus
highlight only the reported typically unrecognized dyslexic, mood/anxiety
and balance/coordination/rhythmic difficulties found to be part and parcel
of this syndrome.

Joey is a six-year old who was brought to me by his father for "extreme
restlessness and distractibility." He seemed foggy and preoccupied and
found it difficult to maintain eye contact. In fact, he appeared unable to concentrate when looking and thinking or speaking at the same time. School
discipline and restraints bothered him no end. Indeed, the only times he was
quiet were when he periodically came home spent or burned-out. When he
was controlled at school, he was wild at home. And no two days were the
same, although the overall pattern was similar. Sometimes he would bounce
around from hyper- to underactive in the same day. Most of the time, these
variations would occur at intervals of several days.

Joey was short and stocky—strong, *but clumsy*. As a result he found it
difficult to run off his energy without *tripping or falling. Speech functioning
was delayed and evidence of articulation problems were still apparent.* In
fact, he was too impatient and lacked the persistence to complete sentences
and thoughts. Were it not for an intelligent glint in his eyes and facial
expression, one might have thought Joey's IQ to be below average, especially
as he also evidenced severe *learning disabilities in school affecting reading,
writing, spelling, math, memory, grammar, and sense of direction and time.*

Although Joey's mother was greatly concerned about his impaired overall functioning, his father seemed quite confident—even overconfident. "I
used to be just like him, perhaps worse. And now I'm practicing urology.

The only thing different about me was that I was never fearful. Joey *is fearful of heights*—he was always that way, since he was an infant. Bouncing him up and down terrified him. And he would even get *motion sick, too! Stairs terrify him*, especially going down. Sometimes he just slides his way from step to step on his backside. And see-through steps are the worst for him. The same is true with *escalators. He panics going down them.* And his nights have been terrible since infancy. He has had *night terrors* since birth. And sometimes I think he is *afraid of strangers* and *has day terrors* as well.

Some Additional Clinical Considerations

Are the dyslexia/LD, speech, anxiety and balance/coordination, psychosomatic (motion-sickness) symptoms characterizing Joey's ADD/ADHD part and parcel of one overall syndrome caused by one common denominator? Or are those separately named "disorders" or groups of symptoms linked to ADHD by chance and thus derived from separate origins?

The Total ADD/ADHD Syndrome

The neurophysiological examination of more than 35,000 children and adults like Laurel and Joey have revealed that:

- More than 96% of children and adults with ADD/ADHD examined neurophysiologically indicate balance/coordination/rhythmic signs and symptoms diagnostic of only inner-ear/CV dysfunction.

- Over 90% of individuals with typical symptoms of ADD/ADHD also evidence associated dyslexic/LD, mood/anxiety as well as balance/coordination/rhythmic and psychosomatic (headaches, dizziness, motion-sickness, tinnitus [ear buzzing]) symptoms.

- Over 90% of patients referred with a primary diagnosis of dyslexia/LD or Anxiety Disorder manifest significant degrees of overlapping or associated symptoms of ADD/ADHD and balance/coordination/rhythmic disturbances.

Only inner-ear/CV mechanisms can explain *all* the signs and symptoms characterizing ADD/ADHD, dyslexia/LD, mood/anxiety, psychosomatic and balance/coordination/rhythmic disorders.

Last but not least, all the stimulant medications helpful for ADD/ADHD and all the anti-anxiety/antidepressant medications were shown by NASA-related research to have antimotion-sickness potency. Since the antimotion-sickness antihistamines were shown by my research to be helpful for all the dyslexia/LD, psychosomatic and balance/coordination/rhythmic symptoms as well as for ADD/ADHD and mood/anxiety disorders—it appears reasonable to view all these diverse groups of medications as inner-ear/CV-enhancers.

Considering all the above insights, it appears reasonable to assume and even conclude that ADD/ADHD and related learning and mood/anxiety disorders are part and parcel of one syndrome resulting from one and the same inner-ear/CV dysfunction. Clearly, the diverse overlapping symptoms characterizing individuals and groups with ADD/ADHD will depend on the specific pattern and degree of primary CV mechanisms impaired, their secondary connections to various CNS processors (i.e., frontal lobe, parietal lobe, occipital lobe, etc.), as well as the ability for CNS compensation.

In summary, the total ADD/ADHD syndrome will comprise an additional group of hundreds of typically unrecognized symptoms affecting 13 major areas of non-concentration/activity dysfunctioning. These dysfunctioning groups include: *Reading, Writing, Spelling, Mathematics, Memory, Direction, Time, Speech, Grammar, Balance and coordination, Phobias and related mental and behavioral disorders, Psychosomatics, Self-esteem and body image.*

The Traditionally Recognized and Accepted Symptoms and Definition of ADD/ADHD

For the typically recognized symptoms of ADD/ADHD, readers are referred to pages 78-95 in the DSM IV manual, Attention-Deficit/Hyperactivity Disorder, as well as the summary in this book on pages 33-35. According to the DSM IV criteria, a diagnosis of Attention-Deficit/Hyperactivity Disorder is made statistically. One must have:

- 6 or more of 14 attention deficit symptoms lasting more than 6 months, and/or
- 6 or more of 14 hyperactivity-impulsivity symptoms dating back before age 7.

A New Classification of ADD

Although the DSM IV definition of Attention-Deficit/Hyperactivity Disorder has significant research value insofar as the need for standardization to facilitate comparison of diverse data derived from similar samples, it has major clinical drawbacks. Thus, for example, as any clinician knows, just about all medical disorders occur in mild, moderate, severe, and even compensated (clinically unrecognizable) forms. ADHD is no exception to this rule. According to my clinical experience, individuals may have only 1,2,3,4, etc. symptoms – and still have ADHD, irregardless of the DSM IV criteria. Indeed, the prior DSM III version required 8 of 14 symptoms for a "sanctioned" definition. I have little doubt that future DSM changes will recognize the above stated clinical reality. Moreover, the response to medications of individuals with ADHD having "6 or more symptoms" and "less than 6 symptoms" are identical – clearly suggesting that the DSM IV statistically determined diagnostic cut-off is "artificial" and deprives the vast majority with this disorder of an accurate diagnosis and meaningful treatment.

Since similar appearing and even overlapping symptoms of ADD and hyperactivity may stem from differing origins, it seemed reasonable to devise a diagnostic classification based on determining mechanisms rather than merely the number of symptoms present. As a result of such a classification, each unique determining mechanism and corresponding symptom can be specifically isolated and more effectively treated. By contrast, the DSM IV "diagnosis by the numbers" masks any such clarification, since all the differing underlying mechanisms and corresponding overlapping symptoms are statistically lumped together and appear as if one.

Eventually my research efforts recognized *four* primary types of concentration disorders (CD) and *one* secondary type based on mechanisms of origin rather than on descriptions of the symptomatic fall-out. According to this new classification:

- *Type I CD* is due to realistic emotional trauma.
- *Type II CD* is due to unconscious neurotic conflicts.
- *Type III CD, or ADD,* is due to primary neurophysiological and/or neurotransmitter dysfunction of the cerebellar-vestibular system (CVS), or inner-ear, as well as interconnected circuits of the alerting and concentration modular centers.
- *Type IV CD, or ADD,* is due to a primary non-CVS neurophysiological and/or neurotransmitter dysfunction of the reticular activating and concentration modulating systems of the brain, perhaps with secondary or associated involvement of higher centers as well as the inner-ear. This disorder may account for those with extremely severe and pervasive symptoms and tends to have a poorer prognosis than Type III ADD.
- *Type V2 CD* is due to the secondary effects of "energy drain" resulting from a variety of conditions such as anemia, or metabolic or chemical disturbances.

As a result of this classification, all patients and all symptoms can be clearly defined in terms of their specific and even overlapping origins. Now all symptoms, depending on their respective origin, can be more effectively treated. In other words, all concentration-related symptoms can be more easily understood; the mild, the severe, and even the transient and reversible normal Freudian-like slips of functioning that periodically affect us all.

Needless to say, a similar classification holds true for hyperactivity and impulsivity as well.

Explaining All the Symptoms — Ten Simple Mechanisms

In order to readily explain all the typically recognized and previously unrecognized symptoms comprising the total ADD/ADHD syndrome, I was led to condense all the many and varied inner-ear/CV mechanisms so that *ten* might be used for explanatory purposes.

1. The inner-ear acts like a guided-missile's computer system — guiding our eyes, hands, feet, and various mental and physical functions in space and time.

2. The inner-ear system also acts like the vertical and horizontal holds on a television set. It fine-tunes all motor (voluntary and involuntary) responses leaving the brain and all sensory responses coming into the brain.

3. The inner-ear is a three-dimensional compass system. It reflexively tells us spatial relationships such as right and left, up and down, and front and back.

4. The inner-ear serves as a timing mechanism, setting rhythms to motor tasks.

5. The inner-ear acts as a dynamic filter — significantly blocking-out maladaptive sensory-motor and mental backgrounds.

6. Integration of sensory-motor functioning is also inner-ear related.

7. The inner-ear, via its connection to various mood, anxiety, motor-energy, and autonomic nervous system centers of the brain, modulates these and various other functions.

8. The inner-ear serves as a gyroscope for the brain.

9. The inner-ear processes tone and gravity signals.

10. The inner-ear was also assumed to facilitate the processing of starting and stopping functions.

Because these mechanisms are thoroughly discussed in my other works (*Total Concentration* [1990], *Phobia Free* [1986], *Smart But Feeling Dumb* [Revised 1994], *A Scientific Watergate – Dyslexia* [1994]), I will merely use three of them here to highlight their explanatory capabilities: *Inhibition, Filtering, Modulation (Fine Tuning)*.

Hyperactivity/Impulsivity – can be explained if we merely assume an impaired *inhibitory* or braking mechanism. Thus, for example, a difficulty in properly braking the activity center of the CNS may lead to abnormalities varying from hypoactivity to hyperactivity and variable fluctuations thereof. Similarly, difficulties with controlling or *inhibiting* action—mental and/or physical—will lead to impulsive verbal and/or motor events.

Distractibility – can be explained by a dysfunctioning in background *filtering* for visual, acoustic, tactile, smell, and even internal physical and mental/emotional stimuli. It's as if there were "holes" in our filtering system allowing "leakage" of excessive internal and/or external stimuli that otherwise would have been screened-out.

Impaired Concentration – results when signal scrambling or impaired *fine-tuning and modulation* of sensory-input signals trigger secondary processing difficulties and avoidance. *Improper modulation* of the reticular activating system also results in faulty arousal which is too little, inconsistent and/or too persistent—the latter contributing to overfocusing, perseveration of thoughts and actions, as well as insomnia and other sleep disturbances.

Diagnosing CV Dysfunction — and Type III or CV-Determined ADD/ADHD

Because over 90% of individuals manifesting symptoms of ADD/ADHD evidence CV dysfunction, testing is aimed at highlighting or diagnosing this neurophysiologically determined difficulty. Since the CV testing techniques are discussed in my other works, I will list them here. These tests include: *Optokinetic Tests, Electronystagmography (ENG), Neurological Testing, Posturography (Balance) Testing, and Bender Gestalt & Goodenough Figure Drawings.*

For a diagnosis of CV-based or Type III ADD/ADHD to be made, both CV signs and symptoms and determining mechanisms must be present. As noted, various contributing or types of ADD mechanisms may co-exist, and thus, their differentiation and selective treatment are essential. Once again, these specifics may be found within the pages of *Total Concentration* (1990).

Theories of ADD/ADHD

To date, there are almost as many theories of ADD/ADHD as there are experts (including the theory that this disorder does not exist as a clinical entity). As with the diverse theories of dyslexia and anxiety disorders, the value and validity of any conceptualization rests entirely on its ability to encompass and explain all other theories, as well as all the data and variations characterizing the corresponding disorder, while leading to new and unexpected discoveries.

Since the CV system is a *fine tuner, filter, inhibitor*, etc. to the brain, it can readily explain all the concentration/distractibility/activity symptoms characterizing ADD/ADHD as well as the associated dyslexic/LD, and mood/anxiety and balance/coordination/rhythmic symptoms and all their variations. By virtue of differences in degrees of signal-scrambling and compensation, it is even easy for the CV theory to explain the "non-existent" theory of ADD/ADHD.

Before leaving this topic, I will quickly note how CV-determined poor eye and hand coordination can explain the typical visual fixation and tracking reading and dysgraphic writing symptoms characterizing dyslexics. And the reported speech-based symptoms can be similarly understood. Additionally, poor CV-determined balance and coordination can readily explain fears of falling and height phobias whereas inner-ear impaired motion processing may trigger fears of moving elevators, escalators, trains, planes, buses and even walking.

Treatment

By understanding the specific CV-related mechanisms triggering all the many and varied symptoms characterizing ADD/ADHD, it is now possible to obtain a greater than 75-85% success rate by using only CV-enhancing medications. As is well known, the CV-enhancing stimulant medications tend to significantly improve the typically recognized concentration/activity sector of the total ADD/ADHD portrait and panorama. By contrast, the CV-enhancing antimotion-sickness antihistamines and nutrients tend to more significantly improve the "typically unrecognized" dyslexic/LD sector. Since both groups of medications have synergistic and overlapping effects, the combined use of these differently named CV-enhancing medication groups offers most patients the best possible chance of the best medication-based improvements.

Having treated more than 35,000 children and adults over the past three and a half decades, I can assure all readers that this type of medical treatment can work well—and without risk. However, one must know how to properly "drive" the medication program, just as one needs to know how to safely drive a car, boat, plane, etc. By using very small doses and avoiding all side effects, we can reduce the negative risks to almost zero, while obtaining rapid and often dramatic improvements in a wide range of *all* the symptoms characterizing this previously mystifying disorder. By contrast, the risk of non-treatment is significant.

Since a wide range of anti-anxiety and antidepressant medications were also shown by NASA-related research to be CV-enhancers, it is no wonder that these and other groups of medications can often be helpful "team mates." Moreover, by facilitating normal and even above average signal transmission and processing, it is possible for a wide range of nutrients to further maximize the benefits this type of therapy can offer.

Clearly, the greater one's comprehension of the mechanisms determining ADD/ADHD, the more flexibility a clinician has in designing and utilizing overlapping helpful non-medical treatment modalities. Thus behavior modification, biofeedback, various nutritional supplements, and avoidance of neurotoxic substances, etc. can be significantly helpful—especially when combined with the previously described medical approach. One can often assume that most reported helpful therapies indeed help. Our aim as therapists is to discern clinically how and how much each therapy works so that the best possible combined or "team approach" can be developed and implemented per patient.

New and Unexpected Discoveries

As noted above, a valid theory invariably leads to new and unique insights. Accordingly, my research led me to recognize that the inner-ear/CV system often plays a hidden co-existing minor role in such major disorders as mental retardation, cerebral palsy, autism, pervasive developmental delay, schizophrenia, etc. Thus by treating the CV component mixed-in the above disorders with CV-enhancers, there often results significant improvement, although the primary cause and effect of the major impairment persists. Needless to say, any improvement in a major disorder —however minor—is significant, especially to suffering individuals and all those interested in helping them.

Summary

As noted, the aim of this chapter was to provide readers with new and unique insights into the inner-ear/CV basis of ADD/ADHD and related learning/mood/anxiety disorders. Since this content is highly summarized, it was only possible to skim its surface. Were each of the subtitles properly expanded, you would more readily grasp the diagnostic/therapeutic benefits of the CV-based formulations of ADD/ADHD versus those contained within DSM IV and most other texts. Indeed, the CV concepts of ADD/ADHD are sufficient to include and integrate all the traditional and even non-traditional ideas and reported data while formulating a scientifically holistic and meaningful treatment program—ensuring that each and every individual with ADD/ADHD can maximize his or her potential and achievement.

In conclusion, I hope this chapter serves as a catalyst for all individuals —especially therapists—interested in understanding and helping patients with this previously mystifying and oversimplified disorder. Clearly, a synergy is created when all disciplines can be united under a common theoretical format. Hopefully, this CV-based content will facilitate this synergy.

Publisher's Note

For 35 years, Harold N. Levinson, M.D., has been improving the quality of life for thousands of people with ADD, hyperactivity, dyslexia, and other disabilities.

The medical-pharamaceutical establishment labeled him a "heretic," along with many other unflattering comments and labels. They shunned his insightful methods, which have now produced what they would call "35,000 allegorical examples" lacking scientific credence. Numerous scientific studies exist, substantiating the concepts and therapeutic approaches of Harold N. Levinson, M.D., for ADD, hyperactivity, dyslexia and related learning disabilities. They validate his work and draw to your attention the importance of becoming well enough informed to decide for yourself.

Selecting what works best—which approaches may be the safest and most effective, which tools to use to deal with these conditions—involves many personal and practical decisions only you can make. We urge you to check the bibliography at the back of this book to discover references that will help you become better informed and able to work with your physician or qualified health care professional, to establish the foundation of logic and select the most appropriate approaches and tools.

We, too, use this foundation of logic to help you help yourself. We share with you some methods, natural choices and techniques that may seem unusual at first, but history may prove to be valid.

How many more men, women and children could have been saved from years of unnecessary pain if all health care providers approached health and healing with an open heart and mind? In Chapter 2, you will be treated to Dr. Michael Lyon's brilliant leading edge information on "The New Science of Functional Medicine." You will discover each chapter is basically self-contained, like a solid summary of a book on each subject, except they are pared down to the bare bones, giving you what you need to know now. These are excellent starting points for discovering self-health care approaches and options you may have never heard about before.

The DSM IV* Diagnostic Criteria

I would like to include the typically recognized ADD/ADHD symptoms included within the DSM IV here so that readers may clearly understand the symptoms needed for a traditionally accepted definition.

---

* Reprinted with permission from the *Diagnostic and Statistical Manual of Mental Disorders,* Fourth Edition, Copyright © 1994, American Psychiatric Association.

Diagnostic Criteria for Attention-Deficit/Hyperactivity Disorder

A. Either 1) or 2)

    1) Six (or more) of the following symptoms of **inattention** have persisted for at least 6 months to a degree that is maladaptive and inconsistent with developmental level:

    Inattention

    a) Often fails to give close attention to details or makes careless mistakes in schoolwork, work, or other activities.

    b) Often has difficulty sustaining attention in tasks or play activities.

    c) Often does not seem to listen when spoken to directly.

    d) Often does not follow through on instructions and fails to finish schoolwork, chores, or duties in the workplace (due to oppositional behavior or failure to understand instructions).

    e) Often has difficulty organizing tasks and activities.

    f) Often avoids, dislikes, or is reluctant to engage in tasks that require sustained mental effort (such as schoolwork or homework).

    g) Often loses things necessary for tasks or activities (e.g., toys, school assignments, pencils, books or tools).

    h) Is often easily distracted by extraneous stimuli.

    i) Is often forgetful in daily activities

    2) Six (or more) of the following symptoms of **hyperactivity-impulsivity** have been persisted for at least 6 months to a degree that is maladaptive and inconsistent with developmental level.

    Hyperactivity

    a) Often fidgets with hands or feet or squirms in seat.

    b) Often leaves seat in classroom or in other situations in which remaining seated is expected.

    c) Often runs about or climbs excessively in situations in which it is inappropriate (in adolescents or adults, may be limited to subjective feelings of restlessness).

    d) Often has difficulty playing or engaging in leisure activities quietly.

    e) Is often "on the go" or often acts as if "driven by a motor."

    f) Often talks excessively.

    Impulsivity

    g) Often blurts out answers before questions have been completed.

    h) Often has difficulty awaiting turn.

    i) Often interrupts or intrudes on others (e.g., butts into conversations or games).

- B. Some hyperactive-impulsive or inattentive symptoms that caused impairment were present before age 7 years.
- C. Some impairment from the symptoms is present in two or more settings (e.g., at school [or work] and at home).
  D. There must be clear evidence of clinically significant impairment in social, academic, or occupational functioning
  E. The symptoms do not occur exclusively during the course of a Pervasive Developmental Disorder, Schizophrenia, or other Psychotic Disorder and are not better accounted for by another mental disorder (e.g., Mood Disorder, Anxiety Disorder, Dissociative Disorder, or a Personality Disorder).

Code based on type:

314.01 Attention-Deficit/Hyperactivity Disorder, Combined Type: if both Criteria A1 and A2 are met for the past 6 months.

314.00 Attention-Deficit/Hyperactivity Disorder, Predominantly Inattentive Type: if Criterion A1 is met but Criterion A2 I not met for the past 6 months.

314.01 Attention-Deficit/Hyperactivity Disorder, Predominantly Hyperactive-Impulsive Type: if Criterion A2 is met but Criterion A1 is not met for the past months

314.90 Attention-Deficit/Hyperactivity Disorder, Not Otherwise Specified: This category is for disorders with prominent symptoms of inattention or hyperactivity-impulsivity that do not meet criteria for Attention-Deficit/Hyperactivity Disorder.

Coding note:
For individuals (especially adolescents and adults) who currently have symptoms that no longer meet full criteria, "In Partial Remission" should be specified.

Healing the Hyperactive Brain Through the New Science of Functional Medicine

Dr. Michael R. Lyon, M.D., B.Sc.
Director of Research and Education
Oceanside Functional Medicine Research Institute

Basic Principles of Functional Medicine

Functional Medicine is not a new medical specialty. In fact, Functional Medicine is practiced by a wide range of health-care professionals and can be considered, in its most basic form, a medical philosophy or an intellectual method which uses important principles as a guide in the assessment and treatment of patients. Most medical treatments are considered satisfactory if they simply reduce or eliminate the symptoms of a disease, or even just alter the results of a laboratory test. In many instances, little consideration is given for the overall quality of patients' lives or their ability to function as productive members of society.

In contrast, Functional Medicine is defined as patient-centered, science-based health care that identifies and addresses underlying biochemical, physiological, environmental and psychological factors to reverse disease progression and enhance vitality. Rather than depending on single, powerful treatments such as drugs or surgery, Functional Medicine relies more upon intelligent and individualized combinations of treatments or protocols.

Getting to the Root of the Problem

When dealing with complex, multi-factorial conditions such as Attention Deficit Hyperactivity Disorder (ADHD), a healthcare provider versed in the principles of a Functional Medicine practitioner will approach the patient in an organized, systematic fashion. This process begins by a thorough historical interview and physical examination and is often followed by selected laboratory tests to help better define the set of problems unique to that individual. In a sense, the practitioner is a skilled detective in search of clues to piece together the mystery of why that individual patient suffers from his or her particular set of signs and symptoms. To those practicing Functional Medicine, it is not sufficient to randomly prescribe a treatment for ADHD.

Antecedents, Triggers, Mediators

The Functional Medicine practitioner begins to assemble an orderly list of problems suspected to be at the heart of ADHD in that particular patient. In most cases, ADHD is multifactorial, that is, it is the result of a collection of underlying medical problems which have additive effects and may lead to ADHD symptoms. This problem list is divided into antecedents, triggers and mediators, any of which can lead to the signs and symptoms of ADHD.

Antecedents are risk factors which precede the onset of symptoms and which predispose the individual to the development of ADHD. These risk factors often begin at conception, during pregnancy or during infancy and early childhood. Common antecedents might include such things as genetic factors, environmental toxins, head injury or stresses within the family. In essence, antecedents set the stage for physical imbalances and internal disorders by weakening a person's basic physiological foundation.

As well, the Functional Medicine practitioner begins to consider the triggers present within each individual with ADHD. Triggers are physical or biochemical problems arising out of the weakened or susceptible physiology in a person with various antecedents that have been exerting stressful influences upon organ systems, cells, or molecules. Common triggers might include such things as food allergies, intestinal parasites, or chronic infections. In general, triggers are more likely to occur in an individual who already has certain antecedents. For example, food allergies (trigger) are much more common if a person has a genetic predisposition to allergies (antecedent).

These triggers, in turn, lead to imbalances of other critical substances known as mediators. Mediators are those physical factors which lead to or mediate the actual signs and symptoms of the disorder. The disturbed mediators in ADHD are primarily brain neurotransmitters such as dopamine, serotonin, and norepinephrine. Imbalance in these biochemical mediators then lead to the signs and symptoms of ADHD.

The search for antecedents, triggers, and mediators can involve repeated visits, sophisticated laboratory testing and extensive patient education. However, when these critical underlying factors are identified and dealt with effectively, the results are often extraordinary and the long-term prognosis for the ADHD patient may be greatly improved. Overall, this approach relies far less on symptom suppressing drugs and instead relies more on safe, natural therapies to address the underlying causes of the disorder.

Assessing The Patient With ADHD

In Functional Medicine, the primary goal is not to simply make the diagnosis of ADHD and then prescribe an appropriate treatment based solely on this diagnosis. Although this approach (often referred to as the "disease-centered approach") is appropriate for certain diseases, it does not address the vast individual differences among patients with complex conditions such as ADHD.

It is becoming quite clear that the disease-centered approach lacks effectiveness in the management of many chronic conditions. Not every human ailment can be placed neatly into a classification system, which then automatically dictates an appropriate method of treatment. For example, ADHD is not a specific disease "entity" with a single, identifiable cause that needs to be poisoned, removed or suppressed.

The disease-centered approach often fails to appreciate that certain conditions like this one are an expression of symptoms resulting from a collection of underlying medical problems exerting their effects upon a highly unique individual. In fact, because ADHD cannot be neatly classified as a distinct disease entity by specific and objective diagnostic tests, there are still some mental health authorities who question whether or not it actually exists at all! Certainly these disease-centered experts have not grown up with ADHD nor have they experienced what it is like to raise a child with this very real condition.

In a disease-centered approach, it is common for the practitioner to make a rapid diagnosis followed by a specific prescription. Although this makes for quick office visits, it often leaves the needs of the patient unmet. This is certainly a common occurrence in the treatment of ADHD. In many cases, the school requests that a child be evaluated for ADHD and then he or she is seen by a pediatrician over a few brief visits. Various questions are asked and perhaps a questionnaire or two is administered until a "conclusive diagnosis" is made. Once the "disease" has been properly identified and classified as ADHD, a prescription for Ritalin® or Dexedrine® is often given. The child is then seen on follow-up and if his or her behavior has improved, the treatment is considered a success. If the child's behavior has not improved, either the dosage is increased or a new drug is tried. Although this disease-centered approach effectively improves certain symptoms in the majority of children, it has some very real limitations and it will probably be viewed as obsolete in years to come.

Patient-Centered Medicine

One of the core principles of Functional Medicine is that healthcare practitioners must become patient-centered rather than disease-centered— focusing where appropriate upon the needs of the patient more than on the name of the disease. Patient-centered practitioners must view health as the presence of wholeness and vitality rather than just the absence of a definable disease.

This has some very important implications. For example, studies indicate that stimulant drugs are effective in about 75 percent of children with ADHD. However, if these "successfully treated" children were examined more closely it might be clear in some cases that their behavior and school performance may be improved but their quality of life may be no better or even worse.

A patient-centered approach would give high priority to the side effects of medication and the long-term implications of its use. As well, the overall wellness of the child on the medication would be an important criterion for judging its success; it is not enough to be satisfied that the child's behavior and school performance has improved. The fact that only a minority of children are willing to stay on stimulant medications over the long-term suggests that, from the child's point of view, treatment is not always a success.

It is also consistent with the patient-centered approach to help those individuals who seek help even if they do not fit the strict criteria for the diagnosis of a specific disease process. Many individuals suffer with some of the troubling features of ADHD but may not have a sufficient number of symptoms, or their symptoms may not be severe enough to accurately establish a diagnosis. In a disease-centered approach, these individuals would simply be reassured that there is nothing really wrong and then told that they will have to live with their problems. However, such people might have underlying physiological problems similar to those with ADHD and their function and quality of life may improve significantly by identification and correction of these problems.

For instance, we have a daughter who has always had a tendency to be aggressive and hyperactive. She has never fit the strict criteria for ADHD but her aggression and hyperactivity has repeatedly caused problems in her life. Many years ago, we discovered that she has significant food allergies and intolerances. Since then, we have found that as long as she abstains from junk foods and the foods to which she is allergic or intolerant and gets regular exercise, her hyperactive and aggressive tendencies are greatly minimized.

Whether she does or does not have ADHD is irrelevant if her function and quality of life is excellent. Unfortunately, for every child or adult who clearly has ADHD there are probably two or three others who suffer with some of the features of this disorder but never receive help because they are told that they really have no problem or that they will just have to learn to live with it.

In the disease-centered approach, you either have a "disease entity" or you do not. Although this principle certainly holds true when it comes to the diagnosis of pregnancy or an infestation of tapeworms, it is not often so clear-cut in conditions like ADHD. Individuals with ADHD are suffering from various underlying problems, most of which can be considered to be somewhere along a spectrum of severity rather than completely present or completely absent.

The Wonderful Uniqueness of Humans

One of the most important concepts in Functional Medicine is that all individuals are all biochemically unique. In fact, humans have more biochemical individuality than they have differences in facial features or fingerprints. The power of biochemical individuality has been recognized in the science of criminology where one hair or one drop of blood can be used to separate one person from every other human on the planet. Our uniqueness is now known to extend to thousands of different biochemical processes and physiological functions.

There are many important implications for this concept of Functional Medicine. For example, individuals may vary as much as perhaps onehundred-fold in their ability to effectively excrete toxic metals. Thus, a level of exposure that would be completely harmless to one person may be seriously toxic to another. Similarly, an individual's need for various nutrients may differ significantly from the Recommended Dietary Allowances (RDAs) adopted to suit the needs of the average healthy individual. Research is increasingly demonstrating that nutritional requirements vary enormously from person to person especially in individuals who are suffering from a disease or disability.

In recognition of this concept of biochemical individuality, the Functional Medicine practitioner should always ponder two questions when dealing with a patient:

Does this person lack something for which he or she has an unusually high requirement in order to thrive?

Does this person have something in his or her body that is preventing him or her from experiencing optimal wellness and vitality (i.e. a stressful or toxic influence)?

These two questions require that the Functional Medicine practitioner evaluate each patient as biochemically unique with a set of special nutritional needs and a distinctive list of stressful or toxic influences underlying his or her condition. Through the process of careful interviews, skillful examination and selected testing, the Functional Medicine practitioner gradually formulates a clear picture of the underlying factors which eventually led to the signs and symptoms for which the patient is seeking assistance.

Solving the ADHD Puzzle

Successful management of ADHD begins by gathering and organizing relevant information pertaining to the ADHD sufferer. This can be likened to gathering up all the pieces of the ADHD puzzle. There are rarely any real shortcuts when it comes to solving a complex puzzle. If you simply start randomly grabbing puzzle pieces and try to force them to fit together you will probably just end up frustrated.

Successfully solving a puzzle starts by carefully studying the picture on the puzzle box and then placing all the pieces in full view on a large table. As you carefully scan the pieces eventually, you begin to see how certain pieces belong together. With persistence, small sections of the picture come become clear until the whole puzzle is solved. I have observed many people who have successfully assembled their ADHD puzzle. With few exceptions, this process requires patience, persistence and often requires the assistance of one or more competent healthcare professionals to be fully successful.

The most skillful puzzle masters will always assemble a puzzle using a proven method; a systematic approach. For instance, they may start from the top of the puzzle and then work down. Likewise, when efforts are being made to uncover the significant factors which are contributing to the signs and symptoms of ADHD, it is critical that this process be conducted in an organized, systematic fashion. Too often, individuals with ADHD are subjected to a random series of visits to different professionals followed by this or that medication. Perhaps a test will be thrown in here or there and maybe a couple of nutritional supplements will be tried. Then there might be a consultation with an alternative practitioner followed by a special diet for a while. At the end of all of these efforts, there may be little improvement in the ADHD symptoms and not much has been discovered about the real factors that are contributing to the patient's condition.

In our own facility, we have observed the value in approaching each ADHD subject in an organized and systematic fashion. This is much like starting a successful business by first compiling and then sticking to a well researched business plan instead of simply opening your doors and trying to "make a go of it." Those with an organized plan will always have a greater chance of success.

Clinical Assessment of the ADHD Patient

The initial step toward solving the ADHD puzzle involves a competent and thorough clinical assessment. Ideally, this should begin with an evaluation by a competent psychologist or other professional who is qualified to perform learning, behavioral and neuropsychological evaluations. These tests can be used as a gauge to assess the severity of ADHD symptoms and to look for learning disabilities, psychological, neurological or psychiatric problems. Such testing may also reveal some real surprises.

For example, as a child, a friend of mine was labeled as a "slow learner" and was placed on Ritalin for hyperactivity. However, when neuropsychological testing was done he was found to have an IQ over 140! Today he is a brilliant and successful computer programmer working for a successful, worldwide organization. If he had not had neuropsychological testing, he may never have had the confidence to excel at anything and might not have been encouraged to pursue a highly academic path.

It is not uncommon for potentially gifted kids, with or without ADHD, to be identified as disruptive, hyperactive or pathologically inattentive when they are primarily under-stimulated and bored out of their minds. In other cases, kids may be labeled as lazy or stupid when they actually have a very definable learning disability. Many of these problems can be minimized or effectively eliminated with proper treatment. Likewise, it is tragically too common for children with visual or hearing problems to be labeled as "slow" when, in fact their sensory deficits are the primary cause of their problems.

The next step in the assembly of your ADHD puzzle should involve an organized method for gathering relevant medical information. Conducting a proper medical history and physical examination followed by performing pertinent medical tests is referred to as the "medical workup." A properly conducted medical workup is the primary means by which a healthcare provider is able to determine the antecedents, triggers and mediators which are contributing to the symptoms of ADHD in each individual.

It is also important to note that a thorough medical workup is necessary to "rule out" highly serious medical problems which could lead to symptoms typical of ADHD. For instance, if a home has faulty ventilation, carbon monoxide may pollute the air inside the home and family members may suffer from some degree of carbon monoxide poisoning. In less severe cases, children may develop cognitive and behavioral problems identical to ADHD and may be quite inappropriately put on symptom suppressing drugs instead of being treated for the medical problem responsible for the symptoms.

Similarly, lead poisoning, thyroid disease and several other potentially very serious medical problems should be considered in the medical workup and, if indicated, appropriate tests conducted to rule out these possibilities. In some cases, such as lead poisoning, there is a high chance that symptoms can be largely reversed if the problem is detected and treated early on. However, if detection and treatment is delayed too long, permanent brain damage may take place.

Summary of an appropriate clinical assessment in patients with ADHD

Initial Assessment

(Goal is to define current disabling ADHD associated problems)

• ADHD questionnaires and rating scales
   (DSM-IV for children and adults; ADHD Monitoring System; Jasper-Goldberg Questionnaire; Conners' Parent Rating Scales and Conners' Adult ADHD Rating Scales)

• Recommend complete neuropsychological evaluation.

Medical Workup

• Directed history and directed physical exam.

• Establish a differential diagnosis and rule out serious medical problems.

• Begin to define underlying antecedents, triggers and mediators of ADHD in that individual.

Functional Testing in the Assessment of the ADHD Patient

There is no substitute for a thorough medical history and physical exam. They are the foundation upon which to build a patient centered diagnosis. Through a properly conducted clinical assessment, the pieces of the puzzle start to come together and some parts of the picture may become clear. However, there are also many factors that cannot be detected by history and physical exam alone. Sophisticated laboratory testing may provide further invaluable information.

In the Functional Medicine assessment of ADHD, several unique laboratory tests are often performed. The clinical judgment of the healthcare provider and the unique nature of the patient will determine which tests should be done and in what order they ought to be performed. Functional testing may include:

Gastrointestinal Assessment

• Intestinal permeability testing
• Comprehensive Digestive and Stool Analysis with Comprehensive Parasitology (especially looking for sIgA level, stool probiotic and potentially pathogenic bacteria; fungal organisms and parasites)
• Helicobacter pylori immune assay
• Candida antibodies
• Urinary organic acids profile
• Urinary peptides
• Breath testing (post lactose and post glucose or lactulose)

Nutritional Assessment

• RBC/serum minerals; vitamins
• Urinary or serum amino acids
• Essential fatty acids (red blood cell)
• Urine elements
• Hair elements
• Intracellular minerals

Allergy Assessment

- Airborne (skin prick testing; RAST; ELISA; MAST)
- Diet/symptom diary
- Open food challenge process
- Formulation of a long term diet with ongoing observations

- Food allergy/intolerance
- Dietary history
- Elimination test diet
- Testing (ELISA; MAST; Provocation-neutralization; AK™)

Toxicology Assessment

- Toxic susceptibility (functional liver detoxification testing)
- Toxic metal testing
- Hair toxic elements
- Fractionated porphyrins
- Post provocative (post chelation) urine testing
- Direct measurements (organic toxin panels using blood, urine or adipose tissue)

- Chemical sensitivities (anti-chemical antibodies)
- Whole blood lead
- Stool toxic metal assay
- Non-metallic toxin testing
- Urinary D-glucaric acid; mercapturates testing

Of course, there is no situation in which most or all of these tests are done on any given individual. Good clinical judgment, based upon the practitioner's knowledge, experience and the suspicions derived from a thorough medical history and physical exam, will determine which tests should be performed. In some cases, tests are done one or two at a time until several are performed over a period of many months.

Even one or two well-chosen tests might uncover some very important causative factors, which could then lead to highly effective treatments. In any case, a laboratory test should only be performed if the results of that test are likely to significantly influence the way a patient is treated. Otherwise, the test is only of academic interest and will provide little tangible benefits for the ADHD sufferer. When appropriately chosen, the laboratory testing unique to Functional Medicine can reveal hidden problems and causative factors that can greatly assist in the establishment of a highly effective treatment program.

Patient Centered Treatment of ADHD

The primary purpose of Functional Medicine is to help people achieve optimal function and quality of life through therapies that seek to achieve more than just a suppression of symptoms. Although these lofty goals are not yet achievable for all human disorders, they are certainly possible in most people with ADHD. Some healthcare professionals who utilize the principles of Functional Medicine may still prescribe drug therapy for ADHD under certain circumstances, or they may be called upon to work with individuals who are already on medications. In Functional Medicine, if symptom suppressing medication is used at all, it is generally considered just a means to "buy some time" while a better, and more long lasting solution can be discovered for that patient.

To comply with the ideals of Functional Medicine, a given treatment or set of treatments should:

- Carry no risk of doing harm and should be free of unpleasant side effects.
- Improve symptoms as well as the overall function and quality of life.
- Help to correct the underlying causes of the disorder.
- Improve the long-term prognosis for the patient.

Functional Medicine treatments of ADHD may include:

Botanical Medicine:

- Begin with 2 AD-FX twice per day on an empty stomach (200 mg American ginseng ginsenoside extract combined with 120 mg Ginkgo biloba 24% extract).
- If necessary, add additional Ginkgo biloba (24%) extract to total 300 mg per day (especially for cognitive effects).
- You may also utilize St. John's wort (.3% hypericin) 900-1200 mg per day (especially for moods and behavior).
- Green tea may also be of benefit to cognition.

4-R Program of Gastrointestinal Rehabilitation:

Remove
- Allergic/intolerant foods and junk foods
- Intestinal parasites; potentially pathogenic bacteria and fungi; bacterial overgrowth (gut fermentation) syndromes.
- Drugs, other damaging chemicals and pollutants.

Agents useful in the "Remove" phase:
- Colostrum, lactoferrin
- Antimicrobial herbals (e.g. garlic, goldenseal, Pau D'arco, Echinacea, Wormwood (Artemesia annua), black walnut hull, citrus seed extract, oregano oil)
- Cold-FX (concentrated glyconutritional oligosaccharide fraction from American ginseng; strengthens gastrointestinal immunity)
- Probiotics (proven strains which strengthen gastrointestinal immunity, kills gut pathogens)

Replace
- Digestive enzymes, gastric acid (betaine hydrochloride, stomach bitters or histadine)
- L-glutamine/L-glutamic acid (rice protein, glutamine supplements)

Reinoculate
- Probiotic bacteria (proven strains)
- Prebiotics: FOS; Dietary fiber (oat fiber is the best prebiotic)
- Immune support (Cold-FX)

Repair
- L-glutamine/L-glutamic acid (rice protein, glutamine supplements)
- Micronutrient support (vitamin A, zinc, B vitamins)
- Essential fatty acids (Omega 3 and Omega 6)
- Fiber (FOS; oat fiber)
- Probiotics
- Detoxification support

Feeding the Hyperactive Brain:

Diet should be optimized for individual needs but should always be a whole foods based diet with high nutritional density. Start with the basics:
- Tolerable whole grains
- Increased quantities of (pesticide free) fruits and vegetables
- Fermented dairy products or other sources of calcium
- Adequate quantities of high quality, low allergy potential protein throughout the day (especially breakfast – rice protein based smoothies are great)
- Minimize bad fats (hydrogenated, saturated, deep fried)
- Supplement with contaminant-free essential fatty acids and related brain beneficial phosphatidylserine
- Break bad food habits and help to build good ones (consider holding community classes and lectures with cooking demonstrations and "pot-luck (bring your own food) dinners").
- Offer healthy snack ideas (nutritious "smoothie drinks" rice protein based) are favorites with kids.
- Ensure adequacy of all brain-critical nutrients (protein, essential fatty acids, iron, zinc, B vitamins, water)
- Provide antioxidant support (vitamin C, vitamin E, grape seed or green tea extracts)

Restoring Strength to the Battered Immune System

- Identify and eliminate or diminish total underlying stressors (antigenic (food/microbial) stress; toxic stress; infectious stress; physical stress; electromagnetic stress; nutritional insufficiencies; psychological stress)
- Provide positive immune system support
- Exercise training (moderate)
- Immunonutrition
- Balanced macronutrients (especially adequate protein)
- Optimized micronutrients (especially zinc; magnesium; selenium; copper; vitamins A, D, B6, folate; vitamin E; vitamin C)
- Essential fatty acids
- Dietary fiber (prebiotics stimulate the colonization of immune supportive probiotic bacteria – FOS, oat bran)
- Probiotic supplementation (with proven strains)
- Glyconutritionals (carbohydrate nutrients that improve immune system function)
- Supports glycoprotein synthesis
- Oligosaccharides act as "receptor decoy" in gut to prevent adhesion of microbes
- Cold-FX (rare oligosaccharides)

Immunotherapy

- Conventional "allergy shots" (only proven useful for inhalant allergies)
- Provocation-neutralization (very time consuming with temporary effects)
- Enzyme potentiated desensitization (EPD) (safe, effective for food allergies and intolerances, double blind study demonstrated efficacy of over 80% in treatment of ADHD)

Purifying the Toxic Brain

- Identify and remove from sources of toxic stress
- Optimize nutritional status for improved detoxification
- Provide balanced macronutrients (esp, protein)
- Optimize intake of nutritional minerals (toxic metals are "chemical competitors" with nutritional minerals)
- Increase fiber intake
- Increase (toxin free) fruits and vegetables
- Optimize lifestyle for more efficient detoxification (exercise and stress management)
- Optimize gastrointestinal function through the 4-R Program

- Consider an intensive therapeutic detoxification program for 2 to 12 weeks.
- Toxin/allergen free diet (oligoantigenic diet)
- Add specific nutrients to support gut and liver detoxification (rice protein, N-acetyl cysteine, L-glutathione, glycine, taurine, inorganic sulfate)
- Herbal supplements which promote detoxication and provide antioxidant protection for liver (milk thistle (80 % Silymarin), artichoke, turmeric extract, taurine)
- Exercise daily
- Hyperthermic therapy (steam bath, hydrotherapy, sauna)

Empowering the Hyperactive Brain Through Exercise

All patients with ADHD must exercise regularly! Properly conducted exercise provides many physical benefits including:

- Improved immune system function
- Improved gastrointestinal function
- Improved detoxification capabilities

Properly conducted exercise provides many benefits to brain function including:

- Enhanced mood, decreased depressive symptoms
- Increased resistance to stress, decreased anxiety levels
- Increased production of dopamine (the most important neurotransmitter in ADHD) throughout the brain
- Enhanced executive center functioning
- Improved confidence and self esteem
- Family recreation builds bonds between parents and children

Focusing the Hyperactive Brain Through Biofeedback, Prayer and Meditation

- Focusing is a learned skill which can be mastered by those with ADHD.
- EEG biofeedback (neurofeedback) is the most potent therapy to train self-regulation of abnormal brain electrical activity.
- As effective as Ritalin in comparison trials
- Effects are probably lifelong after a course of 20 to 40 sessions
- Expense and relative lack of certified professionals are the only drawbacks
- GSR (galvanic skin response) biofeedback is an effective method to help the patient diminish anxiety levels and manage stress
- Some improvement in cognition and behavior can be demonstrated

- Equipment inexpensive and can be purchased by the patient for less than $200.00
- Requires minimal training to help patients to use this therapy effectively
- Prayer and/or meditation can provide benefits if training and commitment is intensively followed.
- Highly effective as a component of maintenance therapy in those who have successfully undertaken neurofeedback training

Keys to a Productive Life — ADHD as Friend and Ally

- Poor parenting skills and an ADHD child are a recipe for disaster
- Become acquainted with books to help parents raise a strong-willed child
- Help parents to avoid the most common parenting mistakes
- Teach parents about the importance of helping their child to become structured and organized
- Adults need to create external structure through schedules and organizers
- Adults with ADHD need to live by a personal mission statement (the "Principle-Centered Life" of *7 Habits of Highly Effective People,* by Stephen Covey, published by Simon & Schuster, is made to fit for adults with ADHD)
- Adults need to become aware of their weaknesses and be willing to change with humility
- Many ADHD adults need to be approached in the same way as alcoholics or drugs addicts.
- They need to come out of deep denial and follow a spiritual path of recovery (a 12 Step approach to spirituality) A simplified version of the 12 step program is in *The Ultimate Power,* by Ken Vegotsky, AGES Publications™. Ordering information is in the back of this book.
- Specific treatments need to evolve into a lifestyle that works and which enables the ADHD individual to consistently experience productivity and happiness and to avoid personal catastrophe

Harnessing the Power to Heal

Central to Functional Medicine is a recognition of the awesome order and complexity of the human body. Ingrained in this philosophy is also an appreciation for the intelligent healing power which is intrinsic to every one of our trillions of cells. Essentially, Functional Medicine recognizes that our bodies want to be well and the therapeutic strategies used in this field reflect this recognition. Rather than focusing on killing disease with various chemical and surgical weapons, Functional Medicine seeks to remove the various chemical, biological and emotional stresses that are impairing the healing process while providing sophisticated nutritional, botanical, emotional and even spiritual support to assist the natural healing process. Many of the high-tech drugs and surgical procedures so revered today will be obsolete in the future. However, as research progresses, natural principles of hygiene, nutrition, lifestyle and spirituality will become permanently embedded in the doctrines of an increasingly evidence based healthcare system.

Functional Medicine may be slightly ahead of its time right now, but in years to come these principles will likely overshadow virtually every aspect of healthcare.

Note: Further Reading: ***Healing the Hyperactive Brain; Through the New Science of Functional Medicine;*** Michael R. Lyon, M.D.; Focused Publishing, 1999, 596 pages; available through bookstores, Amazon.com or fxmed.com.

Contact information

For parents, adults and care-givers who would like a referral to a trained practitioner in Functional Medicine, contact the Institute for Functional Medicine c/o HealthComm International Inc., P.O. Box 1729, Gig Harbor, Washington 98335 USA. Tel: (253) 851-3943 or through their web site: www.fxmed.com.

Those healthcare providers who would like to obtain further training in the emerging field of Functional Medicine are encouraged to explore the educational resources available through the Institute for Functional Medicine in Gig Harbor, WA. (www.fxmed.com). This organization offers comprehensive full-credit courses such as ***Applying Functional Medicine in Clinical Practice*** as well as pertinent published material and audiovisual programs. ***Functional Medicine Update*** is a monthly audio program produced by Dr. Jeffrey Bland, Ph.D. which is heard by thousands of subscribers from around the world. As well, the fully (continuing medical education) accredited International Symposium on Functional Medicine is an annual scientific conference attended by well over 1000 professionals and features some of the world's most sought after scientists and clinicians. For more information about Functional Medicine and healing the hyperactive brain, you can access www.PureLiving.com.

A Refreshing Overview of Some Natural and Complementary Choices

Dorothy Marshall, Ph.D., N.D., N.H.C., and C.E.O. of International Academy of Natural Health Sciences

As the morning crowd pushed through the gates at the amusement park, my son, who was visiting the park for the day, observed a boy, about the age of 6, along with his younger sister in a stroller and his Mum & Dad. The boy had caught my son's attention in the ticket lineup due to his constant movement, whining, and attempts to do anything but stand in line with his parents. These attempts included swinging around a tree and stepping beside each of the flowers in the flower bed.

Once inside the park, the first purchase by the parents was a snow cone to pacify the young lad's requests for a treat, and then off they went for their day in the amusement park.

By coincidence, the young family attended the same Dolphin & Sea Lion show, and later ate lunch in the one of the amphitheater styled cafeterias. The young boy's behavior pattern continued to be unruly, always squirming about in his seat with little focused attention on anything, including the dolphins. As my son watched the family eat lunch, he observed the boy devour his french fries and ketchup, along with a large cup of soda pop, but noticeably he left his half-sandwich on the plate, basically playing with it, rather than eating it. As they left the park at the end of the day, the parents had grown tired of the boy's lack of attention to their words of guidance, and perhaps were disappointed that it seemed all of their hopes and efforts to please him and make him happy just weren't enough to satisfy him. Kind words had become irritated in tone. The little boy was in tears and yet, at the same time, he was eating an ice cream bar.

At our next family gathering, my son asked me whether this was an example of a classic case of hyperactivity and attention disorder, or a case of a young boy dealing with the emotional highs and lows of a sugar-based diet. The reality is that it is not an easy question to answer without actually spending time with the boy and his parents to determine his overall behavior, the influence of his diet and body chemistry, his sleeping patterns, his social interaction with playmates and family members, his participation at school, the type of TV or video programs he watches, and his physical environment. Each of the foregoing can create the impression of a child being hyperactive, but in fact, the behavior is being created by one of those components. Thus, it is not necessarily a lifelong situation that requires medical treatment—just a change in the administration of one or two, of those components in his daily life.

Before focusing most of this section on nutritional and natural means of dealing with hyperactivity, let's take a quick look at the likely amount of sugar this young boy was absorbing in his day.

First of all, breakfast may well have been a sugar-coated cereal lacking fiber and meaningful protein. Food ingredients are listed on the package in order of "quantity." Most children's cereals will start off the ingredient list like this: flour/cereal grains/flaked milled corn, and then the next ingredient listed is "sugar." On occasion, you will find "sugar" listed ahead of the flour component.

At the park, there was the "snow cone," or frozen water with sugar and artificial flavor.

At lunch, the french fries with ketchup were another example of a high intake of sugar. Not only could sugar be premixed with the salt for flavor, sugar is the second ingredient next to tomato paste in the manufacture of ketchup. Drinking soda pop is the same as drinking flavored sugar water. Pop, no matter what make, contains a high level of sugar. For example, Coke Classic® contains about 9 teaspoons of sugar in a 12 oz.can (in metric, about 39.8 grams in a 355 ml can). As a rule of thumb, one can estimate that between 8 to 13% of a non-diet soft drink will be sugar.

Experiment for a moment by pouring 9 teaspoons of sugar on a plate, and then visually experience that amount of sugar entering the body. As a second experiment, take a chicken bone and set it in a glass of pop for about 3 weeks. At the end of the 3 weeks, you will find a bone that is the color of the pop and bends just like a rubber band. The strength of the bone has all but disappeared, and due to the porous nature of bone, the color additives will have dyed the color of the bone.

One has to ask oneself what is happening to childrens' bone density and strength if they flood their bodies with pop everyday?

Again, the end of the day at the park, "ice-cream" was further sugar reinforcement, as sugar is typically the #2 ingredient after "water," or "milk ingredients," depending on the type of iced product being consumed.

So the child's behavior in this case, could simply be a matter of the young boy trying to deal with the constant "peaks" and subsequent "valleys" caused by his sugar intake. If it isn't flushed from his system by bedtime, a restless night lies in store for the whole family. At the rate of daily consumption of sugar by this boy, he could exceed his entire body weight in sugar each year.

The foregoing sets the parameters for our discussion of the basic principles and importance of good nutrition in helping to control hyperactivity. At the outset, it should be stated that this is not a discussion based upon the premise that sugar, salt and carbohydrates must be eliminated. In fact, the body needs these elements to function. However, it needs to absorb them from the right sources and in a controlled manner. One should always keep in mind the phrase, "moderation supports body balance."

Can a change in nutritional in-take and proper stimulation of the body's electrical circuits help to control and improve a child diagnosed with "attention deficit disorder with hyperactivity?" The answer in many situations is "yes." It can even help in situations in which the child has an attention deficit disorder without hyperactivity.

I will always recall the visit of a frantic young mother who was facing the loss of her child through the court systems, as she was about to be deemed an unfit mother by a community child care agency. Her son was in preschool and about to enter grade one in the next term. The boy had been having significant social problems with his classmates and was totally unruly in class. In the course of events, the school involved the child care/protection agency, who conducted interviews with all parties and then determined that while the boy and mother loved one another, she was unable to handle him and provide him with an environment in which he could improve. The recommendation was that the boy should be placed in a foster home. The case was to be heard before the courts in the next week, so there was little time to bring about change.

After an in-depth review with the mother about the child's eating habits and menu, it was determined that with a 100% commitment to making changes, it just might be possible to have her son undergo sufficient modification to his body chemistry to bring about alterations in his personal characteristics.

As the new food program was set out, the mother acknowledged she had never really thought about what to feed her son because food in their house just "kind of happened," but she did undertake to administer the new program with diligence.

The end of the story was very gratifying, because within one week, when the young boy and his mother appeared in the court, he was well behaved and in control. After some discussion, the judge turned to the child care protection agency and asked why they had brought the case forward. The judge then ruled to leave the boy in his mother's care.

While we have lost touch today, for years afterwards the mother maintained a conscious attitude toward her son's food menu, and he progressed well in school and in his social environment. In perspective, the mother was provided with knowledge and she accepted the responsibility for using the new information to help her family situation. This is the case with everyone: one must accept personal responsibility for his or her own individual health and consciously participate in maintaining health balance. It is not a doctor's or a health practitioner's responsibility to keep you healthy; it is solely your personal responsibility to do the best you can for yourself and your family, with well informed guidance.

Water

One of the easiest ways to begin to safely impact children's body chemistry, even though they may still be on medication, is to assess their water consumption. Sufficient water density within the body is a key requirement to creating the internal environment to initiate change in the body's chemical balance. Additionally, all unbalanced conditions of the body can be traced to dehydration.

The quality and content of the water consumed is important. In past years, there has been an increasing concern with the quality of city tap water, and more recently, a growing awareness about the contents of wellwater. While well-water was viewed as having many minerals that we need, it has been determined that many wells contain minerals the body does not need, or contains contaminants due to seepage of chemicals into the ecology system. Both portable and installed home water purifiers have become more affordable as demand and competition have increased, and are viewed as a positive step to obtaining a convenient source of drinking water. In the absence of a purifier, bottled water is recommended. (See Chapter 16 Water: A Source of Problems and Solutions)

Dr. Bernard Jensen's studies on body tissue composition depict the following levels of water in vital areas of the body:

Vital Areas	%Water	Vital Areas	%Water
Muscle	75	Bones	22
Blood	79	Liver	74
Brain	78	Skin	66

Water is an absolute requirement for living, yet we often overlook its value and the need for it within our bodies to help it perform to its highest potential. One must drink about 64 ounces over the day—ideally, at a rate of not more than 4 ounces in a half hour. At a faster rate, the body fails to absorb much of the water for its use, and it generally simply flows through. Even though we are conscious of how much water we should be drinking, we often tend to permit ourselves to allow our personal psyche to fool us. We become convinced that since drinks such as tea, coffee, alcohol, wine and manufactured beverages all contain water, we can include them in our count. Unfortunately, the folly in this attitude is that each of those drinks actually depletes the personal water table, as they are diuretic (tending to increase the flow of urine). When they move through the body, the water in them cannot be absorbed and it quickly moves to the bowel for exiting. However, this water drags along some portion of existing water held within your system, and as such, your water table goes down.

Does it really exit that quickly? One unusual study conducted in the Seattle area would support this timing. In the analysis of their sewer system, the city tracks the flow of waste that escapes through cracked sewer pipes and into bodies of water. Because caffeine is produced uniquely by humans, waste containing it could only have come from sewers or water treatment plants. They have determined that peaks in caffeine flow occur just before 9 AM, when caffeine levels are nearly eight times as high as usual: this was the outcome of everyone getting rid of that first cup of coffee between 8 and 8:30 AM.

To flood the body with water can also be detrimental. When that guilt conscience takes over and one simply wants to make up the deficiency, there is a tendency to accelerate water intake. The result is a peaceful mind, but a body that is going to be further depleted of needed minerals that will not have had the full value and use of the water before it is excreted.

Water acts as the body's conduit for transferring nutrients and energy flow. Cells need to be filled with adequate water to maximize their growth and performance. Nerves must be moist in order to flow the needed data to think or communicate with other parts of the body. While the brain may represent only 2% of your body's makeup, it is said to utilize approximately a fifth of the total blood flow. Without adequate water in your system, body functions simply do not operate to their highest level of efficiency, nor can you adequately flush out unneeded waste products that begin to collect at various points within the body. This will produce a future source for the spawning of disease.

So by initiating discipline within the family to monitor the proper amount and quality of water in-take, there will be a number of noticeable changes that will become evident. Some family members will experience reductions in weight without dieting, others will begin to feel better and suffer fewer periods of fatigue, those enduring high levels of constipation will experience positive change, and the level of hyperactivity in a person will also reduce, as his or her body chemistry moves slowly towards a balance in the scales.

Water is so often overlooked as we search for solutions to help those diagnosed with ADD and Hyperactivity. Yet it is a vital component of our composition and an integral need for all functions and organs.

How can you tell if your child is getting enough water? A quick check of the color of their urine will give you an acid test. If it is a heavy yellow and has an odor, they need more water. The goal is for urine to be a light yellow and without odor.

Another means to use "water" for a person with ADD and Hyperactivity is to encourage him or her to take warm baths using approximately 1 cup of epsom salts and a teaspoon of bath oil. The warm bath will relax muscles and tensed nerves and soothe the body. The epsom salts will work to draw toxins out of the body through the pores of the skin. As toxins in the body are a major factor in trying to reduce the levels of hyperactivity, this cleansing process is a vital and yet very easy step to introduce into the overall treatment plan. Ideally, the bath should be taken before the individual goes to bed as an aid to inducing a relaxing sleep, and thus helping achieve a situation of body regeneration. With time, the degree of hyperactivity should lower, as the benefits from toxin elimination, as well as the right amount and type of sleep, begins to accumulate.

Exercise

Another technique that can be utilized to help control hyperactivity, is to establish a morning routine of controlled exercise. While at the outset a parent may be saying, "This child doesn't need more exercise—he is like a spinning top all day," controlled exercise patterns will have multiple benefits.

First of all the child typically does not resist if the exercises are made to be fun or are made to be challenging as long as it is a personal challenge and not engaging other children. Involving others during the time of establishing a routine will only serve to distract, reducing the child's focus and attention and increasing the control challenges.

Exercise has at least two key purposes from a health perspective. One is that the circulation it generates will force nutrients to move into tissues. At the same time, it will help expel waste from the body. In practical terms, exercise becomes the catalyst to move blood and take care of the lymph stream of fluids, allowing for the development of a good circulatory system. Additionally, exercise oxygenates the body, a process required to produce energy. The good "circulation" created by exercise goes hand in hand with the words "body life force." An old adage is still very appropriate. "To keep the body well, we must put the body through a series of exercises everyday."

Typically, when we think of exercise, we do not think about the lymph system, yet it is an important aspect of maintaining good health. Lymph vessels are located all over the body, just under the surface of the skin.

Waste is picked up and carried to the lymph nodes (which are like little processing factories). Physical exercise will help activate the lymph process. You can awaken them and prepare them for movement by beating them lightly with your hands. Movement of this slightly yellowish alkaline fluid derived from the body tissues will only occur when you engage in exercises that impact them. The creation and movement of this fluid is integral to the efficient operation of your body's specific immune response system.

Dr. Francesco Contreras describes it in his book *Health in the 21st Century* this way: "The specific immune system develops after birth as a response to microorganisms and their toxins. A gigantic task that can only be given to the awesome lymphocytes. They are so called because they are produced by lymphatic ganglia. A fourth of all white cells are lymphocytes and are divided into three branches, T-Cells, B-Cells, and killer cells, which are distributed strategically according to specific needs throughout the body. T-Cells (80%) intoxicate invaders through chemical warfare, B-Cells(15%) maintain the memory of specific chemical substances which will destroy a specific invader and the killer cells (5%) are the SWAT team as they charge, with brute force, invaders or aberrant cells like cancer or cells infected with a virus." In essence, unknown to many, the lymph system and its fluids are our personal assault troops when outside invaders put us in danger. While some cells will float in the blood system, others plant themselves in vital organs, and still others corral invaders into the lymph nodes, which serve as execution chambers for these negative cells. Its proper functioning only serves to increase the odds of maintaining sustained good health.

The question I am asked continuously is what kind of exercise I recommend. Those charged with dealing with hyperactivity are trying to reduce, not stimulate, physical behavior patterns.

One of my personal exercises every morning involves the use of a "rebounder"—a mini trampoline. Three to five minutes on the rebounder is equal to about one mile of jogging, and every muscle in the body is exercised without subjecting the joints or bony structures to the striking impact that takes place when running or jumping. Exercises done on the rebounder are tension-relaxation exercises. The process is simple. Our bodies tense as our feet land on the flexible center of the rebounder and relax as we go into the air. The main purpose of these exercises is to move the lymph and carry off the broken down products of fat metabolism. These movements firm the buttocks, help reduce the waist and strengthen the legs and generally exercise the whole body. Having the exercises done to music adds a level of enjoyment and rhythm to the activity. Because the activity takes only about 5 minutes, and there are as many as 15 different exercises that can be done, the child enjoys time on the rebounder and sees it as a fun time.

The best book I've read on the values of rebounding and types of exer-cises is "Dr. Jensen's Favorite Exercises." (The book and rebounder can be purchased via visiting www.vitabest.ca)

Reflexology

Another method to help improve the body's two main nervous systems, the "sympathetic and the parasympathetic," is through the gentle practice of "reflexology."

The sympathetic system is the one you control, i.e., you decide to make certain body movements, to stand up or sit down. The parasympathetic is the one over which you do not have control i.e., the digestive system's continuous operation, or the peristaltic action in the bowel's alimentary canal.

Reflexology works on the parasympathetic system and is based on the principle that there are reflexes on the body that correspond to every organ and gland within the system. Compression techniques are used on these reflexes to stimulate the organs and glands, unblocking congestion, stimulating circulation and elimination, reducing stress, and normalizing body rhythms. Hand and foot reflex therapy has proven very effective in treating a variety of body imbalances.

In reflexology, the pad of the thumb presses gently, but firmly, on a specific point, and then a "down and in-circular" motion stimulates the reflex. To gain a better understanding of it, using your hands, try the following technique on your arm:

> Use the flat pad of the thumb (not the tip) and press the thumb pad of the right hand on to the soft inner side of your left arm (if you are left handed just reverse the situation).
>
> Depress with a degree of firmness.
>
> Keep the thumb on this spot and rotate 5-6 times. Then move about the width of the thumb to another spot and repeat the pressure and rotation.
>
> Continue this action as you work over the entire area of the inner side of the arm. (You can work on the other side of the arm as well, but for practice purposes you get a better feel for the action of the therapy on the softer tissue.)

Be experimental so that you can experience changes in applied pressure, which should be firm but not so deeply penetrating so as to cause pain.

Now as we have already learned, there are points on the feet and hands that link to every part of the body. In treating those with ADD, we need to work on the brain, the pituitary and adrenal glands, the inner ear, and the digestion.

Visualize the following:

The big toe represents the "head," and the "brain reflex" is on top of the big toe. The pituitary gland is also in the head, so the big toe is a primary focus in the treatment. The reflex points for the digestive system are found on the soles of both feet, on the softer fleshy parts. The adrenal gland reflexes are also located within this fleshy area, just under the big toe pad. The ear reflexes are located at the base of the toes.

With the reflex points identified, try the following on your feet:

> Hold the big toe steady with one hand, and then press and rub with the other hand.
>
> As the brain reflex is on top of the big toe, use the circulating rub and pressing action to cover the areas over and around the big toe.
>
> As mentioned, the pituitary gland is also in the head, so you will also cover it as you complete step #2.

You will note that as you look at and touch the sole of the foot, just underneath the toes there is a bony structure. Down a little bit further, it becomes a softer, more fleshy tissue, and then you come to another boney part at the plate of the heel.

For the digestive system work your thumbs over all of the fleshy parts of the sole, pressing and rubbing, moving a little at a time until you have reflexed the whole area. The adrenal gland reflex will also have been covered, as it is located on the soft tissue, just below the big toe pad.

Now work on all the other toes, tops, bottoms, sides. This will cover the brain and ear reflexes (sinus & eyes, too).

It is quite safe to continue pressing and rubbing over the whole foot, but the purpose of this exercise is to focus on specific areas most helpful to ADD. There is no danger of over-stimulating or under-depressing, or doing any harm, as reflexology serves to help the body create its own natural balance and normalize functions to optimum levels.

There are many good books available as an introduction to reflexology. A 24 hour course from a certified teacher would also provide enough guidance to meaningfully help family members. (For assistance: email: iamnhs@istar.ca and refer to Appendix A: Key Information Resources)

I recommend reflexology to help those with ADD because the person sees it as quality time, spent with the individual attention of a parent or one who cares for him or her. Because there is a physical sensation for the recipient, it keeps his or her focus and attention rooted for the pleasant 10 minute treatment. The activity will have been exhilarating within itself, as it stimulates the body's actions, however, it will also bring about a sense of calm, peace, and restfulness. Thus, it would be good to do prior to bedtime.

Nutrition

On one of my travels, I had the occasion to fly over the flat crop fields of the Midwest; the meandering river below reminded me of how many of us approach our food practices. We meander without specific purpose, without personal health objectives, and without conscious understanding of food values. We often eat without thought of adding value to our body or to the regeneration of our cells. *Personal health objectives* are plans that bring balance to our body, work, and the social, physical, athletic and family demands of our day to day lifestyles and environment. *Conscious understanding* means that with just a touch of knowledge, thought, and care about our food in-take, we could enjoy better longer term physical, emotional, sexual and mental health.

We are into the next century and the natural evolution is to do things or to eat things that are easier, faster, more convenient or simply "trendy." And yet, the way in which our body processes food hasn't changed!

You do not need to become a food nutrient guru or a social outcast within your family or social framework. You must only decide to have the self-will and desire to experience the fruits of living in a healthy body.

While we are dealing with a nutritional approach to helping those with ADD and Hyperactivity, what is being set out is beneficial for the whole family, and as such, is knowledge to help you and your family move towards an improved healthy body balance.

If any part of your body system is not functioning at its optimum performance level, then it likely has become "demineralized" or mineral deficient. The entire body has a need for calcium and within the physical framework, each organ has specific mineral needs. Maintaining a focus on ADD and Hyperactivity, one must determine which minerals feed the brain. Those are potassium and phosphorus based on content. If one feeds the body the correct nutrients, it has the opportunity to perform at its optimum level.

Since our objective at this time is to build a global body balance with an emphasis on improving the performance of the brain, the following foods should become part of the family's food menu on a regular basis:

Global Body Benefit – Calcium Foods

Vegetables	Fruits	Miscellaneous
Broccoli	Apples	Almonds (raw)
Cabbage	Apricots	Buttermilk
Carrots	Lemons	Cottage Cheese
Dandelion Leaves		Dried beans
Lettuce (not iceberg)		Eggs
Okra		Garlic
Parsnips		Molasses

Global Body Benefit – Calcium Foods (continued)

Rutabagas
Spinach (raw)
String Beans
Turnip

Raw Nuts (not peanuts,
or cashews)
Sesame Seeds
(best if ground)

Brain Performance – Potassium Foods

Vegetables	Fruits	Miscellaneous
Beets	Apricots	Dulse
Cabbage	Bananas	Garlic
Carrots	Cherries	Kelp
Cauliflower	Lemons	Milk(dry skim/powder)
Celery	Oranges	Goat's Milk
Eggplant	Pineapple	Olives
Leeks	Raisins	
Onions	Watermelon	
Parsley		
Spinach(raw)		
Squash		
String Beans		
Turnip		
Watercress		

Brain Performance – Phosphorus Foods

Vegetables	Fruits	Miscellaneous
Asparagus	Blackberries	Brazil Nuts
Brussel Sprouts	Black Figs	Buttermilk
Carrots	Cherries	Eggs
Cauliflower	Grapes	Fish
Corn	Limes	Garlic
Cucumber	Oranges	Lentils
Dandelion Leaves		Milk(dry skim/powder)
Kale		Goat's Milk
Leeks		Pumpkin Seeds
Lettuce(not iceberg)		Rice Bran
Lima Beans		Squash seeds
Peas		Walnuts
Savoy cabbage		Wheat Bran
Squash		Wheat Germ
Turnips		
Watercress		

As you can see, there is plenty of variety for developing a broad menu for meals throughout the week. Eating healthy, beneficial foods is by no means a diet per se, just a good food regimen to work towards the opportunity for your body to function at its top performance levels, with the best circulation possible.

There are some foods that should be avoided, as they detract from optimum body performance and work to slow up body circulation:

Scavenger Fish
These fish are higher in toxicity levels than other fish, and as such, impact the performance of blood circulation and digestion:

- Crab, shrimp, lobster, scallops, mussels, and all shell fish.
- Skin fish (fish without scales) such as sole, flounder and tuna (except albacore).

The fish you should eat must have "scales," as scales perform the task of kidneys in the fish, cleansing and filtering the flesh of the fish. (It is important to descale the fish before preparation and wash it thoroughly).

Iceberg Lettuce
Iceberg lettuce is a hybrid, and as it contains natural opium, it slows down the action of the digestive tract.

Pork/Pig Meat
The combustion rate of this food as it is processed by your body is too rapid and as such it actually depletes the body rather than feeding it. This doesn't mean it tastes bad or won't give you that pleasant after dinner satisfaction; however, pork foods will take from your own energy store in order to process it through the body. This action causes a reduction in value for the body and leaves the body at a lower energy level than it was before it was fed.

To some of you, the above list will be disappointing but to many, other than the iceberg lettuce, the eliminations are common to their daily life patterns and cultural or religious philosophies.

Pot Pourri

Efalex
One of the products that I recommend for anyone with ADD or difficulty concentrating, studying for exams, or driving for long periods, is Efalex® by Nutricia™/Efamol®. This product has produced results that suggest it helps eye and brain functions with its fatty acid nutrients. (For a fuller discussion about essential fatty acids, refer to Chapter 17, Essential Fatty Acids: Fats that heal).

I asked the manufacturer to explain why it helps eye and brain functions, and they provided the following explanation, which I would like to share with you.

Approximately 60% of the human brain is composed of fat: a large portion of this fat is fatty acids. Fatty acids are the building blocks of phospholipid membranes around and within cells. The brain is the most membrane-rich tissue in the body. The most abundant fatty acids in the eye and brain are docosahexaenoic acid(DHA) and arachidonic acid (AA). DHA is required for normal nerve cell and eye membranes. AA is required for the normal transmission of messages along nerves and for the development of the short term memory. Therefore, an adequate supply of the right fatty acids helps to maintain healthy brain function. A nutritionally complete diet that includes a combination of certain fatty acids can play a vital role in the development of vision, learning ability and coordination.

Essential fatty acids must be derived from the diet—hence the term 'essential.' In order to be useful to the body, the essential fatty acids go through a series of conversions within the body to produce long chain polyunsaturated fatty acids(LCP's or LC-PUFAs). The body's ability to convert dietary essential fatty acids into the necessary-LCP's is often blocked at the 'first step' due to various factors: stress, viral infection, excess saturated fat consumption.

Fatty acid deficiency has been found in some individuals with Attention Deficit Disorder (ADD) or Attention Deficit Hyperactivity Disorder(ADHD). These deficiencies could be the result of difficulty with the metabolic conversion process. The fatty acids present in Efalex bypass this first step since they are already in a form the body can use and metabolize further.

The key ingredient of Efalex is Tuna oil, selected from a specific part of the fish due to the high DHA content. Such oil reduces the amount of vitamin A, vitamin D, dioxins, and heavy metals, typically found in fish liver. Rich in Omega 6 fatty acids, Efamol's high quality, extensively tested evening primrose oil is a main ingredient. Vitamin E is added as an antioxidant.

Note: Many topics covered in this chapter are expanded upon in other chapters of this book. To find a specific topic or condition, refer to the Table of Contents or Index.

Environmental Factors:
Organic Acids and Hyperactivity
Richard S. Lord, Ph.D.
Director of Education
MetaMetrix Clinical Laboratory

Organic Acids in Urine — Introduction

You can't see them, but, when your body runs low on vitamins or minerals, your urine contains high levels of organic acids. They are there because the food you eat is not being converted cleanly into water and carbon dioxide. Making the process of breaking down food run smoothly is what essential vitamins and minerals do. Without them, the "burning" of food by your metabolism is not clean, but sooty like the plume from a storm lantern that is not getting enough air to burn the fuel. Organic acids in urine are like metabolic soot. Children with developmental disorders frequently have heavy "soot," and many doctors who treat patients with these disorders use organic acid testing to determine what levels of nutrients are needed.

There are hundreds of intermediates formed as your cells start to break down the molecules of carbohydrate, fat and protein. It is somewhat like pulling apart a wooden tinker toy structure one stick and ball at a time to collect the pieces in a bag. Sometimes the parts are stuck together, so you need a pair of pliers to help pull harder. Without the pliers, larger pieces wind up in the bag. Likewise, without the force that the vitamins supply, larger pieces wind up in your urine. The analysis of organic acids in urine measures how many and which large pieces are present.[1, 2] A 4.5-year-old boy with chronic progressive encephalopathy had levels of one piece called alpha ketoglutarate elevated in urine 210 times normal.[3] This is one of the pieces that must have B complex vitamins for conversion.[4]

Since the food you eat is much more complex than a wooden tinker toy, there are many possible large pieces. Biochemists have worked out the pathways of metabolism in such detail that we know where each possible piece comes from and what vitamin or mineral is necessary for the next step that pulls each piece apart. For the breaking of the simple carbohydrate glucose, a simplified sequence of reactions looks like the one shown in Figure 1. Each intermediate from cell glucose to succinate represents a step in the breaking of the chemical bonds of glucose necessary to release the energy to power cell activities. Many of the steps require a vitamin to form the "pliers" necessary to break a bond.

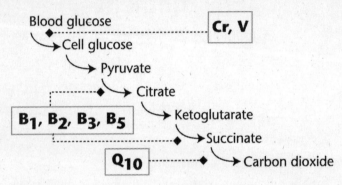

Figure 1
Vitamins and minerals in carbohydrate breakdown

If chromium and vanadium (Cr, V) are deficient, then blood glucose accumulates and spills into urine.[5] (In this case the essential minerals are not used to break a bond, but to help insulin attach to target cells.) If there are inadequate B complex vitamins, then pyruvate and ketoglutarate are not broken[6] and if coenzyme Q10 is deficient, then succinate spills into urine.[7] The B complex vitamins and coenzyme Q10 are analogous to two types of pliers used to handle molecular pieces. Using modern instrumental analysis, dozens of such compounds can be accurately measured. Each one shows a specific point where the essential nutrient "pliers" are not keeping up with the cellular demand. This information is used to reveal which vitamins you need to increase through the use of food supplements or diet modifications. In addition to essential nutrient needs, the organic acid levels show important aspects of waste (toxin) removal, neurotransmitter turnover, and intestinal health.

How To Collect The Specimen

Most of the research that has been done on organic acids was based on a first morning urine specimen.[8] Your body goes through a metabolic transition in the last part of your sleep period. The overnight rebuilding is quite suddenly interrupted by the hormonal shifts that set your daily cycle. Just before you wake, your adrenal glands start making much more cortisol and your cells respond by increasing the flow rate of many metabolic pathways. The urine that passes into the bladder during this period is especially revealing. It also is less likely to be diluted by having consumed large volumes of liquid.

If you sleep through the night, a simple mid stream urine sample will do. If you wake up and urinate after a few hours of sleep, then you should catch all of the urine until after you awake for the normal daily activities, mix it, and take a portion for the test. The specimen should be frozen as soon as it is collected and shipped promptly to the laboratory.

The Laboratory Analysis

Extracting the entire group of organic acids and converting them into chemical derivatives that vaporize when heated mildly prepares the urine specimen for analysis of abnormalities.[8] A solution of the derivatives is injected into an instrument called a gas chromatograph that separates each compound. As they pass out the other end of a long thin tube, they enter a mass spectrograph that identifies and measures the amount of the compounds. The delicate, highly technical procedure must be performed by professionals trained in clinical and analytical chemistry who know how to maintain the instruments and handle the data. Calibrations and quality control specimens must be checked frequently. The technical difficulty of the procedure explains why only specialty laboratories and the largest pediatric research hospitals offer the testing.

The specimen is analyzed for the exact amount of about forty compounds. The report will show which compounds are in acceptable ranges and which are out of range. The compounds are grouped according to classes of information. Specific compounds have been identified as markers of essential nutrients like vitamins and amino acids.[9] There are several other types of information contained in the organic acids that appear. Some compounds come from processes of detoxification in the liver.[10] Others are the waste products of neurotransmitters like epinephrine and serotonin.[11]

Deficiencies of any of the following will be seen as abnormal levels of compounds in urine.

B Complex vitamins[6,12]	Carnitine[20]
Vitamin B_{12}[13-17]	N-Acetyl cysteine[10]
Biotin[18]	Glycine[21-23]
Coenzyme Q10[19]	Branched chain amino acids[24]

Still other compounds that are not produced in your tissues at all may appear in your urine; they are the products formed as the bacteria in the bowel act on undigested food and digestive juices.[25] Abnormal overgrowth of even good bacteria will show up as increased levels of these compounds, and such overgrowth is a factor leading to vitamin depletion.[26] Overgrowth of bacteria in the small and large intestine is frequently found in people who have digestive disturbances or who have had repeated treatments with antibiotics. Each of these classes of compounds can give valuable insight about basic health-sustaining processes.

Detoxification is just getting rid of the metabolic trash. Sometimes we add metabolic trash in what we eat and the air we breathe. Another source of such trash is those microbes always present in the gut. Ammonia is by far the most dangerous normal waste product of human and microbial metabolic activity. There is a special metabolic pathway called the urea cycle that is designed just to assure that ammonia is totally removed. This pathway has an essential nutrient requirement: the amino acid, arginine. Arginine deficiency blocks ammonia removal by the normal pathway. Because of the high toxicity of ammonia (the brain stops working if ammonia gets too high), there is a secondary pathway that is somewhat wasteful, but necessary. It produces the organic acid, orotate. High orotate in your urine means your ammonia detoxification is under stress and you may have a deficiency of arginine. (See Chapter 19, Amino Acids & Proteins, for more information about arginine.)

Another major liver detoxification activity is the removal of drugs and cell debris by attaching sulfur. The sulfur may be in the form of glutathione or simple sulfate. If you are not producing enough glutathione, a compound called pyroglutamate spills in urine. If your liver is running out of sulfate, then urinary sulfate will be low. For those who need a comprehensive review, a recent publication gives complete descriptions of the significance of the compounds that are reported.[27]

A Case Of Childhood Hyperactivity Disorder

After being kicked out of three day care centers for violent behavior, three pediatricians had seen three-year-old Johnny and told the parents, "He has behavioral problems and needs to see a psychologist. The psychologist reported that the child was an ADD candidate and added, "Wait two years before beginning Ritalin." The parents brought him for an examination to find an alternative to Ritalin.

The initial examination found itchy ears with drainage, itchy eyes with dark circles, nasal and sinus stuffiness and mucus, and a broad skin rash on the abdomen. Stuttering speech was noted and a symptom questionnaire completed by the parents had a high score of chronic symptoms.

A first morning urine specimen was sent to the lab for organic acid testing. A very abnormal pattern was found with thirty-one out of thirty nine organic acids above the normal range limits. The abnormalities included markers of impaired fatty acid and carbohydrate metabolism, multiple vitamin deficiencies including carnitine and biotin, poor ammonia clearance and high levels of several compounds formed by bacteria and yeast in the intestinal tract.

The abnormalities revealed deficiencies of B-complex vitamins, vitamin B_{12}, biotin and coenzyme Q10. Increased turnover of neurotransmitters was shown as well as multiple sources of toxicity that can affect brain chemistry (ammonia toxicity and elevated levels of bacterial and fungal products).

A high potency multiple vitamin, mineral formula was used morning and evening at dosages commensurate for the size of this child. Additional supplements of carnitine and biotin were used to overcome the metabolic blocks indicated by the elevated markers. To gain control of the intestinal microbial populations, herbal antibiotics and grapefruit seed extract were used to suppress the toxin-producing strains followed by lactobacillus strains to allow colonization with favorable bacteria.

A follow up test four weeks later showed normalization of energy pathway markers, and all dysbiosis products were within normal limits. The mother reported a dramatic improvement in behavior, and the symptom questionnaire was at a score less than half that found initially. Johnny had stopped wetting the bed and was sleeping through the night. He had started telling jokes and was back in preschool, getting along well with teachers.

The mother reports: "He seems happier. Before, when he became upset, nothing would keep him from getting more and more angry. The other day, he got angry at me for changing the radio station in the car. I told him, 'We are not going to do this.' And he actually stopped, looked at me and said, 'O.K.' Now that sounds like a little thing, but it is really a MAJOR improvement for him."

Although the precipitating events are unclear in the medical history of this three year old, the combination of multiple chemical markers of bacterial and fungal overgrowth in the upper gut revealed endotoxin and constant immune challenge to deplete nutrient reserves. Impaired central nervous system (CNS) function is suspected from the toxic bacterial and yeast products accompanied by multiple deficiencies of vitamins that form coenzymes critical for central energy pathways.

The rapidity and completeness of response to simple re-introduction of nutrients along with mild measures to normalize intestinal function shows the effectiveness of this approach as an alternative to Ritalin. Improvements in follow-up laboratory test results attest to the restoration of metabolic normalcy.

The Program For Correction

In order to help your doctor make decisions about how to correct the pathways that have abnormalities, the report contains a table showing the nutrients that can help for each case. Once you know which vitamins are lacking, a program of food supplementation that will overcome the deficiency can be set up. You can focus on those vitamins that are lacking and use maintenance levels of other vitamins to make sure that a new weak point does not develop. Special customized powders of vitamins are available from some compounding pharmacists. Otherwise, multivitamin products can be used with additional amounts of nutrients that need to be supplied at higher levels. "Free form" amino acids or small peptide mixtures are the best way to assure the availability of the amino acid for digestion in the small intestine. This is different from the use of protein supplements that may never be absorbed into your tissues if digestion is impaired.

In addition to vitamins and amino acids, the detoxification information tells if you need support for the liver in its role of removing toxins. The most often-used direct nutritional support are with special amino acids. Glycine, for example, is not needed if you are healthy, but extra amounts can assure the removal of many drugs and toxins from the internal and external environment. Some people need a special amino acid, N-acetyl cysteine, to form glutathione when the test shows that this critical detoxification and cell control compound is inadequate. Elevation of one of the compounds is a signal that a very high intake of vitamin C will be beneficial. For the bacterial or yeast overgrowth problems, the approach should achieve the following:

1. Reduced populations of toxin-producing organisms
2. Assurance of normal digestive function
3. Establishment of favorable microbe populations
4. Restoration of the integrity of the barriers that protect the tissues from the flow of toxins from the gut.

Powerful antibiotics are sometimes used, but they can exacerbate the problem by killing helpful bacteria. More gentle herbal compounds that suppress bacterial and yeast growth can be effective when used with strains of lactobacillus and other favorable organisms that can establish colonies to keep the proper balance. Dietary fiber and supplemental polysaccharides provide what the good bacteria need in order to multiply. The growth of favorable bacteria actually stimulates healthy intestinal tissue formation. This process can be enhanced by appropriate additions of the amino acid, glutamine, which is the primary energy source for the cells that line the small intestine.

Follow up

The levels of organic acids that appear in urine offer a sensitive test for detecting early signs of disturbances that undermine normal metabolism and the maintenance of healthy tissues. The patterns of abnormalities show where attention should be focused. Restoration of normality depends on the history of each case and the nature of the problems detected. B-complex vit-amin deficiencies are usually one of the easiest problems to overcome because of the ease of absorption and rapidity of tissue response when intake is increased. Normalization of metabolic markers may be seen in three to four weeks.

Detoxification problems may take longer because they usually are accompanied by toxin-mediated loss of cell controls and tissue turnover, including immune system signaling. If dysbiosis has been a long-standing problem, then extensive deterioration of digestive, immune, and absorptive function retards improvements in multiple ways and can self-limit the rate of progress. The rapidity of restoration in the little boy previously discussed attests to the relative short history of the problem and to the power of restoration inherent in children. Follow-up testing is normally spaced at three to four months when these problems are known, and have been present for many months or years.

Conclusion

The metabolic "soot" represented by high levels of organic acids in urine is a complex mixture. Individual components that may appear in the mixture can be routinely measured by modern analytical methods. Doctors can interpret abnormalities on laboratory reports of organic acids to determine how to overcome metabolic problems. The problems may be due to nutrient deficiencies, detoxification support, neurotransmitter synthesis, or intestinal microbial overgrowth. Corrections of these factors can remove underlying biochemical blocks in childhood development and neurological function.

Parasites and Detoxification:

Important Aids in Self Healing for ADD and Hyperactive Children and Adults

Aleks Radojcic, Dr. Ac., R.N.C.P.

There are many avenues of healing for the conditions known as ADD/ADHD. These include acupuncture (laser, traditional and auricular/ear acupuncture), energy healing such as Reiki and Therapeutic Touch, dietary changes, nutritional supplementation, and homeopathy.

From the perspective of the holistic health-care practitioner, any healing process begins with detoxification of the body. Contemporary lifestyles and environments contain many elements that weaken the immune system; elements such as an overuse of antibiotics, exposure to environmental toxins, pesticides in food, use of dental amalgam (an alloy of mercury combined with another metal such as silver, copper, tin or zinc) fillings, exposure to radiation from various sources such as hydro power lines, television, computers, and cell phones, poor elimination, and the presence of parasites in our bodies. These factors compromise the body's ability to eliminate all the accumulated toxins it has absorbed.

Bernard Jensen, N.D., D.C., a well-respected naturopathic doctor and author of numerous books, states in *Tissue Cleansing Through Bowel Management*: "Detoxification is often neglected, overlooked or underestimated in the healing art, despite the fact that all health professionals realize that a sick body is a toxic body." If the body is full of toxins, the best nutrition and supplements cannot be fully utilized. Thus, relying solely on the use of nutritional supplements with the hope of bridging the gap between what our bodies need and what may be missing is not sufficient for bringing about a better state of health.

The beginning of any cleanse must focus on the reality of parasitic infection.

Parasites are not only a problem in underdeveloped countries and tropical climates as it is commonly believed. On the contrary, many health practitioners have found that body parasites are at the root of scores of health problems in industrialized countries as well, and numerous books and articles have been published over the last few years on the topic of parasites.

Authors such as B. Jensen, N.D., C.D., Rev. Hanna Kroeger, A.L. Gittlemen, H.R. Clark, Ph.D., N.D., M. Walker, D.P.M., and Skye Weintraub, N.D., are just a few of the writers who have brought about a greater awareness of this subject.

Dr. Hulda Clark, Ph.D., N.D., has been especially instrumental in raising public awareness about parasites in her books *The Cure for all Cancers*, *The Cure for HIV/AIDS*, *The Cure for all Diseases*, and *The Cure for all Advanced Cancers*. Dr. Clark has found that parasites can be present anywhere in the body, and that they are one of the major causes of many health problems today. Dr. Bernard Jensen shares the same understanding as Dr. Clark. In his book *A Guide to Better Bowel Care*, Dr. Jensen states that parasites are the number one health enemy in the world. Many media reports corroborate the claims of Drs. Clark and Jensen.

A March 1995 headline in Health Freedom News USA reads: "Beware of Parasites in Your Drinking Water!" The Economist's November 1996 Science and Technology column, headlined "Checkmating Parasites" states: "The sex lives of parasites are not the stuff of scandals or fantasies. But they may have a crucial role in the evolution of disease in the age of AIDS." On June 23, 1998, a Toronto Star headline article reported a cyclospora outbreak. The possible culprit? Raspberries from Guatemala. The Toronto Star again reported on parasitic activity on June 30, 1998 in the article "China's Invisible Enemies." According to the article, an estimated 700 million Chinese harbor parasites. On August 1, 1998, the Toronto Star headline read "Parasites in Tap Water Create Panic in Sydney." The accompanying article explained that tap water in Sydney, Australia, was tainted by two dangerous parasites, giardia and cryptosporodium. Giardia produces gastrointestinal problems while cryptosporodium causes flu-like symptoms that can kill those with a weak immune system, such as the very young and elderly.

Numerous factors encourage the spread of parasites: increasing use of day-care centers; increasing international travel; contaminated water

> "The sex lives of parasites are not the stuff of scandals or fantasies.
> But they may have a crucial role in the evolution of disease in the age of AIDS."
>
> – The Economist

supplies; the use of tap water for colonics, enemas or cleaning contact lenses; the popularity of household pets (children playing in parks can get parasites, such as worms—naked soft-bodied parasites—through contact with freely roaming pets); walking barefoot on beaches or fields where animals or birds roam; the increasing popularity of exotic foods; excessive use of antibiotics and immunosuppressive drugs; eating in fast food restaurants; eating microwave-cooked food; eating sushi or any raw or undercooked food; eating pickled fish or smoked foods; failing to wash with soap and water before eating, after using the washroom, or after handling a pet; and unsafe sex. The warning signs of a possible parasitic infection are constipation, diarrhea, gas and bloating, irritable bowel syndrome, skin conditions, allergies, sleeping problems, memory problems, joint and muscle aches and pains, nervousness, anemia, sore mouth and gums, teeth grinding, and chronic fatigue and other immune problems. One option for eliminating parasites is the use of anti-parasitic drugs. In emergency situations, this may be initially preferable to herbal remedies. However, the lifespan of many parasites is 90 days (from egg to larva to full grown adult laying down the next generation of eggs), and using medical drugs for that long may be very hard on the body. This may be especially true for patients who have more than one kind of parasite and need to use several different drugs in combination. In many cases, anti-parasitic prescription drugs do not prove effective because symptoms disappear temporarily, only to reappear later on. Moreover, while the drugs destroy the parasites, they also destroy healthy intestinal flora.

There are several herbal options. The research and clinical experience of Dr. Clark has identified wormwood, cloves, and black walnut as having excellent deworming properties. A very effective herbal formula that also works well is a mixture of Wormwood, Thyme, Quassia, Centaury, Tansy, Elecampane, Blue Vervain, and Self-heal African birds pepper, along with cloves and immature hulls of green black walnut fruit. These herbs can also be used as a preventative treatment, whether or not an actual infection is present. Most herbs, in fact, have a multifaceted ability to spark positive changes in people's lives. In addition, there are a number of foods that can serve to prevent parasitic infection and to eliminate them once infection has occurred. These foods are garlic, onions, sauerkraut, horseradish, ginger, raw pumpkin seeds, raw beets and carrots, figs, raw papaya seed, pomegranate and cranberry juice.

After the parasite-detoxification program is completed, patients can proceed to cleanse all the other major elimination channels: skin, lungs, large intestine, kidneys/bladder and liver. The skin eliminates water, salts and waste products. The lungs eliminate carbon dioxide and water. The intestines eliminate roughage, water, salt, and dead cells. Kidneys eliminate salts, urea, uric acid, metabolized hormones, and water. The liver transforms toxins from fat-soluble to water-soluble compounds before the kidneys eliminate them. The importance of liver cleansing cannot be overestimated. The liver is like a sponge that soaks up toxins, sorts them out, and directs them toward other channels of elimination. If the bowel is overloaded with toxins, the liver takes over in order to detoxify it. If the liver itself is overburdened, toxins spill over into the blood stream. This impairs circulation, causing allergies and skin conditions to develop. The liver also stores and distributes nourishment for the entire body and aids in the metabolism of carbohydrates, fats and proteins. Some examples of foods that can be used for strengthening and detoxifying the liver are dandelion, black radish, carrot, black cherry, artichoke and beets, and all greens that are rich in chlorophyll. An effective herbal formula for the liver consists of milk thistle, black radish, yellow dock, liverwort, sorrel, turkey rhubarb, sage, and rosemary.

After we have cleansed the liver and completed the parasite elimination program, we can now cleanse another very important organ of elimination: the large intestine. An imbalance in the large intestine can manifest as any of the following or a combination of these symptoms: an irregularity in bowel movements (constipation, diarrhea, candidiasis), pressure in the head and sinuses, headaches, sore throat, coughing, recurrent bronchitis, psoriasis, eczema, food sensitivities, hemorrhoids, and prostate problems. In order to facilitate bowel elimination, we must increase our intake of high fiber foods: salads, raw vegetables, raw beets, carrots, sauerkraut, walnuts and linseed, figs, prunes, et cetera. We should also consume eight to ten glasses of water per day, exercise, and use herbal laxatives with fibers until regularity is achieved and continued for a while. These measures eliminate sluggish bowel problems by increasing the regularity of bowel movements.

Another good adjunct for the herbal part of a bowel cleansing program is the use of bentonite clay. Bentonite is a ground-up volcanic ash. It is insoluble in water and swells up to 12 times its original volume when added to water. It can absorb toxins like a magnetic sponge and pick up or remove these from the intestinal tract. Bentonite also helps remove bacteria and parasites from the intestine. Its action may also remove some nutrients from the intestinal tract, and what is left of a good flora. Therefore, use of supplements and bacterial culture (acidophilus/bifidus) will bring the colon into an optimal state of health. The use of a high enema or colon hydrotherapy is another good adjunct to the use of herbal remedies for promoting healing of the intestinal tract. Dr. Max Gerson, Dr. Bernard Jensen, and Dr. Norman Walker (who lived to be 109), were among many doctors who have employed these methods of healing in their practice. Colonic irrigation is usually administered by trained practitioners in holistic clinics. The process cleanses the colon of toxins not eliminated through the use of herbs, diet, and herbal laxatives.

The next step is to cleanse the kidneys and bladder for a period of two weeks or longer. These two organs are closely related and must be treated together. Some foods that are traditionally used to support the kidneys are parsley, dandelion, lecithin, fresh cranberry and apple juice combined, watermelon (and its seeds), and a fresh juice combination of carrot, parsley, garlic, and ginger. These juices can be taken at any stage of the herbal detoxification program. There are a number of herbs that have been traditionally used for balancing and cleansing the kidneys, such as corn silk, uva ursi, buchu, and golden rod. An effective herbal formula can contain a mixture of hydrangea, gravel root, cleavers, marshmallow root, white birch, knot-grass, juniper berries, shave grass, and Vitamins B_2, B_6, A and C. Potassium and the amino acids L-arginine and L-methionine are also useful for improving urinary tract functioning. (For more information of the role of amino acids, refer to Chapter 19, Amino Acids and Proteins). In the case of a urinary tract infection, garlic is one of the most powerful antibiotics available.

When the whole body cleanse has been completed, the final step is to rebuild the system with good nutrition and the supplemental use of digestive food enzymes such as lactobacillus-acidophilus flora, greens, micro algaes such as spirulina, chlorella, and sea weeds, essential fatty acids, bee pollen, and lecithin. Human micro-flora should be particularly emphasized because it is a crucial part of the immune system. The function of human intestinal flora is to provide a barrier to infection by protecting the immune system, removing toxic substances and carcinogens, and creating nutrients such as B-vitamins, short chain fatty acids and amino acids, and enzyme production from lactase to l. acidiophilus. This often results in a normalization of sugar and serum cholesterol levels. The most common causes of micro-flora imbalance are malabsorption of nutrients, overgrowth of potential pathogens due to diarrhea, constipation, the use of antibiotics and oral contraceptives, parasites and fungal overgrowth, radiation, chemotherapy, and heavy metal poisoning. It takes only ten days to destroy most of the good flora through the use of antibiotics, and it takes approximately one year of living a healthy life style to replenish lost bacterial flora. It is important to use quality supplements with a high quality count of acidophilus/bifidus bacteria, and it is important to be aware that most commercial yogurt, with the exception of Bio K Plus, have little or none of the bacteria needed to replenish flora.

An important part of detoxification, one that is not well understood, is the healing crisis. It is a natural consequence of removing toxins from our bodies. The process of detoxification causes toxins to pass into the bloodstream for elimination by way of the liver, kidneys, spleen, skin, bladder and colon. During the healing crisis, whatever symptoms have been suppressed through the use of antibiotics, surgery, poor nutrition, and exposure to environmental toxins, will reappear again for a short time. Persons under-going the detoxification process may become frustrated with the process if they do not have an appreciation of this phenomenon, along with the guid-ance and support of a health practitioner during critical stages.

The symptoms of a healing crisis may include nausea, headache, sleepi-ness, fatigue, diarrhea, colds, ear infections, boils, or skin eruptions. These symptoms can last from a few hours to a few days, and in very rare cases can even last 1 to 2 weeks. The length of the healing crisis will depend on the amount of toxins the body needs to eliminate, and it can occur at any point during the detoxification program, often just at the time when the patient has regained some vitality and has begun to feel better. In addition, there may be several "plateaus" in the healing crisis during which sup-pressed symptoms may resurface. After going through the first plateau, patients begin to feel better—until they reach the next plateau. Knowledge, patience and perseverance will all pay off during the healing crisis. It should also be understood that mental functioning and emotional clarity are insep-arable from one's state of physical wellness.

A thorough, whole-body cleanse can produce exceptional levels of phys-ical healing, as well as improve all levels of mental and emotional health. For the child or adult with ADD/ADHD, internal cleansing is an essential com-ponent in any treatment program since it will allow both mind and body to be more receptive to other healing modalities.

Product sources are listed in Appendix E. This is not an endorsement of these products, as declared in the Publisher's Note in this book's front matter.

The Thyroid and Hyperactivity

– Paul Richard Saunders, Ph.D., N.D., D.H.A.N.P., C.C.H.

Your body contains several different endocrine glands, each with a vital role for your daily survival and functioning. The thyroid gland is located in front of your throat just below your Adam's apple. The two principal functions of the thyroid gland are regulating protein metabolism and regulating the body's use of oxygen. The result is that the thyroid, much like the thermostat for your furnace, sets the rate at which your body (furnace) uses food (fuel) and consumes oxygen to create heat or body warmth. This is referred to as your basal metabolic rate.

If the thyroid is over-active, as in hyperthyroid conditions, then one can be agitated, hyper, and always hungry and always eating but never gaining weight and often losing weight. If the thyroid is under-active, as in hypothyroid conditions, then one is often lethargic, slow mentally, and may gain weight or retain fluid. In the hyperthyroid state the body is metabolizing protein and using oxygen at a faster than normal rate, thus the thinness or weight loss. In the hypothyroid state the body's rate of metabolism is very slow, food is slowly utilized to build protein, and therefore oxygen requirements are reduced. Of the two extremes hyperthyroidism is much less common and if a thyroid storm ensues (fever, weakness, muscle wasting, extreme restlessness, confusion, psychosis or coma) this is a medical emergency that can be life threatening.

Hypothyroidism is much more common and may affect 15-20% of the North American population in subclinical to more significant forms. The most common symptoms are weakness, dry skin, coarse skin, lethargy, slow speech, edema (swelling) around the eyes, feeling cold, decreased sweating, cold skin, thick skin, coarse hair, paleness, impaired memory and constipation. Conventional medical diagnosis requires a blood serum test demonstrating an elevated sensitive thyroid stimulating hormone (sTSH), and a decreased T3 and/or T4. T4 is the less active, precursor hormone produced by the thyroid gland. T3 is the more active hormone and converted form of T4 that directly effects the metabolic rate of all body organs and systems and their cells.

Naturopathic physicians and many of the conventional medical physicians who employ complementary and alternative medical (integrative medicine) practices such as nutrition will also concurrently use the above blood serum test and the basal body temperature test pioneered by Dr. Broda O. Barnes, Ph.D., M.D.. Dr. Barnes found that a low basal body temperature (armpit temperature on first morning waking) correlated with signs and symptoms of hypothyroidism.

How does this relate to a person with ADD/ADHD? Clearly you can see a correlation between hyperthyroid and the hyperactive. But this is not a common occurrence. Much more common is hypothyroid and ADD/ADHD. "How can this be?" you ask.

Hypothyroid people are often dull, apathetic, and less active and less socially interactive and developed. Paradoxically they can also, especially as children, be nervous, hyperactive, aggressive, emotional and prone to temper tantrums. They will have shorter attention spans, moving from one activity to another in a second, have more colds, ear infections, influenza or other childhood illnesses, and sleep longer or have poorer sleep habits. This is probably related to fatigue, something a child cannot easily express or understand—it is as if the hyperactivity acts to combat the fatigue. As these problems escalate and the child enters school, the lack of self confidence and social skills present as restlessness, and an inability to sit and focus for any length of time, resulting in poor performance and the label of "problem" student by the teacher.

In girls, the onset of menarche (first menstrual period), which is alarmingly earlier in North America compared with the rest of the world according to *Time Magazine* (Oct. 30, 2000), can lead to anemia and further fatigue, poor concentration and lack of resistance to infections. While the typical hypothyroid person is thought of as shorter in stature, critical timing of the low thyroid function can result in a taller individual. The increased height is because the long bones do not get the signal to stop growth, so the person continues to grow.

When a hyperactive child becomes an adult, he or she can be mislabeled as neurotic or hypochondriacal, with poor social skills, memory and functioning. They may be prone to headaches, circulatory problems and symptoms of hypothyroidism.

Treatment is different for each individual. Nutritional supplements may be given to aid the conversion of T4 to T3. Iodine or desiccated (completely dried out) thyroid will be given in cases where the essential iodine or hormone cofactors are missing. Dietary modification is often required to ensure the proper balance of proteins, fats and carbohydrates within meals and across the day and week. Junk food needs to be removed from the diet. Caffeine can be a negative stimulant to an under-active system and may be abused by these individuals. Appropriate exercise can help increase the basal metabolic rate, but sleep, that essential time for your body's renewal that so many are forfeiting, must be also be given considerable attention or fatigue will continue. Visualization is also important for creating calmness, positive self-image and addressing deeper emotional issues. Remember, assessing thyroid function is one part of the larger issue of ADD/ADHD.

Acupressure:
Use of Acupressure Beads in the Treatment of ADHD
Dr. Michael O. Smith, M.D., et al.

At the Lincoln Hospital Recovery Center in Bronx, NY, we have used ear acupuncture as a treatment for drug and alcohol abuse for the past 25 years. In 1997, we began to expand our clinical practice to include the treatment of attention deficit hyperactivity disorder (ADHD) on a pilot basis. We have used a type of acupressure bead (called "ear magnet seeds" in Chinese) that is easily applicable to the surface of the ear by adhesive tape. The bead is a round metallic object that is coated with gold. It is somewhat larger than most acupressure devices. There is often a clear sensation of Qi when this bead is applied.

We use a treatment location on the posterior surface of the external ear that is just the opposite of the "shemmen" location on the anterior surface. This location is above the superior end of the "depression groove." One can frequently observe distended veins, moderate erythema, and poor skin tone at this location, suggesting a need for tonification treatment. These beads merely rest in place; they do not need to be pressed or manipulated. The beads must be replaced whenever the adhesiveness of the tape becomes inadequate.

Treatment is more or less continuous for the duration of the patient's problem. We have trained colleagues in several clinics to use this technique on a pilot basis. Most of the ADHD patients come to us when they are taking medication, but continuing to have very significant symptoms. We never suggest that medication be changed when the beads are applied. Medication should only be changed on the basis of clear changes of the clinical picture by the primary prescribing physician. The following colleagues contributed to this report: Cindy Walsh-Briolat, LPN, Memphis MI; Karen, L.Ac, Everett WA; and Jo Ann Lenney, Lincoln Hospital, Bronx NY.

Many of the anecdotal results have been impressive.

1. DB was placed on Ritalin 30mg/day at age 4. He was an angry
    child who destroyed anything in his way. He had an attention span
    of less than 5 seconds. On daytime medication, DB sat unproduc-
    tively most of the day. In the evenings he was restless, tearful, and
    hyperactive. By age 14, DB was taking Dexedrine, Lithium, and
    Catapres. His blood pressure was 150/90. The medications ren-
    dered him sometimes somnolent and sometimes hyperactive,
    unable to have a productive life on any dose of medication. His par-
    ents had tried numerous additional remedies to no avail.

    At age 14 (in 1996) DB responded immediately to his first ear
    acupressure treatment. His sleep and activity patterns normalized
    within a week. His blood pressure and symptoms of depression also
    subsided within weeks. Soon DB was using acupressure seeds and
    beads on a regular basis. His school performance improved steadily
    even as the Dexedrine was being discontinued. In 1998, DB partic-
    ipated in drivers' education classes, rode horses, maintained a part-
    time job, mentored kindergarten children, and was able to study for
    hours at a time. He has become a charming, relaxed young adult
    who is quite aware of his educational deficits and is seeking to
    improve himself on a daily basis. DB is able to tell his mother when
    he needs to have a follow-up acupressure bead treatment.

2. GH is a 5-year-old boy living in a therapeutic residence because of
    his mother's clinical status. GH would stomp frequently and
    required 7 "time-outs" per day for social management. After one
    week of acupressure bead placement, GH could sit calmly and no
    longer required "time outs" for social control. His teacher says he
    completes his homework and "now learns so fast." The beads
    "make me happy" GH says.

3. DK was abandoned at the age of 2 and entered foster care. He was
    developmentally delayed and placed on Ritalin and Ativan. At age
    12 (1998), DK was living with his aunt and doing poorly even in
    special education classes. After the acupressure beads were applied
    in May 1998, DK was able to focus in school, and his bouts of
    anger decreased. Soon DK began to talk about his mother in a
    hopeful manner. He visited her each weekend over the summer and
    will now be able to live with her in a constructive manner. DK no
    longer takes medication and is able to ask for acupressure beads
    whenever he feels it is necessary.

4. Often our youthful patients ask that their parents have the same
    acupressure treatment. Here is a report by the mother of AT: "The
    beads have helped tremendously. I have been able to stay focused

and my mind has stopped spinning. My son has been able to stop being so wild. He has calmed down a hundred percent."

Most of the ADHD children have responded favorably to this treatment within the first week of bead placement. Their responses seem independent of the family's motivation or other psychosocial variations. Treatment effects also seem to be unrelated to the use of medication. Obviously, a controlled randomized outcome study would help us clarify the potential value of this treatment. Furthermore, it should be noted that we have only one point location and one method of stimulation. Results might be improved by using different clinical procedures.

This report is a preliminary anecdotal finding. Nevertheless, it is quite encouraging to see apparently unmanageable chronic patients respond favorably to a safe, inexpensive treatment.

For patient treatment and professional inquiries about the use of acupressure beads in the treatment of Attention Deficit Hyperactivity Disorder (ADHD), contact:

Lincoln Medical and Mental Health Center
Recovery Program Center
234 Eugenio Maria De Hostos Blvd.
Bronx NY 10451
Tel: (718) 993-3100

A Cure for Autism and the ADD/Hyperactivity Connection

Chip Dopson, President, Chisolm Biologic Labs
Pam Floener, P.T., R.M.A., C.N.C., C.T.

Our scientific work in the field of immunology began in 1976 under H. Hugh Fudenberg, MD. From this early work, our ever-accumulating knowledge of autism has evolved to our current understanding that these children are plagued with multiple social and health issues, not the least of which includes an over-burdened, dysfunctional immune system. Many of these children are suffering from sub-clinical viral, bacterial, fungal and parasitic diseases – all of which only manifest in the immune compromised individual. In search of a common denominator, Dr. Fudenberg hypothesized in 1988 that these children were injured in some way by vaccine therapy – particularly the measles-mumps-rubella (MMR) vaccine. He further suggested that these children might benefit from preparations of dialyzed lymphocyte extracts (DlyE) derived from inhabitants of the same household.

More recently, Dr. Andrew Wakefield demonstrated the presence of live measles virus in intestinal lymphoid tissue of autistic children suffering from inflammatory bowel disease.

Our own extensive work in the area of diagnostics and therapeutics for Lyme disease over the past few years led us to hypothesize that this pandemic bacterial infection may also contribute to the autistic condition. To test our theory, we randomly selected 4 children from a group of 20 autistic children and tested them for Borrelia burgdorferi. All four tested positive. This is significant since none of these children were infected via the usual vectors, nor did they ever display the acute symptoms of Lyme disease.

Current data appears to indicate Autism is a multi-faceted condition existing in multiple "layers" of accumulated infective agents, and complicated by an impaired ability to detoxify through the usual pathways.

If these babies are infected in-utero with herpes type 1 and 2, Lyme disease, EBV, and CMV as has been suggested, this implies an already weakened immune system present at birth. The implication would be that these children are born with a chronic condition that prevents a normal immune response – including their response to MMR vaccine. Is autism an immune response gone wrong? Most parents of autistic children report the symptoms appeared after the first MMR vaccination was administered. If MMR is the proverbial "straw" that broke the camel's back, can the effects be reversed?

It was our burning desire to answer this question that motivated us to develop protocols to reverse the autistic condition through practical approaches of penetrating the layers of bacterial, viral, fungal and parasitic infections so frequently found in this population. We have observed dramatic improvement in 50-60% of the children treated with Transfer Factor (TF).

Our knowledge and skill lies in the ability to create specific Transfer Factors which address pathogens that are commonly found in the autistic population. The success to date with our latest TF product has been very promising. Currently we are in the final development stage of an autism specific Transfer Factor that will address the various pathogens that encumber the immune system of autism victims.

Our immediate project is the development of a measles-specific Transfer Factor. We anticipate complete eradication of the live measles virus in autistic children. This will serve as further proof and documentation that antigen specific Transfer Factors are a valid adjunctive therapy in the treatment approach to reverse autism.

ADD and Autism — Is there a connection?

Before ADD was identified and recognized, the condition of autism already existed. It seemingly came from no where and the medical community was at a loss as how to treat it. Dr. Bernie Rimland, considered the "father" of research into autism, was the first to suggest that autism may be an expression of an adverse reaction to vaccines. Most autism victims appeared to develop and behave normally until the first MMR (measles, mumps and rubella) vaccine was administered. In 1988, Dr. Hugh Fudenberg, a renowned immunologist, also suggested a correlation between vaccination and autism.

Over the next ten years, scientists in the U.S. and Japan, operating on the hypothesis that vaccines were connected to autism, began to test autistic children for viral and bacterial antigens. The majority of these children tested positive for active measles virus in the blood as well as other viral and bacterial antigens such as Epstein-Barr virus and the Borrelia burgdorferi spirochete (Lyme disease). Japanese researchers reported at the 1999

Defeat Autism Now Conference (DAN) that their research revealed the measles virus strain found in autistic children to be genetically identical to the attenuated measles strain used in the MMR vaccine given to children at 18 months of age. It would certainly appear that in some children, the MMR vaccine had triggered the autistic condition, causing an "acquired "or pseudo-autistic condition. The question now is, were these children already immune compromised and the vaccine was the proverbial "straw," or did the vaccine cause the immune system to become weakened allowing secondary chronic infections? Is autism an adverse reaction, or a latent sub-clinical immune deficiency condition brought on by the vaccine?

It is difficult to ferret out the statistics in the US population since America has had a vaccination program in place for more that 30 years. In fact, the Federal Government requires 90% compliance in the vaccine program and accomplishes this goal through the schools by tying compliance to federal funding. The vaccine manufacturers and federal regulatory agencies deny that there is any connection between autism and the vaccine. Even though there have been no safety studies on the vaccine, they insist the vaccine is safe based on years of use. It would appear, however, that a drop in the mandatory 90% compliance rate would appreciably affect their bottom line.

In less than ten years after implementing the U.S. vaccine protocol, the incidence of autism in Kuwait rose from 1 in 10,000 births to 1 in 300 births —a rate similar to that reported in the U.S. and other countries which adopted the U.S. model of vaccine therapy.

To better evaluate the implication of vaccine injury, let us examine the statistics in the children of Kuwait. Prior to the Desert Storm operation, this country did not routinely vaccinate its children. The incidence of autism was 1 in 10,000 births. After Desert Storm, the U.S. vaccine protocol was implemented and the autism rate soared to 1 in 300 births in less than 10 years – about the same as the incidence of autism in the U.S. population and other countries that have adopted the U.S. model of vaccine therapy. These countries implement the program under the assumption that vaccines have been safety tested by the U.S. FDA. The fact is there are no safety studies on MMR vaccine.

The subjective data collected from the mothers of autistic children tells us that these children's immune systems may have already been weakened by an infection present at the time or shortly before the MMR vaccine was administered. Some of the mothers recall that the child had an ear, upper respiratory, or some other type of infection at the time of vaccination. This may have altered the child's immune response to the vaccine, allowing the attenuated measles virus to manifest as a low level chronic infection which expressed itself as the autistic condition or a pseudo-autism since these children showed no symptoms of autism from birth to 18 months of age.

But what about the autistic children that did not have an obvious infection at the time of vaccination? A large majority of these children tested positive not only for the measles virus, but also for other viral and bacterial infections such as Epstein-Barr virus and the Lyme disease's spirochete. These same organisms are also present in high percentages of persons afflicted with ADD, ADHD, Chronic Fatigue syndrome, ALS (Lou Gerhig's Disease), MS (Multiple Sclerosis), Fibromyalgia and Rheumatoid Arthritis as documented by Lida Mattman, Ph.D., during her tenure at Wayne State University.

Once thought to be carried only by the deer tick, Lyme disease, caused by the Borrelia burgdorferi spirochete, is carried by other vectors as well. One can unwittingly be infected by the bite of fire ants, mosquitoes and black biting flies from coastal areas and contaminated water. The spirochete is also present in the milk of infected nursing mothers. Infections of Lyme disease by one of these carriers appear to cause low level chronic infections, as contrasted with the acute symptoms caused by a tick bite. Dr. Mattman documented that the spirochete becomes cell-wall deficient and lives in a cyst form inside the red blood cell preventing the immune system from creating antibodies that are normally carried in the blood and detected by routine serum antibody tests. This also raises concerns that blood transfusions and sexual contact may result in transmission of this spirochete to others. A large percentage of individuals tested for Lyme disease through a relatively newly-developed antigen test on urine and blood culture show positive results even though there is no history of tick bite. The serum antibody test for Lyme disease usually renders a false negative with this type of infection, steering the competent physician away from an accurate diagnosis and appropriate therapeutic treatment.

It is estimated that approximately 80% of the US population has been infected with the Epstein-Barr virus (EBV). This virus is believed to cause mononucleosis or the "kissing disease" as it is most common among adolescents and young adults. It has also been implicated in Chronic Fatigue Syndrome. Classic symptoms of an EBV infection are that it is almost always preceded by a strep infection of the throat with flu-like symptoms, fatigue that ranges from mild to debilitating, and low-grade fever. There are those in the medical community who theorize it is actually the strep infection that is present first. The strep infection weakens the immune system, and EBV, they say, is merely an opportunistic virus that is only able to invade an already-weakened immune system. This may also be the case with other viruses like measles. If a child's immune system is already weakened by another infection, does the introduction of another weakly viable virus cause an altered immune response in a weakened host? This is yet another question to be answered by science.

Immunological theory has always maintained that once you have been infected with a virus, your immune system makes antibodies against that virus and retains a memory of the virus so that theoretically, you never again have an acute infection from the same virus. It is now being considered that an immune system, already taxed by another infectious agent and unable to mount a complete immune response, would allow a superimposed low level infection to exist and to thrive.

It has always been assumed that once the antibody attaches itself to the antigen (live virus), the virus becomes inactive or dies. Since most infections from viruses are short lived, the detection of the active antigen is often difficult and tests for antigens often are negative due to the short time period of the virus's activity. Antibody tests were developed to detect immune response to various infectious agents so that past infections could be detected. It does seem plausible, given the limitations of testing, that live viruses never become completely inactive or die, but merely fall below an activity level detectable by current test methods. Further, in an already compromised immune host, antibody levels (assuming that any were made) may not be numerous enough to be detected by the antibody test. Therefore, you would get a false negative on both the antigen and antibody tests leading to the incorrect assumption that the suspected virus had not infected the host. Thus, the virus could be transmitted to others with weakened immune systems.

Additional questions, burning in the minds of progressive research scientists, is whether ADD is merely a milder, less severe form of autism?

Individuals suffering from Chronic Fatigue Syndrome, Fibromyalgia, Multiple Sclerosis, and ALS (Lou Gehrig's Disease), as well as ADD and Autism, have at least one thing in common—a compromised immune system. The etiology of these conditions is unknown, but continued research reveals similar symptom patterns. These individuals are usually infected with multiple viral, bacterial and fungal infectious microbes. Biochemically there are similarities in allergic patterns to environment and food, intestinal parasites, amino acid deficiencies, fatty acid imbalance, and exposures to and accumulations of environmental toxins including heavy metals and pesticides. Here too, the vaccination question looms over these conditions.

Science Offers Hope

While one group of scientists is exploring the cause and effect of disease states, there is yet another that searches for treatments or cures. This is also true with ADD and autism. One very promising area of research recently introduced to the US is Transfer Factor (TF). It is literally the transfer of immunity from one model to another. Since diseases can be transferred –

why not immunity? The theory of transferred immunity was documented as early as 1949. Transfer Factor (TF) helps the individual's own immune system learn to recognize foreign invaders and to create antibodies against the invading organism. Immunomodulators have been used to boost the immune system in general, but does not cause specific antibodies to be created against specific antigens. Antigen specific Transfer Factor (TF) appears to educate the immune system creating a specific immune response directly targeted at the invading organism. Additionally, Transfer Factor (TF) helps the immune system retain "memory" against the specific antigen.

Transfer Factors (TF) are small, low molecular weight proteins found in colostrum – the first substance produced in lactating females prior to milk production and in white blood cells of animals and humans. TF in itself does not kill or cure specific antigens. Its function is to "train" the immune system to recognize antigens so the immune system can create the antibodies that attack the antigen. The immune system is supposed to do this on its own, but in some individuals, it appears to lack the ability to recognize, memorize and produce antibodies for some low level antigens. It is as though the immune system has lost its "memory."

TF's have been developed for EBV, Lyme disease, CMV, hepatitis, and viral cancers. These are all reported in the literature. The most recently developed Transfer Factor addresses measles, mumps and rubella viral loads. Early clinical outcomes have been very encouraging. Use of antigen specific Transfer Factor for MMR in several autistic children appears to have diminished their viral titers. These children have become more aware of their surroundings and more normal in their behavior. Several of the children in the TF project have completely recovered normal behavior and are now attending regular school. A larger clinical study needs to be organized to further document the affect Transfer Factor has on true autism (present at birth) versus pseudo-autism that appears in the second year or later of life.

To this author's knowledge, TF therapy has not been tried on children with ADD. If the hypothesis that ADD is merely a milder form of autism is accurate, TF should cause these children to show improvement as well.

Diseases that have appeared in the latter 20th century are a puzzle to which all the pieces have yet to be found. They are a mystery to unravel through the careful and tedious task of gathering information and relying on scientific methods and new technology to yield direction and answers. It has only been in the recent past that laboratory technology has advanced enough to develop some of the newer tests that help identify stressors of the immune system and chronic low level infections that previously were undetectable by the testing methods available.

This technology is relatively new and few physicians are familiar with the implication of vaccine injury or Transfer Factor therapy. This has, to say the least, been frustrating for the suffering individual as they are often first to discover information through books or the internet, but find deaf ears when they approach their health care provider.

Newer treatments, such as those with Transfer Factor, are also new to the traditional doctor and often discounted since most of these treatments come from small independent laboratories and not major pharmaceutical companies from which physicians have come to consider the "authority" on treatments. The few doctors that are familiar with this approach are scattered throughout the US. If you feel you have exhausted all your avenues, you may want to broach the subject of TF with your current physician. Physicians may contact Chisolm Biological Laboratories in South Carolina at 803-663-9618 for an information package on ImmunFactor® products. Consumers refer to product and source information in Appendix E in the back of this book.

Chisolm Biological Laboratories produces several ImmunFactor® products designed to support the immune system against candida albicans, chlamydia pneumoniae, cytomegalovirus, Epstein-Barr virus, staphylococcus, measles, mumps and rubella virus, as well as several others. Their principal scientist and President, Minter Dopson, has been making TF products since 1978. CBL is recognized among its peers as a main leader in the cutting edge field of nutritionals for immune modulation and support. For the past 20 years, they have been involved in the processing of animal blood plasmas for Bectin-Dickinson and the Centers for Disease Control.

Mercury Poisoning:
A Cause of Learning Disabilities
Wayne Obie

Chelation Therapy:
A Way to Deal With Mercury
Dr. Fred Hui, M.D.

Mercury Poisoning and "Silver Fillings"
Wayne Obie

Mercury, the most toxic, non-radioactive substance known to humanity, is passed by unsuspecting mothers to their newborn children through the placenta, and through breast milk. Incidence of mercury poisoning in children is found to be substantially increased when a mother with mercury amalgam fillings has dental work performed during her pregnancy.

Fillings that are black, gray or silver in color are mercury fillings, without exception! Fillings that are called "Silver Fillings" or "Amalgam Fillings" are in all instances mercury amalgam fillings. Each mercury filling contains between 48% and 52% mercury. The average filling weighs one gram.

While cavities resulting in the placement of mercury fillings in children are

Challenge and fecal analysis performed by diagnostic laboratories on children with learning disabilities in the U.S., Canada and Europe have demonstrated that a very large percentage of children with learning disabilities have elevated levels of mercury in their systems.

generally on the decrease, this does not seem to be true for children with ADD, ADHD and autism.

We have found through our work that children with learning disabilities and autism have more mercury fillings than any other group of children. We strongly suspect that this is due to the fact that mercury toxicity is a major factor in creating or worsening these conditions.

While there is a growing number of mercury free dentists throughout North America and around the world who provide scientifically recognized safe amalgam-free dental care for adults, the same does not hold true for children, more particularly children with ADD, ADHD and autism.

> Health Canada, in their 1995 Position Paper, stated that mercury amalgam fillings should not be used in the primary teeth of children.

Health Canada, in their 1995 Position Paper, stated that mercury amalgam fillings should not be used in the primary teeth of children. However, five years later, dentists are still using mercury as the filling material of choice.

Health Canada's Position Paper also indicated that mercury fillings should not be mixed at any time with other metals in the mouth. However, we have found that eight out of ten children with learning disabilities and mercury fillings also have crowns and other devices made of nickel and other alloys in their mouths. The galvanization of this mixture of metals can result in ringing ears and a myriad of various symptoms which would be instrumental in further compromising the child's condition.

Extremely concerned about the growing number of children adversely affected, CFMR (Canadians For Mercury Relief) recently contacted over 200 mercury-free dentists in the U.S.A. and Canada, inquiring as to whether or not they do treat, or would consider treating, children with autism and behavioral problems. Of our 200 inquiries we could not find one single mercury free dentist willing to provide treatment. In every single instance, they referred me to a specialist that they used.

Our observation: Most of the good biological mercury free dentists are extremely busy, with appointments booked up to six months in advance. While some do handle children, none were equipped or inclined to deal with the challenges that are presented with that of many special needs children. This is something that will change with the elimination of mercury in dentistry, and as mercury-free dentistry becomes more competitive.

Next, I started contacting the specialists that the mercury free dentists were referring us to. Without exception, from Los Angeles to New York and from Montreal to Vancouver, all of these so-called "Specialists" used mercury. My conclusion, was that the only thing that made these dentists

"Specialists" in dealing with these children was that they had the restraints, anesthetics, and in many cases access to hospital facilities that they felt were necessary to fill the children's heads with even more mercury and silver. None of these dentists were members of any biological dental associations, and most considered mercury to be absolutely safe.

Our efforts to help these mercury toxic children appeared helpless, until just before publication of this book when we convinced one of Canada's original mercury free dentists to get involved. Effective September 2000, Dairy Lane Dental Associates in Huntsville, Ontario, is accepting children with ADD, ADHD and autism for treatment, in a one-of-a-kind North American Clinic which will feature not only bio-compatible dentistry for these children, but also accommodations for the children and their parents specifically geared to servicing their special needs. Plans are already underway to add a research and educational facility in the next year, which will be devoted to training biological dentists and providing detoxification support for patients.

The Bottom Line

If your child has ADD, ADHD, suffers from hyperactivity or autism, or has any other behavioral or learning disability, and he or she has even one mercury filling, GET IT OUT! Mercury is poison!

Mercury and Vaccinations

Mercury is used in vaccinations as a preservative (Thermisol). Over the past number of years, we have heard from many parents with children who developed an increase or sudden appearance of symptoms associated with hyperactivity, ADD and autism after vaccinations.

If your child is affected by any of these symptoms, it is important that your child be tested for mercury poisoning and treated. Treatment consists of getting the mercury out of your child, and this is not by any means a simple matter as mercury crosses the blood brain barrier and is absorbed by the body's tissues.

There is much controversy about chelation (a process by which mercury is pulled out of the body), and many of the doctors themselves do not agree as to what is the correct method to detoxify.

Some treatments seem to take years and offer little if any benefit, while other treatments are said to be invasive with many side effects. The fact is that not enough research has been done.

While there are a number of researchers, scientists and doctors working and learning more about heavy metals and treatments, for the most part none of these efforts have had the support of the mainstream medical establishment. The ADA (American Dental Association) is still saying that mercury amalgam fillings are the best filling material, based on the fact that they have been used for over 150 years, in spite of the fact that there are hundreds of thousands of adverse reaction reports. The AMA (American Medical Association) and other medical governing bodies are suppressing information and still disciplining medical doctors who are exploring alternative therapies to include in their treatment protocols. Therefore, many of the various protocols proposed for the treatment of heavy metal toxicity should be considered as experimental.

The Food and Drug Administration on January 12, 2001, issued a warning for pregnant mothers and those planning to become pregnant to not eat shark, swordfish, king mackerel and tile-fish due to high levels of mercury, which could damage the brains of unborn baby's. Calls to put tuna on the do-not-eat list were rejected by the FDA. Young children and nursing mothers were also warned to avoid these mercury-high fish.

Mercury is treated as hazardous waste material before and after it is put into your mouth by the dentist. Mercury is on a complete phase-out program in Canada for environmental reasons. This initiative is by Canada's Ministry of the Environment. Mercury has been banned from use in hospitals and is no longer used in thermometers in most jurisdictions. Mercury should not be injected into your child.

If your child is experiencing any kind of developmental difficulty, you owe it to him or her to look at mercury as a source for the problem. If, in fact, you determine that mercury could be a concern - do your research!

If the child has mercury fillings, be sure that the dentist utilizes a safe protocol for the removal of the fillings. Failure of the dentist to utilize a number of certain precautions could result in your child being subjected to dangerously high levels of mercury in the filling removal process.

If you are considering chelation therapy, do your research! There are various techniques being experimented with for this therapy. Find out what your options are. Talk to many doctors involved in these treatments, and check the internet and your local library. Learn the pros and cons of the various treatment protocols, and then, and only then, determine which option is best for your child.

The American Dental Association still maintains amalgam is safe. However, a major manufacturer, Dentsply/Caulk, has listed contraindications on their web sites:

1. www.caulk.com/MSDSFU/DispersDFU.html
2. www.caulk.com/MSDSDFU/UnisonDFU.html
3. www.caulk.com/MSDSDFU/MegalloyDFU.html

Chelation Therapy —
A Way To Deal With Mercury (and other heavy metals)
Dr. Fred Hui, M.D.

Unlike other day-to-day toxins and pollutants that get into our body, mercury presents a difficult problem that must be eliminated. Mercury has the ability to bind very tightly to tissues, especially the nerve tissues, and in particular, to those that contain a receptor for sulphur. Unless we use a stronger agent, one with the ability to release mercury's attachment, the mercury will remain in the body forever. The damaged cells' functions will never recover unless the binding effects of the mercury can be released.

The following describes a reasonable approach to the problem:

Confirmation and testing for the presence of mercury:

Blood tests are not useful for confirming the presence of mercury as mercury does not circulate freely in the blood stream.

Hair analysis shows the presence of most heavy metals, but tends not to show the presence of mercury. As inorganic mercury (from dental amalgam and industrial exposure) does not integrate, or will not leach itself off the tissues, it is attached onto the formation of hairs. Some organic mercury (e.g. from contaminated fish) may show up in hair.

DMPS challenge is the most reliable and standard way of confirming the presence of mercury. DMPS is an effective mercury-chelating agent. Usually a standardized dose is slowly administered intravenously over half an hour. It is then followed by a collection of either six hours or twenty-four hours worth of urine. This measures the amount of mercury and other heavy metals that were bound and excreted. This gives a reflection of the body's burden of the various heavy metals.

DMSA challenge: For those people who have difficulties receiving injections (such as children), oral DMSA can be substituted as a challenging agent.

Herbs and natural supplements:

Before even proceeding with the challenge, and subsequently throughout the process of detoxification, it is recommended that patients take lots of *onion, garlic, and chives,* which contain high amounts of sulphur. It is easier to replace displaced mercury from the sulphur-binding site of the tissues if there is an abundance of substitutions ready to move in. The same applies to minerals. Supplementing *trace minerals* is recommended because mercury can be more easily flushed out of its binding site when a benign substitution is readily available.

It is also a good idea to put certain substances that have strong affinity for mercury into the gut. The main venue for detoxification of mercury is the liver, which excretes through its bile juice into the bowel. Without a strong mercury-binding agent in the gut, every molecule of mercury will re-enter back into the body because of its powerful penetration through the bowel walls. By taking ample amounts of *cilantro* (parsley), *chlorella* (a form of algae) or *chitosan* (the exoskeletons of small shell fish), the heavy metals will be escorted out of the body through bowel movements.

Dental Removal of Amalgam
(cautions, pre and post procedures recommendations)

Since amalgam is the primary and most significant source of mercury, one should remove the source of contamination rather than just performing detoxification.

Once you realize the possible harm of dental amalgams, you shouldn't ask just any dentist to remove the silver fillings. An improper removal procedure may cause more spillage of mercury into the mouth. The drilling may cause vaporization of the mercury, which is inhaled by the patient. Ask the dentist if he or she is trained and aware of all the precautions for removing dental amalgam. Ask if he or she uses rubber dams, oxygen masks, and high-speed suction. Patients can search for dentists in their area through IAMB (International Academy of Oral Medicine and Toxicology), an organization that trains dentists in the proper removal of dental amalgams.

One should prepare 1 week before the scheduled dental procedure by taking chlorella tablets (available from health food stores). Gradually increase your intake every day, up to 10 tablets on the day of the procedure. The chlorella will help absorb any spillage of mercury.

On the morning of the procedure, if you have access to a chelation doctor in your area, you can ideally do a DMPS chelation in the morning immediately before proceeding to the dental office. I.V. administered DMPS will circulate for 6 hours, in case there is any absorption of mercury into the blood. If DMPS is not easily available before the procedure, some practitioners suggests that the patient have an intravenous Vitamin C and glutathione infusion on the day after the dental procedures. Vitamin C will help protect your system from the transient increase of mercury. Glutathione is a strong anti-oxidant that helps the liver cells detoxify.

If one has access to both DMPS and Vitamin C Glutathione drip, it would be ideal to have both done. If I.V. DMPS is not feasible in the morning before the procedure, then one can receive an intra-muscular injection of DMPS within 72 hours prior to the dental procedures. (Intravenous IV gives a higher dose of DMPS in circulation that lasts about 6 hours.)

Chelation Procedures — A series of chelation

Intravenous DMPS chelation is the method of choice to progressively detach mercury from the body. It can be done once every 1 to 3 weeks. The total number of treatments depends on the total burden that is inside the body. Periodic testing using the DMPS challenge followed by urine collection will give an estimation of one's progress.

DMSA chelation: Given orally this is an easier method of administration. It has the advantage of being able to cross the blood/brain barrier, and therefore cleans the mercury from the brain. It is used as a second stage of the chelation program when the total load of mercury in the body system has decreased to a certain safer level. If used at the beginning stage, when the peripheral tissue level outside the brain is still quite high, there is a theoretical concern that the pheripheral mercury can be carried in by the chelating agent and detach itself in the brain. Each extra molecule of mercury carries the potential for more harm to the delicate brain.

EDTA chelation: It is famous for its treatment of blocked arteries. Talk to any patients that have gone through EDTA chelation, and you'll hear enthusiastic stories about the success and gratification they experienced in the treatment of their angina, heart failure, and blocked arteries in the limbs and brain. EDTA is a good comprehensive chelating agent that removes toxic metal such as lead, aluminum, cadmium and copper from the body. These elements contribute to arterial blockage, deterioration of cell functions, and degenerations of nerve cells and nervous functions. If a patient has concurrent cardiovascular or circulation problems, getting EDTA chelation, as a follow up series or as an inter-mingled treatment among DMPS chelation, will have a potential beneficial effect.

For further information about chelation, please visit the website www.drhui.com.

Chinese Medicine:
An Ancient Approach to Dealing With ADD and Hyperactivity
Dr. Elvis Ali, B.Sc., N.D., Dipl. Ac., M.R.N.,R.N.C.P.

Because of growing dissatisfaction with mainstream medicine's use of pharmaceutical products, there is much interest in complementary medicine, such as Chinese medicine, naturopathy, and nutrition. Complementary medicine encourages active communication between patients and their practitioners so that patients can be proactive in their own healthcare. A definite advantage of complementary medicine is its individual attention to patients. The open communication fostered by the holistic approach encourages patients to fully discuss their symptoms and to understand the treatments administered.

In Chinese medicine, practitioners possess an ancient art that incorporates the five-element theory, meridian(s) pathways, accupuncture points and pulse-tongue diagnosis. Human beings can be viewed in many aspects: as a soul inhabiting a physical body, as a set of chemical reactions, as an intermingling of force fields, and as a self sustaining machine of blood, muscles, bone and organs. Our knowledge of the physical world, however, is far in advance of our medical thinking. It is said that "between Heaven and Earth there is but Law and energy." Here we have a statement asserting that all elements, from the most refined to the most coarse, are made up of energy and the laws governing its manifestation.

Chinese medicine expresses the two fundamental charges of this energy as "yin" and "yang," which are regarded as the negative and positive properties of the same force.

Because of its early emphasis on intrinsic energy rather than outer form, China tended to base its philosophy of medicine on the interaction of forces that govern human health and behavior. Disease was regarded as a blockage or distortion of vital energy. Therefore, ideas about the causes of disease tended to focus on forces such as emotional stress and climatic change rather than viral and bacterial infection. In Chinese medicine, diagnosis is not the naming of a specific condition, but rather a defining of the "inner climate," that is, the state of the energies within a person.

According to traditional Chinese medicine (TCM), disease is caused by an imbalance in the system of flow within some part of the body. The aim of Chinese medicine is to effect changes in the way the energy is distributed and utilized through the body. Treatment is intended to restore equilibrium (balance) when there is an imbalance of energy, known as "chi." The word "chi" indicates energy that has a determined direction, quality, function, or purpose. The air we breathe and food we consume are converted into vital energy. There are many forms of chi, and three forms of energy must unite to create human life. The first and second forms have a physical presence; they are the male sperm and the female ovum.

The third form of chi is the cosmic, universal life force, the "The Spirit of Heaven." There are many forms of chi, which are categorized as follows:

Chen chi	nourishing energy	Cheng chi	kidney energy
Ching oh	energy circulating in meridians	Hsien-t'ien chi	inherited ancestral energy
Ku chi	physiolocial energy from food	Tsung chi	lung energy
Yuan chi	active part of Hsien-t'ien chi	Wei chi	defensive energy of body

In addition to chi, there are four additional substances in Chinese philosophy: Blood, Jing, Shen and other fluids, (sweat, saliva, gastric juices, urine, etc). In addition to chi, a healthy individual requires fluid (food and liquid) and blood.

The yin-yang theory is the foundation of Chinese medicine. It recognizes a number of internal organs classified into yin organs (heart, lung, spleen, liver, kidneys pericardium) and yang organs (gallbladder, stomach, small intestine, large intestine, bladder and triple warmer). Another theory includes the "Five Elements:" wood, fire, earth, metal and water. They are conceived in terms of processes and change rather than as things. The five phase theory as a means of describing clinical processes and interactions was first described in the fourth century B.C. All five elements relate to a specific organ: wood–liver; earth–spleen; water–kidneys; fire–heart; metal–lungs. With regard to treatment, the methods of cure are divided into four major sections: Herbalism, Exercise, Psychology, and Acupuncture. The aim is restoration of inner energies to their primal state, one of home-ostasis. The Chinese medical system has many unique features. Both in theory and in practice it can trace a path stretching from the modern day back into pre-history.

To understand Chinese medicine, we must be familiar with the many aspects of its theory. These aspects place great emphasis on the relationship between humanity and its environment. In studying anatomy and physiology, it is not enough to study the location and functions of the internal organs. It is also essential to recognize their inter-connectedness through the meridians, and how they communicate with the external environment. We must also study how disease can travel from one part of the body to another, and the relationships of the organs during times of pathological change as well as in health.

The study of these internal and external communications and the inter-relationships of organs constitute the central objective of all Chinese medical theory. Acupuncture has become especially interesting to many health-care practitioners over the past five decades. In the 1970s, extensive research into the mechanisms of clinical analgesia and the phenomenon of propagated sensation along the channels were documented. In Beijing China in June 1979, the National Symposia of Acupuncture and Moxibustion and Acupuncture Anesthesia were held. These symposia included participants from thirty-one countries, five hundred and thirty-four abstracts, and three hundred research papers.

According to TCM, traditional acupuncture is one method of treatment. Unlike western science which tries to look behind phenomena to find their cause, acupuncturists focus on the order and pattern of phenomena. The yin and yang are dynamic, inextricably mixed together in nature, and compensate one another to preserve equilibrium. The meridian (channel) system carries and distributes the chi, vital energy. Disease is said to be present when the flow of vital energy is blocked or disrupted. The acupuncture points are specific and represent maximum influence on the flow of chi through the meridians. Once the internal balance of yin and yang is disrupted, it causes abnormal flow of chi, resulting in disease(s). There have been at least seventy-one meridian (channels) described, but only fourteen of those, the ones with acupuncture points, are of importance in treatment. Of the fourteen, twelve are paired (6 yin organs, 6 yang organs), and two unpaired (conception vessel and governing vessel).

The 6 yin organs are Liver (LIV), Kidney (KID), Spleen (SP), Lungs (L), Heart (HT) and Pericardium (P). The 6 yang organs are Gallbladder (GB), Stomach (ST), Large Intestine (LI), Small Intestine (SI), Bladder (B) and Tripple Warmer (TW). In addition to the twelve main meridians and two extra meridians with acupuncture points, there are an additional six meridians without discrete points. This makes a total of 8 extra meridians. There are also 15 Lo meridians, 14 Lo or linking meridians, and 1 great Lo meridian of the spleen. There are 12 connecting meridians joining each pair of main meridians at the extremeties, both yin and yang; 12 divergent meridians from main meridians; and 12 muscle-tendon meridians from the

Ching point of each main meridian. There are approximately 365 acupuncture points overall, yet in practice not all points are used in treating patients.

According to the knowledge and wisdom from Huang Ti (called "the Yellow Emperor," 2697-2597 B.C.), the author of the *Ne Ching* (Book of Internal Medicine), diseases are to be attributed to external, emotional and dietetic factors. The following table summarizes which organ or meridian can be damaged by each factor.

External cause of disease	Emotional cause of disease	Dietetic cause of disease	Organ – Element Affected
Warmth, Heat	Excessive Joy, Irresponsibility	Bitter flavors	Heart – fire
Humidity, Dampness	Indecision, Brooding	Too much sweetness	Spleen – earth
Arid, Dryness	Sadness, Excessive mourning	Too much spicy food	Lung – metal
Cold	Worry, Fear	Too much salt	Kidney – water
Wind	Repressed Anger	Sour food	Liver – wood

TCM considers that emotions are governed by individual organs. It refers to the brain or subconscious as one entity. According to the table above, each organ is correlated with an emotion. For example, the lung is said to be the organ impacted by sadness and grief. From a TCM perspective, it is difficult to be objective about the treatment of disorders involving emotions such as anxiety and hyperactivity because of the difficulty in assessing them objectively.

Acupuncture points to consider when dealing with anxiety and nervous tensions:

Heart 7, Spleen 7, Pericardium 6, Taiyang and Paihui: Auricular (ear points): Subcortex, Shenmen, Heart and kidney.
Others: Governing vessel 12, Gallbladder 20, Conception vessel 6, 7, Heart 3, 7

In order to determine which acupuncture points or herbal points are useful, Chinese practitioners view diseases as being associated with or caused by, three classes of influences: environment, emotions and lifestyle. The Yellow emperor Huang Ti, who composed the *Nei Ching*, incorporated thoughts of preventive medicine. He stated that we can be protected against disease by adapting to environmental changes along with proper diet, rest, work, and keeping a calm mind and heart. The following is a list of acupuncture points used to treat illness.

	Acupuncture Points	Illness
1.	GV 14, LI 11, LI 4	Common cold, malaria
2.	LI 4, K 7	Hypohidrosis, Hyperhidrosis
3.	LI 11, LI 4	Headache
4.	GV 26, GV 16	Unconsciousness
5.	LI 15, LI 11	Stroke and hemiplegia (upper extremity)
6.	GB 30, GB 34	Stroke and hemiplegia (lower extremity)
7.	LI 11, B 54, ST 39	Arthritis (upper-lower limbs)
8.	LI 11, GB 34	Chest and Abdominal distension
9.	LI 11, SP 6	Female problems, venereal disease
10.	ST 36, SP 6	Leg pain and numbness
11.	GB 34, ST 36	Indigestion, muscle pain (leg)
12.	LI 4, LIV 3	Poor circulation
13.	ST 40, GB 34	High blood pressure, constipation
14.	CV 6, ST 25	Neurasthenia, Irregular menstruation
15.	CV 12, ST 36	Stomach problems
16.	L1 4, ST 36	Indigestion
17.	ST 36 (Bilaterally)	Increasing nutrition energy
18.	P 8, ST 36	Nausea, Hiccough, Tiredness
19.	SP 6 (Bilaterally)	Abdominal pain, diarrhea, female problems
20.	SP 1 (Bilaterally)	Abdominal distension weakness
21.	LIV 1 (Bilaterally)	Hernia, Metrorrhagia
22.	GV 14, P 6	Hydrothorax
23.	P 6, SP 6	TB, Cough, Night-Sweats
24.	L 10, K 3	Cough, Fever, Hemoptyss
25.	B 10, B 11	Headache, Stiff neck
26.	K 27, L 2	Cough, Asthma
27.	CV 6, CV 4, CV 3, Extra Point Zigong	Barrenness
28.	LI 4, SP 6	Miscarriage
29.	L 9, LI 4, LI 1	Sore Throat, Tonsillitis
30.	P 3, B 54	Cholera, VD

Herbal medicine in TCM has a long history, and one of the oldest elements is the Pen Ts'ao Ching, in which the Red Emperor, Shen-ung, described various medicaments and included instructions. Chinese practitioners treat with a variety of herbs patients suffering from a variety of emotional problems correlated with stress, tension, nervousness and insomnia. In addition to acupuncture, a variety of fruits and vegetables are encouraged on a daily basis, as well as the elimination of junk foods. These should be replaced by wholesome organic, well balanced meals, and adequate exercise and rest.

In the human body, three factors can cause illness according to TCM. In normal conditions, yin and yang energies in the body are balanced. If any pathogenic factor destroys the balance, it will cause illness.

Disease-causing factors based on their etiologies

1. **Six external disease-causing factors**: The external disease-causing factors come from outside the body and they are mainly climatic: wind, cold, heat, dampness, dryness and fire like heat.

2. **Seven internal disease-causing factors**: They come from inside the body and are mainly emotional; joy, anger, grief, anxiety, worry, apprehension and fright.

3. **The other disease-causing factors include**: improper dietary intake, traumatic injury, fatigue, sexual indulgence, animal-insect bites, and stagnation of blood and phlegm (Tan Yin). The expression of mental state is used to describe the outward appearance that reflects a person's well-being. In TCM, the mental activities of an individual have a close relationship with wellness.

Under normal conditions, the seven emotional states will not cause illness because joy, anger, anxiety, worry, grief, apprehension and fright are parts of life. However, if any one of these emotional states is intense and persistent, it will lead to illness. The diseases caused by the seven emotional factors often lead to dysfunctions in the internal organs and disturbances of blood and energy circulation.

The following table shows organs correlated with emotional states, symptoms and treatments.

Emotion	Organ Affected	Signs & Symptoms	Herbal Remedies
Excessive Joy	Heart	Absentmindness, weakness, palpation, insomina, and mental confusion	Dinq Xin Wan, Tieh Wang Pu Hsin Tan, Ansenpunace Tablet, Cinnabar sedative pills
Anger	Liver	Flushed face, red eyes, headache, and hematemesis	Xiao Yao Wan, Shu Kan Wan, Tanzhi Xiao Yao Wan Lung Tan Xie Kan Wan
Anxiety and worry	Spleen, Stomach	Epigastric fullness and distension, abdominal distension, and loose stool	Liu Junzi Tablet, Aquilaria stomachic pill, Aplotaxis Amomum Pills

Grief	Lungs	Chest pain, shortness of breath, and sneezing	Ginseng pills, Wuchaseng pills
Apprehension	Kidney	Fecal or urinary incontinence, spermatorrhea	Bu Shen pills, Sexaton pills
Fright	All internal organs	Disharmony of yin and yang or blood and energy	

In dealing with cases of ADD and hyperactivity, there are specific herbs to consider as natural remedies. The following table list some herbs and their uses.

Chinese Herb	English Name	Uses
Chi-Hsueh-Ts'Ao	Catnip	Nervous irritability insomniaia
Lu-Ts'Ao	Hops	Active ingredient (lupulin), Works as a nervine, stomachic, tonic soporific (induces sleep) and anodyne (relieves pain)
Ma-Pien-Ts'Ao	Vervain	Strengthener of nerves
Wu-Chia-P'i	Eleuthero	Tonic - mental alertness, nervousness and stress
Mi-Tieh-Hsiang	Rosemary	Soothes nerves, Relieves mental fatigue, Congestive headaches
Ai-Hao	Mugwort	Brain tonic

Note: To access information on Chinese Medicine and practitioners, refer to Appendicies A, D and F in the back of this book. Many Naturopaths also have training in the field of Chinese Medicine.

Section Two

Diet, Additives,
MSG and Aspartame,
Soft Drinks, Water, Sugar,
Essential Fatty Acids,
Herbs, Amino Acids

Let your food be your medicine,
your medicine be your food.
– Hippocrates

11

The Feingold Program — Diet

Jane Hersey, National Director, et al.
Feingold Association of the United States

Food does more than alleviate hunger. What we choose to eat can have a direct effect on how we feel and how we behave. This is something many mothers and observant individuals have long known. The connection is gaining recognition today, but it was not given much consideration by traditionally trained physicians in the 1960s.

Ben P. Feingold, M.D., was Chief of the Allergy unit at Kaiser Permanente Medical Center in San Francisco in 1965 when he saw a patient with a very bad case of hives. Suspecting she was aspirin-sensitive, he told her to eliminate aspirin, as well as some foods and food additives that are chemically similar to aspirin. Not only did the hives disappear, but her belligerent behavior disappeared as well. The change in her personality was so swift and profound that her psychiatrist called Feingold to ask him what he had done. Feingold was both puzzled and intrigued, and at first did not understand the stunning implications.

When sensitive individuals eliminated certain foods and synthetic chemicals, there were dramatic improvements in their behavior, when they ate them again, their behaviors swiftly reflected negative personality changes.

Over the years, Feingold's practice had shifted from pediatrics to allergies, so he was not seeing the rapidly increasing number of children being labeled as hyperactive. In his medical training, the textbooks described "hyperkinesis" (or related labels such as minimal brain dysfunction, etc.), but these children were considered a rarity. By the late 1960s, the youngsters with out-of-control behavior were no longer a rarity; they were showing up in pediatricians' offices with puzzling frequency.

Although allergists had reported adverse reactions to additives, they focused on physical symptoms such as hives and asthma, not on behavioral effects. Feingold began expanding his use of the aspirin-free regimen, or what he called the "K-P Diet" for allergic patients, including children. Some of the parents of these children reported that not only did the allergies improve, but their children calmed down and began to function normally. Gradually Feingold refined the dietary regimen and began to seek out children who he called "the failures of the medical community," children who had not been helped by drugs or counseling. He was able to improve the behavior of many of these children who had been written off as hopeless.

After eight years of clinical work, writing and publishing, Feingold presented his findings at the 1973 Conference of the American Medical Association. He connected the growing number of hyperactive children to the increased use of synthetic food additives, pointing out that both began roughly after the end of World War II. Dr. Feingold did not believe that the foods/additives caused the symptoms, but that they played an important part in triggering symptoms in sensitive individuals.

Initially, Feingold's work received the AMA's overwhelming support; here was one of their esteemed colleagues who had clearly identified a major factor in this mysterious disorder. Within a short time, however, they would withdraw support, with no explanation. Even before the 1973 medical conference, the food and chemical industry lobbies were hard at work providing damage control. They used a variety of questionable tactics to protect the vast financial stake their employers had in the continued use of synthetic chemicals in food. Later, the pharmaceutical interests would see how their bottom line was related to this disorder, which was treated as a medical abnormality without having been proven as such.

Random House asked Dr. Feingold to write a book directed to parents; the result was his 1974 book *Why Your Child is Hyperactive*. Studies were initiated later, but most were plagued with design flaws and poor compliance. In 1982, the National Institutes of Health (NIH) held a consensus development conference to evaluate these studies. The NIH found them to be an inadequate test of Feingold's program. But despite their limitations, a close look at the published studies showed nearly all of them offered very supportive data. The early Harley study at the University of Wisconsin included ten preschool-age, hyperactive children. Contrary to what is often written about the study, it confirmed what Feingold had been reporting; all ten of the mothers of these children rated them as improved on the K-P Diet.

Later studies avoided some of the worst mistakes of those from the 1970s and early 1980s. In 1985, Egger et al. published their double-blind placebo-controlled test and found that most of the hyperactive children in their study reacted adversely to yellow dye No. 5. Using a very loose version of the Feingold regimen, Kaplan et al. had a positive response from 58% of the children tested. Boris and Mandel brought the success rate up to 73%, and Rowe & Rowe documented a clear reaction to yellow dye, with a dose response effect observed.

Despite these and many other studies, the lobbies that represent various vested interests still claim that diet has been proven to be ineffective in the treatment of hyperactivity. In 1989, the National Institutes of Health again held a consensus development conference. Documentation of the effectiveness of the Feingold Program was presented, and the panel concluded that the evidence warranted further research. It did not surprise long-time observers that, at least to date, nothing more has happened.

The heart of Dr. Feingold's program, however, is not found in the studies, but in the everyday lives of the families who use it. Support groups formed spontaneously as many parents saw dramatic changes in their children. When two or more such parents met, the first question was, "What can your child eat?" Trial and error lead to a small listing of brand-name processed foods that were being used successfully by the youngsters. A parent's mistake, a misleading label, or a sudden change in ingredients meant a 3 to 4 day reaction in sensitive children. So, parents learned to be careful of what they bought, and suspicious of food labeling.

In May of 1976, representatives of these parent groups met to form a national organization, and chose the name Feingold Association to honor the man who had made such a difference in their lives. One of the first tasks was to develop a systematic method for finding out what is actually in brand name foods—not just what is listed on the label. This has grown into a fairly sophisticated technique, with the production and frequent updating of "Foodlist" books for the seven regions of the United States. These books run to nearly 100 pages of brand-name products which have been researched by the Association, and found to be free of the unwanted additives. This information is updated ten times a year in Pure Facts, the Feingold newsletter.

Being on the Feingold Program no longer means cooking from scratch. Instead of making her own mayonnaise, the member need only turn to the section on condiments in her Foodlist. She will also find a listing of the acceptable ice creams, potato chips, mixes, candy, beverages, et cetera. What was once a change in lifestyle is now primarily a change in one's grocery shopping list.

After the child (or adult) has avoided the troublesome additives for several months, most develop the ability to tolerate occasional infractions. Gradually, new products can be tested, and eating out becomes less of a problem as the child or adult learns to make informed choices. There's a comprehensive section on eating out in the book *Why Can't My Child Behave?*

Many people are hung up on terminology. Giving a set of symptoms a label serves some important purposes; it is a way people can all be sure they are talking about the same thing. But too often the labels children receive get in the way of finding answers. Just being given a name for a condition does not tell parents how to help their children. To make matters more confusing, the labels change often. Parents may be told their child has one of the Dee-dees (as one mom referred to it). There's ADD, ADHD, ODD, OCD, PDD, and you might even run into the older MBD.

Having been involved with the Feingold Association for nearly a quarter century, I have spoken with more parents than I can count. In virtually every case, they tell me about a child who is bright and really sweet at heart, but who gets upset too easily. In my experience, the "short fuse" is the one universal characteristic of the chemically sensitive individual.

Dr. Feingold taught us that if you are sensitive to something, the reaction can come in many forms. Some people will experience a behavioral effect. An adult may get very irritable, drive too fast, or reach for a beer to help him feel better. A child might throw a tantrum. If the effect is cognitive, an adult might get easily confused or distracted; a child might forget the spelling of words he knew yesterday. For some people the most noticeable effect is physical. It might be a headache, sleep disturbances, ringing in the ears, sinus problems and even nasal polyps. Any medical text that describes symptoms of aspirin sensitivity will give you an idea of the wide range of effects food additives and natural salicylates can have on an individual who happens to have a particular sensitivity.

The people my colleagues and I have helped are perfectly normal folks, but they simply don't have the same ability as others to eat some pretty disgusting chemicals. If you got sick from eating a bug killer, you wouldn't give yourself a label and wonder if there was something wrong with your body. If polluted air made you feel sick, you wouldn't conclude you were abnormal. If you drank a LOT of alcohol and acted rather funny, you would not be diagnosed with a "standing up straight disorder."

What are these chemicals I'm speaking about with such disrespect? And why are they being added to our food? (Now that's the subject of a very long book.)

The Feingold Program eliminates:

- artificial (synthetic) food colorings
- artificial flavorings (aspartame, saccharin & cyclamates are also eliminated)
- three antioxidant preservatives: BHA, BHT, TBHQ

When people learn that those food dyes and preservatives are derived from petroleum (as in gasoline), it seems like a small sacrifice to give them up. Although these additives are used in most of the processed food in the United States, there is also a huge assortment of acceptable brand name products. In many cases, the food company that makes products with these additives also has a few varieties without them. For the occasional hard-to-find product, such as natural marshmallows or natural food dyes, the Association provides a listing of specialty mail order resources. Other additives which are of concern to some families include:

- MSG (monosodium glutamate)
- nitrites
- corn syrup
- sodium benzoate
- fluoride
- sulfites
- calcium propionate

Foods containing these substances are not eliminated, but when any of these additives are in a product on the Foodlist their presence is noted.

The artificial sweetener aspartame is not on this list since should it be eliminated from everyone's diet. Refer to Chapter 13, The Secret World of Flavor Enhancers: MSG and Aspartame – The Deadly Duo.

During the first weeks of the Program the "natural salicylates" are removed, and non-salicylates are used in their place. Once the individual is doing well on the Program, the salicylate-containing foods may be reintroduced one at a time and tested. The "salicylates" which are temporarily removed are:

- Almonds
- Apples (also cider & cider vinegar)
- Apricots
- All berries
- Cherries
- Cloves
- Coffee
- Cucumber & pickle
- Currants
- Grapes & raisins (also Peach wine & wine vinegar)
- Nectarines
- Oranges
- Oil of wintergreen
- Peppers
- Plums & prunes
- Tangerines
- Tea
- Tomatoes

Aspirin and medication containing aspirin are also removed.

The following non-salicylates, which are tolerated by most people, may be used:

- Avocado
- Artichokes
- Asparagus
- Alfalfa sprouts
- Banana
- Bamboo shoots
- Bean sprouts
- Beans (all types)
- Eggplant
- Figs
- Grapefruit
- Guava
- Kiwi
- Lemons
- Lettuce
- Lentils
- Pears
- Peas
- Persimmon
- Pineapple
- Pomegranate
- Potatoes (white & sweet)
- Pumpkin

- Beets
- Broccoli
- Brussels sprouts
- Cabbage
- Cantaloupe
- Carrots
- Cauliflower
- Celery
- Coconut
- Dates
- Limes
- Mushrooms
- Mangoes
- Melons (all types)
- Okra
- Olives
- Onions
- Papaya
- Parsley
- Parsnips
- Radishes
- Rhubarb
- Rutabaga
- Spinach
- Squash
- Turnips
- Water chestnuts
- Watercress
- Watermelon
- Yams

Salicylate sensitivity is a very big problem and often goes unrecognized by doctors. Many are well acquainted with aspirin-sensitivity but are not aware that grapes or tomatoes can have just as serious an effect on someone who is sensitive to them. Some families don't like to remove these wholesome foods, even for a short time. If they can just get rid of the unwanted additives, that's a very big step in the right direction, but we remind them to consider a test in the future to see if any of the salicylates are causing problems. They're sneaky little devils!

The focus of the literature provided by the Association is geared to the early weeks when the new family is learning to substitute pear juice for apple juice (many juices contain apple or grape juice as fillers and for flavoring), to use pecans in place of almonds, et cetera. We call this period "Stage One." The first half of the Foodlists contain just Stage One foods, and the second half lists products that are free of the unwanted additives, but which contain one or more of the natural salicylates. This is called Stage Two.

If a person is sensitive to one salicylate it doesn't necessarily mean she will have to avoid the others. This is an individual thing and the Association shows people simple steps to determine their sensitivities. Even if a child is found to be sensitive to one of the natural salicylates, it doesn't mean she will have to eliminate it permanently; most children (and many adults) can later reintroduce the food and tolerate it well.

Most foods can be purchased at local supermarkets. Others are available at health food stores or through mail order. There are several companies that cater to the Feingold members and offer items such as candies, mixes and over-the-counter cold medicines. Personal assistance is available from volunteers. There is a wealth of information in the *Feingold Handbook*, the recipe book which accompanies it, and in newsletters. Even more detailed suggestions and information are found in the book *Why Can't My Child Behave?* which is available from the Association and is also found in some libraries.

Another area to consider is the use of additives in non-food products: toothpaste, vitamins, medicine, as well as topical products such as lotions and colored play dough. The Association provides information and guidance on how to find what you need. Parents often realize that their child is being exposed to synthetic additives in their toothpaste, but believe these additives don't have any effect since the youngster doesn't swallow the toothpaste (usually). But additives can be absorbed through the tissues in the mouth and through the skin. Medicine designed to get into your system rapidly is placed under the tongue, and we know that drugs can be delivered into our bodies via skin patches. But in the case of non-foods too, the emphasis is on all of the acceptable products that can be used, not on the things that must be avoided. Virtually all of the things needed by a family using the Feingold Program are available, but you won't be able to do all of your shopping at one store.

People typically find that it takes about two weeks to feel comfortable in the new routine. The program is not difficult but it generally involves some changing from one product to another. Once parents see a difference in their child's behavior or ability to cope or other positive benefits, the effort required seems insignificant in comparison. Many families have used very restrictive diets or expensive therapies with little or no benefit; many begin the Feingold Program convinced that this will be just another failed approach and are delighted to see that such a simple change can yield dramatic results.

The length of time it takes before an improvement is seen varies widely, but the typical time is between three days and three weeks. If no improvement is seen, the member is encouraged to contact a volunteer who can work with him or her; in most cases something has been overlooked and can be easily corrected. But while most people report a significant improvement, there are some who do not, even though they have followed the program carefully. Parent volunteers may be able to suggest another nonprofit organization or direct the family to the appropriate professional. The Feingold volunteer is trained to appreciate the limitations of her role and never offers guidance that could be interpreted as medical advice.

What parents can effectively do is share tips that have worked well for them as they used the program in their families. They can suggest strategies for things such as gaining a child's cooperation, selecting foods at a restaurant, and adapting favorite recipes. They do this, confident that the Feingold Program offers no risk and no danger of adverse side effects.

The Association was formed way back in 1976, and since that time, we have watched children grow up on its Program. We have seen them go through school, go on to college, and experience success in all facets of their lives. When they have their own children we often hear back from them; these new parents want to be spared the problems their parents experienced. If they begin the Program in preschool they are likely to avoid the social skill deficits that are so troublesome for the older children.

Many of us started out thinking it was unfortunate that we were sensitive; we wished we could be like others and continue to eat the familiar foods. But as my family began to enjoy the results of eating good food, we changed our minds and stopped feeling sorry for ourselves. My kids were the ones that did not get ear infections, frequent colds, cavities, asthmatic attacks, etc. Maybe it was a coincidence that my daughters' chronic ear infections stopped as soon as we began Feingold, but I doubt it. Going to the pediatrician became something of a joke. When we went in once a year for the school physical, the doctor would stare at us for a moment, thinking "who are these folks?" He would look in his folder and express amazement that we had not been there since the last check up a year ago. Each year he told me how remarkably healthy my two daughters were, and how I should keep doing whatever it was I was doing. When I tried to tell him what we were doing, he would brush me off, finish up and hand each girl a bright red lollipop!

My kids got a lot of lollipops and other assorted junk from many people, but it really was not a problem. They knew they could swap them for other wonderful treats: naturally colored lollipops, chocolate candies, ice cream, cookies, soda, et cetera. It wasn't so bad having to eat Haagen Dazs! I was able to find a natural (delicious!) substitute for virtually every kind of treat, except jelly beans. Today there is even a natural jelly bean. This is the way most of the moms approached the Feingold Program. We didn't deny our kids the treats they enjoyed, but when we could, we would sneak a little more of the good foods into their diet, and often found healthy things they really loved. I was amazed at how much my daughters' preschool classmates enjoyed the cucumbers and dip I once brought in.

We adults found ourselves eating and enjoying things we hadn't really considered before. Instead of the Feingold Program limiting our diet, it actually expanded it, and we gradually began to incorporate the steamed broccoli and other good-for-you things. But the best news for me was that (pure) chocolate was allowed, so I never had to sacrifice anything. I consider the Feingold diet to be more like a gourmet diet because it prescribes pure, high quality foods. It's the way a master chef cooks, and I am convinced that no chef worth his wooden spoon would use dyes or MSG. When I have helped plan the food for our conferences I just ask the chef to cook for us the same way he cooks for his own family, and we have not had any problems.

I once would have thought I was being deprived because I could not eat yellow 5 (a dye made from petroleum). Now the question is "Why on earth would I want to eat yellow 5? It's a second cousin to gasoline. Is there a daily requirement for petroleum?" I no longer believe that I am on a special diet; I think the poor folks who consume dyes and MSG are the ones on the special diet.

In the years since Dr. Feingold devised this elimination diet, other doctors have added their own recommendations. Parents are sometimes told that in addition to removing the additives, they should also eliminate sugar and refined flour, milk, chocolate, wheat, corn, nuts, and all processed foods. Sometimes they are directed to continue using the natural salicylates. While there is much to be said for eliminating sugar, refined foods, et cetera, it is a very difficult task for most families, and not popular with the children.

The Feingold Association's approach is a pragmatic one; we don't focus on whether a substance is healthful or not, but only if it can be tolerated by the majority of children. We have seen in our children and in those we have helped, most of the youngsters can eat the approved brands of candy and junk food if they don't overdo it. By not removing things they are accustomed to having, and at the same time offering delicious alternatives, it isn't hard to gain and keep their cooperation. We try to focus on all of the foods the family can enjoy, rather than on what they must avoid. This approach is used because it has worked so well for us for so many years. For those children who must further restrict their diets, volunteers help the family to do so, and we refer them to the many excellent books and qualified professionals who can guide them. For these children the Feingold Program is only the first step, but we believe it's an essential one.

Nobody would expect a person to change from being a "couch potato" to a marathon runner in a matter of days. But many families are asked to make equally drastic changes in the food they eat, and the task is equally daunting. People who have excellent diets themselves sometimes forget that the overwhelming majority of Americans are accustomed to eating the types of nutrient devoid-foods that line the aisles of supermarkets. If this food didn't sell, it would not be in the supermarket. The preferred vegetable for most American children is the french fry, and they live in homes where Taco Bell is considered to be one of the four food groups. Parents of hard-to-raise children need lots of help and encouragement, and for the non-cooks, the need is even greater. These families find that they can follow the Feingold approach, and that once they have removed the dyes, artificial flavorings and preservatives, the change in their child is likely to be dramatic. Once they have this first introduction to nutrition—once they understand that food really matters—they are on their way to making the gradual improvements at a pace that is right for them. These convenience food freaks really do evolve into aware consumers: I know it's true because I'm one of them.

Note: If you are interested in the Feingold Association, its materials or books on the subject, refer to the bibliography and resource sections at the back of this book under Appendix A: Key Information Resources

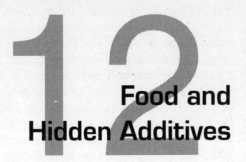

Food and Hidden Additives

Additives defined • What have scientific studies of additives indicated? • What is the purpose of food additives? • Sulfites • Artificial sweeteners • Antioxidants • Food dyes (colors) • Flavor enhancers • Antimicrobial preservatives • Fats substitutes • Hydrogenated fats • Other additives • Indirect additives • How to report an adverse reaction to an additive • Suggestions for Avoiding Additives in Your Diet • At-A-Glance Quick Reference™ List of Specific Additives and Groups of Additives to Avoid

Additives Defined

Americans ingest approximately 140 to 150 pounds of additives each year. Some additives can be more harmful than others, especially for children and adults who are more sensitive to additives. Yet nutritionists and food scientists say most additives are basically harmless if consumed in the tiny amounts regulated by the Food and Drug Administration (FDA).

A "food additive" was defined by the Department of National Health and Welfare as "any substance or its byproducts, the use of which results, or may reasonably be expected to result in, becoming a part of or affecting the characteristics of food." For this government body, these substances are usually chemical in nature, and do not include spices, seasonings and flavorings. For the sake of clarity, we consider anything added to food which alters any of it natural properties to be an additive. This is important because they can affect the health of our citizens.

In America, over 10,000 chemical and food additives are legally approved. The majority of additives are safe, some are harmful, but too many have not been adequately tested. A problem is that highly processed foods usually contain the most additives. These foods are usually nutritionally deficient and loaded with calories. In addition, the possibility of interactions between various food additives lacks sufficient study. The monosodium glutamate and aspartame interaction, discussed in detail in the following chapter, is an excellent example of what can go wrong when two food additives from different sources are consumed.

Excessive processing of foods results in significant lose of nutrients and requires that more things be added to foods, in some cases to lessen the impact of these deficiencies. How the additives are used, rather than the additives themselves, causes many problems. A food coloring or flavor may be safe in itself, but problems arise when they are used to simulate real foods like fruits, or when additives are used together, causing harm to people sensitive to these additives.

To avoid food additives, you would have to grow your own foods and prepare all your meals from scratch. Time deprived Americans usually choose processed and packaged foods to meet their dietary needs, which means additives are a necessary ingredient in food manufacturing. Unfortunately, the use and overuse of food additives is obscured by concerns, controversy and questions.

What have scientific studies of additives indicated?

Science has proven that some additives can cause reactions. The younger a person is, the greater the likelihood of food additives affecting their developing nervous systems, causing irritation or damage. Children become more susceptible to accidents, especially if hyperactivity is a result of their sensitivity to additives. Difficulties may occur in their abilities to speak, balance, and learn, regardless of their level of intelligence as measured by IQ tests. The theory that food dyes can affect children's ability to learn is being corroborated by numerous studies.

According to Dr. Michael Lyon, M.D., in his seminal work, *Healing the Hyperactive Mind: Through the New Science of Functional Medicine*, (Focus Publishing, 2000) "One of the antecedents or predisposing causes at the heart of ADHD may be an inherited or acquired decrease in an individual's ability to adequately process and excrete certain types of chemicals. It is not uncommon to discover that someone with ADHD is hypersensitive to food additives."

Dr. Lyon goes on to point out these are not true allergies, but sensitivities often resulting from the reduced ability of the liver "or other systems of the body to detoxify these common chemical substances." As a result of this inability, the body allows some food-derived chemicals or their resultant byproducts, to cause malfunctions of cellular processes, by accumulating in the body and raising the possibility of adverse reactions.

Dr. Lyon concludes that "...simply eliminating man-made pesticides and chemical additives in the ADHD diet may significantly reduce the total toxic load on the individual's brain and body and may pay valuable dividends in terms of health, cognitive performance and behavior."

The Great Ormand Street Hospital study in Great Britain found a link between hyperactivity and the processed foods and chemically-laden water children consumed. Many parents and school boards resisted further examination of this problem even after it was brought to their attention. What the hospital did was supply families of hyperactive children organically grown foods, without any additives, and distilled re-mineralized water. The results were astounding. Within two weeks all the children in the study had dramatic improvements in their behavior.

Dr. Ben Feingold states over 50 per cent of hyperactive children are sensitive to synthetic flavors, artificial food colors, preservatives, phenolic compounds and naturally occurring salicylates. This is based on his observations of over 1,200 cases of learning and behavior disorders, which significantly improved with the elimination of food additives from their diets.

The University of Melbourne's Royal Children's Hospital studied the effects of synthetic food coloring on the behavior of hyperactive children. Two hundred children were put on a six-week diet, free of any synthetic food coloring. Behavioral improvement was noted in 75 per cent of the children. When artificial colorings were reintroduced into the children's diets, their behavior worsened. The greater the amount of synthetic food colorings a child ingested, the longer the duration of undesirable behavior lasted.

In this study, observers noted irritability, restlessness and sleeping problems when a yellow coal-tar based dye was consumed by the children. The more they ingested, the longer the problems persisted. Other coal tar derived dyes were not included since they had related chemical structures and are chemically similar to the yellow dye used in the study. Different ages exhibited different reactions:

- The reactions of children aged 2–6 included persistent crying, irritability, restlessness, sleep problems, and tantrums.
- The reactions of children aged 7–14 included aimless activity, irritability, lack of self-control, unhappiness and being whiny.

The children who were sensitive to the yellow dye shared certain common health challenges, including allergic runny nose, asthma and eczema. In addition, they all tested positive for one or more reactions to eight common food allergens.

In 1979, an interesting test program was tried by the New York City pubic school system. They decided to do a series of elimination diets, progressively removing more food additives at each step. Eight hundred and three schools were involved in the project. The base line established the students academic performance at the 39th percentile range on standardized achievement test scores, compared to other American public school systems. Here's what happened:

- **First,** the school feeding program significantly reduced the sugar content of the foods served, as well as banning two synthetic food colorings. Achievement test scores improved to the 49th percentile.

- The next step removed all synthetic flavorings and colorings from the food program. Achievement test scores improved to the 51st percentile.

- Finally, BHA and BHT, two commonly use preservatives, were added to the list of substances removed from the food program. Achievement test scores improved to the 55th percentile.

By improving the quality of the food program in the New York City public school system, a dramatic academic improvement of 16 percent was noted!

What is the purpose of food additives?

According to the FDA, a food additive is any matter that becomes part of a food product directly or indirectly during preparation, storage, or packaging. "Direct additives" are purposely added to a food product to preserve or replace a specific feature. They can be from natural or synthetic materials. "Indirect additives" are found in tiny amounts and get into foods during growing, storing, and packaging.

Approximately 3000 additives are used in foods today. Most are used in very small amounts. About 1000 flavorings are from naturally occurring sources; the minuscule amounts used generally lessen the need for concern.

Food additives are used to prevent spoilage and extend shelf-life, make foods more attractive or tastier, provide palatability and consistency, and replenish lost nutrients or improve their nutritional value.

Very common additives are sugar, salt, corn syrup, baking soda, citric acid, pepper, mustard, and vegetable colors. The FDA states these additives account for almost 98 percent of all food additives used in this country. In fact additives have been used for thousands of years: spices and herbs to enhance flavor, sugars to preserve fruits, salt for preserving meats and fish, and vinegars to pickle vegetables. During the last century, many additives were invented. They usually have complex names. Most of them are derived from naturally-occurring substances.

Not all things are as they seem.

One must also be wary of claims such as "pure and natural" since it does not mean the food product is free of additives. For example, white sugar is bleached to make it look bright white and pure. Red dyes are sometimes illegally used to enhance the visual appeal of meats, even though USDA regulations are in place to prevent meat processors and retailers from doing this. Pyroligneous acid is used to create a "smoked" flavor in foods, and FDA labeling requirements allow processors to call it "smoked."

A smoke screen of sorts is used to meet legal labeling requirements. Partial truths, using commonly understood language as the tool, results in inadequate and misleading food labels.

Add to this the indirect and hidden additives such as recombinant bovine growth hormone (RBGH) to increase milk production, which is approved for commercial use in America by the FDA. The Canadian Health Protection Branch has not allowed this hormone to be used by their milk producers, primarily because of its negative affects upon the health of the cows.

The use of herbicides and fungicides for crops, which get onto and absorbed into the plants themselves, are a hidden source of additives. None of these substances appear on food labels or on the non-organically grown vegetables and fruits in your supermarket, nor do they have to. The FDA regulates food safety, but it relies primarily on the data the chemical producers supply, and does not guarantee the safety of the additives they approve.

Compounding this problem is the use of dangerous substances directly and indirectly in many non-food products we use daily. Alone, minuscule amounts may have no affect upon people. What is becoming evident is that their cumulative affect may be significantly worse then ever suspected.

According to Sam Graci, author of *The Power of Superfoods* (Prentice Hall, 1999), over 100,000 xenobiotics (foreign chemicals) are in use today. "While the thousand or so new chemicals created each year may individually test negative for causing birth defects or cancer, their affects upon reproductive systems and the human endocrine system are unknown, as well as their affects on the ecosystem. These chemicals are believed to be responsible for many wildlife and human health problems."

(Portions of the above text excerpted from *Natural Remedies and Supplements*:
The All-in-One Guide to™ series, AGES Publications™, 2000,
ISBN 1-886508-28-3 and 1-886508-33-X)

Other examples of this problem exist. For example, highly toxic chemicals are used to create chemicals added to detergents. According to Aubrey Hampton, author of *Natural Organic Hair and Skin Care: Including A to Z Guide to Natural and Synthetic Chemicals in Cosmetics,* (Organica Press, 1987), many commonly used cosmetic ingredients have potentially harmful effects upon humans. He recommends consumers not buy any products containing chemicals from this list of ten synthetic ingredients he wants banned, and explains why:

1. Butyl- and ethyl- and methyl- and propylparaben are used to extend the shelf life of products since they inhibit microbial growth. They cause skin rashes and allergic reactions. Alone they are toxic; in combination with benzoic acid they combine with the methyl family of chemicals and become highly toxic.

2. Diazolidinyl urea and imidazolidinyl urea are commonly used preservatives. The American Academy of Dermatology has established them as a leading cause of dermatitis (skin inflammation). Germall II and Germall II5 are two trade names for them. Neither is a good antifungal, necessitating their combination with other preservatives. Over 10 degrees, Germall II5 releases formaldehyde. They are toxic.

3. Petrolatum is used in lip products to protect against chapping, sunburn and so on. It is a mineral oil jelly which can cause numerous skin problems such as photosensitivity. Photosensitivity promotes damage from sunshine and interferes with your body's natural moisturizing process, resulting in dry skin and chapping. Manufacturers use it because it is incredibly cheap.

4. Propylene glycol, when it is made from a combination of natural substances such as grain alcohol and vegetable glycerin, is okay. Unfortunately, synthetic petrochemical formulations use it as an humectant (substance that promotes the retention of moisture) and it has produced many instances of allergic and toxic reactions.

5. PVP/VA copolymer is used in wave sets, hair sprays and other cosmetics. This petroleum-derived chemical is considered toxic, because tiny particles become foreign bodies in the lungs, causing problems for people sensitive to them.

6. Sodium lauryl sulfate is used in shampoos for its foaming and detergent actions. This synthetic substance causes hair loss, eye irritation, skin rashes, a condition similar to dandruff called "scalp scurf," and allergic reactions. It is commonly used in fake natural cosmetics, and disguised on the label with the description "derived from coconut."

7. Stearalkonium chloride is used in hair creams and conditioners. This toxic chemical causes allergic reactions.

8. Synthetic colors are used to dress up cosmetics and make them look "pretty." Along with hair dyes, they should be avoided at all cost. Labeled as D&C or FD&C, followed by a color and number (e.g. D&C Green No.6 or FD&C Red No. 6), they are thought to be cancer-causing substances.

9. Synthetic fragrances are problematic because a cosmetic may use as many as 200 ingredients to produce a synthetic fragrance. Labels state "fragrance" so there is no way one can know what the components are. The list of side effects from synthetic fragrances includes headaches, dizziness, hyperpigmentation, rashes, violent coughing, skin irritation, vomiting and so on. Do not buy cosmetics that list "fragrance" on the label.

10. Triethanolamine (TEA) is used to adjust the pH balance of cosmetics. It is also combined with fatty acids to convert acid to salt (stearate), which is then used as a base for cleansers. TEA causes eye problems, dryness of skin and hair, and allergic reactions, and may be toxic when absorbed by the body over long time periods.

Two companies whose body care products may be of benefit to you are:

Aubrey® or Aubrey Organics® – a line of 100 per cent natural and organic hair, skin and body care products found in better health food and nutritional stores. Founded in 1967, they never used animal testing, nor source products they determined as being safe based on animal testing. They only use products that have been tested on humans for safety and effectiveness, and that have many years of safe use. Their products are internationally recognized as the most natural herbal body care, hair and skin products available.

Thursday Plantation's Zero Lice Kit™ is an all-natural and non-toxic complete lice and nit removal kit available in the marketplace. Laboratory testing rated it 100% effective at removing lice and their eggs. Tea tree oil has the maximum kill rate against lice. The solution breaks down the cement-like bond that nits use to attach themselves to the hair shaft. The kit includes everything needed to safely and effectively remove lice and nits. Their products are distributed internationally through pharmacies, health food stores, and retailers. (For more information about tea tree oil, refer to the book available in the back of this book.)

This is not an endorsement of their products,
nor a guarantee of their effectiveness.

What is the government's role in the regulation of food additives?

Today, food additives are significantly more regulated than ever before. Before the Pure Food and Drug Act of 1906, food manufacturing was virtually unregulated. Before this, food processors used to preserve milk with formaldehyde, preserved meat with sulfurous acid, and butter with borax. The 1906 act gave the government some control over the safety of the food supply chain. In 1938, The Food, Drug, and Cosmetic Act added additional powers to the FDA's control over the ingredients in food and labeling of foods.

In 1958, the Food Additives Amendment was passed, requiring manufacturers to prove an additive's safety, and it called for FDA approval of any additive before its use in foods. Two groups of substances were exempted from the regulatory amendment: those deemed as safe prior to the 1958 amendment were designated "prior sanctioned" (for example potassium nitrite and sodium nitrite), and those identified as "generally recognized as safe" (GRAS) based on their long period of use and substantiated by published scientific evidence. The following are GRAS substances: sugar, salt, MSG, vitamins, and additives derived from other foods like cornstarch. A review of exempted substances, produced due to reports of adverse reactions or additional evidence, resulted in some additives meeting strict labeling requirements, as is the case for sulfites and saccharin, or being banned, as is the case for cyclamates. Continued monitoring efforts by the FDA of all GRAS and prior-sanctioned substances, hopefully, ensures their safety.

An important provision in the 1958 amendment is the Delaney Clause, which prohibits the approval of additives that cause cancer in humans or animals, even when consumed in the tiniest of amounts.

In 1960, the "Color Additives Amendment" was passed, requiring prior approval by the FDA of all dyes used in foods, cosmetics, and drugs. Of the original 200 color additives, only 90 were approved for continued use, and of those only 9 were approved for use in foods!

Now, prior to approval of a new additive, manufacturers must show that an additive does what it is designed to do and is harmless to humans in the amounts being proposed for use in products. The manufacturer supplies the scientific information to the FDA, which then reviews it and makes a determination based on this information. The studies usually are based on animal testing, using large doses of the substance over long time periods. If the FDA determines the additive is safe to use, they issue regulations specifying which food types it may be used in, how food labels identify the additive, and the maximum amount allowed to be used; this is usually listed in parts per million or ppm.

The Adverse Reaction Monitoring System (ARMS) is an FDA operation where complaints arising from particular food additives are investigated so that appropriate actions or warnings can be taken. The March 1997 warning issued by the FDA for people sensitive to sulfites to avoid eating canned tuna is a good example of how this system works. The tuna industry discovered that sulfites had inadvertently been added to the fish through the use of a raw material that contained "hydrolyzed vegetable protein" to enhance flavor. Asthmatics and sulfite-sensitive people can have severe reactions to sulfites. Products containing sulfites must be appropriately labeled to meet FDA requirements for additives. In this case, the manufacturers choose to voluntarily discontinue using sulfite containing materials.

Avoid These Food Additives

Sulfites

Sulfites are now recognized as potentially harmful to asthmatics and anyone who has had a previous adverse reaction them. Sulfites are one of eight additives known to cause adverse reactions. Prior to 1986, they are believed to have resulted in at least seven deaths. That's when the FDA banned their use on fruits and vegetables intended to be eaten raw, like salad bars. According to the Center for Science in the Public Interest (CSPI), a consumer advocacy group focusing on nutrition and food, sulfites are known to destroy Vitamin B_1. A year later the FDA ordered that foods specifically using sulfites as a preservative must be labeled regardless of how much is used in the product. Foods containing sulfites as part of processing and not as a preservative must be labeled when they contain in excess of 10 parts per million (10 ppm) of a sulfiting material.

Food processors and restaurants serving fresh or frozen peeled potato products can use sulfites without any warning or labeling required. In the late 1980s food processors successfully blocked the FDA's attempts to regulate this use. Plans to ban their use on potato products are being made by the FDA. It asks anyone having an adverse reaction to potato products to report it to ARMS. On food package labels sulfites are disclosed under the following names: sulfur dioxide, sodium sulfite, sodium and potassium metabisulfite, and sodium and potassium bisulfite. Sulfites are regularly used in processed potatoes, processed or fresh-frozen seafood, dried fruit, and wine.

The Center for Science in the Public Interest's *Guide to Food Additives* states "A simple general rule about additives is to avoid sodium nitrite, saccharin, caffeine, olestra, acesulfame K, and artificial colors. Not only are they the most questionable additives, but they are used primarily in foods of low nutritional value."

In addition, the CSPI issued warnings against the most frequently used additives: sugar and salt. Though essentially they are not toxic, the large quantities they are consumed in is of great concern. Salt is a concern because it can cause high blood pressure, a big factor in heart disease. Sugar contributes to tooth decay, obesity, and nutrient deficiencies. Sugar constitutes about 20 percent of teenagers' diets, which is derived mainly from nutritionally deficient foods. Adults consume slightly less sugar in their diets. The immediate and long-term effects of this can greatly affect one's quality of life.

Potentially dangerous additives identified by the American Academy of

Allergy and Immunology (AAAI) include the artificial sweetener aspartame, BHT, BHA, food colorings, MSG, nitrates and nitrites. In addition, sulfites also destroy Vitamin B_1.

Sulfites are found in beer, canned vegetables, dehydrated vegetables, dried fruits, peeled and processed potato products, shrimp, wine and other food products.

Artificial Sweeteners

Controversy still surrounds artificial sweeteners such as aspartame, saccharin, and acesulfame K, even after decades of use. For over 20 years, saccharin has been controversial. The FDA still questions the possible cancer-causing aspect of saccharin. In November 1999, the FDA published a consumer report on artificial sweeteners, stating that it "knows for certain that (saccharin) causes cancer in animals."

In contrast, the National Cancer Institute says that adults ingesting saccharin within normal levels exhibit no signs of cancer. Warning labels used to be required on saccharin containing foods, but this has been recently changed.

NutraSweet®, the brand name for aspartame, has questionable effects upon humans. Concerns about it possibly causing brain tumors have arisen since its approval in the 1970s. At that time, the FDA determined there was no relationship between aspartame and brain tumors and allowed the use of the additive. The National Cancer Institute's data indicates no marked increase in brain tumors since its approval. What is now known, is that there is a negative interaction between aspartame and monosodium glutamate (MSG), which we discuss in the next chapter.

The American Academy of Allergy and Immunology (AAAI) has studies indicating that aspartame may cause swelling of the eyelids, feet, hands, and lips. The AAAI indicates these are rare occurrences, requiring additional study. Excellent documentation shows that people suffering from the rare, inherited metabolic disease PKU (phenylketonuria) need to strictly control their diet, and must avoid aspartame. Pregnant women are encouraged to not ingest aspartame.

In 1988 the sweetener acesulfame K was approved after more than 90 studies showed it was safe. There are indications that the tests may have been poorly done, and that this artificial sweetener is best avoided by consumers.

In 1998 sucralose, a new sweetener, was approved. Over 110 studies in animals and humans were designed to identify reproductive, neurological, or cancerous effects. The studies did not discover any.

A study of those who drank artificially sweetened drinks before a meal showed they ate about 11 percent more in terms of calories at meals than those who do not drink artificially flavored drinks.

Artificial sweeteners are found in diet products, soft drinks, some fruit drinks, and other processed foods.

A safer, natural sweetner is Stevia, also known as "sweet grass." It is approximately 200 to 300 times sweeter than sugar. Coke-Cola used it as the sweetener for Diet Coke® in Japan. When they decided to standardize Diet Coke's formulation around the world, Stevia was dropped in favor of an artificial sweetener. It is an approved noncaloric sweetener in Japan, and can be used instead of sugar for cooking and baking.

Stevia is gentler on the body then sugar or artificial sweeteners. It does not provoke the insulin problems that sugar does.

Stevia is recommended to people wanting to reduce their sugar intake. It is extremely sweet, and only a pinch is needed. When artificial sweeteners cannot be used, Stevia is acceptable for cooking and baking products.

Antioxidants

Antioxidants prevent the fats in foods from becoming rancid. Butylated hydroxytoluene (BHT) and butylated hydroxyanisole (BHA) are commonly used antioxidants. Even though BHA was approved as a GRAS substance, some animal studies have shown very high doses of BHA causes cancer of the stomach. The FDA continues to review the new scientific research on it, but has concluded that the levels of BHA in food for human consumption are safe. The AAAI indicates that BHA and BHT cause skin rashes and hives in those sensitive to the additives.

Propyl gallate is a commonly used antioxidant preservative with BHA and BHT. Studies indicate, but have not proven, that propyl gallate may have cancer-causing properties. This leads the CSPI to recommend you avoid this additive because of the lack of proper testing.

Color Enhancers

Food coloring (FD&C) additives continue to be controversial. Any foods using FD&C additives must be labeled.

The coloring Yellow No. 5, also known as tartrazine, has created the greatest concern. Those sensitive to it may get hives or have severe asthma attacks. Yellow No. 5 is the second most frequently used food coloring. People sensitive to aspirin have had mild allergic reactions to it. Yet, the FDA indicates there is little evidence supporting such claims, expressing the opinion that Yellow No. 5 causes hives in less than one in 10,000 people.

The most commonly used and tested food dye is Red No. 40. The FDA is investigating the approved Red No. 3 because tests on rats have caused thyroid tumors.

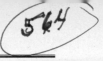

The top six food coloring offenders

1. Blue No.1, derived from coal-tar or petroleum. Used in baked goods, candy, cereals, desserts, drink powders, gelatin, ice cream, ices, soft drinks, puddings, plus other foods.

2. Citrus Red No. 2, used to color the skin of Florida oranges. May damage internal organs. Known as a lesser cancer-causing agent.

3. Green No. 3, used in baked goods, candy, cereals, confections, frozen desserts, mint-flavored jelly, plus other foods. Possibility of allergic reactions.

4. Red No.3, derived from coal-tar or petroleum. Used in baked goods, candy, canned fruit cocktail, cereals, cherry pie mix, maraschino cherries, gelatin based desserts, and puddings. Possibly interferes with the brain's neurotransmitters.

5. Yellow No. 5, also known as tartrazine. Derived from coal-tar or petroleum. Used in baked goods, breakfast cereals, candy, confections, powered drinks, it is an ingredient in most processed foods, ice cream, puddings, sherbets, and spaghetti. Sadly, about half of aspirin-sensitive people and tens of thousands of others are sensitive to it. Asthmatic symptoms can result from ingesting it. Approximately 60 per cent of prescription and over-the-counter drugs such as antibiotics, antihistamines, sedatives, and steroids, contain Yellow No. 5. It causes a deficiency of zinc and hyperactivity in children.

6. Yellow No. 6, derived from coal-tar or petroleum. Used in baked goods, candy, carbonated drinks, confections not having oils or fats in them, drink powders, gelatin desserts, puddings, tablets.

Food dyes were originally derived from coal-tar oil, but today they generally are made from petroleum. Some third world and industrialized countries may still use coal-tar oils to produce food dyes for their products.

One of the underlying principles of the "Feingold Diet" (see Chapter 11) is that the source of a food dye or coloring could be an underlying cause of ADD and hyperactivity. It separates them into natural source dyes. For example a vegetable based coloring will be easier on the body than one produced as a byproduct of coal tar or petroleum. Many people have successfully treated themselves or their children using the "Feingold Diet" and making simple changes like only using foods like cereals that contain certain natural food colorings.

Food dyes are found in baked goods, candy, drink mixes, fruit juices, gelatin desserts, maraschino cherries, pet food, and many other processed foods.

Flavor Enhancers

One of the most commonly used flavor enhancers, monosodium gluta-mate (MSG), causes reactions such as nausea, headaches, sweating, and burning sensations in the upper arms and neck of people sensitive to it. The percentage of people suffering this sensitivity is unknown. Labeling laws require that MSG and other glutamates such as disodium guanylate, dis-odium inosinate and hydrolyzed vegetable protein must be labeled. An important issue is the various interactions between different food additives. In the case of glutamates, aspartame increases the possibility of an adverse reaction, as we shall later discover in this and the next chapter.

MSG is found in bouillon cubes, hot dogs, frozen foods, instant soups, poultry, restaurant foods, salad dressings, sauce mixes, seafood, stews, plus other processed foods.

Antimicrobial Preservatives

Nitrates and nitrites are typically used as a preservative in processed meats such as bacon, bologna, and hot dogs. They should be avoided unless used in combination with erythorbic or ascorbic acid. When nitrates and nitrites are added to foods they may form tiny amounts of nitrosamines, known cancer-causing chemicals. Erythorbic and ascorbic acids inhibit the formation of nitrosamines. The nature and quality of the fatty, salty, and processed meats nitrates and nitrites are used in, is generally not beneficial. This in itself is a good reason to avoid such foods. Obviously, vegetarians have little to be concerned about when it comes to nitrates or nitrites.

These substances are found in bacon, bologna, corned beef, ham, hot dogs, luncheon meats, smoked fish, and many other processed meats. If you purchase these products, make sure they contain erythorbic and ascorbic acids, which to a degree counteract the negative effects of nitrates and nitrites.

Fat Substitutes

The Proctor & Gamble fat substitute Olestra™ is an additive that must be avoided for at least two reasons. First, it causes mild to severe gastroin-testinal problems such as stomach cramps, diarrhea, and loose stools in many people. Second, it inhibits the body's ability to absorb carotenoids and the fat-soluble vitamins A, D, E, F and K. Olestra™ is a combination of sugar and vegetable oil which are processed to pass through the body with-out being absorbed, thereby leaving no fat or calories behind.

When Olestra™ transits and exits the body, studies show that it removes those valuable fat-soluble vitamins. It also inhibits the absorption of carotenoids from foods eaten at that time. Carotenoids are thought to pro-tect against heart disease, cancer and blindness in the elderly. While manufacturers fortify products containing Olestra™ with fat-soluble vitamins, the carotenoid issue still lingers.

In addition to this, the body needs fats to function properly. For example, the brain is about two-thirds fat. Your nerves are protected with an outer layer made up of fat. Your body is wrapped in a layer of fat, critical to helping it keep you at the right temperature. Recent studies proved ADD and ADHD can be positively influenced with nutritional supplementation using essential fatty acids. Eating the right fats can even help you lose weight. Over time, a body slowly robbed of the right fats and nutrients will exhibit illnesses, diseases and eventually death.

Olestra™ is found in chips, crackers and other processed foods.

Hydrogenated Fats

Recently, the hydrogenated fats commonly known as trans-fatty acids have been gaining recognition as a source of health related problems. The process of hydrogenation solidifies liquid oils, making them less susceptible to rancidity and creating these trans-fats. They are commonly found in crackers, cookies, margarine, snack foods, and vegetable shortenings. Trans-fats increase LDL blood cholesterol, the cholesterol that can become "bad" due to excessive homocysteine levels in the body. This process increases the risk of coronary heart disease.

Hopefully, FDA labeling regulations will make it easier for consumers to know when they are consuming products with trans-fatty acids. In Canada, food labeling shows total fat content and specific fats, but when one adds up the specific fats listed, one finds a small discrepancy between total fat content and this number. The difference is mainly the hidden trans-fatty acid content of the processed foods. Consumers should avoid this fat in processed foods, especially fried foods and restaurant meals.

Trans-fatty acids are found in baked goods, chips, margarine, vegetable shortening, and many processed foods.

Other Additives

Phosphates and potassium bromate are two other additives you may want to avoid. Potassium bromate is an additive used in making bread dough. According to CSPI studies, potassium bromate causes tumors in animals. Since 1991, the FDA has chosen to request bakers not use it, but has not banned it. Some manufacturers still use potassium bromate in their products. In California, products containing potassium bromate must have a cancer warning. Potassium bromate is banned in Canada and the United Kingdom. Avoid breads that have "potassium bromate" or "bromated flour" on their labels.

Excessive consumption of phosphates may be a contributing factor to the development of osteoporosis. Phosphate additives are a small amount of the total phosphates in most people's diet—the majority come from diary products and meat rather than additives.

High salt (sodium) intake increases blood pressure, which leads to heart disease, vision problems and a host of other health challenges. Excessive salt intake can cause imbalances in other trace minerals, like lithium and potassium. This can greatly affect one's health. When dehydrated, sufficient salt levels are critical for maintaining and retaining body fluids. Salt is found in most processed foods including crackers, meats, potato chips, and soups.

Sugars, including dextrose and corn syrup, contribute to diabetes, tooth decay, obesity, poor nutrition, hyperactivity and many other health related problems. Over consumption is very easy as sugars are labeled under many different names. Sugars are found in breads, cakes, cookies, fruit juices, soft drinks, syrups, snack foods and most processed foods.

Carrageenan is a derivative of Irish moss, and has a salty taste and seaweed-like odor. Currently there is concern about this food additive. It is undergoing additional studies. Carrageenan is used as an emulsifier and stabilizer in artificially sweetened jams and jellies, cheese foods, cheese spreads, chocolate products, chocolate milk, chocolate-flavored drinks, confections, evaporated milk, French dressing, frozen product syrups, ice cream, pressure-dispensed whipped cream, syrups used in frozen products.

Xanthan gum is derived from the fermentation of corn sugar using Xanthomonas campestris bacterium. It reduces the ability of the body's thirst mechanism to function properly. In addition, it causes the stomach to continuously produce acid.

Indirect Sources of Additives

A major source of additives is modern farming methods. Foods grown using modern growing methods may contain up to 100 agricultural chemicals, excluding fertilizers, and over 50 food processing additives. They include pesticides, fungicides, fertilizers, herbicides, and genetic alterations, which create an incredible amount of potential toxic sources hidden in foods. Added to this is the use of untreated sludge, usually excrement from large agribusinesses such as hog producers, and the use of dead animal carcasses to feed livestock.

"You are what you eat" applies to humans, animals, eggs and produce. Pulitzer Prize-winning author, Richard Rhodes, in his book *Deadly Feasts* (Simon and Schuster, 1997), deals with mad-cow disease. He points out that countries banning the use of dead carcasses as animal feed eventually see mad-cow disease disappear. Unfortunately, this disease can take 25–30 years before the signs and symptoms become apparent in humans, and up to 7 years in livestock. Hogs are slaughtered when they are 2 or 3 years old, so the underlying assumption that they do not get mad-cow disease is a

faulty one, since the disease takes 7
product containing dead animal mat
roses, may be a carrier of mad-co
kosher meats cannot be fed dead anir
organically-grown livestock, the bette

Nichole Fox, author of *Spoiled:*
what we can do about it, (Penguin, 19
monella carriers, such as chickens a
chicken producers' farms grew from
100,000-plus range for livestock farm
ated marketing campaigns to manipula
of salmonella poisoning was their own .... food preparation. Just fifty
years ago, the possibility of salmonella was minuscule. Today, it is estimated
that up to 85% of newborn chicks and eggs have salmonella.

These indirect sources of additives used to nourish plant and animal life
become part of the foods we eat. As the number of food production options
increases in profit-driven agri-businesses, we may see increasing amounts of
negative impacts upon our health. The result is an ever-increasing demand
for organically-grown and certified foods, which use only natural nutrients
and methods for growing crops and raising livestock.

In addition, imported foods may contain banned or excessive amounts
of additives, and may nevertheless be allowed into the United States or
Canada. Some imported foods contain residual amounts of hazardous
chemicals, which can be harmful to you.

How to report an adverse reaction to an additive?

The FDA needs you or your health care provider to report the problem.
This is a voluntary process. When symptoms are not recognized as resulting
from an additive, or the individual is not medically treated for the problem
because he or she does not consult with a doctor or health care provider,
nothing happens.

The FDA's Adverse Reaction Monitoring System gathers and acts on
problems or complaints about all food ingredients. If you have an adverse
reaction to any food or food product, first contact your local office of the
FDA listed in your local phone directory, or call their emergency hot line at
(301) 827-7250 or (301) 827-7240 or toll free 1 (800) 332-1088.

In addition, send a written letter to the Adverse Reaction Monitoring
System (HFS-636), 200 C St. S.W., Washington, DC 20204. To access the
FDAs Adverse Reaction Monitoring System on the web try:
www.ora.fda.gov

Canadians should first contact their local Health Protection Branch
Canadian Food Inspection Agency office listed in your local phone

4 hour toll free emergency food hot line at 1 (800)
also try their web site at www.cfia-acia.agr.ca
send a written letter to the Minister of Health Canada,
ture, A.L. 0913A, Ottawa, Ontario, Canada K1A 0K9
1 (613) 957-1820

ome suggestions for avoiding food additives in your diet

- Eat only fresh, wholesome foods such as fresh vegetables, fruits and whole grains.
- Eat less of foods with labels, which are processed foods tending to have more fat, sodium, and additives.
- Eat organically grown fruits and vegetables, and organically raised livestock and eggs. Another good choice is kosher meats.
- Read the labels on processed foods to avoid the additives you do not want to consume.
- When buying unlabeled bulk foods, ask the store staff to check or show you the list of ingredients.
- When eating at restaurants, ask your server to check if the foods contain any of the additives you want to avoid.
- Photocopy the list of additives below, and check off those you don't want to consume. Carry it with you at all times as a quick reference and to show others what to look for.

At-A-Glance Quick Reference™ List of
Specific Additives and Groups of Additives to Avoid

ADD and Hyperactivity: The All-in-One Guide to™ series

Check off the additives:

❏ acesulfame K	❏ artificial colors
❏ aspartame	❏ baking soda*
❏ BHA (butylated hydroxyanisole)	❏ BHT (Butylated hydroxytoluene)
❏ bromated flour	❏ caffeine
❏ carrageenan	❏ citric acid
❏ corn syrup – a sweetener	❏ dextrose** – a sweetener.
❏ disodium inosinate***	❏ disodium guanylate***

Food colorings:

❏ Blue No. 1	❏ Red No. 40
❏ Blue No. 2	❏ Red No. 3
❏ Citrus Red No. 2	❏ Yellow No. 5 – also called tartrazine
❏ Green No. 3	❏ Yellow No. 6
Other_____	Other_____
❏ hydrolyzed vegetable protein***	❏ hydrogenated fats
❏ MSG	❏ nitrates
❏ nitrites	❏ NutraSweet® brand name for aspartame
❏ Olestra™	❏ orris root extract
❏ phosphates	❏ potassium bromate
❏ potassium nitrite	❏ propyl gallate
❏ saccharin	❏ salt (sodium)
❏ sodium nitrite	❏ sorbate
❏ sucralose** – a sweetener	❏ sugar

sulfites:

❏ sulfur dioxide	❏ sodium and potassium metabisulfite
❏ sodium sulfite	❏ sodium and potassium bisulfite.
❏ trans-fatty acids	❏ xanthan gum
Other_____	Other_____
Other_____	Other_____

*   baking soda contains aluminum, an agent suspected of causing Alzheimer's disease.
**   Ingredients ending is "ose" are usually sugars.
*** Contains or is MSG – monosodium glutamate

The Secret World of Flavor Enhancers

MSG and Aspartame — The Deadly Duo

After salt and pepper, the drug glutamic acid is the third most used flavor booster in America. The most frequently used form is monosodium glutamate (MSG). The Food and Drug Administration, as well as Canada's Health Protection Branch, classify it as a food additive. It can have drug-like effects on many people.

Everyone is vulnerable to glutamate's toxic effects. Glutamates are common neurotransmitters in the brain, responsible for the movement of chemical signals from one neuron to next. Minute quantities are rapidly released and reabsorbed. If the bloodstream has high levels of glutamates, it may cause misfiring neurons, resulting in psychological and physical problems. In extreme instances permanent damage can occur.

Foods in which naturally occurring protein-bound glutamates are found include aged cheese, mushrooms and tomatoes. For centuries, Japanese cuisine has been using seaweed sauce. Monosodium glutamate was first discovered in seaweed as the active ingredient which gave seaweed its powerful potency.

A Japanese scientist discovered MSG in 1908. Since then it has come into widespread use in oriental cooking. It wasn't until a conference in 1948 that all the major US food companies found out about MSG. Its properties as a food additive to improve pleasant tastes and lessen unpleasant ones, especially in canned and frozen foods, was a significant discovery for the prepackaged food industry.

"Glutamates are glutamates," says the Glutamate Association, a lobbying group for the multi-billion-dollar food industry. According to the Association, chemical additives are metabolized in the same way as all natural glutamates present in foods. They claim that MSG is, "therefore, safe for most people." Biological availability is the major difference between glutamates naturally found in foods and those used as additives.

The major difference is the rate at which natural glutamates, as con-trasted with chemical additives, are digested and absorbed. Both the natural and chemical additive glutamates are absorbed in the intestines in the same way. The critical difference is that protein-bound natural glutamates are absorbed more slowly. The glutamate additives are not bound to other pro-teins, causing them to be quickly and easily absorbed. This results is in a spike of glutamate in the blood.

Glutamates and asparate, aspartame's active ingredient, are closely related. Both are very powerful free radicals (substances that cause damage to the body) generators. Unprocessed natural glutamates are escorted by antioxidants, substances which decrease or nullify the effects of free radicals.

Together aspartate and glutamate are synergistic, thereby increasing the probability of nervous system problems. Because the myelin sheath that pro-tects nerves from damage is not fully developed in young children, they are more likely to suffer damage from these chemicals. Children's bodies are more sensitive and can suffer a toxic reaction at smaller dosage levels. Unfortunately, the fast foods and lunch meats enjoying increasing popular-ity with children may be high in MSG, and combined with soft drinks (pop) containing aspartame (aspartate), may result in a powerful potentially toxic cocktail.

Evidence is mounting that attention deficit hyperactivity disorder and the accompanying emotional problems may be a partial result of consuming glutamate additives. Eliminating MSG from the diets of many "problem" children has resulted in remarkable changes.

Evidence indicates MSG contributes to or causes the following problems:

asthma attacks	memory and learning loss
behavioral disturbances	mood swings
depression	obesity
hormone changes	paranoia
heart irregularities	stunted growth
infertility	seizures

In addition to these problems, evidence is mounting that aspartate and glutamates are factors that contribute to the development of neurodegener-ative diseases such as ALS (Lou Gehrig's disease), Alzheimer's, and Parkinson's.

How do you diagnose a child's or adult's sensitivity to MSG?

This is difficult to do, since there can be a significant time lag between a MSG-laden meal and the onset of symptoms. Individual sensitivities, and other factors such as age, sex, and the extent to which the body has been exposed to foods in which the MSG content has been masked, contribute to the body's inability to cope with the internal assault of MSG. The following is a partial list of possible symptoms:

an asthma attack   hyperactivity
behavior problems in children   mimic of a heart attack or stroke
depression   seizures
flushing of the face and neck   stuffy nose
headache – usually migraines

The list of potential problems may also include more subtle and long term affects, not mentioned above.

Avoiding MSG in your diet may be difficult to do. Why? Monosodium glutamate is described in many ways. Hydrolyzation is a process that frees aspartic acid and glutamic acid from the protein which causes them to act the same way as MSG does on the brain. The following list describes sources of MSG and their legally acceptable descriptions on food labels: Permission is granted to photocopy and distribute this list from *The All-in-One Guide to*™ *ADD and Hyperactivity,* ISBN1-886508-29-1, AGES Publications™.

• monopotassium glutamate, found in low sodium foods
• hydrolyzed vegetable protein contains up to 20 per cent free glutamate and aspartate
• hydrolyzed plant protein contains up to 20 per cent free glutamate and aspartate
• "natural flavorings" may contain glutamates
• spices may contain glutamates, even those labeled "all natural"

Take this list with you when shopping so you will know when food processors use it in their products. Restaurant foods generally have MSG in one form or another in the prepackaged condiments, main courses, and other products they serve. Ask to see the packaging label, and if there is no label, assume the food contains MSG.

What can you can do to decrease your MSG consumption?

Eat as many organic, fresh foods as possible, since they contain no additives. There are some MSG-free sauces, seasonings and soups, generally found in the organic food section of your supermarket, as well as health food and organic food stores.

When preparing food, instead of using MSG if the recipe requires it, substitute fresh juice from organically grown lemons.

Make your own soup stock and sauces—yes, even ketchup—in large quantities. Use ice cube trays to freeze them into single meal servings. Once frozen, put the cubes into plastic freezer bags or containers.

Create a food preparation network with a group of friends. Each week, every person prepares a large batch of a single food, which is divided up equally among the members of the group. This is an inexpensive way to get chemical-free foods, that are good for everyone. In addition, you build a sense of community which is very valuable for the sake of your children.

Avoid fast foods, restaurants, and processed foods.

The Problems With Soft Drinks

14

Gayle Alleman, M.S., R.D., in her book *Save Your Child from the Fat Epidemic: 7 Steps Every Parent Can Take to Ensure Healthy, Fit Children for Life* (Prima Publishing, 1999), writes about the problems with the foods in our diets, soft drinks being one of them. In pursuit of profits and income, schools and drink manufacturers have teamed up to put them in our schools.

Consider Coke® and Pepsi®, store brand colas and pop, or soft drinks in general. They usually contain one or more chemicals harmful to human health such as caffeine, phosphoric acid, sugar, and aspartame. (see the preceding chapter, MSG and Aspartame—The Deadly Duo). Drink manufacturers are putting caffeine into soft drinks that previously did not have them, in the hopes of stimulating sales. At the same time, they are not labeling their products as containing these additives, or they are listing the additives as if they were naturally-occurring food flavorings.

At low levels, these substance may not affect an individual, but the accumulation of the additives in a child's or adult's body may trigger problems, or even worsen preexisting conditions.

A teenage boy drinks 3.5 cans of pop each day. The industry's statistics show that it produces enough for the average American to drink 54 gallons a year.

Over-consumption of soft drinks can cause problems

Healthier and more nourishing drinks such as low-fat milk and water, are replaced with soft drinks.

A regular can of Coke® has approximately 150 calories; a large 32 ounce soft drink has over 300 calories. Obesity can result from this. You drink less of what your body needs clean unadulterated water.

Phosphoric acid is a major component in many soft drinks. It leaches calcium from bones. Eventually the body develops problems due to this, such as osteoporosis, kidney stones, weakened teeth, et cetera.

Caffeine destroys, depletes or prevents the body's ability to properly utilize many nutrients. These are some of those nutrients it affects according to the authors of *Natural Remedies and Supplements: The All-in-One guide to™* (AGES Publications, 2000, ISBN 1-886508-28-3 and 1-886508-33-X): vitamin B_1 (Thiamine), vitamin B_3 (niacin, nicotinic acid, niacinamide, nicotinamide), vitamin K, Biotin (part of the B vitamin complex, also known as Coenzyme R or Vitamin H), inositol, calcium, iron, potassium, zinc, glucosamine and Omega 3 fatty acids.

In addition to this, when a 40 pound child drinks a 12 ounce, caffeine-loaded soft drink, it is the equivalent of a 175 pound man drinking 2 1/2 cups of regular coffee. The difference is that a 40 pound child's body is significantly less able and more sensitive to it than would be the grown man. Age, weight, gender, physical disposition and diet are just a few of the variables determining how caffeine affects someone.

One typical 12 ounce soft drink is equal to the maximum amount of sugar a person should have each day, about 10 teaspoons. American food guidelines suggest we should eat a maximum of 10 per cent of our daily intake as sugar. That means a teenager or adult eating 2,000 calories a day should not have more then 12 teaspoons of sugar.

Excess sugar intake can create all sorts of problems, such as elevated cholesterol and triglyceride levels and weight gain which can result in adult-onset diabetes and heart disease. Sugar may compromise the immune system's ability to function properly. Sugar becomes an excellent medium for growing bacteria, such as Candida Albicans, which results in yeast infections and excessive levels of yeast, something much easier to diagnose in girls and women than in boys and men. Yeast problems can occur in both genders, and it is hard to permanently resolve. An overabundance of yeast can affect one's mood, immune system and a host of other bodily systems and organs. And so on and so on...

Other things Coke® or Pepsi® are good for, is removing rust: crumple up aluminum, dip it in either product, then rub away those nasty rust spots. Pour a can over your battery terminals and watch the corrosion bubble away. It is also a great degreaser; just pour a can into your laundry load of greasy clothes, add your regular detergent, use a regular washing cycle, and presto, clothes without grease emerge.

The phosphoric acid content in these soft drinks produces a pH of 2.8, which is strong enough to dissolve metal nails in days. Put your child's baby teeth in a glass of Coke® or Pepsi® and watch them disappear over time. They eat right through the enamel of teeth.

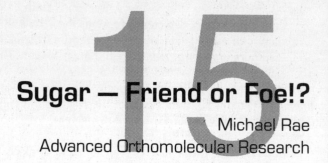

Sugar — Friend or Foe!?
Michael Rae
Advanced Orthomolecular Research

We have a difficult relationship with sugar...

On the one hand, our bodies use glucose as one of its principal fuels. In fact, the brain runs almost entirely on glucose, and cannot directly use protein or fat for its energy. Because it is a quick energy source, glucose is also good for quick bursts of energy, and our body thus releases a flood of glucose for immediate use in "fight-or-flight" emergencies. We've all experienced the problems of low blood sugar: sapping of energy, low motivation, and even wooziness as the brain is deprived of its energy source. On the other hand, high blood sugar is a major health problem, too—and not just for diabetics.

Glucose is a chemically active substance, not an inert, neutral fuel. One of the things to which it likes to bind is protein. When blood sugar is high, it tends to react with the proteins in our cells, forming structurally-ruined protein/sugar complexes known as Advanced Glycation End products (AGEs). This sticky refuse is appropriately named. The slow buildup of AGEs over the years stiffens our arteries, clogs our cells with the waste product lipofuscin, reduces the functionality of our kidneys, slows nerve transmission, and clouds over the lenses of our eyes. AGEs are a major source causing the complications of diabetes, but they are also implicated in the aging process itself.

Mention the word "sugar," and most of us immediately think of soda pop and candy bars. But actually, all the carbohydrates in our diet are made up of sugars, from starches to monosaccharides. The differences in the carbohydrates present in our foods come down to two basic factors: the length of the chain of sugars strung together, and the chemical structure of the individual sugars making up the chain. All carbohydrates are made up of a fairly small number of very simple, isolated sugars called monosaccharides.

From a dietary perspective, the most important of these is glucose. It is glucose that your body uses as fuel for the brain, and glucose is the most important sugar circulating in your blood. Other simple dietary sugars, such as the fructose in grapefruits or the galactose which forms part of the sugar content in milk, are "isomers" of glucose: they have the same number and type of atoms in them, but these building blocks are arranged differently. But most of the carbohydrates in our diet do not come in the form of monosaccharides: instead, we get our sugars in longer or shorter chains, from the basic two-sugar-molecule disaccharides like the lactose in dairy products (which is made up of one glucose molecule bonded to one galactose molecule) to much longer sugar chains—the so-called complex carbohydrates, like the starch in wheat or potatoes (composed of long strings of glucose molecules). But when you break it all down, it all comes back to those three simple sugars.

So when, decades ago, doctors were first asked what changes diabetic patients could make in their diets to help keep their blood sugar levels stable, the answer seemed simple: more of the longer-chain carbohydrates. Complex carbs (so the theory went) would take longer to break down in the gut, and would thus give a "time-release" glucose supply, lowering the glucose spike and helping to fill in the blood sugar valley. It was a great-sounding little story. It made intuitive sense. In fact, it made so much sense that the story was preached as received truth, and accepted as a proven fact, when it was never anything more than an hypothesis—an hypothesis that had never been put to the test. The myth of the complex carb became so entrenched in mainstream medical thinking that it just didn't seem worthwhile to invest the money and time to see just how quickly those sugars were really being released into the blood.

> The myth of the complex carb became so entrenched in mainstream medical thinking that it just didn't seem worthwhile to invest the money and time to see just how quickly those sugars were really being released into the blood.

All this changed in the early 1980s. Starting in 1981, scientists like Thomas Wolever of the University of Toronto and Dr. Jennie Brand-Miller at the University of Sydney began giving subjects foods with equal amounts of carbohydrate in them and measuring just how much glucose was released into the bloodstream. And whether they used healthy volunteers, diabetic patients, athletes, or people with heart disease, the results were essentially the same: the simplicity or complexity of the carbohydrate bore almost no relationship to the glycemic response. The "complex carbohydrate" story turned out to be a complete myth.[3]

Make no mistake: there are real differences between the rate at which different foods release their sugars into the blood—that is, between the glycemic indexes (GIs) of different foods. But looking at a ranking of tested foods[2] is like staring into the looking glass: not only does the table not look like the ranking predicted by the "complex carb" story, the glycemic index tables look like the expected tables turned on their head. Wheat, rice, and potatoes, for instance, are among the fastest sugar-releasers yet tested; by contrast, many foods we think of as "sugary" because of their sweetness — such as black cherries and grapefruit—are extremely low-GI foods. Even candy bars and table sugar, while relatively high-GI, still beat an equal amount of carb in the form of whole wheat bread or rice cakes in terms of how quickly the sugars they contain spike—and crash—blood sugar levels. This does not make table sugar any more nutritious (table sugar is empty calories, void of nutritional value) but it does mean that many foods that are both sweet and nutritious are better food choices than starches—which are neither.

As it turns out, our GI tracts are a lot better at breaking down carbohydrate than anyone had guessed. True, there are some carbohydrates—dietary fibers—which the gut can't break down at all (although some of these fibers are digestible by our friendly bacteria). But when scientists looked at the digestible carbohydrate content of foods, they found that the GI tract made fast work of them, indeed. Chain length made no difference: irrespective of its "complexity," a carbohydrate is broken down into simple sugars in mere moments. What makes the difference is not the length of the carbohydrate chains involved, but the components of the chain. The starch in potatoes and rice is made up entirely of glucose, which is released directly into the bloodstream. By contrast, the simple sugars in a grapefruit are dominated by fructose, which must be converted into glucose in the liver before it is released into the blood. And the lactose in milk is composed of 50% quick-release glucose, but also 50% galactose, which is converted and released as slowly as fructose.

Fiber content also makes a difference—but it depends on the fiber type. The insoluble fibers typically present in grains have little effect on GI, so that white bread and whole-wheat have almost identical ratings. But soluble fibers—the gums and pectins found in legumes and many fruits—make the digested meal more viscous, slowing the emptying of the stomach and thus the release of the sugars in the food. Another nutrient which slows gastric emptying, and thus lowers GI, is fat content, so that adding a little high-quality fat to a meal can help curb glycemic response. Other factors—from the amount of processing of a carbohydrate (mashed vs. whole kidney beans, for instance, or parboiled vs. sticky rice), the "superstructure" of starches (amylose vs. amylopectin), and even the presence of GI-lowering fruit acids like citrate and malate—also affect glycemic index.[6,10]

The GI of a meal thus plays a major role in controlling our blood sugar, determining whether we get a sugary rush followed by will-sapping hypoglycemic doldrums on the one hand, or smooth sailing on the other. And this, in turn, affects a variety of parameters, from insulin sensitivity and glucose tolerance,[4] to how much food we will eat at our next meal,[5] to our capacity for endurance sports.[1,9] Further, because fast-releasing sugars drive up insulin levels, studies also show that there is a relationship between GI and risk of diabetes: the higher the GI of the carbs a person eats, the greater his or her risk of developing diabetes.[8,9] Because elevated insulin is a very powerful risk factor for cardiovascular disease, there is a strong argument to be made that high-GI carb eating may contribute to the development of this major killer too.[6]

Representative Foods' Glycemic Indexes:

100 Glucose	59 Pastry	36 Yogurt
98 Baked Potato	59 **Table Sugar**	36 Lima Beans
97 Parsnips	51 Bran	34 Pears
87 Honey	51 Green Peas	32 Skim Milk
80 Cornflakes	51 Potato Chips	32 Strawberries
72 Whole Wheat Bread	51 Sweet Potato	29 Lentils
72 White Rice	50 White Spaghetti	29 Kidney Beans
70 Mashed Potatoes	49 Slow-Cook Oatmeal	26 Peaches
69 White Bread	46 Grapes	26 Grapefruit
68 Mars Bar	44 Oranges	25 Plums
67 Shredded Wheat	42 Whole Wheat Spaghetti	23 Cherries
66 Brown Rice	42 Whole Grain Rye Bread	20 Fructose
64 Beets	38 Apples	15 Soybeans
64 Raisins	38 Tomatoes	13 Peanuts
62 Bananas	36 Ice Cream	8 Chana Dal
59 Corn	36 Chickpeas	

Glycemic Index refers to the rate at which a food's sugars get released into the blood

For sources of "Glycemic Index" lists, refer to this web site http://www.mendosa.com/gilists.htm

Another concern that has been brought up is that some foods, because of their sweetness, may trigger an unhealthily strong insulin response despite their low GI. This effect—the so-called cepalic-phase insulin response—has been extensively documented in lab animals: because of a response similar to that in Pavlovov's famous dogs (which had been served food after hearing the dinner bell so often that they would begin to salivate as soon as the dinner bell rang), the mere taste of some artificial sweeteners can cause an insulin response, even when the sweetener itself has no direct effect on the insulin-releasing cells of the pancreas. While this effect has been shown to be a real issue in lab animals, and while humans can be trained to respond this way,[11] two human studies[12,13] have found that the effect doesn't happen spontaneously in humans: people drinking the equivalent of a can of artificially-sweetened soda, or tasting sweetness equivalent to a slice of apple pie, show no measurable insulin response. While many would prefer to wait for more careful studies, it does appear that, for humans at least, insulin levels are only spiked by the objective sugar in your blood—not the subjective sweetness in your mouth.

So don't fall for the fairy tale. Consider cutting back on the bagels, pasta, bread, rice, and potatoes, and eating more of most fruits, vegetables, and legumes. See how you like oatmeal as a breakfast cereal instead of Special K. You don't have to ride the blood sugar roller coaster.

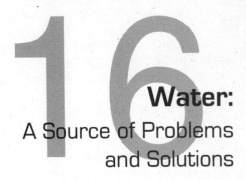

16

Water:
A Source of Problems and Solutions

the ALL-IN-ONE GUIDE to
NATURAL
REMEDIES
and
SUPPLEMENTS

Vitamins • Minerals
Enzymes • Amino Acids • Fats
Herbs • Aromatherapy
Flower Remedies • Homeopathic Remedies
Leading Edge Supplements
Phytochemicals • Nutraceuticals

Dr. Elvis Ali • Pam Floener • David Gershowitz
Dr. George Grant • Fred Hui, M.D. • Gordon Ko, M.D.
Dr. Joseph Levy • Dorothy Marshall • Selim Nakla, M.D.
Alvin Pettle, M.D. • Ken Vegotsky

Water: Water everywhere, and not a single drop to spare!?

Water makes up about 66% of your body's composition. It is critical in helping the body maintain its homeostasis—its internal balance. As a primary source of well being, clean water is critical for the transportation of nutrients (vitamins, minerals, essential fatty acids, etc.) into and throughout the bodies of ADD and hyperactive children and adults. Soft drinks, fruit and vegetable juices are poor replacements for water.

Contaminants such as arsenic, mercury, asbestos, aluminum and *E. coli 0157* are just a few of the thousands of substances finding their way into our water supplies. The Environmental Protection Agency has targeted several major sources of noxious and deadly chemicals that are fouling our air and water; these result from industrial manufacturing processes and the large farm factories for hogs, chicken, cattle and other livestock.

Numerous studies are pointing to side effects which usually first appear in the workers in these businesses and spread out to the community. Water tables, lakes, rivers and streams are being destroyed. The costs to clean them up are significantly greater than taking preventative measures to ensure the quality of these critical resources for our health and well-being.

David Korten in his critically acclaimed books *When Corporations Rule the World* and *The Post-Corporate World* clearly shows how businesses do not directly bear the costs of these problems. You and every other member of society bear the costs, and in so doing, help corporations to build and maintain their profitability. He expands on this by showing that the United States is not the only country experiencing this massive distortion to, and destruction of its environment. It is a global problem.

In Canada, the University of Alberta's David Schindler, one of the world's leading experts on water and our ecology, indicated in a recently published scientific paper that pollution from agriculture combined with other sources will end all fresh water fishing by the middle of this century in Canada, and that Canada's drinking water will be totally compromised during this century.

During the Spring and Summer 2000, deadly outbreaks of *E. coli 0157* infection and other problems started occurring with increasing frequency in the provinces of Ontario, Alberta, Quebec and Manitoba, indicating that those provinces' massive factory farms are having deadly affects on their water supplies. Add to this the indiscriminate use of the untreated toxic waste and untreated manure from these agri-businesses, and you have a recipe for the total destruction of their water and food supplies. And the news gets worse.

> **"If bread is the staff of life, then water is the wine of life."**
>
> – Bahir Ben Ken,
> *The Prophet Revisited,*
> by Ken Vegotsky

Toronto, Ontario has the worst air pollution in Canada. Los Angeles and New York City are beginning to look pristine in comparison. According to *The Toronto Star*, the province of Ontario is the second or third most polluted environment in the U.S.A. and Canada, just behind the number one leader for the most pollution, Texas. The results are increasing cases of asthma, heart attacks, deaths and other problems attributable to the stresses on the body caused by air pollution and water contamination.

Each year, in excess of 1,800 children and adults die in Ontario, Canada, due to air pollution. Of those, 400-plus of these deaths happened in Toronto during the summer of 1999. Ineffective regulations, or none at all, combined with lack of personnel to enforce them, are allowing businesses to destroy what used to be the one of the best environments in the world, while downloading the costs to the citizens of this province. Inertia is caused by a blame game played by politicians, each pointing their fingers at the other saying the pollution is coming from the others' states or provinces. This finger-pointing is accompanied by the rally cry of "cost cutting." All the time, the most vulnerable citizens, the children, develop physical problems such as asthma that seem to go hand in hand with many cases of ADD and hyperactivity.

Clean water is essential for optimal health and healing. Directly and indirectly it may be a cause of ADD and hyperactive symptoms in our populations. The benefits of clean water include its ability to promote lubrication of body parts, transporting nutrients, energizing people, and as a medium to expel toxins through sweat. Water helps cleanse by taking waste products out of your body. It helps maintain and keep your biochemical balances on an even keel. It is a critical component of the heating and air conditioning system that maintains your body temperature. Water performs a host of other essential functions too numerous to list here.

The type and quality of water you get can significantly affect your health. This may be especially true for the ADD/Hyperactive child or adult. Protect yourself and your loved ones. Contact your elected officials and ask them to protect your water and food supplies from the short-term economic interests of businesses and trans-global mega-corporations that are not currently accountable for their actions. The subject of food is covered in numerous other chapters in this book. Here's a quick guide to water, and what you can do:

Tap water and safety issues

The advantages of tap water are ease of access, low cost and hopefully constant monitoring and accurate testing by public authorities. The disadvantages vary, depending on where you live—in the city, on a farm or in the country. Drinking, bathing, swimming and showering in water are the key ways you absorb some of these potentially hazardous chemical. Here are some of the negative aspects of tap water:

Chlorination – Chlorine has numerous negative health side effects, from skin irritation to possible cancer causing properties that are as yet unexplored. Europeans, whose water resources are significantly fewer than ours, use ozonation as their primary method of cleaning water from swimming pools, tap water, and other sources. This method reduces the number of chemicals that can potentially invade and toxify your body.

Fluoridation – The unnatural fluorides used in our water supplies are very dangerous and difficult for our bodies to handle. They are linked to and may be the cause of mottling of the teeth (discoloration and bumpy surfaces called dental fluroditis), as well as cancer, and possibly, Downs Syndrome. Recent studies indicate that it does not reduce the incidence of cavities, and may even cause a loss of bone density over time, resulting in osteoporosis and osteomalacia.

The two types of fluoride generally used to treat water are fluorosalicic acid and sodium fluoride. Both are man-made, industrial by-products not found in nature. They are so toxic that they must be stored in special containers. They are, moreover, ingredients found in rat poison. Unfortunately, the naturally occurring non-toxic calcium fluoride is not used in our water supplies.

Fluoride is now found in most of the processed foods we consume, since it is in our water systems. This may result in more and more symptoms of fluoride overloading being discovered in the coming years. Methods do exist to remove most of the fluoride from your water: they are distillation, reverse osmosis, and activated alumina filtration systems.

Ignorance – Be it a blatant disregard or a simple lack of knowledge or understanding of the water cycle, ignorance leads to many abuses of and threats to our water supply. Here are a few examples:

- Inappropriate dumping of industrial and household wastes into the water system, such as laundry detergents, cleaning products, paint, solvents, left over food, et cetera. The potential for dangerous chemical interactions keeps increasing as we keep spoiling the valuable and limited life-giving resource that water is.

- Careless handling, storage and disposal of toxic chemicals that are used in or become the byproducts of manufacturing, such as arsenic.

- Spreading untreated farm sludge, which is a breeding ground for disease and illness since it is composed primarily of the waste matter from over crowded agri-business farms.

- Excessive or unnecessary use of fertilizers, pesticides, insecticides and other similar products that get into the water table and become part of the water system.

- Air pollutants and chemicals that return, carried on the backs of raindrops, to the water table, which feeds the municipal water systems.

- Parasites that use the water system to survive.

This is a sampling of what we are doing to our water and what may be coming out of our taps. Water analysis may give you a picture of only some of the hazardous chemicals, parasites, and other agents lurking in your water. Part of the problem is that water analysis cannot test for everything. The message is clear: you would not clean your floors, food plates or car with dirty water, so do not expect your body to maximize its healing properties if all you use is polluted and/or dirty water. You do have choices.

Soft Versus Hard Water — It's all about mineral content!

Hard water refers to water with higher amounts of the minerals magnesium and calcium. The result is water that does not let soap develop suds or lather easily, and that leaves a filmy deposit on any surface it comes in contact with. Some believe the magnesium and calcium in hard water are beneficial for the arteries, bone and heart: others do not believe this to be so. In addition to this, the taste of the water is affected by magnesium and calcium.

Soft water may be hard water that is treated to remove the magnesium and calcium, or it may be naturally soft. Water treated to make it soft is problematic in several ways. It has a greater chance of dissolving pipe linings than hard water. In the case of lead pipes, this can be a serious threat to your health. A similar threat exists in galvanized or plastic piping that contains the toxic heavy metal cadmium. Artifically softened water can also leach out of the arsenic, copper, iron and zinc found in copper piping.

The issue here is that your water can be the underlying cause of toxic illness or disease. Your body may have to constantly work to counteract the affects of toxic overload. This prevents it from performing other activities required to achieve optimal health.

Ways to Improve Your Tap Water

Hardware and general merchandise stores carry many types of water filtration systems. They can be easily added onto your existing water system at home. However, some just remove chlorine and other chemicals that cause it to taste bad. Here are the options we suggest:

- Boil your tap water to a rolling boil for at least five minutes to kill parasites and bacteria. Unfortunately, this may cause other byproducts to become more concentrated in the water, as well as requiring time to cool down in your refrigerator. Leaving water exposed for hours or using a blender to aerate it can reduce the taste caused by chlorine and other chemicals. They do not really clean the water.

- Filtration is the way nature cleans water. The bacteria is deposited into rocks and the water is remineralized with trace minerals such as magnesium and calcium from the rocks. Many man-made systems use this idea to produce cleaner water. Here are three:

  1. absorbent filters, using carbon to remove impurities from the water. They may be attached to the water system or used in containers that you store in the refrigerator.

  2. micro filtration systems, where you run the water through the tiny pores of the filtering system, so it picks up and gets rid of the contaminants.

  3. ion-exchange and other specialized methods using various media to clean the water.

- Reverse osmosis and ceramic filtration systems are widely used and considered to be among the best for most household water purification methods. It should be noted that none of these systems can get rid of all the impurities in your water.

What other choices and treatment methods do you have?
Bottled water

Bottled water is classified by its source, mineral content and/or by the method of treatment. It could come from a variety of places, such as a spring, spa, well, even your municipal water supply! The mineral content indicates a minimum of 500 parts per million of dissolved parts. If the water has been steam-distilled, demineralized, deionized or undergone any type of treatment, the bottle's label should indicate this. The major problem with bottled waters is that they are not regulated and tested like the public system water is. California has some of the strictest requirements for bottled waters; most other government bodies take a very lax attitude in terms of pollutants in the water, such as arsenic and bacterial levels. This can result in misleading labeling and potentially false claims on the labels.

Demineralized and Deionized Water
— an electrifying choice!

Demineralized and deionizing mean neutralizing the electric charge of a water molecule. The process of deionization removes the nitrates, magnesium, calcium and heavy metals such as barium, cadmium, some types of radium and lead.

Mineral, Natural Spring and Sparkling Waters
— *C'est la vie*! Translation: *This is the life*! or is it?

Years ago Perrier, one of the world's top brands of mineral water, had to recall all of its bottled water because a breakdown in its filtration system prevented the removal of benzene, a carcinogen, from its water source used for bottling. Yet this and other less notable incidents have not stopped the growing popularity of bottled waters. If you are using mineral waters as a dietary source of minerals, you should read the labels and make sure you are getting what your body needs. Drinking mineral waters that contain minerals your body does not lack can cause you harm. Moderation is the key.

Many mineral waters are carbonated, yet they are called mineral waters because the producer added citrates, bicarbonates and sodium phosphates to distilled or filtered tap water. Club soda is an example of a sparkling carbonated mineral water—and usually a lot cheaper then other packaged brands.

The term "natural spring water" indicates that the mineral content of the water has not been manipulated or changed. It may or may not have been treated. It may or may not have come from a spring. All the above problems arise due to legal definitions and requirements or lack thereof. Read the label to discover the source of the water and its mineral content.

Sparkling water is water that has been carbonated. Plain, without fillers such as sugars, artifical sweeteners and other additives, it is a healthy choice compared to a daily consumption of soda pop and alcoholic drinks.

Some carbonated waters are natural, some are man-made. This does not reflect on the quality of the water or its mineral content. Check out the labels before buying it.

Warning: If you suffer from ulcers or intestinal problems, do not drink sparkling or other carbonated waters as they can cause irritation to the gastrointestinal tract.

Steam-distilled Water
— really cleaning up your act!

Distillation is the process of heating water and condensing the resulting steam to produce a more nearly pure water. It removes nasty impurities like parasites, bacteria, chemicals, viruses, pollutants, and unfortunately, some helpful minerals. A carbon filter is recommended for preventing organic gases, such as benzene, carbon tetrachloride, trichloroethylene and tri-halomethanes, from reentering the distilled water. When consumed, distilled water helps cleanse the body's systems by leaching inorganic minerals from the tissues and cells.

Remineralizing the water with low sodium Concen-Trace® Trace Mineral drops is recommended. Use a quarter of a teaspoon (20 drops) for each gallon of water. Other healthy additives include lemon juice and organic apple cider vinegar. Both lemon juice and apple cidar vinegar add flavor and aid the digestive system.

The preferred storage medium for distilled water are glass bottles or stainless steel containers. Plastic containers may have compounds leached from them by the water. Distilled water when used in a controlled manner can help restore the body's homeostasis (internal balance).

Portions of this chapter are excerpted from *The All-in-One Guide to*™
Natural Remedies and Supplements, Elvis Ali, et al, AGES Publications™
ISBN 1-886508-28-3 and 1-886508-33-X
Ordering information in the back of this book.

Essential Fatty Acids:
Fats that Heal the ADD/Hyperactive Brain

Nancy L. Morse, B.Sc. (Hons), CNPA

More emphasis has been put on clinical studies investigating the potential implications of long chain polyunsaturated fatty acids (LC-PUFAs) in infant foods than for any other group of micronutrients, according to Dr. Koletzko from the University of Munich, Germany.[1] This is because research is increasingly proving the importance of these substances in brain and eye development. A study just reported by Dr. Eileen Birch and associates at the Retina Foundation of the Southwest in Dallas says the LC-PUFAs docosahexaenoic acid (DHA) and arachidonic acid (AA) are critical during the first 4 months of life.[2] They found that babies fed formula supplemented with DHA and AA performed significantly better in mental development and visual acuity tests than babies not provided with these fatty acids. But what are these mysterious nutrients that have gone unnoticed by modern society to the point where our children are suffering the consequences of our lack of awareness?

LC-PUFAs are a special group of fatty acids that are derived from the essential fatty acids (EFAs). Fatty acids are the building blocks of fat. Fat is considered in conventional terms to be a macronutrient because our bodies use fat as a source of energy similar to the way we use proteins and carbohydrates. But fatty acids have a much more important function in the body besides just supplying energy. They are structural components within all the cells in our bodies and therefore impact on how those cells function. For example, they can effect the fluidity and the flexibility of cell membranes and modulate the behavior of various membrane-bound proteins such as receptors, enzymes and ion channels. They are involved in the transport and disposal of cholesterol from the body and are responsible for the impermeability of the skin to water and possibly for the regulation of permeability in the gut and other tissues. In addition, they are precursors for a family of hormone-like substances that regulate a number of body processes including blood pressure, inflammation and other aspects of the immune system. These regulatory molecules include the prostaglandins.

There are two special fatty acids called essential fatty acids (EFAs) that are viewed with higher regard because they are much like vitamins. That's because these fatty acids cannot be made in the body and so we must eat a certain amount of them everyday in order for our bodies to function properly. These are linoleic acid (LA) and alpha-linolenic acid (ALA). LA is the major fatty acid in safflower oil and is also present in varying amounts in all vegetable oils and in nuts and seeds. ALA is also present in many vegetable oils but usually in lower amounts than LA. It is a major component of flax seed oil.

LA is from the Omega 6 series of fatty acids and ALA from the Omega 3 series. The terms Omega 3 and Omega 6 refer to the position of the first double bond in the molecule starting from the carbon atom at the methyl end of the molecule. Fatty acids are frequently referred to by numerical nomenclature. For example, LA is also called 18:2n-6. The number before the colon describes the number of carbon atoms in the molecule (18 in this case). The number after the colon defines the number of double bonds in the chain (2 in LA) and the n-6 indicates that the first double bond is on the sixth carbon from the methyl end of the molecule. This number nomenclature is important for a scientist because it immediately provides insight into how the body can utilize that fatty acid and what other materials can be made from it in the body.

Both LA and ALA are eighteen carbon chain fatty acids and are called polyunsaturated fatty acids because they contain more than one double bond in the chain. Fats that contain lots of LA and ALA, such as vegetable oils, are liquid at room temperature. Fats that contain primarily saturated fatty acids (with no double bonds) are solid at room temperature and include things like butter and lard. Double bonds can exist in either a *cis* or a *trans* form.

Figure 1: The Configuration of Cis and Trans Double Bonds

The *cis* configuration is the natural form of the double bond and the one that the body recognizes and uses for proper function. Unfortunately, the processing techniques that are used to improve the shelf life of most commercial vegetable oils tend to convert the *cis* form to the *trans* configuration.

Since the body does not utilize these fatty acids in the same way as the natural form, it becomes starved for or deficient in the natural form and all the fatty acids that are derived from them. For this reason, many people are turning to high quality fatty acid supplements that ensure daily requirements of the natural *cis* form.

   LA and ALA can be used in the body to make a whole range of other fatty acids (Figure 2).[3] The process involves a series of alternating desaturations (removal of two hydrogen atoms and insertion of a double bond) and elongations (addition of two carbon atoms). It is generally believed that the enzymes in this metabolic pathway are the same for the Omega 6 and Omega 3 series. However, this should not be misunderstood to mean that the Omega 6 fatty acids can be converted to the Omega 3 fatty acids and vice versa. The two series are not interconverted in mammals. In fact, sharing the enzymes in the metabolic pathway results in a competition between the two series. Overall, the enzymes have a higher affinity for the Omega 3 series so that at each step in the pathway the Omega 3 fatty acids are preferentially metabolized relative to the Omega 6 fatty acids. This is why researchers recommend a daily intake of 4 parts Omega 6 fatty acids and 1 part Omega 3s.[4] Various other interactions between the two series have also been discovered. However, these are not particularly relevant to the subject of this book and so will not be included here.

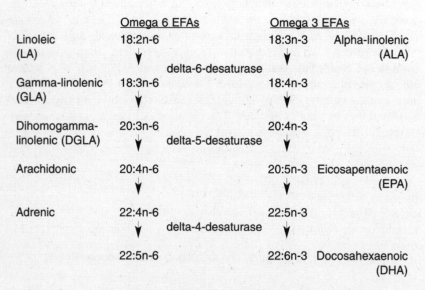

	Omega 6 EFAs		Omega 3 EFAs	
Linoleic (LA)	18:2n-6 ↓		18:3n-3 ↓	Alpha-linolenic (ALA)
		delta-6-desaturase		
Gamma-linolenic (GLA)	18:3n-6 ↓		18:4n-3 ↓	
Dihomogamma-linolenic (DGLA)	20:3n-6 ↓	delta-5-desaturase	20:4n-3 ↓	
Arachidonic	20:4n-6 ↓		20:5n-3 ↓	Eicosapentaenoic (EPA)
Adrenic	22:4n-6 ↓		22:5n-3 ↓	
		delta-4-desaturase		
	22:5n-6		22:6n-3	Docosahexaenoic (DHA)

Figure 2:   Metabolic Pathway for conversion of LA and ALA
                   to their corresponding metabolites

Various vitamins and minerals are required as co-factors for the enzymes in the fatty acid metabolic pathway. For example, zinc and magnesium are required for the enzyme called delta-6-desaturase (D6D) and vitamin B_6 for the elongase that converts GLA to DGLA. The two rate limiting enzymes in the pathway are D6D and delta-5-desaturase.

Research over the last twenty years has identified factors that can affect the activity of D6D in particular. When D6D is not functioning properly, the body's requirement for fatty acids changes to include the metabolites of LA and ALA. These metabolites include everything below D6D in the pathway, for example GLA and AA on the Omega 6 side and EPA and DHA on the Omega 3 side. Unfortunately, dietary sources of GLA are rarely available in sufficient levels to compensate for the quantity of GLA that would normally be made from LA if D6D were functioning properly. So dietary supplementation becomes an option using products like evening primrose oil that contains significant quantities of GLA. In the same way, it is useful to supplement with Omega 3 metabolites like EPA and DHA found in fish oil to compensate for the body's inability to convert ALA through to its corresponding metabolites.

> When D6D is not functioning properly, the body's requirement for fatty acids changes to include the metabolites of LA and ALA.

The influences that govern the effectiveness of D6D to perform its job include genetic and lifestyle factors. Dietary habits like inadequate intake of zinc and magnesium can hamper the ability of the enzyme, as can too much saturated fat or trans fatty acids in the diet. Stress can also impact D6D because the body produces cortisol and adrenaline in response to this stimulus and both these hormones reduce the activity of the enzyme. But genetics seems to be one of the biggest predictors of abnormalities in fatty acid metabolism.

People who have inherited disorders like atopic eczema, asthma, migraine headaches and allergies have a defect in their D6D.[5] This apparent decreased ability to convert dietary LA and ALA into their corresponding metabolites has also been observed in a number of other disease conditions including diabetes,[6] premenstrual syndrome,[7,8] multiple sclerosis[9] and rheumatoid arthritis.[10] The presence of this problem is determined by measuring the blood fatty acid levels in patients with these conditions. If the levels of LA and ALA are normal or elevated and the levels of all the metabolites are significantly below normal, this indicates an inability to convert the dietary EFAs into their corresponding metabolites. Abnormalities of fatty acid metabolism or intake can sufficiently alter the body's biochemistry to orchestrate massive abnormalities in structure and function of all body systems.

In recent years, abnormal fatty acid patterns have been measured in children with attention deficit hyperactivity disorder (ADHD).[11,12] The initial study completed by Dr. Laura Stevens and Dr. John Burgess at Purdue University, Indiana, measured the blood fatty acid levels in 53 children with ADHD. They also measured levels in a control group of 43 children of similar age who did not have ADHD. Parents were asked to evaluate signs of possible EFA deficiency including extreme thirst, frequent urination, dry skin, dandruff, and brittle nails, and to report on complaints such as headaches, stomachaches, diarrhea and constipation. A diet record was also maintained for each child. This was used to identify any differences in dietary intake between the control subjects and the children with ADHD that might account for differences in blood fatty acid composition.

The researchers found that the children with ADHD had lower than normal levels of DHA and AA in their blood. In addition, the LC-PUFA levels were the lowest in the ADHD children that had the most severe signs of EFA deficiency. Examination of the dietary fatty acids consumed showed there was no apparent difference between the diets of the ADHD children and the diets of the normal children. These two observations suggest that either children with ADHD are not able to efficiently make fatty acids like AA and DHA from the EFAs they eat, or they are very quickly using up what they do make. Either way, it leaves them without enough of the LC-PUFAs, AA and DHA.

> Ask you doctor
> to measure the levels of
> LA, ALA and
> metabolites,
> as well as
> DHA, AA and
> LC-PUFA levels,
> to see if these are
> problem areas.

What are the consequences of having insufficient body stores of AA and DHA? Looking at the fatty acid composition of various tissues within the body may give us some clues about where deficiencies may impact. LC-PUFAs make up a large part of the brain and eyes. The brain is about 60% fat and a high proportion of this fat is made with the fatty acids DHA and AA.[13] DHA is also extremely important for vision. It is a major constituent of the membranes in the cone and rod cells in the eye. These are the cells that are responsible for transmitting light messages to the nerves that supply the brain. If there is not enough AA and DHA being made in the body, the supplies of these two fatty acids in the brain and eyes may be reduced and so they may not function properly. Therefore, it's logical to conclude/surmise that fatty acid metabolism may be involved in learning disorders like ADHD.

In fact, the idea that fatty acids might be involved was first proposed by two British women in 1981—Vicky Colquhoun and her daughter Sally Bunday who founded the Hyperactive Children's Support Group in Britain.[14] They came to this revolutionary conclusion after completing a survey of a large population of mostly male, hyperactive children in West Essex, UK. The purpose of the study was to determine what characteristics were common to hyperactive children. They found the following:

1. Many had atopic disorders like eczema, asthma, allergies, repeated infections, and colic.

2. They were always thirsty.

3. Many were zinc deficient.

4. Eating foods containing certain additives and salicylates caused rapid behavioral deterioration.

These common characteristics within the children lead them to believe that EFAs were somehow involved with the problem for the following reasons:

1. People with atopic conditions have difficulty metabolizing EFAs.

2. Most children with ADHD are males and males need more EFAs than females, so a partial EFA deficiency would show up more quickly in males than females.

3. Thirst is one of the first signs of EFA deficiency.

4. Zinc is a co-factor for D6D, so if a person is zinc deficient, he or she cannot efficiently convert EFAs into their corresponding metabolites.

5. Salicylates block the conversion of fatty acids to prostaglandins.

Along with a summary of these findings, Colquhoun and Bundy reported that hyperactivity may be the result of EFA deficiency. However, they also realized that these apparent deficiency symptoms were unlikely to be caused by a dietary lack of EFAs since often only one family member was affected even though they were all eating the same types of food. They reasoned the problem might result from a failure to convert dietary EFAs (LA and ALA) into LC-PUFAs (like AA and DHA).

Subsequent research, like the Stevens study mentioned above has confirmed their conclusion. We now know the problem is a *functional EFA deficiency*. In other words, the body is not able to use the EFAs that are supplied in the diet. Therefore, even though these children may be eating lots of LA and ALA, their bodies are not able to maintain sufficient body stores of the LC-PUFAs derived from them. Consequently, children with ADHD have all the classic symptoms of EFA deficiency, even though they are eating enough

EFAs in their diets. This means that what is crucial for eye and brain function is not the EFA's themselves, but the way the body is able to use them. And if the body is unable to use the EFAs efficiently, then it needs to be provided with the LC-PUFAs directly. Supplying fatty acid supplements like flax oil that contain mostly LA and ALA and no LC-PUFAs are unlikely to provide any benefit to these children.

Drs. Stevens and Burgess have since done some follow up studies in children with ADHD. They have found that children with higher amounts of DHA in their blood have better mathematics ability and overall academic ability. These children are also less prone to behavior problems like temper tantrums and sleep disturbances. Children with ADHD who have the lowest levels of DHA and AA in their blood suffer the most severe anxiety, impulsivity, hyperactivity and misbehavior. Children with lower amounts of AA seem to have more colds, and their reported use of antibiotics is greater than in children with near-normal AA levels.

Another interesting observation that was made in the first study completed by these researchers involved dietary intake during infancy. Children with ADHD were less likely to have been breast-fed, and if they had been breast-fed, it was for a shorter period than the children in the control group. A similar observation was made by one of the world's leaders in nutrition, Dr. Jacqueline Stordy, who proposed a biological link between learning disorders like ADHD, ADD, dyslexia and dyspraxia.[13]

Dr. Stordy observed that in families with more than one person with dyslexia, those who had been breast-fed the longest had fewer or less severe symptoms of dyslexia, and in general their problems became apparent later in childhood. Interestingly, human breast milk is an excellent source of DHA, AA and GLA,[16] and it has been suggested that dietary intake of these fatty acids may provide a protective effect for children who are genetically predisposed to the condition. A subsequent survey to determine the types of fatty acids that were being eaten by two groups of mothers during pregnancy indicated that mothers of dyslexics were eating diets containing less DHA than mothers of nondyslexic children.

Following these early observations, Dr. Stordy set up a study to determine if dietary supplementation with DHA might be beneficial to dyslexics.[17] Previous research had indicated that DHA was important for ensuring proper functioning of the rod cells in the eye. These are required for proper night vision and are particularly important for dark adaption—the ability to see quickly when going from light into dark. Dyslexics have difficulty doing this because their eyes adjust too slowly. Dr. Stordy used this abnormality to devise a test that would measure any improvement in dark adaptation in dyslexics after taking DHA.

Five dyslexics and five nondyslexic controls were given 4 capsules per day of fish oil containing 120 mg of DHA per capsule for one month. Dark adaptation was measured in both groups before taking the capsules and following treatment. The DHA produced a significant and consistent improvement in the dyslexics, but no change in the controls.

Following that Dr. Stordy completed a study with a local group affiliated with the Dyspraxia Foundation in the UK.[13] The aim of this study was to determine the children's ability to complete a defined test before and after treatment with a fatty acid supplement containing DHA, AA and GLA. The product, called Efalex® was a mixture of evening primrose oil, tuna oil, vitamin E and thyme oil, and the children were given this product for 4 months. The test involved throwing a ball up, clapping a specified number of times and catching it. At the end of the study there was a significant improvement in the children's scores for manual dexterity, ball skills, static and dynamic balance and total impairment. The recommended dosage for the Efalex® by Nutricia™/Efamol® is eight 500 mg capsules per day for twelve weeks followed by a maintenance dose of as little as two capsules per day. The recommended dosage for Focus by Swiss Herbal Remedies™ is nine 434 mg capsules per day for twelve weeks followed by a maintenance dose of as little as two capsules per day.

Dr. Stordy's study confirmed that dietary fatty acids could have an effect on brain function most likely on account of their ability to alter the fatty acid make-up of the membranes. Subsequent research by Dr. Alex Richardson and her associates has shown that membranes within the brain cells of dyslexics are different from those of people without the condition.[18] This was determined by measuring the difference in membrane phospholipid turn over in the brains in dyslexics and nondyslexics. Membrane phospholipids contain fatty acids that are periodically being replaced with new fatty acids as part of normal cellular function. In dyslexics, the rate of turn over or replacement of these membrane phospholipids is abnormal. This study has provided concrete evidence that a real physical abnormality is responsible for this and possibly other learning disorders.[19]

The cause of impaired fatty acid metabolism in children with ADHD and related conditions is still under investigation. Dr. Rodolfo R. Brenner in Argentina believes that our modern lifestyle may be partially responsible for the inability to convert dietary EFAs to LC-PUFAs. Our typical Western diet is high in saturated and processed fats and lacking in certain vitamins and minerals. This may be slowing or partially blocking the conversion of EFAs to GLA, AA and DHA. These dietary factors can effect the development of a person's brain not only during childhood, but even during fetal development since selective uptake of fatty acids by the brain takes place through the placenta during gestation and via breast milk in the first 6 months to 1 year of life.[21] In fact, the fetal brain increases 4 to 5 times in weight during the last 3 months of pregnancy when there is a rapid accumulation of DHA and AA in the eyes and brain cells of the fetus.[22,23] In fact at this stage, the fetal brain increases 4 to 5 times in weight. It is possible that ensuring a sufficient supply of DHA and AA in the mother in order to meet the needs of the fetus may reduce the likelihood of the child developing a learning disorder later in life.

According to a leading fatty acid researcher, the average adult daily requirement for EFAs is about 3% of total calories.[24] This requirement increases to about 4.5% during pregnancy and up to 7% during lactation. The Canadian Ministry of Health recommends an average adult intake of 1.36 grams per day of DHA and 7.9 grams per day of Omega 6 LC-PUFAs.[25] Even prior to this, reports containing similar information had been trickling in, including one from the University of Flinders in Australia in 1996. In this study, babies were fed formulas with or without the addition of LC-PUFA. After 30 weeks, the group that had been given LC-PUFA's had better sharpness of vision than the group deprived of LC-PUFA's.[26-33]

A collaborative study from the Universities of Washington and Chile was published in early 1998 that demonstrated the effects of infant formula with added DHA on eye and brain function in the recipients.[34] The authors concluded that DHA deficiency in preterm infants in particular could alter brain function and may account for the development of learning disabilities and visual problems. They recommended further research along these lines and suggested that infant formulas should be formulated to supply adequate amounts of Omega 3 and Omega 6 LC-PUFAs.

Interestingly, North American infant formulas usually contain the EFAs, LA, and ALA as their primary fatty acid components. They do not normally contain LC-PUFAs, unlike some other countries such as Japan where commercially available infant formulas contain evening primrose oil and fish oil as sources of DHA, AA and GLA. This is cause for concern considering the North American tendency towards bottle feeding, the negative impact that LC-PUFA deficiency can have on brain and eye development, and the increasing prevalence of learning disorders in our society. It is especially thought-provoking because studies have shown that babies fed formulas supplemented with LA and ALA alone can only modestly increase their body levels of LC-PUFAs through their internal metabolism.[35] That observation is not at all surprising to most lipid researchers. According to Dr. Stephen Cunnane at the University of Toronto "Over the first 6 months of life, DHA accumulates at about 10 mg/day in the whole body of breast-fed infants, with 48% of that amount appearing in the brain."[36] To achieve that level, breast-fed infants need to eat at least 20 mg DHA/day. In addition, formula-fed infants not eating DHA would need to convert 5.2% of their ALA intake into DHA to reach the DHA amounts achieved in breast-fed babies. That would be a substantial feat for an infant considering the fact that adults can only convert about 3.8% of the ALA they eat into DHA at the best of times[37] and babies naturally have a reduced ability to convert dietary LA and ALA into AA and DHA.[38]

Some studies have shown that problem solving ability in infants may be enhanced by LC-PUFA supplementation. These include two reports from the University of Dundee, Scotland where researchers found LC-PUFA supplementation enhanced problem solving abilities in infants.[28,29] They concluded that LC-PUFAs may be important for the development of childhood intelligence. Reports like these and others with similar findings provide evidence to suggest that preventive measures may be a means of reducing learning disorders in our population. Research can provide the knowledge, but it's up to all of us to use that information wisely.

Summary

Ask you doctor to measure the levels of LA, ALA and metabolites, as well as DHA, AA and LC-PUFA levels, to see if these are problem areas.

For ADD, ADHD and dyslexics, the initial recommended dosage for Efalex® by Nutricia™/Efamol® is eight 500 mg capsules per day for twelve weeks followed by a maintenance dose of as little as two capsules per day.

The initial recommended dosage for Focus by Swiss Herbal Remedies™ is nine 434 mg capsules per day for twelve weeks followed by a maintenance dose of as little as two capsules per day.

Children or adults with ADD and/or Hyperactivity should take the following supplements and amounts daily.

	Children	Adults
Evening Primrose Oil	1-3 gm	3-6 gm
Flaxseed Oil	3-5 gm	5-10 gm
DHA (Docosaxexaenoic Acid)	1-3 gm	3-5 gm
Vitamin B Complex	10-50 mg	100-150 mg
Zinc (citrated or chelated)	10-20 mg	50-90 mg
Magnesium (citrated or chelated)	200-400 mg	250-500 mg

Caution: Epileptic Children should take safflower oil, vitamin C, vitamin E, Zinc and vitamin B-complex instead of Evening Primrose Oil.

Essential fatty acid products for ADD/Hyperactivity include Efalex® by Nutricia™/Efamol®, and Focus by Swiss Herbal Remedies.™

(This table is an excerpt from *The All-In-One Guide to*™ *Natural Remedies and Supplements,* AGES Publications™ ISBN 1-886508-28-3 and 1-886508-33-X.)

Herbs:
Botanical Approaches to ADD/ADHD
Paul Richard Saunders, Ph.D., N.D., D.H.A.N.P.

Plants, both as food and medicine, are our oldest forms of food and nutritional supplementation. In fact, perhaps 40% of today's prescription drugs are derived from or based on plant medicines or plant constituents. Today's reemphasis on plant-based medicine is a healthy choice by many, but needs to be done in the broader context of an appropriate workup and diagnosis, and an overall plan for good nutrition and healthy lifestyle choices.

Herbalists often look at plants as representing a personality or set of signs and symptoms. This helps to distinguish one herb from another. These distinguishing differences are based on years of clinical use, and are a representation of the ecological environment and constituent differences of each plant. Consequently, the herbs below are presented as scenarios of people or symptoms.

Botanical medicines are available in many forms: tincture, fluid extract, tea, capsules, dried, freeze dried, standardized capsules, etc. The new standardized capsules assure the consumer that the actual herb is in the capsule, and allow consumers to compare the dose (usually in milligrams, mg) to the dose of a standardized preparation in a clinical study. The difficulty with standardization is that most herbs are not available in this format, or this format was not used in a study. Many herbalists also argue that standardization, if it is due to a complex extraction technique, may exclude other constituents of the herb and reduce the synergistic effect provided when all the constituents are present at one time.

Personally, I prefer water-alcohol extractions because of their long history of successful use, standard method of preparation, and ready absorption. These methods are described in many standard pharmacopoeia such as the British Herbal Pharmacopoeia and American Pharmacopoeia.

Essentially, a pre-measured amount of herb is soaked in a known mixture of water and alcohol. The ratio of water to alcohol is different with each herb, and based on historical use both of what has worked and what will preserve the resulting tincture or fluid extract.

The issue for many is the presence of alcohol from 15-90%. Alcohol evaporates at a low temperature. Pouring boiling water over the dose and allowing it to cool so it can be consumed will cause the alcohol to evaporate. If the ADD/ADHD person is very sensitive to alcohol or its residues, or the active herbal components include volatile oils, this evaporation process is not recommended. Known or admitted alcoholics should also avoid all tinctures and fluid extracts.

Doses of herbs will vary with age, sex, vitality, weight, and chronicity and severity of the condition. They may also vary based on concurrent medications. The decision regarding dosage is best left to a cooperative venture with your herbalist, naturopathic physician or other skilled practitioner. In general, herbs are taken with foods—indeed, they are food. If they should be taken otherwise this will be noted in the instructions provided to you. Beneficial effects can take as long as four to eight weeks to manifest, so do not despair if your child is not better the next day. Allow time for healing.

Oat straw (Avena sativa) is a nutrient tonic for the nervous system. People needing oat straw have trouble keeping their mind focused on a single subject, instead flitting amongst many subjects. Often there is a nervous exhaustion that can manifest as hyperactivity in an effort to resist the need for rest, mental relaxation, sleep, or recovery. Headaches may be present as a result of this mental overwork. They typically occur at the vertex (top of the head) or occiput (back of the head). An excellent way to take oats in children is as freshly prepared oatmeal at breakfast or during the day. If a sweeter flavor is desired, add a few pieces of fruit, but not sugar, honey, molasses, corn syrup or maple syrup. The latter are significant contributing factors to ADD/ADHD.

Gotu Kola (Centalla asiatica) is a low creeping plant from the Southern Hemisphere. It is very useful for nervousness, insomnia, mental agitation or disturbed emotions that lead to poor memory and tremors of various types. It has been used for epilepsy in India. In the yogi tradition, gotu kola is taken to calm the mind so that one can meditate with greater focus and less disturbance from the events of the surrounding world. It is also useful for infections that effect the tonsils or cause sore throats. Often hyperactive children present with frequent infections of the ears and throat, making this herb all the more indicated.

Yellow jasmine (Gelsemium sempervirens) is a native perennial vine of Central America. It has a long history of use in the native medicine and eventually found its way to North America where it was also used effectively by the eclectics. These individuals are often very hot, irritable, restless, nervous, may suffer from headaches (arterial throbbing, migraine type headache), and have insomnia. These symptoms can become significantly worse with fever, especially a high spiking fever. *Yellow jasmine is a powerful botanical that may interact with a number of drugs that impact the central nervous system, including aspirin. For this reason, you should not take it on your own or give it to your child without supervision by a knowledgeable naturopathic physician or herbalist.*

Hops (Humulus lupulus) is a climbing vine grown in Europe and North America to flavor beer. It has a sedative effect, helping with tremors, restlessness and a brooding irritability. Often the strobiles (female flower) were placed into pillows to help children and others suffering from insomnia sleep at night. The herb is distinctly bitter, thus the amount and variety used gives beer its flavor, and must be hidden in other foods. It will not make children prone to drinking beer or alcohol, as some have said. *It should not be use by anyone who is depressed.*

St. John's wort (Hypericum perforatum) grows in Europe and North America, and its perennial yellow summer flowers will brighten any garden. While much has been written and said about it in the last decade, its use goes back to ancient times and was popularized by the eclectics in the late 1800s. The clinical picture for St. John's wort is depression with anxiety. The person may have also suffered from a severe blow or trauma that has shocked or concussed the nervous system. Bed-wetting is often present at any age. The dilute tincture can be use for cuts or scrapes, and the oil can be applied to bruises. *Recently, there have been a few warnings in the press about the use of St. John's wort with conventional antidepressant therapy and medications given to patients on cardiac drugs. The interactions are theoretical, but potentially serious. If you are in either of these two categories, do not take St. John's wort without appropriate supervision by a naturopathic physician or qualified herbalist.*

Wild lettuce (Lactuca virosa) from Europe and the United Kingdom has a long history of use for restless and excitable children, and insomnia in adults who overwork. It was used during both world wars for pain relief on the battlefield, and to help with the pain and irritation of chronic coughs. It has even been shown to relax animals and induce sleep. It is quite bitter tasting and thus has not received much attention.

German chamomile (Matricaria chamomilla) from Europe and Asia is often use by mothers to calm irritable teething babies. In children, the picture is one of irritability, restlessness, peevishness, impatience, and difficulty to please. Pain, whether from trauma, an earache or a cold, can make these children difficult to manage and be around. This soothing tea could spell the difference between an angry, unmanageable child and one who is calmed and able to focus and pay attention. The flavor is spicy, but pleasant.

Passion flower (Passilfora incarnata), a tropical plant, made its way to Europe in 1570 with the Spaniards who conquered Central and South America. The patient is often exhausted but unable to sleep because of over-exhaustion, nervousness or excitement. He or she may also worry a lot, and can suffer from headaches and occasional tremors. It combines well with oat straw or chamomile. If pregnant or on medications affecting the central nervous system, this herb should only be used with appropriate supervision by a naturopathic physician or qualified herbalist.

Kava kava (Piper methysticum) from Polynesia and Micronesia was used in ancient times with the passage into adulthood to induce dreams that were part of the vision quest and the receiving of an adult name. Today, we recognize its use for anxiety, despondency and insomnia. Anxiety prevents these people from focusing, or they may become fixated on a toothache or earache and unable to focus on what is occurring around them. *If one is taking medications effecting the central nervous system, this herb should only be used with appropriate supervision by a naturopathic physician or qualified herbalist.*

Valerian (Valeriana officinalis) is another herb with a long history of use that has recently been popularized. Insomnia and nervousness associated with depression are keynotes. Often there is a history of a death in the family that was especially significant to the affected individual. Because of the grief and sadness, their sleep is poor, their focus is disturbed and they often act up to gain attention. Death of one so close can be a hard for some children to accept. Valerian, with its distinct odor that carries over many meters, is an example of why herbs in capsule form are usually the most palatable.

What should be the daily dosage of an herbal medicine?

On each bottle of product there are instructions for the daily dosage of that same product, or a recipe on how to use it. If the right medicine is chosen, it should be able to bring about some changes as a catalyst in the person's state of health. These changes may not look initially like pleasant or positive ones at first. The "healing crises" has been addressed in more detail in chapter 5.

Dosages are guidelines, but for those who are impatient and results-oriented or suffering from some chronic condition, they may have to take a lot more than the recommended amount. This should be done gradually, or at the beginning of treatment, with the help of your naturopath or herbalist.

Why not use the same recipe for each one of us? It's because we are all different and unique. Are we ill, or are we using a product preventively? We are at different levels of health and constitutions, weights, sizes, ages, and levels of emotional/mental stress. Experiment with natural medicine, be intuitive, and listen to your inner voice. I have used herbal medicine for approximately 25 years on myself, my loved ones, and my patients, and I have not yet seen negative results with the use of dosages higher than recommended. For 25 years, I have personally used and have given to patients mixed products for various issues to be taken together. There are, however, situations in which some herbal medicines are better taken alone. If you are in need of guidance from a health practitioner, use one who has some kind of testing procedure for dosages of recommended products.

Children's dosages

Children's dosages are based on the same principles as adult dosages. These principles are age, weight, level of health, constitution, parents' understanding of healing crises, and so on. If we prefer to start with recommended dosages, but the product lists dosages for adults only, parents can follow the following fomula: divide the child's weight by 150 (the weight of the average adult). The resulting figure represents the percentage of the adult dose the child needs. For example, if the child's weight is 50 lb., divide 50 by 150. The child's dose in this case would be 1/3 of the adult dose.

Alcohol in herbal tinctures: is it good or bad?

Technically speaking, herbal tinctures are fluid extracts of herbs. Water is used to extract medicinal properties of herbs in infusion or decoction, and alcohol is added to water when we want to make tinctures. Alcohol is by far the most efficient medium for preserving and extracting herbs' active ingredients, both known and unknown. *Alcohol-based tincture gives almost indefinite shelf life; guaranteed potency is at least five years.*

Making herbal tincture is an ancient method of producing herbal medicine. Even though many chemical properties do dissolve in water, there are some important properties that do not, examples are: essential oils, steroids, alkaloids, resins, etc. There are companies that make glycerin-based tinctures. Glycerin is, however, inferior to alcohol since it allows for more oxidation and decomposition of plant ingredients. The medicinal properties of herbs in tincture go very quickly into the bloodstream—almost instantly. The effects may be noticed within minutes. This is not the case with infusions, decoctions, tablets, or encapsulated herbs.

Tinctures are also excellent first aid in emergency situations. A well-made tincture, two to three drops, can be higher in medicinal properties than an entire cup of tea. The alcohol used in tincture is vodka or pure grain alcohol. The amount of alcohol content found in tincture is insignificant. If someone were to take 30-60 drops of tincture per day, the alcohol content would be less than in some mouthwashes. This amount is also safe for anyone in a 12-step program, such as Alcoholics' Anonymous. The number of people sensitive to this amount of alcohol is probably less than 0.01% of the population.

For those who still have some concern about alcohol in tincture, but would also like to experience the benefits of tinctures for themselves or their child, they can try adding the drops of tincture to a little bit of hot water (not boiling), or herbal tea.

19
Amino Acids and Proteins
Keeping the body's systems in balance

Dr. Elvis Ali, B.Sc., N.D., Dipl. AC., M.R.N.

Pam Floener, P.T., R.M.A., C.N.C., C.T.

David Garshowitz, B.Sc. Phm., F.A.C.A.

Dr. George Grant, M.Sc., M.Ed., Ed.D., C. Chem., R.M.

Dr. Fred Hui, M.D., C.C.F.P., C.A.F.C., Diplomat I.B.C.T.

Dr. Gordon Ko, M.D., C.C.F.P. (EM), F.R.C.P.C., F.A.A.P.M.R., C.I.M.E., N.MD.

Dr. Joe Levy, B.A., B.PhE., M.S.W., Ph.D.

Dorothy Marshall, Ph.D., N.D., N.H.C.

Dr. Selim Nakla, M.D.

Dr. David Newman, B.A.,B.Sc.,D.C.

Dr. Alvin Pettle, M.D., F.R.C.S. (C) (OBY GYN)

Ken Vegotsky, B.Sc., et al

Amino acids are popularly called "the building blocks" or chemical components of proteins. They are the nitrogenous organic acids that form proteins necessary for all life. They are the building blocks of peptides, polypeptides and proteins in our bodies. Twenty-six of the more than 100 naturally occurring amino acids are used by the body to create the proteins necessary for optimal functioning. Eight amino acids are "essential" for adults: isoleucine, leucine, lysine, methionine, phenylalanine, threonine, tryptophan and valine. Ten amino acids are "essential" for children. "Essential" means the body cannot manufacture or produce them on its own and must obtain them from an external source, such as breast milk, foods, or supplements. All amino acids are necessary;

the "non-essential" ones can be manufactured by the body. When we reach adulthood, our body's chemistry has developed such that only eight amino acids remain essential.

A deficiency of an amino acid in a child or adult can cause problems such as attention deficit disorder (ADD), attention deficit disorder hyperactivity (ADHD), learning disabilities, and a host of problems that are more fully dealt with in this chapter. These problems may be manifested through symptoms such as an inability to fall asleep, which the amino acid tryptophan can alleviate.

Children require two more amino acids from outside sources, since their biological systems are not mature enough to produce them on their own. We cannot stress enough the fact that children need 10 essential amino acids, plus all the others their bodies produce, for optimal health and healing. The liver produces about 80 percent of our bodies' amino acid needs. The other 20 percent must come from our diet. When an essential amino acid is missing, or even just low, the potency of all the other amino acids is proportionately reduced.

Protein is the second most abundant material making up the human body, next to water. Proteins are part of your muscles, tendons, ligaments, glands, organs, nails, hair and body fluids critical to bone growth. The process of protein digestion also creates amino acids as an end product.

Essential to life, proteins are linked chains of amino acids held together by peptide bonds. Each type of protein is unique in its chemical sequencing. Each protein fills a specific need in the body and is not interchangeable with another protein. Proteins in the body are not directly derived from food. Dietary protein is broken down into its amino acid components in the body, then reconstituted as the specific proteins your body needs at that time. This is why the amino acids are considered essential nutrients. The following lists some of the functions amino acids are involved in:

- They act as neurotransmitters or precursors to them; some are needed for the brain to send and receive messages.
- Some can pass through the blood-brain barrier; this barrier exists to maintain the health, chemistry, and other processes of the brain.
- They aid in communication with nerve cells in other parts of the body.
- They empower vitamins and minerals to perform their job.

The following are some of the functions proteins are involved in:
- bone growth
- brain function
- regulation of the body's processes

- disease and illness prevention
- maintenance of correct internal pH and water balance
- nutrient exchange between the tissues, blood and lymph with intercellular fluids
- formation of the structural basis of chromosomes

Some amino acids stimulate the body's ability to produce human growth hormone (somatotrophin or STH). The pituitary gland stores this hormone, releasing it into the body from activities such as exercise, reduced food intake and sleep. As we age, the levels of growth hormone decrease until we finally stop producing it around age 50. With the use of supplementation, you can stimulate your body's ability to produce growth hormone and return to levels you had as a young adult.

The release of human growth hormone from the pituitary gland is regulated by those hormones originating from the hypothalamus. Other biochemical factors influencing the production of human growth hormone include hormones from other sources (e.g. thyroid, adrenal, gonads) and nutrient levels in the blood. The following are the principal health-related actions of human growth hormone:

- Anti-aging
- The conversion of fat into muscle and energy, aiding weight loss.
- The improvement of protein synthesis for building muscles.
- Wound healing, also regenerates heart, kidneys, liver and lungs.
- Restoration of hair growth and color.
- Tissue repair.
- Sharper vision.
- Reduce wrinkles and improve skin elasticity and texture.
- Reduction of urea in the urine and blood.
- Improvement of the quality of connective tissue, and consequent strengthening of ligaments and tendons.
- Strengthening of bones and restoration of bone and muscle mass.
- Increased calcium and collagen levels.
- Increased energy and endurance during exercise and body building.
- Antidepressant action on the brain, elevation of mood, and increased concentration.
- Strengthening the immune system through anti-body production.
- Increased oxygen intake and ability to exercise.
- Improved sleep.
- Reduction of blood pressure and cholesterol.
- Greater cardiac output.
- Powerful aphrodisiac properties for both men and women.
- Alleviation of PMS and eliminates vaginal dryness.

Studies have shown that taking growth hormone directly for up to six months can be beneficial. After that period of time, it is no longer advisable, since it appears to negatively affect some adults. A better option is to help your body release growth hormones naturally using supplementation with amino acids and other nutrients. The amino acids are arginine, glutamine, glycine, ornithine, tryptophan and tyrosine. Their human growth hormone releasing properties are significantly enhanced when taken with vitamin B6, vitamin C, niacinamide, calcium, magnesium, potassium, and zinc. Homeopathic remedies to stimulate an increase in the amount of human growth hormone are now in the marketplace. To find out more about homeopathy, refer to Chapter 21, Homeopathy and Cell Salts.

Note: **Drug interaction with amino acids:**
In 1999, Dr. Jay Seastrunk, who runs a chronic fatigue center, reported that patients using the medication Neurontin, an anti-convulsant and pain drug, have found it does not work well if taken when supplementing with magnesium or an amino acid.

The following is a list of key amino acids.
Those marked with an asterisk (*) are the essential amino acids:

alanine	asparagine	aspartic acid	carnitine
citrulline	cysteine	cystine	gamma-aminobutyric acid
glutamic acid	glutamine	glycine	isoleucine*
leucine*	lysine*	methionine*	ornithine
phenylalanine*	proline	serine	taurine
threonine*	tryptophan*	tyrosine	valine*

arginine* (in babies and children)   histidine* (in babies and children)

An 'L-' used before an amino acid indicates a natural form that is easily absorbable by the body. For example, 'L-alanine' is the amino acid 'alanine' in a more biologically absorbable form.

A 'D-' before an amino acid indicates a synthetic variation of the amino acid.

Alanine

A nonessential amino acid that the body can produce if the necessary materials are available. Beta-alanine, a form of alanine, is a component of coenzyme A and vitamin B_5 (pantothenic acid). Coenzyme A is an important catalyst in the body.

Principal benefits: Improves immune system. Helps metabolize glucose, a source energy for the body, and alleviates hypoglycemia. Reduces benign prostatic hyperplasia (BPH). Decreases risk of kidney stones.

Excessive levels of alanine and low levels of phenylalanine and tyrosine are associated with the Epstein-Barr virus and chronic fatigue.

Food sources: Meat, poultry, fish, eggs.

Non-food source(s): Beta-alanine is found in vitamin B₅ (pantothenic acid) as well as coenzyme A, a vital catalyst.

Arginine

Essential for babies and children. Nonessential for adults who can produce it from within, until about age 30.

Important notice: After 30 years of age, the adult pituitary gland stops producing arginine. Supplementation may be needed.

Principal benefits: Needed for optimal functioning of the pituitary gland. Along with other amino acids, arginine aids the pituitary gland's production and release of growth hormone. Utilized in numerous other hormone and enzyme activities. For example, it is a component of vasopressin, a pituitary hormone, that helps the pancreas release insulin. It is found in high amounts in the skin, collagen and the body's connective tissue. This means it is important for repairing and healing damaged tissues, as is the case with arthritis, connective tissue problems, damaged tendons and building new bone. Increases sperm count. A lack of this component of protein can lead to male infertility, since this amino acid makes up to 80 percent of the protein needed in seminal fluid. Boosts the immune system, which can then slow the growth of cancers and tumors. Accelerates and aids in healing wounds. Tones muscles and metabolizes body fat. Vital for balancing nitrogen levels. Helps improve liver function by healing fatty liver and cirrhosis of the liver. Detoxifies the liver, by neutralizing ammonia. Fosters mental alertness. Promotes physical readiness. Boosts thymus gland function and size, which results in more production of the vital immune system component called T-cells (T lymphocytes). If you have suffered physical traumas, eat more arginine rich foods. Under medical supervision you may want to combine L-arginine and L-ornithine to stimulate weight loss.

Food sources: Brown rice, carob, chocolate, coconut, dairy products, gelatin desserts, nuts, oatmeal, popcorn, all protein-rich foods, raisins, sesame seeds, sunflower seeds, walnuts, white flour, wheat, wheat germ, whole wheat bread.

Possible signs of deficiency: Impaired liver lipid (fat) metabolism. Glucose intolerance. Improper insulin production and utilization.

Dosages: Use L-arginine. It is available in powder and tablet forms. Take 2000 mg (2 grams) with water or juice on an empty stomach just before going to bed. Body builders and those wanting to tone up their muscles can take 2000 mg (2 grams) one hour before vigorous exercise, on an empty stomach. To enhance male sexual performance take 3000 to 6000 mg (3 to 6 grams) on an empty stomach, an hour before sex.

Warning: Do not give arginine to infants or growing children, since it may cause giantism. If dwarfism is the infant's or child's problem, discuss the options with your health care provider before using any amino acid supplements. Do not give to those with schizophrenic problems. Individuals with herpes should not use supplements or eat foods rich in this amino acid, as it is believed to trigger the herpes virus. To counter-act this reaction, and still be able to take L-arginine, try taking 500 mg of L-lysine, which may inhibit an herpes virus outbreak. Excessively large dosages of 20 or more grams can cause bone and joint deformities. If you take too much arginine over a period of several weeks, your skin can become course or thicken. Reduce your arginine intake to allow the problem to rectify itself.

Asparagine

A nonessential amino acid that the body can produce from within, if the necessary materials are available.

Principal benefits: Maintains and balances central nervous system by helping to prevent extreme conditions of over- or under-stimulation from affecting it. Helps the liver's ability to transform an amino acid from one type to another one that the body requires.

Food source: Mainly meats.

Aspartic acid

A nonessential amino acid that the body can produce from within, if the necessary materials are available.

Possible signs of deficiency: Chronic fatigue and reduced stamina.

Principal benefits: Useful for brain and neural disorders. Aids functioning of all the cells and the carriers of our genetic codes, RNA and DNA. Protects the liver by helping to removing excess ammonia, which is very important for athletes and critical protection for the central nervous system; ammonia becomes very toxic once in the circulatory system. Boosts endurance and stamina. Improves immune system function. Aids metabolism. Increases stamina. Helps remove toxins, such as ammonia, from the bloodstream.

Food source: An excellent source is the plant protein found in sprouting seeds.

Dosage: Aspartic acid salts increase athletic endurance and stamina. The natural and best form is L-aspartic acid. It is available in tablets. Usually it is taken in 500 mg dosages, one to three times a day with water or juice, on an empty stomach, and at least a half hour before meals. Do not take protein at the same time, as it interferes with the body's ability to utilize aspartic acid.

L-Carnitine

A nonessential amino acid that the body can produce from within, if the necessary materials are available. The body needs enough of the amino acids lysine and methionine, plus thiamine (vitamin B₁), pyridoxine (vitamin B₆), ascorbic acid (vitamin C) and iron to make carnitine. Neither lysine or methionine are available in large enough amounts from vegetable sources, which makes it very important for vegetarians to get sufficient amounts. Carnitine improves the benefits of vitamin C and E, two powerful antioxidants.

The form most easily used by the body is called L-carnitine. It is a vitamin-like nutrient found mainly in the brain, heart and skeletal muscles. It plays a vital role in delivering fatty acids to mitochondria, which supply the power for the cell and, in turn, the skeletal and heart cells. The cells are better able to utilize oxygen. Italian researchers have discovered it improves the potency of sperm in men with fertility problems.

Possible signs of deficiency: Confusion, heart pain, muscular dystrophy, muscle weakness, obesity.

Principal benefit(s): Aids conversion of fat to energy in the body. Improves cholesterol metabolism. Can help lower blood triglyceride levels. Helps improve fat metabolism problems due to diabetes and fatty liver caused by alcohol consumption. Beneficial for controlling hypoglycemia and diabetes. Needed for a healthy heart. Reduces frequency of angina attacks. Aids treatment for coronary artery disease. Reduces surgical cardiac damage to the heart. Helpful in treatment of kidney and liver diseases. Increases athletes' endurance time. Supports the skeletal muscular system and improves poor muscle tone as well as neuromuscular problems. Helps alleviate high cholesterol and/or triglycerides. Aids male infertility, caused by weak sperm. May be helpful in treating Alzheimer's disease patients, by slowing, preventing or even reversing the disease.

Food sources: Dairy products, meats, tempeh, soy-based products and grains fortified with lysine, such as cornmeal.

Dosage: Only take L-carnitine products, not D-carnitine, since it is more easily used by the body. On average, take 250 mg three times a day, at least an hour before, or two hours after, a meal. Take up to 1500 mg of tablets a day. There is no recommended daily intake amount for this amino acid. Men need more than women because of their greater muscle mass.

Caution: L-carnitine has no side effects; it is safe. D-carnitine may have toxic side effects. Always consult your health care provider before taking supplements for existing heart conditions. If you take over 1 gram (1000 mg) a day, you may develop a fishy odor. This odor does not occur very often, is not dangerous and quickly disappears as soon as the dose is reduced. Vegetarians may become deficient in carnitine and may consider supplementation, since it is not found in vegetable proteins.

Citrulline

A nonessential amino acid that the body can produce from within, if the necessary materials are available.

Principal benefits: Supports energy production. Increases immune system function. Can be transformed into L-arginine, which detoxifies the liver, by neutralizing ammonia (nitrocen in the blood).

Food source: Liver is the richest source of citrulline.

Cysteine (N-acetyl-L-cysteine)
– see also Cystine

A quasi-essential amino acid because it is sometimes synthesized from methionine or phenylalanine. Cysteine is found in alpha-keratin. Two joined molecules of cysteine make up their close amino acid relative, cystine. Cysteine is not stable and easily converts to L-cystine. L-cystine in turn, easily converts to cysteine. Your body does this on an as-needed basis. Cysteine is more soluble than cystine, which means it is easier for your body to use. That is why cysteine is the preferred form of these two amino acids when used to treat most illnesses. Both of these amino acids contain sulfur. The body's stores of L-methionine form cysteine.

Principal benefits: Powerful antioxidant. Major metal and liver detoxifier. Detoxifies harmful toxins. Chelates, binds with heavy metals, thereby helping remove them from the body. Recommended for treating rheumatoid arthritis, mutogenic disorders like cancer and hardening of the arteries. Anti-aging properties exemplified through the reduction of age spots and prevention of baldness. Beneficial with respiratory tract problems and the treatment of mucus producing illnesses such as emphysema, bronchitis and tuberculosis. Beneficial for respiratory diseases such as asthma, bronchitis and emphysema. May improve allergy and sinusitis conditions. Keeps fingernails, toenails and hair in good condition. Important for collagen production which benefits the texture and elasticity of your skin. Alleviates psoriasis.

People with chronic diseases may need to supplement with cysteine. Important in the activity of the disease-fighting white blood cells. Promotes healing of severe burns and surgical wounds. Protects the brain and liver from alcohol and drug damage. Aids the body's fat burning mechanism. Helps build muscle. Aids in the absorption of iron. Protects against cigarette smoke's toxic compounds. Precursor to glutathione, a key detoxifier of the liver. Helps increase glutathione levels in bone marrow, kidneys, liver and lungs. Found in many digestive enzymes and other proteins in the body. Protects against radiation damage.

Vitamin and mineral co-factors and other benefits: Selenium and vitamin E improve cysteine's free radical fighting properties. Vitamin B_6 is needed to synthesize cysteine. You may use cystine or N-acetylcysteine instead of cysteine for supplementation. N-acetylcysteine and cysteine are beneficial in reducing or preventing side effects from radiation therapy (X-rays, nuclear radiation) and chemotherapy. N-acetylcysteine is a better booster of glutathione levels than cystine or even glutathione supplementation.

Food source: The body synthesizes it.

Dosage: People with chronic diseases may need larger amounts of cysteine supplements, up to 1000 mg, three times a day, for 30-day periods. For drinkers and smokers it is very beneficial to combine three parts vitamin C with one part cysteine.

Caution: It is recommended that diabetics only use cysteine/cystine under medical supervision. When used alone or in combination with vitamins C and B, it can interfere with and deactivate insulin. Persons suffering the rare genetic illness cystinuria, that causes the formation of cystine kidney stones, should not supplement with the amino acid cysteine. Discontinue use if nausea, vomiting, diarrhea or stomach cramps occur, and consult with your physician or naturally oriented healer.

Cystine
– see also Cysteine

Cystine is a nonessential amino acid that the body can produce from within, if the necessary materials are available.

Principal benefits: Stable form of the amino acid cysteine. When metabolized, cystine produces sulfuric acid which helps detoxify the body. It offers effective protection against copper toxicity. Useful for prevention of side effects from radiation therapy and chemotherapy. Aids in prevention of free radical damage due to smoking and alcohol. Helps in eliminating age spots.

DL-Phenylalanine (DLPA)
– see also Phenylalanine

DL-Phenylalanine is not a naturally occurring amino acid. DLPA is another form of phenylalanine combined with equal amounts of synthetic D- and natural L-phenylalanine. This helps produce and activate endorphins, the body's natural pain killers. They are more powerful than opium derivatives and morphine. Endorphins are constantly destroyed by certain enzyme systems in the body; DLPA may inhibit these enzyme systems from functioning, better enabling the endorphins to do their job. Selective in its pain reducing qualities, DLPA can help people with chronic pain, since it does not interfere with the natural short term acute pain defense mechanisms of the body for injuries such as cuts, burns and scrapes.

Principal benefits: Alleviates lower back pain, muscle and leg cramps, migraines, osteoarthritis, postoperative pain, rheumatoid arthritis and whiplash. Powerful antidepressant. Pain relief that gets more effective the longer used, and you do not build up a tolerance to it if taken for up to one month, without additional drugs. Curbs addictive cravings. Sexual stimulant. Has no known adverse interactions with other therapies and drugs and can increase pain killing benefits.

Dosage: The experience of pain is very personal. Individuals who have not achieved pain relief with traditional prescription medications may want to consider DLPA; it works when prescription drugs fail. Finding the best dosage, depends on the condition. In conjunction with your health care provider, start at 375 mg to 750 mg, taken three times a day, half an hour before each meal. Pain relief may occur within four to twenty-one days. After that period, if no relief has occurred, you may want to double the dosage for another twenty-one days. Once you have found a workable dosage, reduce your intake until you get to the minimal amount you need.

Toxicity: None known.

Warning: DL-phenylalanine should not be used by pregnant women. DLPA elevates blood pressure and is not recommended for individuals with hypertension or heart conditions, unless under medical supervision, in which case it is usually prescribed to be taken after meals. DLPA is contraindicated for those with phenylketonuria, an inherited inability to oxidize a metabolic product of phenylalanine and exhibiting severe mental retardation. Persons with malignant melanoma and using antidepressants containing monoamine oxidase inhibitors, should not use phenylalanine.

Dimethylglycine (DMG)
– see also Glycine

Dimethylglycine is derived from the simplest of amino acids, glycine. It is also known as vitamin B_{15} and pangamic acid, although, technically, DMG is not really a vitamin. It is a building block for other amino acids, DNA, hormones, and neurotransmitters. There are no known symptoms of deficiency.

Principal benefits: Supports and improves the immune system (e.g. flu virus, salmonella). Aids function of many organs. Increases mental alertness. **Improves behavior of ADD and autistic individuals.** Helps maintain suitable blood pressure levels. Helps the body sustain high energy levels. Normalizes glucose blood levels. Beneficial in lowering high blood cholesterol and triglyceride levels. May help curb or lessen the effects of epileptic seizures.

Dosage, toxicity: see Vitamin B_{15} (pangamic acid).

Gamma-aminobutyric acid (GABA)

A nonessential amino acid, that the body can produce with the necessary materials. It is formed from glutamic acid, another amino acid. In the central nervous system, it acts as a neurotransmitter. It depresses neuron activity. Prevents nerve cells from overworking. Combined with inositol and niacinamide, it helps stop stress and anxiety messages from reaching the brain's motor centers by occupying the stress and anxiety receptor sites in the brain.

Principal benefits: Vital for efficient brain function and proper metabolism. Analgesic effects. **Beneficial for treating attention deficit disorder (ADD) and epilepsy.** Works like the prescription tranquilizers Valium (diazepam) and Librium (chlordiazepoxide) to calm the body, without the need for concern about addiction. The benefits of being relaxed mean it may improve a depressed or inhibited sex drive. Beneficial for treating hypertension. Helps regulate sex hormones, so it is useful for treating enlarged prostate glands.

Warning: Excessive amount of GABA may increase anxiety. It can lead to shortness of breath or very shallow breathing. Too much can result in tingling extremities and numbness around the mouth.

Glutamic acid

A nonessential amino acid that the body can produce from within, if the required materials are there. It becomes glutamine or gamma-aminobutyric acid (GABA) when needed. It fires the neurons in the central nervous system, brain and spinal cord. Helps the movement of potassium through the brain-blood barrier. The brain uses it as fuel.

Principal benefits: Aids brain functioning. Elevates mood. Converts excess ammonia, which inhibits brain function, into the buffer, glutamine, which is the only amino acid able to detoxify ammonia in the brain. Reduces fatigue. Aids in metabolism of fats and sugars. Reduces cravings for sugar. Beneficial in treating alcoholism, muscular dystrophy, personality disorders (such as schizophrenia), epilepsy, and the diabetic complication caused by insulin, hypoglycemic coma. **Treats behavioral disorders in children.** Speeds healing of ulcers and prostatic hyperplasia.

Dosage: see Glutamine.

Warning: **When used for treating children, always do it under proper medical supervision.** Individuals with a sensitivity to monosodium glutamate (MSG), even though it is not the same as glutamic acid or glutamine, may experience an allergic reaction to them. **Before taking these supplements, consult with a doctor.**

Glutamine

The natural form is known as L-glutamine.

Principal benefits: Glutamine helps produce higher levels of glutamic acid, which benefits brain functioning. It is known as 'brain fuel' since it can pass through the brain-blood barrier. **Beneficial in treatments of senility, schizophrenia, epilepsy and developmental disabilities.**

Glutamine aids the pituitary gland's production and release of growth hormone. Reduces recovery time and possibility of infection for cancer patients undergoing bone marrow transplant treatments. Reduces fatigue. It is the most abundant free-form acid found in the muscles. Helps build muscle mass in people who exercise. It may help reduce sugar cravings, which means it can help dieters. Elevates mood. Aids in controlling alcoholism. Reduces time it takes ulcers to heal. Promotes wound and burn healing. Aids in muscle-wasting prevention, particularly important for those who are bed ridden or chronically ill. Beneficial in treatments for impotence.

Thomas Welbourne of Louisiana State University College of Medicine discovered glutamine raised human growth hormone levels to four times their pretest levels. The results occurred regardless of age, in female and male test subjects ranging in age from 30 to 64.

Dosage: L-glutamine is usually taken in divided daily dosages totaling between 1000 to 4000 mg (1 to 4 grams). Best taken 30 minutes before, or 2 hours after, a meal or at bedtime. When used to treat depression, impotence, fatigue, alcoholism, senility and schizophrenia, seek the guidance of your health care provider.

Warning: **When used for treating children, always do it under proper medical supervision.** Individuals with a sensitivity to monosodium glutamate (MSG), though different from glutamic acid and glutamine, may experience an allergic reaction. Before taking these supplements, speak to a doctor. Do not take if you have any of these conditions: kidney problems, cirrhosis of the liver or Reye's syndrome.

Glutathione

Not an amino acid. It is a tripeptide. The amino acids cysteine, glycine and glutamic acid are involved in the production of glutathione. The liver produces this very powerful antioxidant, which helps detoxify the body, excreting toxins from the body. It is also found in the intestinal tract and lungs. It may have anti-aging properties. As we age, our stores of it decrease, and in turn the aging process accelerates. To counteract this, the least expensive and currently most effective way to increase your glutathione levels is to supplement with the amino acids glycine, glutamic acid and cysteine.

Glycine
– see also Dimethylglycine (DMG)

Glycine is a nonessential amino acid that the body can produce from within, if the necessary materials are there. It is used to build RNA and DNA, our genetic code carriers. It is essential for the production of bile acids and nucleic acids and for the synthesis of some nonessential amino acids. Glycine is found in muscle, skin and connective tissues. When needed, it converts to serine, another nonessential amino acid.

Principal benefits: Aids in treating certain types of low pH in the blood (acidemia), in particular those due to an imbalance of leucine, which manifests itself as bad breath and body odor. Improves low pituitary gland function. Critical for a healthy prostate. Vital for proper central nervous system functioning. Its neurotransmitter dampening affect can be beneficial in treating epileptic seizures. **Useful in treating hyperactivity** and manic-depressive disorder, also called bipolar disorder. Aids in the treatment of muscular dystrophy, due to its ability to produce creatine, which is vital for muscle function. Used in treatment of gastric hyperacidity, glycine is also a component of some gastric antacid drugs. Used in the treatment of hypoglycemia, since it stimulates glucagon production, which activate and release glycogen into the blood stream as glucose.

Caution: While the right amount increases energy, excess amounts may cause fatigue.

Histidine

A semi-essential amino acid, meaning external sources are needed to replenish its levels in the body. It is essential that babies and children get it through food or, if medically prescribed, supplementation. It is vital for the growth, maintenance and repair of tissues. Beneficial for maintaining proper red and white blood cell levels. Protects the nerve cells by maintaining their myelin sheathing, that is, their outer protective layers. Prevents radiation damage to the body. Helps remove potentially toxic heavy metals from the body.

Histidine is important in the production of the immune system chemical, histamine, which improves one's ability to experience sexual arousal and pleasure. To increase histamine levels, combine histidine with niacin (vitamin B_3) and pyridoxine (vitamin B_6).

Principal benefits: Improves rheumatoid arthritic conditions. Helps improve libido, sex drive. Alleviates stress and allergies. Beneficial for indigestion, since it increases gastric juice levels. May help prevent AIDS.

Food sources: Wheat, rye, rice, fish, poultry, pork, cheese.

Caution: Excessive levels of histidine may result in psychological problems, such as schizophrenia and anxiety. Methionine can be used to lower histidine levels. Insufficient levels are associated with nerve deafness. Low levels may result in rheumatoid arthritis. Do not take histidine if you have manic-depressive disorder (bipolar disorder) unless a deficiency has been discovered.

Isoleucine

An essential amino acid, meaning external sources are needed to replenish its levels in the body. Important for regulating and maintaining energy and blood sugar levels. Vital for hemoglobin formation. Isoleucine is metabolized in the muscles.

Symptoms of deficiency: May exhibit similar symptoms to hypoglycemia. Deficiencies are found in some physical and mental disorders.

Principal benefits: Increases endurance and enhances energy levels. Helps repair and heal muscles.

Food sources: Almonds, chicken, chickpeas, cashews, fish, eggs, lentils, meat, liver, rye, soy protein.

Dosage: Take it in a combination supplement. Since it is a three-branched chain amino acid, it should be taken with a two-branched chain amino acid, to maintain a proper balance. Use the most bio-available form, identified by 'L-'. The best ratio in a combination supplement is 1 part L-isoleucine, 2 parts L-leucine and 2 parts L-valine.

Leucine

An essential amino acid, meaning external sources are needed to replenish its levels in the body. It is one of the three-branched chain amino acids.

Principal benefits: Helps protect muscles. Fuels muscles. Can reduce elevated blood sugar levels. Beneficial for bone, muscle and skin healing. Promotes faster recovery from surgery. Can increase human growth hormone levels.

Food sources: Beans, brown rice, nuts, meat, soy flour, whole wheat.

Dosage: Always take in a combination supplement with the following ratio: 1 part L-isoleucine, 2 parts L-leucine and 2 parts L-valine.

Caution: Moderately excessive amounts may result in symptoms of hypoglycemia. Very high levels may result in more ammonia being present in the body and may induce pellagra.

Lysine

An essential amino acid, meaning external sources are needed to replenish its levels in the body. It is necessary for growth and tissue repair. Lysine is a vital building block for body proteins. It maintains an appropriate level of nitrogen in adults. It plays a key role in the production of antibodies, enzymes and hormones.

Principal health benefits: Vital for optimal growth and bone formation in children. Promotes efficient use of fatty acids needed for energy production. May be beneficial for menopausal women, who are at risk of getting osteoporosis, since lysine helps the body use calcium more effectively. Possibly helpful in resolving some fertility problems. Improves concentration. May reduce or prevent the incidence of herpes simplex infection – cold sores and fever blisters.

Studies indicate lysine is beneficial for patients suffering from chest pain (angina); patients were given 6 grams a day and improved enough that they could stop taking their sublingual (under the tongue) nitroglycerin tablets within four weeks, and were able to increase their exercise levels, allowing their hearts to heal faster. Lysine can lower high serum triglyceride levels and high blood pressure.

Lysine is also a beauty aid that keeps skin looking young and vibrant; it does this by encouraging collagen formation, the underlying tissue that supports the surface layer of skin, which is vital for preventing wrinkles and sagging skin, as well as tissue repair. Improves recovery time from sports injuries and surgery.

Symptoms of lysine deficiency may include: Anemia, proneness to bloodshot eyes, poor concentration, dizziness, hair loss, nausea, fatigue, enzyme disorders, irritability, poor appetite, reproductive problems, weight loss and retarded growth. Older people need more lysine, particularly males.

Food sources: Cheese, milk, eggs, fish, lima beans, red meat, potatoes, soy products, yeast, all protein-rich foods.

Dosage: To improve your skin and strengthen your bones, take 500 mg of L-lysine tablets or capsules 1 or 2 times a day, 30 minutes before meals. For an individual having an outbreak of herpes, take 3000 to 6000 mg (3 to 6 grams) a day and eat the lysine-rich foods mentioned above. To prevent recurrence, take 500 to 1000 mg a day. Speak to your health care provider concerning this form of treatment.

Caution: When supplementing for heart conditions, always do so in consultation with your doctor or naturally oriented healer.

Methionine

An essential sulfur amino acid used in the manufacturing of all proteins. Major source of sulfate, aids production of mucous that protects the lining of the stomach and intestine. Methionine is a critical component in tissue development, growth, repair and protein synthesis.

Principal benefits: Functions as an anti-oxidant, anti-inflammatory and methyl donor. A principal source of sulfur. Protective effects against toxins including heavy metals, atrazine, radiation and drugs. Can increase the neurotransmitters dopamine, norepinephrine and epinephrine. Used for hypertension control; reduces allergic symptoms; relieves chronic pain; reduces inflammation; lowers cholesterol; protects from the bad effects of aspirin; beneficial in treatment of Parkinson's and schizophrenia.

Methionine metabolites include taurine, cysteine – aids heart function and detoxification processes. Also glutathione, carnitine, S-adenosyl methionine (SAM), and cystathione. Facilitates availability of selenium.

Deficiency symptoms: Tendencies toward inflammatory conditions, allergies, premature atherosclerosis, folic acid and B_{12} deficiency, depression, chronic pain, fatty liver, weakened immune system. Disease states, poor diet, stress or chronic exposure to toxins increase the need for methionine. Diets low in meat and eggs may contribute to methionine deficiency. Vegetarians may need to supplement with methionine as processed soy protein loses its methionine.

Note: Modern food processing methods destroy methionine. Diets deficient in methionine have a higher incidence of colon cancer.

Food sources: Eggs, meat and unbleached flour products. High heat oxidizes methionine, preventing the body from utilizing it.

Dosages: Babies need 22 mg/Kg (22 mg/2.2 lbs.) of body weight daily (500-800 mg/day); Adults 10 mg/Kg of body weight daily (750-1500 mg/day). Seniors need up to 2.5 grams per day (2000-2500 mg/day). Should be taken as equally divided doses 2 to 4 times per day. Should be taken with either betaine, vitamins B_6, B_{12} or folic acid. These nutrients support the separate methylation pathways of methionine.

Note: Nutritionally oriented practitioners reported positive results in treating cancerous cells with a blend of methionine, grape seed and other nutrients. In one case a lung cancer patient showed no signs of cancer or scarring, after 3 weeks of treatment. The product, 'C-Gone', is available from LifeStar, 2175 East San Francisco Blvd., San Rafael, CA 94901 (415) 457-1400. A dl-methionine product, Redoxal HMF™ and co-nutrients is available from Preventhium International, 5885 Cumming Highway #108-291, Sugar Hill, GA 30518 (770) 831-8605 or (800) 755-1327 (US only). This is neither an endorsement of their products, nor a guarantee of effectiveness.

Ornithine

A nonessential amino acid, synthesized from arginine, which is a precursor of glutamic acid, proline and citrulline. It is found mainly in the connective tissue and skin. Ornithine promotes the discharge of human growth hormone and helps the liver regenerate by ridding the body of ammonia.

Principal benefits: Helps repair damaged tissues and promotes healing. Aids in building muscles. Increases the levels, benefits and potency of the amino acid, arginine. In fact, this is a circular system where arginine is produced from ornithine and ornithine is released by arginine. Releases growth hormone while you sleep which, in turn helps you slim down. Aids insulin secretion and insulin's work as a muscle building (anabolic) hormone.

Food sources: Brown rice, carob, chocolate, gelatin desserts, nuts, oatmeal, popcorn, all protein-rich foods, raisins, sesame seeds, sunflower seeds, whole wheat bread.

Dosages: Most effective when taken with arginine just before bed. Ingest on an empty stomach, in a glass of water or juice, without any protein, which interferes with utilization. It is available in powder and tablet forms. Take 2000 mg (2 grams). Body builders and those wanting to tone their muscles can take 2000 mg (2 grams) on an empty stomach, one hour before vigorous exercise.

Warning: Since ornithine and arginine are best taken together and are so closely related, the following approach is prudent: Supplementation is not recommended for pregnant or nursing mothers, unless medically warranted and suggested by your doctor. Do not give to infants or growing children, since arginine may cause giantism. If dwarfism is the infant's or child's problem, discuss the options with your health care provider before using any amino acid supplements. Do not give to those with schizophrenic problems. Individuals with herpes should not use supplements or eat foods rich in arginine. Excessively large dosages of 20 or more grams can cause bone and joint deformities. If you take too much arginine, over a period of several weeks, your skin can become coarse or thicken. Reduce your arginine intake to allow the problem to rectify itself.

Phenylalanine
– see also DL-Phenylalanine (DLPA)

An essential amino acid, meaning external sources are needed to replenish its levels in the body. Phenylalanine becomes tyrosine, another amino acid. It is intimately involved with the central nervous system. Tyrosine becomes two vital neurotransmitters, norepinephrine and dopamine, that promote alertness.

Principal benefits: Critical to alleviating depression, phenylalanine enables the brain to release the antidepressants norepinephrine and dopamine. Increases libido (sex drive). Helps memory and mental alertness. Aids in appetite suppression. Used to treat menstrual cramps, migraines, obesity, schizophrenia, arthritis and Parkinson's disease. In some forms it relieves pain.

Food sources: Almonds, cottage cheese, lima beans, peanuts, protein rich foods, pumpkin seeds, powdered skim milk, sesame seeds, soy products.

Dosage: Tablets are available in 250 and 500 mg sizes. Not addictive. To increase vitality and alertness, take between meals with juice or water, but not protein. To control appetite, take one hour before meals with water or juice, but not protein. Note: Phenylalanine is not metabolized if you are deficient in vitamin C.

Caution: Do not supplement with phenylalanine during pregnancy or if you have skin cancer (contraindicated for people with pigmented malignant melanomas) or phenylketonuria (PKU). If suffering from high blood pressure or a heart condition, consult with your doctor before using this supplement as it may increase blood pressure. If your doctor okays its use, it is advisable to take it half an hour after meals. *Do not take with antidepressants, MAO inhibitors, St. John's wort and Licorice root.*

Note: DL-Phenylalanine or DLPA is another form of phenylalanine combined with equal amounts of synthetic D- and natural L-phenylalanine. This produces and activates endorphins, the body's natural pain-killer. They are more powerful than opium derivatives and morphine. Selective in its pain reducing qualities, it can help chronic pain sufferers since it does not interfere with the natural short-term acute pain defense mechanisms of the body for injuries such as cuts, burns and scrapes.

DL-Phenylalanine is beneficial in the following conditions: lower back pain, muscle and leg cramps, migraines, osteoarthritis, postoperative pain, rheumatoid arthritis, whiplash. Powerful antidepressant. Pain relief that gets more effective the longer used and you do not build up a tolerance to it – up to one month without using additional drugs. When used in conjunction with other therapies and drugs, it has no known adverse interactions and can increase the pain killing benefits. It is non-toxic.

Proline

A non-essential amino acid, which means the body can produce it on its own.

Principal benefits: Increases ability to learn. Promotes wound recovery by healing cartilage and strengthening tendons, joints and the heart muscle. Acts synergistically with vitamin C, in keeping the connective tissue healthy. Aids the body's ability to produce collagen, which keeps the skin youthful and vibrant.

Food sources: Primarily meat.

Serine

A nonessential amino acid, which means the body can produce it on its own. It can be made from glycine in the body. Serine helps diminish pain. It can mimic the actions of a natural antipsychotic. It is required for efficient metabolism of fatty acids and fats and for proper muscle growth. It facilitates production of antibodies and immunoglobulins, and helps maintain the immune system.

Taurine

A nonessential amino acid, which means the body can produce it on its own, if given the needed materials. It is also known as the "brain amino acid." It is found primarily in heart tissues, the central nervous system, white blood cells and skeletal muscles. It is a building block for other amino acids.

Taurine can improve heart function. Japanese doctors use it to treat congestive heart failure and lower blood pressure. Reduces enlarged prostate. Helps detoxify and alleviate liver congestion. Protects the brain. It utilizes choline which promotes one's ability to think and maintains neurotransmitters. May help in the treatment of brain malfunctions, such as epilepsy and anxiety. It is associated with zinc utilization for the eyes. Vital for fat-soluble vitamin absorption and creation of bile salts in the gallbladder, which are needed for proper digestion of fats. Critical for proper absorption of potassium, sodium, magnesium and calcium. Helps control serum cholesterol levels. Helpful in treating diabetes. Possibly beneficial for eye health and prevention of macular degeneration. It is a useful anti-aging supplement.

Food sources: Eggs, fish, milk, meat. It is not in vegetable proteins, but if there is enough vitamin B_6 in the body, as well as either cysteine or methionine, taurine can be synthesized.

Drugs it may be an alternative for: Phenobarbital and other chemotherapeutic drugs.

Substances and problems that can lead to taurine deficiency: Genetic or metabolic disorders. Excessive consumption of alcohol prevents the body from fully using taurine. Emotional stress, yeast infections (Candida albicans), cardiac arrhythmias, zinc deficiency, diabetes, intestinal problems, improper platelet formation.

Diseases it may help treat: Heart disease, cardiac arrhythmias, Down's syndrome, epilepsy, anxiety, **hyperactivity,** seizures, hypertension, hypoglycemia, edema, diabetes, macular degeneration, muscular dystrophy.

Dosage: Take up to 1500 mg of capsules daily, with water or juice, on an empty stomach at least half an hour before meals. Diabetics should be monitored by their doctor or natural health care professional since they usually need more taurine. Taken with cystine, it may reduce the need for insulin.

Caution: Taurine is a depressant. Large doses may result in loss of short-term memory.

Threonine

An essential amino acid, meaning the body cannot manufacture it on its own and must receive it from an outside source. It is vital for the production of purines, which break down uric acid, itself a by product of protein digestion. An excess of uric acid may be responsible for gout, a form of arthritis, and other health problems. Threonine is also vital for the production of the nonessential amino acid, glycine.

Threonine is found mainly in the heart, skeletal muscles and central nervous system. It is vital for collagen and elastin formation. When threonine is combined with methionine and aspartic acid, it aids lipotropic and liver function. It is very helpful for prevention of fatty buildup in the liver. It boosts production of antibodies, which in turn improves the immune system. Vital for protein utilization in one's diet, as well as maintaining the appropriate protein balance.

Caution: Vegetarians tend to be deficient in threonine, since their principle food sources, such as grains, are very low in it.

Tryptophan
– also called L-tryptophan

It is an essential amino acid, meaning the body cannot manufacture it and needs to get it from an outside source. It is vital for the production of niacin (vitamin B_3). Tryptophan is the precursor to serotonin, which is important for sleep, appetite levels, stable moods and pain sensitivity.

The U.S. Food and Drug Administration (FDA), temporarily banned tryptophan in 1989 due to 26 deaths and hundreds of cases of reported illness in New Mexico, supposedly due to tryptophan. It was later discovered to be a problem at the Japanese manufacturer's plant. A toxic chemical accidentally contaminated a batch of L-tryptophan. According to the Atlanta Center for Disease Control, no one has died or become ill due to properly processed L-tryptophan.

Principal benefits: Antidepressant qualities. Alleviates some alcohol-related chemical body problems. Helps control alcoholism. Reduces nicotine cravings. Natural tranquilizer reducing anxiety and tension. Best utilized with vitamins B_6 (pyridoxine) and B_3 (niacin) and the trace mineral magnesium to help the brain synthesize serotonin. Magnesium and tryptophan may prevent coronary artery spasms. Promotes sleep naturally. Alleviates migraines. **Beneficial for treating hyperactivity.** Promotes the release of human growth hormone.

Food sources: Bananas, brown rice, cottage cheese, dried dates, fish, milk, meat, peanuts, turkey and protein rich-foods.

Dosage: L-tryptophan is available through your doctor. When taking it, you should also take a balanced and complete B-complex vitamin formula that has at least 50 to 100 mg of B_1, B_2 and B_6 with your first or last meal of the day. To induce sleep, take 500 mg of tryptophan a half hour before bed with vitamin B_6 (100 mg), niacinamide (100 mg) and chelated or citrated magnesium (120 to 130 mg). Take it with juice or water, but not protein. As a relaxant, take between meals, during the day, with water or juice, but not protein nor milk. Single dosages over 2000 mg (2 grams) are not recommended.

Tyrosine

A quasi-essential amino acid sometimes synthesized from methionine or phenylalanine.

Principal benefits: Can help suppress appetite. Critical neurotransmitter as it stimulates and modifies brain activity. The mood elevator phenylalanine must first be converted to tyrosine, without which norepinephrine will not be made in the brain, and this would result in depression. Acts as a mood elevator by aiding in neural brain activity by increasing the rate neurons produce the antidepressants norepinephrine and dopamine. Used to control medication resistant depression. Used to reduce the amount of amphetamine a patient is taking. Helps reduce the side effects of cocaine withdrawal such as depression, irritability and fatigue. Improves libido (sex drive). Alleviates stress.

Dosage: The use of tyrosine to alleviate cocaine withdrawal symptoms is more effective when combined with vitamins B_1, B_2, C, niacin, and the enzyme tyrosine hydroxylase, in a glass of orange juice.

Caution: Contraindicated for people with pigmented malignant melanomas. May increase blood pressure. *Not to be taken with antidepressants and MAO inhibitors, St. John's Wort or Licorice root.*

Valine

An essential amino acid, meaning the body cannot manufacture it and must get it from an outside source. It is a branched-chain amino acid, which is important for supplying energy to muscles. One key role is its stimulating effect. It aids muscle metabolism and is concentrated in the muscles. Balances the body's nitrogen levels.

Principal benefits: Aids tissue repair. Helps correct drug addiction-induced amino acid deficiencies.

Food sources: Grains, dairy products (especially cottage cheese), mushrooms, meats, peanuts, soy proteins.

Valine deficiency: May negatively affect the myelin covering of nerves.

Dosage: Always take in a balanced combination supplement having the following ratio: 2 parts L-valine, 1 part L-isoleucine and 2 parts L-leucine. For example, 2 mg L-valine, 1 mg L-isoleucine, 2 mg L-leucine.

Caution: Very high dosages can result in a crawling sensation on the skin, and could even lead to hallucinations. If any symptoms occur, stop taking the supplement and see your health care provider.

Section Three

More
Complementary and Natural
Self-Health-Care Choices

"Whoever destroys one life,
it is as though he had destroyed a whole world;
and whoever saves one life,
it is as though he had saved a whole world."

— translated from *Talmud,* Sanhedrin, Chapter 4:5

Homeopathy and Cell Salts
Laurie Simmons, H.D., D.H.M.S.

History of Homeopathy

Homeopathy was developed by Dr. Samuel Hahnemann 200 years ago in Germany. He developed this new system of natural medicine as an alternative to the harsh and toxic treatments available at the time. Dr. Hahnemann developed over one hundred medicines from natural substances in his lifetime. He wrote extensively on the subject and taught his new system at medical school. Homeopathy spread rapidly throughout Europe, into Asia and North America. Research and use of homeopathy became widespread, resulting in the development and use of over 2000 homeopathic medicines.

The first homeopathic hospital was founded in 1850 in London, England by Dr. Frederick Quin as a result of his own recovery from cholera. Currently in the UK, there are six homeopathic hospitals, and it is the treatment of choice for the royal family. It is used by more than 30 million people in Europe alone, and is prescribed regularly by physicians. It is estimated that 500 million people use homeopathic remedies each year.

Homeopathy was established in the United States during the 1820s by Dr. Constantine Hering and Dr. James Tyler Kent. It became the first system of medicine to be regulated in both the U.S. and Canada in 1844 and 1859 respectively. Homeopathy was taught at universities. Homeopathic hospitals flourished throughout North America. Emily Stowe, the first Canadian female doctor, and the founder of Women's College Hospital in Toronto, was a Homeopath.

Homeopathy has a rich and impressive history. Homeopathic medical schools exist today throughout the world, and exciting new research is coming out of institutions such as the London Homeopathic Hospital and the Glasgow Homeopathic Hospital. Many clinical trials have proven homeopathy effective for various acute and chronic conditions, and their results have been published in many respected medical journals. One such article is a review of 105 controlled studies published by the prestigious *British Medical Journal* in 1991 entitled "Clinical Trials in Homeopathy." This review revealed that 81 of the 105 studies yielded positive results with homeopathy.

Homeopathic medicine is experiencing an explosion of interest and use by both medical practitioners and the public. It is a very appealing alternative to drugs and surgery because of its gentle action. It is particularly popular in the treatment of children because it stimulates healing with safe and natural substances.

How does Homeopathy work?

Homeopathic medicines do not use any synthetic substances. All of the healing properties are derived from plant, animal, and mineral substances. There is no risk of poisoning, addiction, or interaction with other medicines or supplements. Homeopathic medicines are extremely gentle and act as catalysts to stimulate the mind and body to heal itself.

The philosophy of the homeopathic system of medicine stems from Dr. Samuel Hahnemann's discovery that *"like cures like."* The symptoms that a substance can produce in crude doses in a healthy person actually <u>cure</u> those same symptoms when administered in highly diluted doses to a sick person. A simple example of this is to think of the allium plant or onion. Onion contains an oil that causes the nose and eyes to run and burn. A highly diluted dose of homeopathic allium will cure the irritating, watery symptoms in the common cold. Another example is a plant called pulsatilla. Its constituents, when taken whole and without dilution from the plant, cause depression, weepiness and thick mucus discharge. Therefore, homeopathic pulsatilla will cure a cold in a weepy child with thick, nasal discharge.

These two examples of very different cold symptoms being treated with different homeopathic medicines illustrate another element of the homeopathic philosophy. Each person is treated individually with a homeopathic medicine that precisely matches his or her symptoms. Two patients, each of whom has a cold, can receive different medicines. And most importantly, every homeopathic medicine is also prescribed to match both the psychological and physiological symptoms precisely, thereby healing both emotional and physical complaints. The example of the weepy child with the cold mentioned above illustrates this. The pulsatilla will help cure her weepy disposition as well as clear up the thick congestion.

Homeopathic medicines are inexpensive and readily available at health food stores and pharmacies in low potency. Most common are potencies labeled 6c 12c, l5c, or 30c. These products and a simple guide for instructions are very valuable as self-help tools to treat common acute conditions such as coughs, colds, fevers and flus. However, chronic conditions require higher potencies and very precise prescribing for effective treatment. These conditions should be treated by a "homeopathic doctor."

Homeopathic medicines are easy to administer to children. Tiny sugar pellets containing the medicine are dissolved in the child's mouth. Nothing should be taken by mouth 15 minutes before or after the medicine. The pellets must be stored in a dark, cool place and away from strong odors. The low potencies need more frequent repetition. Higher potencies, prescribed by a homeopathic doctor, will usually be administered in a single dose and act for several weeks similar to a time-release action.

Why use homeopathy for ADHD?

Stimulant drugs commonly used in the treatment of ADHD are amphetamines such as Dextroamphetamine (Dexedrine), methylphenidate (Ritalin), and pemoline (Cyclert). Research has demonstrated that these drugs have a calming effect on children for about 4 to 18 weeks in the majority of cases. During this time, the child's behavior may be subdued, but there is generally no improvement in academic performance. Stimulants can cause obsessive over-focusing, and limit the child's awareness of his or her surroundings. Essentially, these drugs dull the child's energy and enthusiasm, making him or her quieter and easier to control.

In addition to the disadvantage of such a short-term improvement of symptoms, amphetamines can have serious side effects. They generally increase heart rate, blood pressure and the risk of cardiovascular disease. In addition to possibly causing heart damage, stimulants can cause insomnia, appetite suppression, tics, depression, memory loss, and liver damage. Furthermore, there have been no studies to investigate the effects of long-term amphetamine use on a child's developing brain. For more specific information on pharmaceutical drugs, refer to Section 5, The Pharmaceutical Drugs.

Homeopathic medicine is a gentle, safe, and non-toxic alternative to stimulant drugs. All homeopathic medicines are made from natural substances, which are highly diluted and generally do not cause any harmful side effects. Homeopathic medicines are safe to use concurrently with prescription drugs, and may enable the child, with the help of a doctor, to reduce or eliminate the use of prescription drugs. The correct homeopathic prescription will have long lasting results, and may provide a permanent solution to the symptoms of ADHD.

Treating ADD and Hyperactivity with Homeopathy

Many health professionals believe the term "Attention Deficit Hyperactive Disorder (ADHD)" is a generic label which is being used to cover a variety of psychological and physiological conditions that children experience.

Homeopathic medicines are extremely successful in treating children with ADHD because they treat each child's unique emotional and physical symptoms rather than the generic condition. Unlike prescription drugs, which are commonly used to treat this condition, homeopathic medicines do not sedate an overactive child. A homeopathic doctor will take a detailed history of the child's behavior, personality, and fears, as well as physiological health complaints such as sleep problems, asthma, and eczema. This complete history will determine the appropriate homeopathic medicine. Detailed case-taking results in a *symptom picture*, which enables the homeopathic doctor to match the child's symptoms precisely with a homeopathic prescription. This precise match will stimulate the healing of those symptoms naturally and gently.

Homeopathic medicines may successfully treat the child's symptoms, enabling him or her to avoid prescription drugs. However, homeopathic medicines are perfectly safe to use when the child is currently on prescription drugs, and may enable the child to reduce or eliminate the prescription with the supervision of his or her medical doctor.

The Homeopathic interview and casetaking procedure.

What happens at your first homeopathic appointment?

Your first visit with a homeopathic doctor will take approximately one and a half hours. It will be a relaxed visit that gives the parents an opportunity to describe the nature of their child. It is an easy and open conversation that enables the homeopath to record the unique details of the child's physical, emotional and intellectual health. The child will also participate in the conversation if he or she is old enough. Younger children will be given toys and art supplies so the homeopath can watch them play and interact with their parents. It is important for the homeopath to know the details of the child's temperament and personality. These details, such as whether the child is shy, outgoing, easily angered, cheerful, calm, anxious or weepy are very important. Parents need to explain the details of the child's relationships with siblings or other children, and their challenges at school.

Parents also discuss the child's food preferences, sleep patterns, dreams, or tendency to having nightmares. The homeopath will want to know everything that frightens the child, and what calms him or her. There may be details discussed about how the child's energy or mood changes throughout the day. Parents will record the child's diet, body temperature, digestive function, and bowel habits.

The homeopath will also meticulously record all physical complaints since birth such as skin conditions, allergies, stomach problems, upper respiratory infections, asthma and chronic ear infections.

Your family medical history will be discussed, as well as the health and emotional state of the parents during the pregnancy and any complications during the birth. The parents will be asked to mention anything that they feel improves or worsens their child's physical or behavioral symptoms.

It is through this meticulously recorded information and the observations of the homeopath that a symptom picture is developed. The symptom picture is individual and unique to each child and determines the correct homeopathic prescription.

Examples of symptom pictures seen in children suffering with Attention Deficit Hyperactive Disorder

Homeopathic doctors develop symptom pictures by gathering detailed information about the child's behavior, physical and emotional health. Throughout treatment, the medicine's potency, frequency of repetition, and prescription will change. For successful treatment of a child's symptoms, the homeopath must carefully monitor the child's reaction to each prescription, and his or her progress. The following symptom pictures of homeopathic medicines are given as an example of the many different ways a child may experience ADHD, and illustrate the variety and uniqueness of children's behavioral symptoms that may respond to homeopathic treatment. Remember that while some symptom pictures may look similar to that of your child, there are actually over 2000 homeopathic medicines from which the homeopath must choose an exact match. It is highly recommended that parents seek professional advice from a homeopathic doctor before beginning treatment. However, if one of the medicines below seems to describe your child, administering a low potency (30c) once a day for one week and then waiting to observe any improvements is a good trial. If the homeopathic medicine does not work, it means you have not used the correct prescription or the exact match.

Kali Bromatum

Children needing kali bromatum are extremely restless. They have very fidgety hands and feet, fiddling with desk items, tapping, or drumming his or her fingers. These children suffer from sleeplessness due to worry and accompanying tossing and turning. They sleepwalk and grind their teeth. They have great fear at night and cannot sleep if left alone. They may have experienced an emotional trauma. They can also be extremely loyal friends, and family is very important to them. They are honest and have a strong sense of duty.

In adolescence, they suffer from acne on the face, back, and chest. This acne leads to scarring. They have poor concentration and memory loss, forgetting words or mixing up words in talking and writing. They are worriers, and their anxiety and restlessness can only be calmed by staying busy.

Lachesis

These children are extremely talkative. They may have mood swings. They may develop a lack of self-confidence that leads to self-criticism, withdrawal, and a feeling of weakness and depression.

They are very jealous of siblings and other people. They are very suspicious and worried that they are being talked about and criticized. They have a preoccupation with others.

These children are very competitive, and this trait, combined with jealousy, results in problematic oneupmanship. They are showy and very concerned with the look of things. They have a love of beauty and nature. They have passionate emotions and are loud, animated and witty. Their minds are full of ideas that they cannot bear to keep them to themselves. They call out in school and are impulsive. They are intense and hyperactive.

Lachesis children hate any physical or behavioral restrictions. They cannot bear tight clothes. They have an extreme aversion to authority. They can have suffocative feelings and may have asthma or frequent sore throats that hurt when swallowing liquids. They have a history of ear, nose, and throat problems, or bleeding problems. They have a hemorrhagic tendency.

Lachesis children are usually females. Their physical complaints are usually on the left side. They may fear snakes and going to sleep. They are grumpy after sleep. This medicine is commonly indicated during puberty.

Lycopodium

These children are bossy and dictatorial and can have tamper tantrums. They are more comfortable with younger children because they can boss them around. They are very concerned about what others think about them. They are more intellectual than athletic.

Lycopodium children are fearful underneath their bravado. They are cowardly but try not to show it. They have a tremendous lack of self confidence and are reluctant to try new things because they have an enormous fear of failure. This deep insecurity causes performance anxiety and a fear of school tests because their weakness will be revealed. Their biggest fear is that a demand will be made of them and they may not be prepared for it. They are fearful of any new situation and worry about the future.

They can be bullying tyrants at home and rude to parents where they feel secure. At school they are more timid, and can be charming to adults in situations in which they are less secure. They try to cover up their mistakes and to appear courageous, which often presents as being quite boastful. They get angry from contradiction.

Lycopodium children frighten easily and will often act quite immature for their age. They are extremely restless and have an inability to sit still and pay attention at school. They are distractible and may be dyslexic. These

children have problems with their gastrointestinal system. They are consti-
pated and have frequent stomachaches, gas, and bloating. They are intolerant to changes in diet or meal times. They react badly to sugar, and all complaints are worse between 4 p.m. to 8 p.m..

Hyoscyamus

These children have boundless energy during the day. They are usually
male. They try to attract attention in whatever way possible. They make
ridiculous gestures to make you laugh, and are very animated and silly. They
have poor impulse control, and smile and laugh at everything. They can be
the class clown, joking, jesting, singing and humming. They show off and
talk too much. Their behavior is foolish and can be promiscuous and sexually inappropriate. They may expose themselves, use bathroom language,
play with their genitals and run around naked.

The hyoscyamus children are extremely afraid of being alone. They are
afraid of being betrayed or deserted by the person on whom they are completely dependent. This gives them a feeling of being unloved, and causes
acute fear and panic reactions. Their fear of being deserted causes them to
tempt to be attractive, although in the most bizarre and shameless ways as
mentioned above.

These children may have episodes of mania and rage that include hit-
ting and screaming. They are extremely jealous, especially of siblings.
Depression can follow the manic stage. They may curse for shock value.
They are suspicious and deceitful.

Their hands and feet are very restless. They pick at their clothes and
plays with their fingers. They suffer from sleeplessness and prefer to be
uncovered. They wake up suddenly and frightened out of sleep, and go back
to sleep without being comforted. They have an aversion to water, and
suffer from stomach cramps and hiccups.

Stramonium

This medicine is for the most fearful children who react in an aggressive and violent way. Often they have experienced a traumatic event.
Stramonium children can have a Jekel and Hyde personality. They can be
sweet one moment and throw a violent rage the next.

Stramonium children are oversensitive to light and noise. They have
mood swings, are hyperactive, and have behavioral disorders. They are jealous, intense and talkative. They speak in a devout, earnest and a beseeching
manner with ceaseless talking. They may stammer until the word finally
explodes. They may talk in a threatening manner, saying things such as,
"I'm going to kill you." They talk loudly, laugh loudly, and may curse. They
may think that they hear voices.

Stramonium children develop rages that are impulsive without fore-thought. They have violent outbursts with striking, biting, and/for stran-gling. Their faces turn red and their pupils dilate during this mania. They can be violent, yet are afraid of violence. They have fear-responses as though they are alone in the dark, surrounded by wild animals that will attack them at any time. They are terrified, and their response is one of rage and vio-lence. They are extremely afraid of the dark and being left alone. They need the light on, warmth and company to calm them. They are afraid that the person they depend on will leave them. They do not feel secure and safe. They may follow the parent from room to room to avoid being alone.

Their fear causes tremendous nightmares and sleep disturbances. They will have frequent night terrors which they awake from screaming and ter-rified. They will not recognize anyone, and cling to their care-taker. They need a night light and company to fall asleep. They are afraid of monsters, ghosts, dogs, suffocation, injury and death.

The stramonium children are extremely thirsty, yet dread water. They desire lemon juice and sweets.

Tarentula

The children who need this medicine want to be noticed, and go to great lengths to attract attention to themselves. They behave in a shameless, las-civious, or threatening manner. Singing, dancing, and hectic activity all help attract attention to themselves. They must be the center of attention. They will be climbing and jumping in order to accomplish this, and mimicking animal behavior.

These children have the urge to move constantly. They exhibit nervous excitability. They are keyed up, tremendously hurried, impatient, impulsive, and distractible. As adults, they are compulsive worriers. In children, it is expressed in constant and hyperactive play followed by exhaustion. There is a constant restlessness of the legs, feet and fingers. These childrens' hands are fidgety and busy. They pick their lips and noses, or have their fingers in their mouths. They touch everything and everyone. They often will use their hands creatively, such as by painting, and are attracted to bright colors. These children need to have things to keep their hands busy and out of trouble.

Their sleep is also restless. They toss and turn, and tie the sheets up in knots. Their legs are also very restless in bed. They find it hard to fall asleep before midnight, and like to lie on their backs with their limbs flexed.

These children are cunning. They are destructive and difficult to con-trol. They are obstinate and disobedient, manipulative, and like to play tricks on people. They tell lies and love to hide. They also have a good sense of humor, a charming nature, and are a little sneaky. They may be destructive and strike very suddenly and intentionally. They enjoy this and afterwards they laugh; it is exciting to them. They can be comic, wild and manic, or a little more subtle and mischievous.

They are willful and can have tantrums or violent rages. They may break things, tear things, or throw things. During these rages they may hit others or themselves. They can be volatile and sensitive to being teased. They will push the limits and can have trouble with authority.

Music will calm these children. They may sit and stare while listening to music, or they may have an irresistible urge to dance. They love loud, fast, rhythmic beats. They will be seen dancing, tapping, and drumming.

This child suffers from a lot of anxiety. They are anxious that things won't get done or that something will go wrong. They have a fear of being injured, assaulted or trapped. They may have anxiety attacks with a sensation of being suffocated. They must have fresh air. Their nervous systems are wounded. There may also have a fear of spiders.

Tuberculinum

Children needing tuberculinum are the most restless of children. They have a constant desire for change. They become dissatisfied with whatever they are doing very quickly. They move from room to room or from toy to toy. These children are unable to stay in one place for very long. They jump on the couch or rock in their chairs. It is impossible for them to complete homework. They lack concentration and have an inability to sit still, which gives them an aversion to studying. They will suffer from physical aggravation such as headache if forced to do it. Homework is agonizing to them. They will procrastinate, lie, and say they are finished or refuse to complete it. Their memory is so weak that they have to relearn things, and they make mistakes in spelling and reading.

It is difficult for parents to keep these children quiet and still. They are very loud, demanding, and capricious. They scream for attention. They will have violent temper tantrums if they are contradicted. They will throw themselves to the floor kicking, pounding fists, scratching, and screaming. They can be deliberately destructive and break things. They may strike others or themselves, as in the characteristic "head-banging." They are irritable and contrary. They will say "no" to everything. They get into many fights with siblings and school friends. They provoke fights with poking or pushing. If they are hit, they will instantaneously and violently hit back (even at a parent). They will lash out at anyone who has authority over them.

Tuberculinum children will become nasty and uncontrollable when sick. They will kick, scream, hit and push their parents away. They are especially irritable in the morning. They have trouble getting to sleep. They wet the bed and have night sweats. They toss and turn in their sleep. They grind their teeth voraciously and bore their head into the pillow.

There is an impish quality to them. They will tease, and be coy and mischievous. These children have a strong fear of cats and/or dogs. They worry over the smallest details and have a fear of new situations. They are very afraid of being alone and of the dark.

They react very strongly to sugar and dairy products, which makes all their symptoms worse. They get frequent ear infections and bronchitis, and can have asthma. They crave cold milk and cured spicy meat.

Other Homeopathic Treatments You May Try

Other over-the-counter homeopathic products you may safely try at home are Tissue Salts (sometimes referred to as Cell Salts), see below, and Bach Flower Remedies, refer to Chapter 21.

Tissue Salts

Tissue salts were developed by the German doctor Wilhelm Schuessler, over 100 years ago. They are pharmacologically prepared in a similar fashion to homeopathic medicines, although they are much milder and their action much more subtle. They are made from mineral compounds, and when prescribed accurately will eliminate symptoms by restoring any deficiencies of these minerals in the body. They are safe to use in conjunction with other treatments, including homeopathic medicines and stimulant drugs. Tissue salts are dissolved under the tongue and must be taken 3 or 4 times a day for several months in chronic cases, and every hour until symptoms subside in acute cases.

There are a total of 12 tissue salts, but only a few are indicated in the treatment of children with attention deficit or behavioral problems. The following cell salts may be useful in the treatment of your child, however, when used on their own, the results will be very subtle. It is best to use these products in conjunction with other treatments, and it is very important to discuss what you are using at home with your homeopathic doctor. This enables the doctor to determine each product's effectiveness on your child.

Calcarea phosphorica

This is prescribed for children who have difficulty concentrating, and who may get headaches from the pressure of school work. It is excellent for improving the growth and nutrition of the blood, bones and teeth, and is often used for chronic growing pains, healing broken bones, delayed teething, and anemia. It is the most commonly used tissue salt for children.

Kali phosphoricum

This tissue salt is used as a nerve nutrient. It is used to sharpen memory and concentration in children who are very nervous and anxious. They will overreact, and cry or scream. They are impatient, talkative and fidgety. They are often depressed or irritable, and may get insomnia from worry. They may suffer from nervous exhaustion and become lazy and irritable.

Magnesia phosphorica

Magnesia phosphorica is very effective anti-spasmodic. It quickly calms muscle spasms, menstrual cramps, colic, stomach cramps, twitching, tics, headaches and even hiccups. It is well-prescribed for children who suffer from any of these symptoms, and who have trouble concentrating and are nervous. These children may also have trouble sleeping.

Finding a Homeopathic Doctor

All professional members of the associations listed below have had extensive education in classical homeopathic medicine. The purpose of these associations is to form a united body of professional homeopathic practitioners who provide safe, effective and professional homeopathic health care.

In the United States, membership with the National Center for Homeopathy ensures the homeopathic practitioner has been trained in classical homeopathy. The accreditation of C.H.C. identifies practitioners certified nationally by the Council for Homeopathic Certification in classical homeopathy, including clinical internship and medical science education.

In Canada, a consumer should identify a homeopathic doctor with the accreditation H.D. This ensures the practitioner has 4 years of postgraduate education in medical sciences, including 2000 hours of training in classical homeopathy and 1100 hours of clinical internship. This is the highest standard of homeopathic medical training in North America.

You may also search each state or province for a local homeopathic association.

To find an appropriately trained homeopathic doctor in your area, contact one of the associations listed below.

United States

National Center for Homeopathy
801 North Fairfax, Suite 306,
Alexandria, Virginia 22314
(703) 548-7790
Website: www.homeopatic.org

The Council For
Homeopathic Certification
1790 Seabright Avenue,
Santa Cruz, CA 95062
Website: http://www.healthy.net/chc

Canada

Ontario Homeopathic Association
6365 Yonge Street, Suite 202,
Toronto, Ontario, M2M 3X8
(416) 222-2995
Website: www.ontariohomeopath.com

Homeopathic Medical Council of
Canada
Website: www.hmcc.ca

21

Bach Flower Remedies

Stefan Ball
Dr. Edward Bach Foundation. UK

Origins of Bach Flower Remedies

In the 1920s a British doctor called Edward Bach began to look into the healing properties of flowers. Bach was already a well-known name in bacteriology and pathology and ran a successful research clinic and a Harley Street practice, but he felt dissatisfied with the treatments he could offer. Medicine was failing, he felt, because of its over-concentration on disease symptoms. He wanted to find medicines that could treat what he believed were the underlying causes of ill-health—stress, fear, and various kinds of personal and emotional conflict.

Using a mixture of intuition and trial and error, Bach prepared and tested hundreds of different flowers over a period of some eight years. He completed his system of 38 remedies, each made from spring water and a single flowering plant or tree, in 1935.

Bach died a year later, but his colleagues founded the Bach Centre at his home in Oxfordshire to carry on making remedies using his methods. From this small corner of England the system has spread all over the world. Bottles carrying Dr. Bach's signature still originate at the Bach Centre. Since the 1970s many new systems of flower essence have been created in imitation of Dr. Bach's work, but the original system remains the best-known and most accessible. Millions of people around the world use Bach Flower Remedies as a normal part of their day-to-day self-health care.

What Bach Flower Remedies do

Each flower remedy relates to a very specific negative mood or personality trait: Pine is used for guilt, Aspen for general, vague anxiety, and Wild Rose for apathy. For one of these negative states to arise there must be a lack of the corresponding positive quality, so if you are in a Wild Rose state you lack interest in and enthusiasm for what is going on around you. Dr. Bach believed the energy captured from each plant resonated with one of these suppressed positive qualities. Taking the right remedy brings out the associated quality, in the same way that sounding a string on one guitar can make the string of the same pitch vibrate on another. Taking a remedy you don't need has no effect because the corresponding positive quality is already present.

Research work carried out in Italy and published in *La Medicina Biologica* in 1999 has supported this view of how Bach Flower Remedies work. Doctors Rossi and Setti added different flower remedies to solutions of phyllosilicates and recorded the resulting changes in structure as the solutions crystallized. They found that each remedy would only affect some solutions, and that different remedies affected different types of solution. The remedies were not forcing change on the solutions from the outside. Instead they were co-operating with specific internal forces that were present in some phyllosilicates but not in others. In other words, the energy in a remedy helped to draw out specific properties that were in some solutions but not in others.

As for research into the remedies' effects on people, a Ph.D. thesis in California and various outcome studies in the UK and Italy have been positive, but the evidence is still largely anecdotal. Nevertheless, an increasing number of nurses, midwives and doctors rely on them as a natural and safe complement to their other therapies.

At least one of Dr. Bach's revolutionary claims, that emotional states are crucial to people's general well-being, is now accepted to the point of being medically commonplace. Researchers in psychoneuroimmunology – the study of the relationship between the nervous system and the immune system – have found that happy, balanced people get sick less often and recover sooner from illness and injury. By helping us take control of our feelings and enjoy a more fulfilling emotional life, Bach Flower Remedies can allow our bodies to find their own natural states of well-being and so have a direct impact on all kinds of health problems.

How to use Bach Flower Remedies

There are three ways of using Bach Flower Remedies. Most people first use them in a corrective way, for example, when a problem has already taken root, and usually when other approaches have failed or have not achieved the desired results. Users take a mix of remedies over a period of time, sometimes changing the mix as emotional layers are stripped away, until eventually they get back to their own personal equilibrium.

If good results happen and the problem gets better, people then move naturally to the second use, that of prevention. This involves taking one or two remedies for short periods of time, as negative moods arise. This allows them to stay more or less in balance all the time, so things don't get out of hand again. This was what Dr. Bach had in mind when he compared taking a remedy against fear to pulling a lettuce from the garden when we are hungry—it is natural and straightforward. It means taking *Olive*—the remedy for exhaustion—at the end of a hard day, or *Star of Bethlehem* when you have suffered a shock.

The third type of use can be described as evolutionary, and again comes about quite naturally as we think about our emotions and personalities as part of trying to select the right remedies. We learn more about how we feel, and this helps us to achieve a real sense of who we are and so contributes to our personal growth.

All three uses start with the basic idea of thinking about how we feel. Selecting remedies is as simple—and as difficult—as matching our moods to a mix of remedies. For full information on the subtleties of each remedy it's best to consult a good book on the subject, but the basic indications are given here as a guide.

Remedy	Emotional State
Agrimony	laughing and playing to avoid facing up to inner torment
Aspen	anxious or afraid but can't say why
Beech	intolerant and critical of other people and their lives
Centaury	likes to help, but can't say 'no' to stronger characters
Cerato	doesn't trust his or her own judgment, looks for reassurance
Cherry Plum	irrational and uncontrolled to the point of violence
Chestnut Bud	can't learn from his or her mistakes
Chicory	loves to be needed, so becomes intrusive and demanding
Clematis	doesn't pay attention, day-dreams
Crab Apple	dislikes his or her appearance, obsessive-compulsive behavior
Elm	overwhelmed by having too many things to cope with
Gentian	despondency after a setback
Gorse	pessimism, defeatism
Heather	self-obsessed, very talkative, incapable of listening
Holly	hatred, envy, jealousy, suspicion
Honeysuckle	regrets, homesickness, living in the past

Hornbeam	tired at the thought of doing something, procrastination
Impatiens	lacks patience, thinks and lives fast
Larch	lacks confidence in abilities
Mimulus	anxiety and fear for a specific reason, shyness
Mustard	feels depressed for no good reason
Oak	slow, methodical, refuses to give in
Olive	tired after some physical or emotional effort
Pine	guilt and self-blame
Red Chestnut	anxiety over the welfare of somebody else
Rock Rose	terror
Scleranthus	indecision when faced with two or more options
Rock Water	self-sacrifice in the name of perfection
Star of Bethlehem	shock
Sweet Chestnut	complete anguish and despair
Vervain	over-enthusiasm, always active
Vine	bullying, forcefulness
Walnut	protection against outside influences, adjustment to change
Water Violet	quiet, reserved, dignified people
White Chestnut	repetitive worrying thoughts
Wild Oat	lacks fulfillment, lacks direction in life
Wild Rose	apathetic, lacks enthusiasm
Willow	self-pity, resentment, bitterness

It you have trouble finding "your" emotion on the list of remedies, ask yourself why you feel the way you do. There is no specific remedy for anger, for example, but there are remedies for the different causes of anger— hatred, intolerance, impatience, resentment, injustice and so on. With a little thought it should soon be possible to come up with the correct remedy or mix of remedies.

For long-standing problems the best way to take remedies is in a personal dosage bottle. This is a 1 oz. (30 ml) glass bottle with a built-in dropper containing spring water and two drops of each selected remedy. You can buy the remedies and an empty bottle at any good health food store or pharmacy and put the mix together yourself. I recommend mixing together no more than seven remedies at once because if you take more you are probably including some you don't need. Once you have put together your dosage bottle take four drops of the mix at a time, four or more times a day.

When taking remedies for short-term problems there is no need to mix a dosage bottle. Instead add two drops of each remedy to a glass of water, and take sips at intervals until the feelings pass.

There is one ready-mixed combination of five remedies that can be used in emergencies and when there isn't time to make a careful selection. It isn't a cure-all but it can help calm things down in the short term. Sold as Rescue Remedy®, you can take it in a glass of water, in a dosage bottle, or neat on the tongue. The dosage in each case is four drops.

Bach Flower Remedies and ADD/ADHD

Attention deficit disorder and attention deficit hyperactivity disorder – ADD and ADHD – are diagnosed according to a list of behaviors. When we look at some of the symptoms we can easily start to match them to likely remedies.

Symptom	Possible Bach Flower Remedies
lack of attention to what is going on	• Clematis – daydreaming, mind on the future • White Chestnut – repetitive worries • Honeysuckle – mind in the past, homesickness
repeats mistakes	• Chestnut Bud – failure to learn from experience • Clematis – head in the clouds
inability to sustain attention at one task	• Impatiens – wants everything to happen fast • Walnut – distracted by outside influences
avoids or dislikes work assignments	• Wild Rose – apathetic, disinterested • Hornbeam – puts things off, tired at the thought of doing something
always active, can't stay still	• Vervain – uncontrolled enthusiasm • Impatiens – trying to do things too quickly
excessive talking and interrupting others	• Heather – overwhelming need to talk to people • Beech – need to criticize • Chicory – wants respect and a show of affection • Vine – wants to dominate and dictate things

This table gives a starting point, but everyone is an individual and you should always select remedies on that basis. Your child's inability to concentrate could be due to a Clematis state, but other possible causes include bullying, lack of confidence, and poor self-image, and each would lead to the selection of a different remedy: Mimulus, Larch, Crab Apple. Some people might avoid work assignments because they are in a Wild Rose state, but others might dislike the type of work assignment set. For example, Impatiens and Water Violet people will both dislike group work.

Bach Flower Remedies are a holistic system, while ADD and ADHD are reductionist labels put on collections of symptoms. If you want to use the remedies well you need to look past the labels at the human being they conceal. You need to identify with his or her specific and personal needs.

Sometimes this can be painful for care-givers, because we may have to accept that we are ourselves part of the problem. The Chicory child who climbs the walls to attract attention may be genuinely starved of attention, and if this is the case giving her a remedy is not the answer. Taking a remedy ourselves might be.

Contraindications

The remedies are preserved in 27 per cent proof brandy, and because of the alcohol content they should always be diluted when given to children. Adults with an alcohol problem, especially those taking drugs to help them stop drinking, should seek medical advice before using the remedies. For most people the alcohol need not be an issue, however, because if you are taking a mix from a dosage bottle the amount of alcohol you consume is about the same as you would get from eating a ripe banana.

Aside from the alcohol there are no problems taking the remedies along-side other medicines, both complementary or orthodox. Most people using flower remedies to address the emotional aspects of a medical or psychological problem will also use other more physically-orientated techniques as a complementary treatment.

Finding a practitioner

Bach Flower Remedies are primarily designed for self-help. Bach included the least possible number of remedies in his system, hoping in this way to make it easy for people to use. Most people can make a start simply by reading a book and matching the way they feel to the correct remedies. Nevertheless, it can be difficult to identify emotions when we are too involved in a situation, so whether we are treating our own ADHD symptoms or trying to help our children it can be helpful to have an objective person guide us through the system. This is where a Bach practitioner can help.

Practitioners are trained to think about different human situations and behaviors in terms of remedy indications. A consultation should be a straightforward process in which you are encouraged to talk through your feelings. If you are seeking help for your child you may be asked to sit at a distance for a time while the practitioner listens to the child. After about an hour the practitioner will mix up a bottle of remedies for you, or tell you where you can obtain them. Don't be afraid to ask what remedies are in the bottle—a good practitioner will be happy to tell you this because it helps you learn for yourself how the system works. If you don't think one of the remedies is a good choice, say so, but at the same time be honest with yourself. There is no disgrace in needing a "negative" remedy. We all go through all of the 38 base negative states at some point in our lives.

If you need help finding a practitioner contact the Dr. Edward Bach Foundation, the Bach Centre's registering organization. The Foundation holds a register of practitioners working in 35 countries around the world. Practitioners using the letters BFRP (Bach Foundation Registered Practitioner) have completed a rigorous training course and work under strict Code of Practice.

The Dr. Edward Bach Foundation

The Bach Centre   Tel: 00 44 1491 834678
Mount Vernon   Fax: 00 44 1491 825022
Bakers Lane   E-mail: mail@bachcentre.com
Sotwell, Oxon OX1 0PZ   WWW: www.bachcentre.com
UK

The Benefits of Exercise for ADD and Hyperactive Children and Adults

Daniel Tamin

The 2 million Americans living with attention deficit-hyperactivity disorder struggle with a variety of symptoms which cause considerable suffering in the lives of those it afflicts. While there are many conventional and non-conventional methods with which to treat the disorder, most are passive. While passive—namely medical—methods can be effective to a certain extent, they do not go far enough in addressing all the needs of ADHD patients. Active methods involving exercise and/or physical activity hold great potential in assisting those dealing with ADD/ADHD.

While there are many indications of the presence of ADD/ADHD , there are three which are of greatest significance:

Inattention. People who are inattentive have a hard time keeping their minds on any one thing and may get bored with a task after only a few minutes. They may give effortless, automatic attention to activities and subjects they enjoy. However, focusing deliberate, conscious attention on organizing and completing a task they don't enjoy, or learning something new in which they aren't interested, is difficult. This inability to focus on activities and subjects that don't interest them impacts their capacity for study and time management. They are unlikely to excel academically, and as adults may have difficulty holding down a job.

Hyperactivity. People who are hyperactive always seem to be in motion. They cannot sit still and may dash around or talk incessantly. Hyperactive people squirm in their chairs or roam around the room. Or they might jiggle their feet, touch everything, or noisily tap their pencil.

Hyperactive teens and adults may feel intensely restless. They may be fidgety or try to do several things at once, bouncing around from one activity to the next.

Impulsivity. People who are overly impulsive seem unable to curb their immediate reactions or think before they act. As a result they may blurt out inappropriate comments or they may run into the street without looking. Their impulsivity may make it hard for them to wait for things they want, or to take their turn at games. They may grab toys from other children or strike out.

These symptoms can be treated, to a degree, with medication. Unfortunately, when people see immediate improvement, they often think that medication is all that's needed. Medications, however, do not cure the disorder, but only temporarily control the symptoms. Although the drugs help people pay better attention and complete their work, they do not enhance overall lifestyle. The drugs alone cannot help people feel better about themselves or cope with the many problems associated with ADHD. These require other kinds of treatment and support.

Sports and exercise are the next step in controlling the effects of ADHD. While medication may be necessary in some cases to control the effects of ADHD, as many as 20% of ADHD patients may experience side effects such as increased heart rate and blood pressure, stomach aches, headaches, irritability, decreased appetite, and sleep problems with the onset of usage, and moodiness, depression, tics, and mild social withdrawal with continued use. Yet, there are many benefits enjoyed by people who get regular physical activity.

According to the National Institute of Health, a mild regimen of daily exercise resulted in helping patients cope with stress, improve self-image, increase resistance to fatigue, counter anxiety and depression, relax and feel less tense, improve the ability to fall asleep quickly and sleep well, and provided an easy way to share activities with friends or family and an opportunity to meet new people. Exercise can help to negate the effects of medications, which, as already stated, cause side effects such as insomnia and irritability. Exercise also allows the release of energy in a focused environment. In a study conducted on children with ADHD, results showed that physical exercise contributed to improvements in disruptive behavior, with running and callisthenics having the greatest effect. This improvement resulted from a release of the hyperactive tendencies during exercise.

While not a cure, regular physical activity increases fitness and, if undertaken appropriately, can result in a decrease of ADD/ADHD symptoms. The inability to participate in work or recreational activities can be a handicap for children and adults alike. Many of the problems facing people dealing with the effects of ADHD revolved around their inability to sustain social and personal order in their lives. While medication may be the first step in controlling ADHD impulses, this alone does not lead an individual out of the ostracism that often accompanies those affected. Reducing the effects of ADD/ADHD through physical activity results in many intangible benefits.

Exercise aids in overcoming the physical effects of ADHD such as hyperactivity and impulsitivity by placating these influence in a proactive and positive manner. In this way, patients are able to gain both self confidence and social skills. In children affected by ADHD, participating with other children in physical activities, be it on the playground or in a gymnasium, allows for confidence-building and the building of friendships. For adults, gaining the discipline to focus their impulses towards physical activity allows them to lead active and full lives in both their professional as well as their personal lives.

Preliminary studies indicate that exercise improves self-esteem, confidence, and psychological and physical fitness. Beyond that, people who exercise have increased latency and decreased motor impersistence, assisting them in the process of participating with others on an equal basis without having the effects of ADHD interfere in their lives.

Today, with proper treatment, those affected by ADHD are able to live happier more productive lives, and participate actively in their communities.

The Benefits of Swimming for ADD and Hyperactive Children and Adults

Kyle Brownell

    I have been involved in aquatics as an instructor/lifeguard for the past six and a half years. During this time I have worked with many children both in integrated classes and in private lessons. Children with attention deficit disorder (ADD) and attention deficit hyperactivity (ADHD) disorder have special needs but are usually taught in integrated classes. Many ADD/Hyperactive children have high levels of energy but difficulty focusing their concentration. Any sport or physical activity can be very beneficial in aiding the release of the stored energy. Swimming happens to be one of the best activities for ADD/Hyperactive children. It is both healthy and safe. Swimming is an important agent which can aid in the calming of ADD/Hyperactive children.

    The instructor for ADD/Hyperactive children needs to be experienced in order to teach them in an integrated class. Often, ADD/Hyperactive learners become easily distracted by the other class members. Well-planned classes will create calmer and more focused swimmers. Parents report that not only do the children want to come to the pool, but that there is a connection between the focus on swimming and the focus on other activities. Some parents say that swimming has resulted in a reduced need for medication.

    Swimming is a unique activity. Unlike other forms of physical activity, swimming allows the ADD/Hyperactive child to keep his or her attention focused on the task provided by the instructor. In swimming, unlike other sports, there is little time for socializing between students, and there are not many distracters at the bottom of the pool. The children must stay concentrated on swimming because if they stop thinking about finishing (the length), they will stop swimming and sink. This provides swimmers with a goal (e.g. a length of the pool) which they are able to stay focused on and accomplish. As they progress though the various swimming levels, the amount of swimming distance increases, thus increasing the length of time they are concentrating on their task. This undoubtedly will transfer to other avenues of their lives by expanding their length of concentration.

I became interested in the special skills necessary to assist ADD/Hyperactive children. There is no protocol for dealing with them in terms of swimming instructions, but during my first year of teaching I learned very quickly how to relate to ADD/Hyperactive children. The trick is to have well-structured lessons which use routines the children become accustomed to. This is comforting for the children because they know what is going to happen. You would expect that this may cause boredom for ADD/Hyperactive children, but on the contrary, most ADD/Hyperactive children thrive in this type of environment even more so than non-ADD/Hyperactive children do. Giving them an itinerary for the next three skills ahead also allows them to prepare for the next set of challenges.

One of the most difficult subjects to teach an ADD/Hyperactive child is water safety, as they normally are disinterested in this. One tool I use and find very effective in teaching water safety for all children is game-playing. The instructor asks a question relating to water safety, e.g. "What do you bring in a boat?" The child who answers first is allowed to perform the skill. This continues until the last child is on his or her way. This keeps the children attentive through the competition of answering questions, and also provides them with the opportunity of hearing what other children are thinking on that topic.

There are many opportunities for ADD/Hyperactive children to be distracted, which normally leads them and others into trouble while they are waiting for the rest of the class to finish the skill. The way to avoid this distraction time is to fill it with simple skills, such as front floating or attempting a perfect handstand. This provides the children a skill in which they are competing against themselves and can always improve. It is imperative that the instructor ask how they are doing, and whether they have finished the skill. This shows the children that the instructor is not just filling time, but is legitimately interested in their performance of that skill. This inspires them to try even harder to improve. Building the feeling of self-confidence often lacking in ADD/Hyperactive children is a major goal.

One of the potential benefits for ADD/Hyperactive children participating in swimming lessons is the learning of a life-saving skill. Learning to swim can save a child's life or that of a friend. This above all else should lead parents to enroll their children in swimming lessons. Most parents feel a lot more comfortable allowing their child to go to a cottage, or go boating or fishing, knowing that their child can swim. This has potential psychological benefits for both the child and parent by reducing anxiety levels. Although municipal pools are well-run, there is a surprising lack of supervision at private pools. Children who can swim feel a lot more confident when water activities are involved, because they also know their swimming abilities and limits. They are taught to make wise choices through the Red Cross program.

The long-term benefits of physical fitness are endless, running from the reduction of bone and muscle loss to the reproduction of brain cells, according to a recent scientific study. Physical fitness may reduce the chance of heart disease and stroke. Swimming is a physical activity that can continue for a person's entire life, and provide a high cardiovascular work out with little to no impact on joints. It is this stress on joints that normally causes people to stop other forms of cardiovascular activities such as running.

Swimming also provides a social setting in which children can meet new people, which is beneficial mentally and spiritually. In this day and age of sports and sports equipment costing parents thousands of dollars, swimming is still one of the most economical participatory sports, as most municipalities offer most swimming programs at quite a reasonable cost. Competitive swimming is one of the cheapest competitive sports there are for both coaching and equipment. Inclusion in class is good for both ADD/Hyperactive children and non-ADD/Hyperactive children. The ADD/Hyperactive children feel more a part of the group and more ordinary, which is so important for young people. It also teaches the others to respect the efforts and success of those who have a greater mountain to climb.

Note: Swimming instructors with lifesaving certification are the recommended choice when looking for a swimming instructor for ADD/Hyperactive individuals.

Section Four

Tools That Empower™ Teachers, Parents and ADD/Hyperactive Children and Adults

Psychological and Other Choices

"A child's spirit is like a child, you can never catch it by running after it: you must stand still, and, for love, it will soon itself come back."
— Arthur Miller, *The Crucible*

24
Neurofeedback for ADD/Hyperactivity

Lynda Thompson, Ph.D., The ADD Center

Imagine a learning technique that makes it possible for people who have trouble paying attention to finally concentrate. It is a kind of learning—called operant conditioning by psychologists—and nothing is done beyond giving them information about their moment-to-moment brain wave activity using game-like displays on a computer. This method of improving concentration involves no drugs or invasive procedures. This technique, called neurofeedback or EEG biofeedback, produces a lasting change in people's ability to focus, to organize their thinking and materials, and even to read or listen without their thoughts drifting. Those who are restless, fidgety, impulsive or hyperactive become calmer.

This learning, which involves a kind of exercise for the brain, helps people stay focused while meeting the demands of boring daily routines. Without it they can concentrate only on things that interest them, or when there is either a payoff or a threat to motivate them. Children with ADD usually have superb concentration for video games, television, or other things they choose to do, and parents may not understand why they cannot focus that way when doing school work. Yet with this learning, both getting down to chores and following through becomes easier for them.

When doing neurofeedback, you monitor a person's brain waves using sensors that sit on the head with a dab of gel. A computer gives information about what brain waves are being produced. Using that information, called feedback, people can learn to modify their own brain waves. Changing immature brain wave patterns—getting them to shift toward a more mature pattern—produces a relaxed yet focused mental state. This empowers the person with ADHD symptoms to do things that were previously very difficult for them. They get better at a variety of things, ranging from doing homework without prompts or arguments, through to keeping their focus in sports. The results with this technique have been published in scientific journals and written about in a few books, and they are uniformly positive, that is, no negative side effects have been reported.

More research, including studies that have placebo controls, will help the field of neurofeedback gain even more scientific credibility. In the meantime, demand is growing because of the results that are observed. Those results are impressive. Changes with neurofeedback include improved academic performance, higher intellectual performance (measured by increases in IQ scores), and decreased ADHD symptoms. On standardized computer administered tests like the Test of Variables of Attention (TOVA), researchers have found improved attention, decreased impulsivity, and faster, steadier reaction times. You can look at the published results in a number of journal articles and books—some are listed in Appendix D, Bibliography/End Notes and Recommended Reading.

You can hear about the latest research and applications of neurofeedback at conferences, including those held by the Association for Applied Psychophysiology and Biofeedback, the Society for Neuronal Regulation, or at the more informal Winter Brain Meeting organized by Futurehealth. Since 1996, there has been separate accreditation for practitioners of EEG biofeedback through the Biofeedback Certification Institute of America. You can check the web sites of these organizations and find references for selected articles about neurofeedback using the listings at the end of this chapter.

To give you the flavor of this exciting field, here is an example of results obtained with one student at our ADD Center. A few years ago a father phoned us about his teenage son. The family lived about a three-hour drive away in New York state, yet this dad was willing to make the trip in order to find a way to help his son do better in school without the use of stimulant drugs. The boy had been on Ritalin for some time, and though he was fortunate in not suffering too many side effects, his father worried that it might affect his growth or have some unforeseen effects in the future. By the time this teenager had done 20 one-hour sessions of neurofeedback training, he was totally off medication. By the time he had completed 40 sessions, his father reported that he no longer had to sit with him every night to get homework done. In addition, the marks gradually moved up from the 80's to 90's. What really delighted the father was the unexpected bonus of his son becoming a top wrestler in inter-school competitions. Though he had always shown talent, he used to lose to inferior wrestlers because he lost his focus. Now he was consistently winning his matches! The following year he led his football team to a championship.

This student's improved results caught the attention of his teachers, administrators at his high school, and even the superintendent of schools. The superintendent took the initiative of investigating what neurofeedback was about, coming with some of his professional staff to the ADD Center and seeing his own brain waves on the computer screen. When he saw that he could control a computer game by maintaining his concentration—he focused on trying to remember and recite the Greek alphabet—he became intrigued. Now he is spearheading a group of professionals (educators, psychologists and doctors) who are working to get funding so they can implement a project to put neurofeedback training into schools in their district. They will be following in the footsteps of others who have put this training into schools in Minneapolis, Minnesota, and Yonkers, New York.

In Yonkers, the neurofeedback program began after the dynamic vice-principal of the Enrico Fermi School, Linda Vergara, saw the benefits with her own child. She had refused to use drugs to treat her son, though that is what was recommended when he was diagnosed with ADHD. Instead she tried neurofeedback, going to a psychologist in New York. Delighted with the changes, such as mornings being less of a hassle and her son starting his homework without being asked, she wanted it for her students as well.

Visiting her school in the spring of 1998, she told me that student attendance had improved among those receiving neurofeedback. The students' parents and teachers were happy with the results, and the school was saving money because the children required less in the way of intense special education and behavioral programs. Since then, the school district has increased the budget for neurofeedback at Linda's school and put it into two more schools. They are riding the wave of the future as people realize that empowering students through neurofeedback—having them learn the skill of being calm and concentrating at will—is both cost effective and good for self-esteem.

Let's now look at who benefits from EEG biofeedback, how assessment and training are done, the history and scientific basis of the field, plus how you can go about finding a practitioner and what your investment will be if you decide that this approach seems right for you or your child.

Good Candidates for Neurofeedback Training — Those with True ADD

The easiest clients to deal with and the best responders to neurofeedback are the bright daydreamers whose main complaint is academic underachievement. This is also the group who have the poorest response to medication, the group with the least research done on them, and the ones who are often diagnosed later in life because people, for the most part, considered them lazy or unmotivated and did not realize there was an underlying problem with attention. Often they are female. The formal diagnosis would be ADHD: Inattentive Type.

As a brief aside on diagnosis, the core symptoms have always centered around inattention, impulsivity and, in some cases, hyperactivity. Thus the most recent (1994) classification scheme in the Diagnostic and Statistical Manual of the American Psychiatric Association (DSM-IV) outlines three sub-types of Attention-Deficit/Hyperactivity Disorder: Inattentive Type, Hyperactive-Impulsive Type, and Combined Type. The diagnosis used in the earlier DSM-III was Attention Deficit Disorder, with or without Hyperactivity. In practice, people use ADD, ADHD or even ADD/ADHD as acronyms for this constellation of traits. (DSM-IV on pages 33-35)

Whatever you call it, here are some important ideas to keep in mind. In the first place, it is not really a disorder, but a difference. People with this diagnosis pay attention differently and there are also differences in their brain function. The EEG shows more slow wave activity in central and frontal locations. PET scans show decreased metabolism in the frontal region. SPECT scans show less blood flow to the frontal region, especially when the person is stressed, for example, by being asked to do math calculations. This makes sense in terms of the symptoms because it is the frontal region of the brain that is involved in the executive functions that include planning, inhibiting what is inappropriate, and problem solving. Being different is not necessarily bad and there are many wonderful traits observed in association with being more in your own world (which parallels having more slow wave activity): spontaneity, creativity, a good sense of humor, and great persistence when keen on something. If we called these traits the Edison Syndrome in honor of Thomas Edison, instead of Attention Deficit Disorder, then people would be reminded of the positive instead of the bothersome aspects of this style.

Second, it is not a deficit in attention because attention is superb for things the person with ADD is interested in. They only appear deficient in attention when someone (like a parent or teacher) wants them to pay attention to something they find boring or slow paced. Just like Tom Sawyer, they may have trouble staying seated in the classroom, but they will happily sit still for hours when fishing. As first discovered when doing my doctoral research in Toronto at the Neuropsychology Research Unit of the Hospital for Sick Children, boys diagnosed with ADD make great goalies. It was the favorite position among the hockey playing boys in my study of hyperactive children. The goalie with ADD may daydream or skate aimlessly when the action is at the other end of the ice, but as soon as the puck crosses the blue line he is in hyper-focus and not even screaming fans can ruin his concentration. Parents are delighted when their goalie makes a great save, but they get frustrated when the same hyper-focus translates into being glued to the TV and they have to call him ten times before he finally comes for dinner.

Attention can shift from scanning mode to hyper-focus when a person gets interested in something. Thom Hartmann likens this to a hunter who looks for something to go after and then locks on when he finds his prey. The term "Hunter Mind," as contrasted with "Farmer Mind" (for those who do well with daily routines), is a wonderful gift that Thom has given to this field, not just because it is an apt analogy, but because it lets people with ADD realize that their style of reacting to the world has merit and value. They just have to learn to harness their energy and use these traits to their advantage. As adults they may be very successful in sales or as entrepreneurs. With today's technology for monitoring brain waves, they can learn how to concentrate like a "Farmer" through neurofeedback, and can then have a full range of attention: from scanning, through to attention to boring details, and on to hyper-focus.

Most people with the symptoms of ADHD are potential candidates for neurofeedback. There cannot, however, be a guarantee of success with any individual client because there are many factors involved. Children, teenagers and adults can benefit from neurofeedback. Most clients are school age (though clients at the ADD Center have ranged in age from 4 to 63.) Client selection is very important because some people with the symptoms have other problems as well and those other difficulties might interfere with a good response.

Dr. Joel Lubar and his wife Judy, a psychologist and social worker respectively, have worked using neurofeedback for over twenty-five years in Knoxville Tennessee where Joel is a Professor at the University of Tennessee. Their guidelines for excluding clients include drug abuse, primary depression, too young for treatment, low intelligence and dysfunctional families. Consideration must be given to the fact that students may be inattentive for reasons other than ADD/ADHD, so you have to make sure that you are dealing with true neurologically based differences in attention before applying neurofeedback. Examples of non-ADHD tuning out would include someone who becomes inattentive in class because the work is beyond their comprehension, or someone who does not have the emotional energy to pay attention. This might be the case if parents were getting a divorce, if a child was abused, if a family member were very sick, or there was a recent death in the family

There are other instances where problems other than ADD/ADHD co-exist and the person is still a good candidate for training, though training may take more sessions. The most common co-existing problem is learning disabilities. It is much easier to address and remediate learning disabilities when a person can concentrate, so neurofeedback can be an especially important intervention for this group. Others who benefit are those who have attentional problems along with Tourette's Syndrome, closed head injury, seizure disorders, Asperger's Syndrome, and even high functioning autism. Each of these may also be associated with tension, anxiety and some emotional and behavioral lability. For these co-morbidities there is a growing body of anecdotal evidence for improvements during their neurofeedback (NFB) training for improving attention span and decreasing impulsivity. However, this evidence has not, at the time of writing, been organized and published, so neurofeedback is still considered an experimental intervention for these disorders.

Only a small number of the students seen at our center have serious behavior problems. (This is perhaps because it is the motivated parent who has been on the look-out for ways to help their child who is more likely to find out about neurofeedback and invest in it.) In many publicly funded clinic settings, however, there are high rates of ADHD combined with Oppositional Defiant Disorder or even the more serious Conduct Disorder. The prognosis for these children is not particularly good with any intervention. Although their self esteem and self confidence improves during neurofeedback, the behavioral problems are a reflection of psychological difficulties and often result from family problems or poor management techniques used at school or in the home. The improvements observed during NFB training sessions may not generalize to home and school unless these psychological and family problems are also addressed. These should be dealt with by appropriate professionals preferably before NFB training begins.

In the brochure from the ADD Center a list of six appropriate groups of candidates are given, along with an objective for training with that group:

1. **Gifted yet Underachieving:**
   Gain a consistent, calm, relaxed-yet-alert, highly-focused state. Learn to concentrate even when work is boring.

2. **Attention Difficulties:**
   Learn to focus for extended periods of time and to reflect and organize your thoughts before responding.

3. **Specific Learning Weaknesses:**
   Improve Reading, Math, Sequencing, Writing, Visual-Perceptual functioning.

4. **Tense/Anxious:**
   Learn to control the physiological indicators of tension. A relaxed but alert state improves all aspects of learning.

5. **Special Problems:**
   Head Injuries: A special 19 lead assessment shows affected areas of the brain and indicates parameters to be used in assisting the brain towards normalization.

- Seizure Disorders: Although relatively unknown in Canada, research beginning in the early 1970s at UCLA led to this being the first use of EEG biofeedback.
- Tourette's Syndrome: EEG Biofeedback leads to improved attention span and may also lead to a decrease in tics.

6. **Athletes:**
   Improve mental flexibility and focus. Top performance requires specific mind/body states.

How Neurofeedback Is Done

Neurofeedback involves making changes to improve brain function so you need to check what a person's typical brain wave pattern is before you start. Thus the first step after the diagnosis of ADD (which is made on the basis of clinical interviews and questionnaires, supported by standardized scores from continuous performance tests and from psychological testing) is to look at the brain wave activity to determine what frequencies to train and where. As noted above, the brain wave pattern found in most people with ADD is excess slow wave activity in the frontal and central area. Note that there are many sub-types, though this chapter is not concerned with all the fine details that a practitioner must know.

The EEG (electroencephalogram) is a measure of electrical activity produced by the brain. Brain waves are described according to the frequencies of the brain waves, that is, how many cycles per second, measured in Hertz (Hz), and also according to their amplitude, expressed in terms of power (measured in picowatts) which is the square of the electric potential (measured in microvolts.) The brain waves that are of interest when doing neurofeedback with students who have ADD are usually the frequencies between 4 and 20 Hz. Slow Theta waves (4 to 7 Hz) indicate an inner state that is rather like going to sleep. Your mind drifts and you are not paying attention to anything in particular. Next are Alpha waves in the 8 to 12 Hz range and they, too, are considered slow waves. They reflect a resting state in the brain rather than activation. You also find alpha activity dominant during some kinds of meditation, and it is increased artificially by marijuana use. Starting around 12 Hz you have fast wave activity that is associated with activation. The 12 to 15 Hz frequency band is called Sensorimotor Rhythm. When it is being produced a person will be still (inhibiting movement or impulsive behavior), and will pay less attention to sensory input. This means that increasing SMR is very helpful for those who are physically restless or impulsive, including those who are verbally hyperactive and blurt things out without thinking. The fastest brain waves that are trained are called Beta, and occur in the 16 to 20 Hz range. If the child is working out a problem or actively reading or listening, you would see quite a bit of these faster waves. Brain waves thus reflect what a person's brain is doing moment to moment.

The location where they are measured is also important. A simple quantitative EEG (QEEG) can be done with an electrode picking up information from the top of the head (a location known as CZ in the international 10-20 electrode placement system) and sensors on each ear lobe. This is considered sufficient by most practitioners for much of the work done with people diagnosed as ADD. A full cap assessment, using at least 19 electrodes placed all around the head, can be used for complex cases or whenever the full picture is desired. The 19 lead/full cap process obviously gives more information, but also adds a lot to the cost since it takes much more time to do (at least an hour, and often more, compared with about 15 minutes for the basic 3-lead QEEG.) Its interpretation also takes a lot of time and most often a professional service is used to read and interpret the huge amount of data collected. This adds at least $400 (U.S.) to the initial assessment, and it can be much more depending on where it is sent for expert interpretation and comparison with a database. It is also more of an ordeal for the child since one must sit fairly still for the better part of an hour.

Once the practitioner has decided on the frequencies to train and at what locations, the client begins his or her training sessions. Schedules can vary, but a common practice is to see a client at least twice a week initially. Training is painless and simply involves the electrodes being placed on the head and ear lobes with a bit of conductive gel in the cup of each sensor. The tiny electrode, which is about the size of the nail on your baby finger, is placed on a site that has first been cleaned with a mildly abrasive solution rubbed on with a finger or a Q-tip. One eight-year-old client compared that part of the procedure to his cat licking his ear—a good comparison because it feels wet and a little rough. The electrodes have slender wires attached and the electrical activity from the head travels along them and into an EEG amplifier which analyses the signal and sends the information to a computer. The computer then displays the information in a way that lets the client learn to maintain concentration and to recognize when they have drifted off.

The method of learning known as neurofeedback is based on the principle that actions that are rewarded are more likely to occur again. Psychologists call this operant conditioning. The way to reward the brain wave pattern that you want to increase is to reward the person through games that work when the person produces that pattern. Things move on the screen (perhaps progress is made through a maze or an animation comes to life) and there are sounds or music when the person is getting it right. For those with ADD, getting it right means less slow wave activity and more fast wave activity. They are activating the areas of the brain needed to inhibit movement and to do some really focused thinking. In addition to this immediate feedback from the computer, at our center we reward the children with tokens when they are working well during each session. They can save up the tokens and exchange them for prizes. We know that little "Hunter" minds like to go after something. The prizes help keep them motivated until they have done enough training to start seeing results in everyday life.

Things to Combine with Neurofeedback

The other thing we add to the feedback is some coaching in learning strategies. Once the person is paying attention for longer periods of time, he or she practices maintaining that attention while they are reading or doing math, or perhaps, working on their time management plan. This helps, we think, to transfer their ability to concentrate to situations in everyday life, such as working in the classroom or at the office.

Neurofeedback can and should be combined with other approaches. You always want to pay attention to the Big Three: diet, sleep and exercise. The food one eats can either improve or worsen the symptoms. For details, look at the chapter entitled "Feeding the Child with ADD" in *The ADD Book: New Understandings, New Approaches to Parenting Your Child* which I co-authored with pediatrician William Sears. There you will find topics that include the best breakfast food for the brain (you need to balance complex carbohydrates and proteins) and comments on the food-mood connection. Watch out, for example, for sugar highs followed by sugar lows. Bill's latest book is *The Family Nutrition Book* and it goes into greater detail on the subject. Section 2 in this book covers diet, nutrition, and additional information on this topic.

Getting a good night's sleep is just plain common sense for the person with ADD because being sleepy is associated with theta waves, and the marker for poor attention is too much theta in the EEG. So if you are tired it is a double whammy—you increase still further the waves you already have in abundance. Though good sleep hygiene appeals to common sense, it is not necessarily common practice, especially with teenagers.

Exercise falls into the same category. It just makes sense to do something productive with the energy if a person has the high activity kind of ADD and it is a good way to ward off depression in the lethargic type. Sports and exercise are also a good way to increase oxygen to the brain.

A good educational setting is of utmost importance, with the most important component being a teacher who treats the child with respect and understanding. Medications can be combined with neurofeedback, and this combination may be both necessary and desirable in cases of extreme hyperactivity. If stimulant medication is being taken when training begins, be sure to inform the physician who will want to monitor the dose. In many cases, it will be possible to reduce the amount of medication as the person learns to self-regulate with neurofeedback. In a series of 111 clients tracked at the ADD Center, 30% of the children were taking medication when they began, and the use of Ritalin medication was eliminated in about 80% of these cases by the time they reached 40 sessions of training. Indeed, only one of the 29 originally taking the drug was on the same dose when retested, and 28/29 had reduced the dose or were off drugs entirely. By far, the majority of our clients decide on neurofeedback training either instead of trying drug approaches in the first place, or because they experienced unacceptable side-effects on stimulants.

Although it takes time (about five months at the rate of two sessions per week, longer if the child has complex or severe symptoms that benefit from more than 40 sessions) and costs money, parents often says it is the best investment they ever made in their child. One grandparent, as he wrote a check for his grandson's training said, "I had planned to spend money on his university studies, but if we don't do this now, he'll never get to university." If you are building a solid bridge to the future for your child, neurofeedback can provide the keystone of that foundation.

The History of Neurofeedback

Although the first publications about the EEG in humans was published in the 1920's by German physician Hans Berger, it was not until the 1970's that neurofeedback developed as a treatment for disorders and not until the 1990's that it became more widely available. The field had to wait for fast and less expensive computers before it could grow outside the research labs.

There are two lines of EEG research that converge on the practice of neurofeedback. One line comes from scientists like Dr. Barry Sterman, now a Professor Emeritus at UCLA. He was the first to establish that brain waves could be operantly conditioned, that is, increased or decreased according to what was rewarded. Starting with basic experiments with cats in 1965 and publishing results in 1967, Sterman was the first to identify some unique characteristics associated with brain waves at 12 -15 Hz. He named those frequencies Sensorimotor Rhythm or SMR because that activity was most easily measured across the sensori-motor strip of the brain (from ear to ear across the top of the head), and because these waves seemed to reflect both sensory and motor activity.

In another series of experiments, he discovered that cats who had been trained to increase the SMR brain waves were resistant to seizures. Sterman and others like him, including Joel Lubar, had pure science backgrounds and were initially doing animal studies. But the observations regarding decreased seizure activity led to SMR training being applied to people who had seizure disorders. Dr. Joel Lubar and others continued the research with children who had ADD and ADHD, but no seizure disorders. Sure enough, with training to increase SMR, their hyperactivity was reduced. Since the publication of the first results with a hyperactive child in 1976, Dr. Lubar, a Professor at the University of Tennessee, and health professionals at other centers have continued to study ways in which neurofeedback can help people learn self-regulation and reduce their ADD symptoms.

The second line of EEG research was not focused on animal studies but, rather, was looking at questions of human consciousness. Dr. Joe Kamiya is a pioneer in this area. He is the psychologist who first studied the mental states associated with alpha waves, and he demonstrated back in 1958 that a person could recognize when they were in an alpha state, even though they could not say how they produced it. Dr. Thomas Budzynski, an engineer turned psychologist who now works at the University of Washington, investigated how to improve learning during "twilight states" and, along with other biofeedback researchers like Elmer Green, was among those who founded the Biofeedback Research Society in 1968. This group became the Association for Applied Psychophysiology and biofeedback. Currently Dr. Budzynski is working on projects that include brain brightening for the elderly using neurofeedback.

Today, when we work with people who want to improve their focus and concentration, we are building on both traditions. They learn through the computerized feedback how to produce and maintain more fast wave activity, that is, how to pay attention to paying attention, and how to become aware of when they drift off into Alpha or Theta. If they want to relax or be creative, Alpha and Theta are good zones to be in. If there is work to be done, they can shift gears and reduce those slow waves.

In the 1990s, smaller EEG equipment was developed and personal computers became cheaper and more powerful so that neurofeedback became a technique that can be used not just in university research centers, but also in psychologists' offices and schools. One of the most common applications is to improve attention problems. More information is available to the public all the time; for example, a readable and informative book "that chronicles the history, struggles and promise of neurofeedback" (as noted on the book jacket) is *A Symphony in the Brain* by Jim Robbins. With even more advances in brain research and technology, the availability of this service should increase. With more practitioners entering the field, it will become easier for parents to find service for their children and easier for adults diagnosed with ADD to learn self-regulation and thereby reach their potential.

How to find a Practitioner

Although the research supporting neurofeedback goes back over twenty-five years, there were relatively few practitioners until the 1990s. The equipment was expensive and there were few sources of training. More powerful, cheaper computers could better handle the huge amounts of data

and myriad calculations required to transform the electrical information
about brain waves into something meaningful on the computer screen. As
we start into the new millennium, there are at least a thousand neurofeedback practitioners around the globe.

Neurofeedback should be carried out by a person who has had extensive hands-on supervised experience with the equipment and who has some
knowledge of how the brain works. The academic background of the trainer
or coach will differ depending on the tasks taken on. For example, teachers
and post-graduate students who are talented coaches may be the preferred
trainers for students who have ADD. For the initial assessment, someone
such as a psychologist with broader training is desirable. Psychologists may
be the preferred choice as therapists or supervisors when NFB is used with
clients who have complex symptoms or some associated disorder in addition
to ADD. For the most part, neurofeedback is a learning technique and thus
an educational intervention rather than therapy. One way of ascertaining
whether a practitioner has had sufficient training is the BCIA certification.
The Biofeedback Certification Institute of America provides certification
that is based on academic learning, practical experience, supervision, and a
rigorous written exam. However, not all competent professionals choose to
take this examination. There are some old-timers in the field who have used
neurofeedback since before the BCIA certification became available.

In the final analysis, there is nothing better than going for an initial
interview and making your own assessment just as you would do when
choosing any professional whether it be a lawyer, a doctor, or a mechanic.
You should not be hesitant about asking questions because qualified people
are happy to share the information with you. They want you and your child
to be comfortable. In addition to how the individual relates to you, or to you
and your child, there are a few observations which may help your decision
making. Don't be afraid to ask practitioners:

- where they received their training.
- who their supervisor was and what had been their experience.
- what journals they read.
- what seminars they have taken in the last 2 years and what
  professional meetings they regularly attend.
- what condition or conditions the majority of their clients have.
- what their results have been on standardized pre- and post-testing
  of their own clients.
- if they check impedances between all their leads when doing the
  EEG assessment to ensure that they had good connections.
- how long they have been offering neurofeedback services.

The Biofeedback Certification Institute of America, located near Denver in Wheat Ridge, Colorado, has a listing of practitioners on their web site (www.bcia.org). They will also send you a list of certified people in your state or province if you write to them (include a stamped, self-addressed envelope) at 10200 W. 44th Avenue, #304, Wheat Ridge, CO 80033-2840 or phone them at 303 420-2902. BCIA is a non-profit organization that was started in 1981 to establish and maintain professional standards for the provision of biofeedback services and to certify those that meet those standards. Starting in 1996, they developed specialty certification for those doing neurofeedback, and there was the opportunity to certify through a grandfathering process until the end of 1997. Since 1998 a formal certification process in EEG Biofeedback has been available.

Another thing you can try is to look in your telephone directory. Practitioners may be listed under Biofeedback, Counseling or Tutoring. You can check with your local Psychological Association to see if they have practitioner referral services. (This is not the only health care area involved. There are many other professionals in addition to psychologists providing this service, but they are the largest group.) In some cases, you may not be able to find a practitioner close to home. One option is to travel to an established center and do a condensed program with daily sessions over a period of time. The Lubars, for example, have offered summer programs at their Southeastern Biofeedback Institute in Knoxville, TN, for many years. Each summer at the ADD Center the number of clients from outside the Toronto area has grown, and in summer 2000, for example, we had clients from Alaska, Quebec, Nova Scotia, Massachusetts, Texas and Virginia. Professionals came to learn about doing neurofeedback from British Columbia, New York and New Jersey.

The field is becoming more international, and both the Society for Neuronal Regulation and the Association for Applied Psychophysiology and Biofeedback have Australian branches. There is also a Biofeedback Foundation of Europe that meets annually. It is a fast growing approach to managing symptoms and helping people reach their potential. If you decide to try neurofeedback to better manage the symptoms of ADD and ADHD, you will be on the cutting edge of using the latest technology, coupled with the latest brain research, to improve your life.

25
Mediation of Cognitive Competencies for Students in Need
The Fuerstein Method
Meir Ben-Hur

Keith, an average fifth-grade student, has just completed an exciting hands-on science unit investigating "planet Earth." It lasted four months. Wanting to assess Keith's new understanding, his teacher engages in a clinical interview with him.[1]

Teacher:	Where is the sun after it sets?
Keith (pausing):	I don't know...
Teacher	Is there anything in our classroom exhibit that can help you think about this?

(...The teacher pointed to the student-made colorful globes with attached labels hanging from the classroom ceiling and to students' pictures and drawings on the walls...)

Reprinted with permission: Presseisen, Barbara (Editor), *Teaching for Intelligence: A Collection of Articles,* pp 305-318, SkyLight Training and Publishing Inc., Arlington Heights, IL, 1999.

Keith (looking around):	No... but I know it doesn't go into the ocean.
Teacher:	How do you know that?
Keith:	Because it would splash the water.
Teacher:	Oh. So where does it really go?
Keith (pausing):	Maybe to China?
Teacher (relieved):	And where is it when it sets in China?
Keith (troubled):	I don't know...

Sound familiar? Have you ever wondered why it is that some student experiences—even rich, exciting, hands-on types of active learning—do not result in real learning of new concepts? Have you wondered how it happens that some students (perhaps as many as half) do not understand what they experience even in the most engaging classes?

Why Learning Needs to Be Mediated

The Piagetian constructivist school of developmental psychology, which views cognitive abilities as a product of the combination of the maturation of the central nervous system and earlier exposures, provides little help to our troubled teacher. She needs to find ways to facilitate the construction of concepts in mathematics, science, and other subjects for the half of her students who cannot build them on their own.

"Meaning" is not implicit in objects and events. Our concept of the world is, for the most part, not a product of our perception of the world. Rather, our perception is generally the product of our concept of the world. What we learn from our direct exposure to objects and events (direct learning) is strictly determined by our preconceived notions of these objects and events and by our ability to relate them to our previous learning. Our concepts, in turn, may be modified by those experiences that are incompatible with them. However, such modifications are unlikely to happen without some form of intervention or mediation. Remember, it took humans millions of years to change their idea that the Earth is flat, and they did not change their thinking until the interventions of maps and exploration provided evidence incompatible with their beliefs.

Keith's learning about planet Earth could not depend entirely upon his own ideas of planet Earth even in a hands-on, exciting, active-learning science class. His perceptions of the objects and events in his science class were entirely different from those his teacher expected.

Lev Vygotsky, a world-renowned social psychologist, argued that the origin of our concepts of the world must be found in our early learning of such things as language, culture, and religion.[2] This learning cannot happen without the help, or mediation, of such people as parents, caretakers, and siblings.

Reuven Feuerstein terms this form of learning Mediated Learning Experience (MLE), as opposed to Direct Learning Experience (DLE). He argues that the "mediators" of our early learning interpose themselves between us and the world to help make our experiences meaningful. Furthermore, he argues that in their deliberate attempts to change our concepts, mediators promote the development of our cognitive systems.

How MLE Promotes Cognitive Development

In an attempt to produce mental models, modalities, and dispositions for our later experiences, mediated learning experiences transform our cognitive systems and facilitate our cognitive development. To "show us the meaning," mediators confront us with and draw our attention to selected stimuli. They teach us how to look at the world selectively, how to "see meaning." They schedule the appearance and disappearance of stimuli, they bring together stimuli that are separated by time and/or space, and they focus our attention on certain transformations in stimuli that we otherwise would overlook. In the process, they teach us how to focus and how to register the temporal and spatial properties of objects and events and the changes that occur in them. They teach us how to compare the same experiences using different criteria and how to sort relevant data from irrelevant data. They help us learn how to label our experiences, and they teach us how to group them by categories. Through MLEs, we learn how to learn and how to think. MLEs prepare us for future learning.

Consider, for example, two groups of parents and children who visit a hands-on, exploratory science museum. In one group, a child skips eagerly from exhibit to exhibit, touching displays and occasionally pressing a button or listening to a recorded message. In the second group, the child and parents walk to each exhibit together. Then the parents direct the child's attention to specific features, they ask questions, they interpret displays, they search for causal relationships, and they eventually help the child formulate concepts about the exhibit. In the first group, there is no comparing of this new experience to what the child already knows, no new insights are gained, and no new learning takes place. In the second group, the parents provide an MLE, and the child learns and acquires meaning.

Children who have not received sufficient MLEs are not prepared to deal with the cognitive challenges confronting them as they enter school, and are thus unable to benefit from the wealth of classroom experiences offered. Even when faced with hands-on, active-learning opportunities, they fail to find the meaning. They may enjoy creating the model planets, but they do not understand the related "whys." They fail to achieve academically, fall behind, and lose interest. These children often experience the world in a random, impulsive way and grasp it episodically. They cannot consider several sources of information simultaneously and do not compare their experiences. They do not form relationships between ideas or look for causes. They do not identify problems and are bored even in classes that teachers believe are challenging. They are children who do not feel a need to reason and draw inferences, children who have difficulties in making representations. Keith was one of these children and, as such, he benefited little from typical classroom experiences.

Why MLEs May Be Withheld

Children may not receive mediated learning experiences as a result of certain biological, emotional, or social factors. Extensive research—such as studies on Down syndrome or emotionally disturbed children—has been done on biological and emotional factors. Indeed, the literature is replete with evidence of their importance in the cognitive development of children. Some of the research shows that even the consequences of biological and emotional conditions can be ameliorated with effective MLEs.

Feuerstein specifically directs our attention to social factors. He points to the social condition of many culturally different children as a determinant of their academic failure. He has observed that it is this population of children—those likely to be deprived of the benefit of a stable cultural context—who do not receive MLEs as a matter of their parents' choice. Because they do not see their own culture as necessary, or even appropriate, for the future of their children, many minority parents withhold MLEs from their children and delegate the responsibility for their cognitive development to the social institutions of the government. Cultural discontinuity, which turns into MLE deprivation, is indeed a growing social problem, as reported in comparative studies with minority children. The population of minority students with learning problems, including the gifted underachievers, continues to grow.

Feuerstein's theory of MLE is tied to his belief that our cognitive abilities are modifiable, that we can change our abilities from the expected course of cognitive development. One of his fundamental premises is that the structure of the intellect can be transformed to enable one to learn better. Feuerstein argues that, regardless of age, irrespective of the cause, and despite a poor level of functioning, humans' cognitive abilities are malleable. This argument is well supported by research on the brain. If a child did not receive sufficient MLEs as part of his or her early childhood experiences, MLEs in the classroom can change the course of the child's early cognitive development.

MLE in the Classroom

Feuerstein's theory of MLE offers a refreshing outlook on education, and many teachers find his humanistic approach exciting. However, he warns against the misuse of his ideas. Good learning is not necessarily mediated, and, according to Feuerstein, mediation is not always good teaching.

A teacher must first decide whether a student needs mediated learning. If mediation is not needed, then it is useless and may even be harmful. Mediation, by definition, replaces independent work. If a student has formed an appropriate goal for his or her science observations (i.e., has formed a relevant hypothesis); can follow written directions; can record, compare, and sort data; can write a report; and can present findings, and if his or her learning requires only these processes, then mediation is not needed. If the student cannot perform any one, or more, of these functions, then mediation should be offered to ameliorate the specific deficiency. Furthermore, mediation should be withheld as soon as the student achieves mastery. Ultimately, all students should be able to benefit from all types of learning opportunities, including direct learning experiences—such as lectures, the Internet, and independent study—because they have learned how to learn.

If you decide to offer MLE, you may want to follow Feuerstein's guidelines for mediators. Feuerstein lists three characteristics that define MLE and distinguish it from other teacher/student interactions.[3] None of these is sufficient by itself; rather, each provides a necessary dimension for MLE. These characteristics are intentionality and reciprocity, transcendence, and meaning.

Intentionality and reciprocity. While children learn much of what they know and can do incidentally, mediation is not incidental teaching. In MLE the teacher interposes himself or herself intentionally and systematically between the children and the content of their experiences. At the same time, both the teacher and the children reciprocate with shared intentions. It is easy to apply this principle when a student initiates MLE—that is, when a student feels a need for the teacher's guidance. In such cases, a teacher intentionally addresses the existing need that engages the student in learning and responds to a child's need for mediation. The more challenging case for mediators is when a child does not feel the need for mediation. How can the teacher's imposed intentions achieve a reciprocal response?

Skillful mediators create student-felt needs by manipulating all the available classroom resources, including the content of instruction, the students' level of alertness, and the teacher's own behavior. The model of Feuerstein's Instrumental Enrichment (FIE) program helped me to understand this idea.

Let us first consider the choice of instructional content and material. The FIE program includes hundreds of problem-solving exercises—all using alternatives to the cultural content (ideas, values, beliefs, vocabulary, traditions, and so on) that is known to foster MLEs naturally in the

childhood environment but that is often absent in the experiences of culturally deprived students. Teachers are always impressed by the students'
excited responses to FIE tasks and by the power of the program to generate
a felt need for mediation. FIE tasks challenge students appropriately both by
their novelty (their unusual appearance and structure) and by their level of
difficulty (not too easy, but progressively more difficult).

Teachers who have access to or are creative in developing and collect-
ing alternative instructional contents usually know how to use variations to
engage students. Such teachers may find or develop a variety of content for
the mediation of specific abilities. For example, a teacher may want to mediate the sorting of data. If a student is not interested in sorting with one kind
of content, the teacher may offer an alternative that does engage the student.

We also need to consider how a teacher's actions help to create student-
felt needs for mediation. As teachers, we often behave in the classroom in
unusual ways in order to keep students alert. We raise our voices, use
exaggerated body movements, and ask direct questions of students who
seem to be drifting off. Other teaching strategies, however, enhance the reciprocity in mediation. They focus on student expectations and intrinsic
motivation. FIE teachers trained in MLE use questions to create a student-
felt need for mediation. Questions are carefully chosen to be as challenging
and rewarding as the FIE tasks are. This model can be applied throughout
the curriculum.

The choice of questions reflects the mediator's expectations of students.
If the expectations are low, the questions are simple. If they are high, the
questions are difficult. If the expectations are wrong, the instructional pace
is too slow or too fast, or the questions are unchallenging, the mediation is
likely to fail. Therefore, the choice of questions must be based on a fair
assessment and analysis of the needs and abilities of the students. The analysis, assessment, and expectations of students must be dynamic, reflecting
the changes sought by the MLE.

We often think about the choice of teacher questions in terms of levels,
such as those represented by Bloom's taxonomy. When a teacher asks students "why" and "how" rather than "what," students need to generate ideas
rather than reproduce and copy ideas. For example, a science teacher whose
students completed a sorting procedure will ask the students to explain how
they did the procedure rather than what the result of their work was.

New learning experiences should always be built on past successful
ones, with a manageable progression between the two. When the challenge
of the teacher's questions is manageable, students become intrinsically
motivated to engage further in MLE. If the questions are too simple or too
difficult, students disengage from the MLE.

The way we choose our questions is related to the time we allow students to think before they respond and to our reactions to their responses.

Teachers often are impatient. The average pause or "wait time" after teachers ask a question in the classroom is two to three seconds. This impatience generally has three negative consequences. First, students may need more time to think a question through carefully. Premature student responses are likely to misguide teachers in forming subsequent questions. Second, short wait time reinforces students' impulsiveness. Third, when students don't respond during the short pause, teachers tend to become uncomfortable and replace the original question with another, lower-level question, thereby reducing the challenge to students, possibly below the optimal level. A mediator's (in this case a teacher's) patience, even an "exaggerated" pause, is critical to the learning experience.

The mediator's response to a student's answer must foster reciprocity in the interaction. Mediators may encourage and invite further elaboration and discussion or probe if initial responses are incomplete, unclear, or incorrect. At the same time, mediators should remain nonjudgmental in their comments. Examples of appropriate teacher responses are "Thank you for your answer," "Interesting answer," "Could you explain your thinking in a different way, so that all the students can understand?" and "Could you think of another answer?" Responses of this kind reflect the reciprocal nature of the interaction between mediator and learner, and they foster intrinsic motivation.

To summarize,
teacher behaviors that foster reciprocity in a MLE include:

- choosing content that students like to think about,
- changing stance, facial and body expressions, and level and inflection of voice,
- asking "why" and "how" questions rather than "what" questions,
- allowing sufficient wait time for student responses,
- responding to student reflections in a nonjudgmental manner,
- encouraging students to offer alternative ideas,
- revealing interest in student learning,
- listening carefully to students,
- showing readiness to spend more time for the benefit of a student's learning, and
- taking special interest in struggling learners.

Transcendence. While it may be an appropriate teaching goal, content knowledge by itself is not the mediator's concern. Content serves only as a means to reach the goals of MLEs. An MLE seeks changes in the way students learn and think. Such changes must transcend the content and context of the MLE. A teacher may use the science class to mediate the process and utility of sorting data by different criteria. However, the teacher's mediation must be aimed at the cognitive behavior and not at the specific data to which the process is applied. In fact, content may be a restrictive factor in an MLE.

Abstract as it may be, content always defines specific contextual, functional, or even conceptual boundaries. In order to ensure the transfer of learning to other content areas and contexts, mediators should attempt to eliminate the boundaries that intrinsically tie the target cognitive behavior in the learning experience to its content; that is, they must decontextualize the learning of cognitive behavior. To do this, mediators need to vary the content while focusing on the same target behavior. For example, if the mediator is focusing on representational thinking, then the classroom model for the rotation of Earth around the sun would be just one instance in which the students discuss the spatial configuration and relationships involved. The mediator would engage the students with other contents that model the same cognitive function. Thus a science teacher might ask students to model eclipses of the sun and the moon and to explain these conditions as observed from Earth, the moon, and the sun. When the students realize that the view differs depending on the point of reference, the teacher would ask them to think of other cases in which the outcome depends on the point of view.

Typical examples of the transcendence principle can be found in mediated learning at home. As parents mediate the concept of organization, they choose different content areas and contexts. These may include the organization of toys, drawings, crayons, chairs, tools, the contents of a school bag, and so on. The organization of these objects will vary with the criteria applied. First, the items might be ordered by size or color, then grouped by function, and, eventually, by age or according to the different relationships between them.

The transcendent goal in these MLEs is to develop the child's need and ability to organize different objects and events by different criteria for different purposes. If the mediated learning of organization is limited to certain objects, certain criteria, and specific purposes, then the transfer or application of this learning will be limited. Similarly, parents use different content and contexts to mediate reflective behavior, comparative behavior, the concepts of space and time, the search for causal relationships, logic, communication skills, and so on. When parents mediate, they foster lifelong learning abilities.

If the goal of MLE is to foster independence and lifelong learning, then teachers, too, must focus on processes rather than content. Just think about the magnitude of change in the world since you were in grade school. If you are currently a teacher, then the amount of knowledge in the world has grown at least eightfold since you went to grade school; school curricula have been changed many times; work has changed radically; life has become vastly different. It is projected that in twenty years, knowledge will double every seventy-three days! Can you imagine how our lives will differ in twenty years? Mediated learning experiences must seek the development of learning and thinking abilities that will be useful with mostly unpredictable content.

The key to teacher mediation is identifying appropriate transcendent goals. Current national and state standards for different academic fields call for the pursuit of such goals. For example, among the standards for science literacy established by the American Association for the Advancement of Science, the benchmarks for the use of patterns and relationships include measuring, estimating, seeing the shape of things, making graphs, comparing two groups of data, analyzing patterns, and so on.[4] These goals describe cognitive processes and dispositions rather than contents. While the content used to achieve these goals may vary, the transcending MLE goals are quite specific. The cognitive processes described by these goals are likely to be applicable even in the unforeseeable future.

Transcendent goals turn MLEs into deliberate and systematic, rather than incidental, experiences. Such goals provide the mediator with a context for structuring learning experiences. However, as indicated above, despite the implicit order in the learning experiences, students still might not make connections between current and previous learning and might not anticipate future learning experiences without the help of a mediator.

Mediators employ several practices to ensure that students understand how their learning is connected to transcending goals. First, mediators help students make a clear connection between a current learning experience and previous ones by asking them to review their past experiences, summarize a new experience, and compare both sets of experiences. Mediation of transcendent goals again takes the form of higher-level questions. Questions that elicit students' insights about "how" and "why" they perform the way they do, help them to connect current and past experiences.

Second, mediators are always instrumental in bringing the learning outcomes to the level of the child's awareness. The typical questions "What was new today?" followed by "How did you change?" provide the vehicle for the production of this awareness of or insight into the learning outcomes.

Third, mediators help students relate current learning experiences to transcendent goals by asking questions that anticipate future uses, such as "What is it good for?" and "Where can it be used?" Student examples of such applications are meaningful because they illustrate the transcendence of the learning experience beyond the specific content. For example, if a child learns to organize his room and is asked to elaborate on the value of organization and to anticipate the future uses of this idea, the child might recognize that he needs to organize his school bag and that, when he is older, he will need to organize his tool box, and so on.

Teacher behaviors that model transcendence in an MLE include:

- selecting a variety of instructional content in accordance with transcendent cognitive developmental goals,
- asking "why" and "how" questions rather than informative "what" questions,
- making a clear connection between a current learning experience and previous ones,
- discussing learning outcomes, and
- relating learning experiences and transcendent goals.

Meaning. The basic tenet of the theory of MLE is that mediation endows the learning experience with meaning. Meaningful learning may be considered the successful product of emotional and cognitive excitement. An MLE provides the student with the emotional excitement of learning and with the feeling of competence. An MLE also successfully targets the "whys" and "what fors" of the learning. Thus the learning experience simultaneously becomes a meaningful emotional experience and a meaningful cognitive one. Mediators do not expect their students to readily "see" this meaning in the learning experience. They guide the students through learning in the search for this meaning.

Much has been said about "making learning fun." I will not discuss this important idea here. Rather, it is my intention to elaborate the cognitive aspect of the mediation of meaning. In this article I am concerned with the common case of students who learn content and procedures and may have fun learning them but are still left without an understanding of why what they learned is important. Tricks, no less wonderful than magic, make such students absorb content and procedures whose meaning they don't understand. Unfortunately, in many cases, and certainly in the long term, even magic does not work, and meaningless learning stops. Students may graduate or drop out of school without ever appreciating the utility of mathematics, the beauty of art and literature, the purpose and process of scientific experiments, the importance of physical education, or the value of a healthy diet. These are the kinds of meanings mediators guide students to find in their learning experiences.

Discovering how our theories apply to our observations—i.e., finding meaning—involves comparing experiences, grouping and regrouping them, considering when and where they occur, and examining relationships between them. Children are not the only ones who fail to do this.

I remember an adult student in the FIE program who suddenly realized that his failure in school had to do with the fact that he did not know how to learn. One day he appeared extremely excited and instructed me to "look at this textbook!" I took the book from him, looked at the cover, scanned its contents, and struggled to find some intelligent comment to match his excitement as he exclaimed, "Look, I highlighted the whole book!" Indeed, his yellow marks covered the entire contents of the book. He said that he never knew that learning is not memorizing. Only now did he understand that to find meaning he needed to reorganize the information he read to fit his theories—or to adapt his theories of "why" and "how" things are or happen. Indeed, many students process their experiences this way only when a mediator guides them to do so. Experienced and independent learners do so automatically. They do it because they learned why and how to do it at some point in the past.

The mediation of meaning is essentially teaching how to learn. First, mediation makes it understood that learning has a target. By asking questions, the mediator helps the student anticipate a learning goal: "What are we looking for?" and "Why is it important?" Then the mediator makes sure that the student compares and classifies the new information or connects it with what has been previously learned, asking such questions as "How is it the same as before?" "What is new here?" and "How is it different?" Then the mediator helps the student construct new meaning, asking such questions as "What did you learn today?" "How did you find out?" "Why is it important?" and "Where can you use what you learned?" Eventually, the mediator will bring the process of learning itself into the student's conscious awareness: "What did you learn about learning [e.g., experimenting, thinking, and so on]?" and "Where will you use it?"

Teaching behaviors associated with the mediation of meaning are:

- discussing learning goals with students,
- repeating concepts in their different applications,
- encouraging students to identify applications for what they learned,
- expecting students to transfer their learning across the curriculum,
- giving explicit value to a given experience,
- changing stance, facial and body expressions, and level and inflection of voice, and
- asking "why" and "how" questions, rather than "what" questions.

Throughout my career as an educator, I have found that Feuerstein's theory of MLE, while "naturally appealing," is more a source of concern for educators than a source of relief. It is more demanding than it is comforting; it makes our expectations grow and our accomplishments shrink. Feuerstein's theory is hard to implement, for it requires the utmost in commitment, continuous learning, and systematic work. At the same time, I have learned that there is no alternative to hard work for enabling children to learn.

The reward for that hard work is well deserved. Keith is now 18 and will graduate from high school this year. The dialogue with Keith less than a decade ago was an important milestone in his teacher's career. She has since become a mediator and has helped many other students in Brooklyn, New York, develop appropriate science concepts. Together, a student and his teacher found out where the sun is before it rises.

The Healing Power of Sound:
Music and Guided Imagery
Naomi Gold

A story about French physician and ear specialist Alfred Tomatis tells of his visit to a French Benedictine monastery in the 1960s, during the time of the Roman Catholic Church's Second Vatican Council. This council introduced significant, often momentous changes into every aspect of Roman Catholic life.[1]

One of the most far-reaching changes instituted by the council was the replacement of Latin, the church's universal language for prayer and liturgy, with local vernacular languages. Another change was the elimination of chant from the cycle of daily prayer practiced by monastic men and women who, according to traditional custom, spent up to seven hours a day in communal prayer. It was thought that in the interests of modernizing certain ancient practices, the long hours required for chanting daily prayers might be better spent on other activities.

In the monastery Tomatis visited, this elimination of the practice of chanting impacted the community in unexpected and discouraging ways. Men who had functioned well, and even thrived, on long hours of work, a largely vegetarian diet, and moderate sleep, became more prone to illness and demonstrated conspicuous signs of listlessness and fatigue. The abbot of the monastery, thinking that lack of sleep might be the culprit, increased the time allowed for sleep, but this did not remedy the situation. Nor did modifying the monastic diet to include more meat.

The state of the monks continued to deteriorate until 1967, when Tomatis was called in to examine the situation. One of his primary recommendations was the restoration of chanted prayer. It is reported that within nine months, most monks experienced full recovery of their former energy and vigor, and most were able to return to the rigorous schedule of daily prayer, long hours of work, short periods for sleep, and vegetarian diet. Tomatis concluded that the practice of chanting "affected the brain in such a way as to give energy to the body."[2]

The idea that certain types of sound, including and especially music, can impact and even transform both physical and mental states, should not come as a surprise. There is evidence that the physical body responds in particular ways to certain tones and frequencies, and many practitioners of complementary therapies and energy healing maintain that the human energy system is decisively affected by sounds. Every culture has acknowledged that music can influence both physical health and emotional states.

The National Association for Music Therapy, Inc. (NAMT) established in 1950, has worked to foster the therapeutic uses of music and related research. At the current time, music therapy is used in almost all types of treatment centers, rehabilitation facilities, and by many individual practitioners.

The influence of music is not limited to formal, clinical settings. In all cultures, including our own, music is used both as a mental stimulant and as a means for inducing feelings of relaxation. For example, so called "club" music is dominated by a continual, pounding rhythm that stimulates long hours of dancing. Many people run or perform other types of exercise to rock music; hip-hop or club music because the rhythmic beat motivates them to keep moving.

At the other end of the activity spectrum, we play and/or sing soothing songs to infants to induce a relaxed state—and, we hope, sleep. We have come to understand instinctually that certain types of music are more appropriate than others for certain activities and developmental stages: we would not think of exposing an infant or young child to the sounds of Led Zeppelin, as much as we, as adults, may find them exciting and stimulating.

In recent years, the calm, often ethereal sounds of Gregorian chant have enjoyed an enormous resurgence in popularity, along with the traditional chants of other religious traditions, most notably those of Hinduism and Buddhism. CD's containing traditional Gregorian chants and eastern mantras set to both traditional and contemporary melodies are readily available. In addition, many varieties of so-called "new age" music are based on the drumming and chanting practiced by such diverse populations as North American first-nations, Africans and Afro-Caribbeans, and Tibetans, who possess their own distinct style of Buddhist devotional chanting. The variety of such music now available demonstrates the reality that all cultures have recognized and utilized music for healing and ritual purposes.

We in the west can understand that music works on our emotions; we are exposed constantly to this principle through the love songs, whether ballad or rock-and-roll, to which those of us who listen to popular music are constantly exposed. We can also probably be persuaded by the idea that music impacts our emotions because it has the power to bypass the logical part of the brain. Altshuler, in 1948, contended that music has a greater impact on the emotions as contrasted with non-musical modes of communication because the brain processes it through a different set of "logic filters" than those used to understand language. He theorized that music was processed in the limbic system, a more primitive part of the brain. We know how we *feel* when listening to certain songs that are particularly poignant, or that we associate with a particular time in our lives.

Unlike the cultures of India, Africa, and the first-nations in North America, we do not usually think of music as containing potential healing capabilities, or the ability to enhance our mental functioning. However, there is now a significant body of research showing that the powerful effects of music go beyond heightening emotion. The research goes so far as to suggest that music can positively impact health and even, according to some researchers, enhance certain levels of intellectual functioning.

Much of this research focuses on the ability of certain kinds of music, specifically the music of Mozart and other composers of the baroque age, to enhance intellectual abilities. To better understand how this is possible, it is necessary to consider some of the theories behind the idea of music and sound healing. A number of philosophical, religious and metaphysical systems posit that everything in the universe is in a state of vibration. Every par-

ticle, including those that make up our own bodies and everything in them, is in motion and produces a sound or frequency. According to many metaphysicians, even thoughts convey vibrations.

Sound, therefore, is a form of energy that can change the vibrational rate of objects. According to those who practice healing using sound and music, diseases of both body and mind can be corrected when an afflicted body part or state of mind is made to vibrate again according to its natural, healthy state. Healing with the use of music and sound involves finding a correct resonant frequency for the imbalanced condition, and causing the disharmonious condition, object, or mental state to resonate with that correct frequency.

Research carried out by the Institute of HeartMath, a nonprofit organization in Boulder Creek, California,[3] claims to show that music can actually boost the immune system. It is reported that exposure to a special type of music developed by HeartMath resulted in participants having up to 140% more of certain immune-system enhancing antibodies in their saliva. The conclusion drawn is that this study may show the ability of music to stimu-late a positive frame of mind, thereby stimulating the immune system and strengthening the body's defenses against disease.[4] Further, a Canadian study carried out at McGill University showed that rats given a painful stim-ulus "exhibited a decrease in neuronal activity when high frequency sound (above 60 hertz) was played." This result is significant because "decreased neuronal activity indicates a reduction in pain,"[5] and it suggests the possi-bility that "any music [inducing] a positive feeling state in the listener increases our general health."

The term "Mozart Effect," according to its official website (www.mozarteffect.com), "...is an inclusive term signifying the transforma-tional powers of music in health, education, and well-being." The website states that The Mozart Effect represents "...the use of music and the arts to improve... memory, awareness, and the integration of learning styles; the innovative and experimental uses of music to improve listening and atten-tion deficit disorders; the therapeutic uses of music for mental and physical disorders and injuries; [and] the collective uses of music for imagery and visualization to activate creativity, and reduce depression and anxiety" (www.mozarteffect.com).

The enthusiasm of the general public for the idea of a "Mozart effect" has sent the CD titled "Music for the Mozart Effect: Vol. 1, Strengthen the Mind" to the top of the classical bestsellers list on Amazon.com. This title is also among Billboard magazine's classical top ten, along with the sequel "The Mozart Effect: Music for Children Vol. 1—Tune Up Your Mind."

The "Mozart Effect" began to receive media attention in 1993 after the publication of a study conducted by Katherine Ky, Gordon Shaw, and Frances Rauscher at the University of California at Irvine. Their study was published in the journal *Nature* (1993, volume 365, p. 611). In the study, 84 college students were divided into three groups, each of which was assigned a specific activity:

1. listening to Mozart's *Sonata for Two Pianos in D Major,*
2. listening to a relaxation tape, or
3. listening to no sound at all.

The students were then given a spatial-reasoning test adopted from the Stanford-Binet intelligence test. The results indicated that those who had listened to the Mozart piece scored 8 to 9 points higher than those in the other two groups. As with many "alternative" or "complementary" healing modalities, however, there is significant controversy regarding research into the "Mozart effect," and some of the experiments have drawn criticism. In particular, subsequent attempts to replicate the findings are regarded by some researchers as producing inconclusive results. Kenneth Steele, an Appalachian State University psychologist, repeated one of Shaw and

Rauscher's key experiments, but found no indication that the music of Mozart improved the scores of 125 subjects, "even when he scoured individual scores for signs of improvement."[6] Another psychologist, Harvard University's Christopher Chabris, examined the results of 16 studies involving 714 subjects, looking specifically for evidence of a "Mozart effect." He claims not to have found it, and concluded that "...the real reason some people do better is what psychologists call 'enjoyment arousal'—music improves people's mood, so they perform better."[7] By contrast, Lois Hetland of the Harvard Graduate School of Education asserts that critics are examining evidence in a very partial way, one that doesn't allow for recognition of the full range of the research. For example, Hetland says that Chabris examined only experiments "that compared Mozart against silence, not against other compositions." Hetland's own examination of the data

"cast a broader net that included every study to date, a total of 1014 subjects."[8] Her findings conclude "Mozart listeners outperformed other groups more often than could be explained by chance, although the effect was usually much weaker than Shaw and Rauscher saw." She maintains, however, that even these "small effects are impressive."[9]

Other resources promoting the multiple healing properties of music are the books *Superlearning* and *Superlearning 2000* by Sheila Ostrander and Lynn Schroeder. These writers discuss the creativity-enhancing properties of the compositions of other composers, chiefly baroque ones such as Bach, Handel, Vivaldi, Telemann, and Corelli. While definitive, predictably replicable scientific evidence for a "Mozart Effect" seems elusive to some researchers, the broad use of music in all cultures, including our own, to stimulate and enhance various feeling-states, and to enrich life at every level, is itself substantial evidence for the power of music.

While the precise nature and mechanism of the "Mozart Effect" may not yet be clearly understood, there is certainly a significant body of evidence to suggest that active involvement in music, such as singing or playing an instrument, can enhance intellectual and cognitive abilities. It is certain, moreover, that these activities enhance one's quality of life. It is therefore very unfortunate, and very much to the detriment of children, that many school systems look upon music and the arts as non-essential. Music and art programs are often the first to be cut with the introduction of spending limitations, and when music and the arts are cut from school curricula, children are deprived of a huge range of the most enriching, creative aspects of human experience.

It is, therefore, very important for parents to take the initiative and attempt to expose their children to music. This exposure doesn't have to be in the form of music lessons. It can be accomplished simply playing different types of music at home—various styles of classical, choral, jazz— from the time children are infants. It is important to keep in mind that exposing children to music is not merely for the purpose of making them "smarter" or improving their school performance, which are the most generally accepted benchmarks of achievement. While all children need and deserve substantial exposure to the music and the arts, it is especially important for children who do not seem to "fit" into conventional school programs.

Like the French monks treated by Dr. Tomatis, children cannot be expected to thrive in an environment that fails to recognize and make provision for activities that are essential to the human spirit and the human condition, but that may seem to some people not "useful" or "practical." There are many excellent resources in both conventional and "new age" bookstores for learning about music, sound healing, and The Mozart Effect. The Mozart Effect official website (www.mozarteffect.com) contains an extensive list of links to online references and resources, including links belonging to specific individuals and organizations concerned with creative arts therapies, music education and music therapy, and, of course, The Mozart Effect itself.

The idea that our thoughts and emotions can contribute to illness is not a new one, but the belief that they can also contribute to our health is not yet well understood, although it is gaining wider acceptance. It is thought by some researchers that many health problems may be emotional, social, or familial in origin, although these problems initially present as physical pain and illness. At the same time, research into biofeedback, hypnosis, and meditative states has shown that people have a powerful range of self-regulatory abilities.

The American Medical Association approved the use of hypnosis as a valid form of treatment in 1958, but there has been little funding provided for the kind of research into hypnosis that is conducted for pharmaceutical products. With the establishment of the field of psychoneuroimmunology, a speciality that studies the relationship between thought and the functioning of immune cells, and the establishment of the National Institute of Health's Office of Alternative Medicine, the value of these and other non-mainstream, mind/body techniques stands a greater chance of being understood.

Although scientific research has not located the precise basis for imagery's healing abilities, there is enough data to prompt researchers to begin theorizing about how it may work. Visual, auditory and tactile imagery seem to be produced by the brain's cerebral cortex, the location of higher mental functions such as language, thinking, and problem solving. (This is in contrast with imagery concerning smell or emotional experiences that arise from more primitive brain centers.) When researchers use a sophisticated technique called "positron emission tomography" (PET) to monitor the brain during imagery exercises, they have found that the same parts of the cerebral cortex are activated whether people imagine something or actually experience it.

This suggests that the picturing of visual images activates the optic cortex, thinking about music (e.g. a favorite piece of music) activates the auditory cortex, and conjuring up tactile sensations stimulates the sensory cortex. Thus, vivid imagery can send a message from the cerebral cortex to "lower" brain centers, including the limbic system, which is the emotional center of the brain. From there, the message is relayed to the endocrine system and the autonomic nervous system, which can affect a range of bodily functions, including heart rate, perspiration, and blood pressure.

Advocates of the practice of guided imagery assert that the imagination has potent healing abilities. Many of us accept the idea that the use of imagery can help us manage stress, tension and anxiety. More than this, however, research into guided imagery also suggests that imagery can relieve pain, speed healing, and aid in the management of depression and allergies.

Practitioners of imagery maintain that it is the language the mind uses to communicate with the body, and constitutes an actual biological connection between the mind and the body. The effectiveness of guided imagery is grounded in this "mind/body connection." As far as the body is concerned, sensory images have nearly the same impact as actual sensory experiences. For example, the body reacts physiologically to the imagined smell of baking bread in the same way it would to walking into a bakery, and mental anticipation of a fearful event can be just as frightening (or even more frightening) than the event itself. Many practitioners of guided imagery believe that the more fully one imagines an event, the more "real" it seems to the brain, and the greater the amount of information sent to the nervous system. Practitioners work from the belief that people who can learn to control and direct the images in their minds can affect physiological as well as psychological conditions.

According to a study at the Rainbow Babies' and Childrens' Hospital of the University of Hospitals of Cleveland, and Tufts University School of Medicine in Boston, exercises involving self-hypnosis and relaxation "...can help children control the frequency and pain of migraine headache episodes." (This article's source for information on the study was found at www.kidsource.com/kidsource/content/news/headaches.5.27.html). It is estimated that 9% of school-aged children experience the symptoms of migraine headache, symptoms such as severe pain, nausea, and extreme sensitivity to sound and light. Children trained in imagery techniques, such as the use of an imaginary control to "turn off" headache pain, suffered from fewer headaches. At the time of the study, Dr. Karen Olness was director of the Pediatric Biobehavioral Center at Rainbow Babies' and Children's Hospital and associate professor of pediatrics at Case Western Reserve University School of Medicine. She said, "We asked children to imagine a favorite place… a place that you know about or can imagine. A place where you like where you are and how you feel. The more you can feel like you're in a place that you enjoy, the easier it is for you to tell your body to do things that are good for you and helpful to you." According to Dr. Olness, the research in this study found that relaxation and imagery techniques "are more effective in eliminating juvenile migraine than preventive medication."

Other studies at Ohio State University, Pennsylvania State University, Case Western Reserve University School of Medicine, and the University of South Florida have studied the uses of imagery for conditions as diverse as the affects of chemotherapy, recurrent canker sores, and stress in patients suffering from bronchitis and emphysema. James Halper of Lenox Hill Hospital in New York City has conducted a controlled study of the benefits of guided imagery for patients with asthma; Mary Jasnoski of George Washington University, Washington, D.C., has examined the effects of imagery on the immune system, with potential implications for use in cancer and AIDS; and Blair Justice of the University of Texas Health Sciences Center in Houston was funded to conduct a controlled study examining the effects of a group imagery/relaxation process on immune function and quality of life in breast cancer patients.

Guided imagery is an activity that draws on the emotional and image-making capacities of the right brain, capacities that can enhance other functions of the right brain: intuition, abstract thinking, empathy, and aptitude for music and art. Because guided imagery brings unconscious and preconscious processes to bear on conscious goals, it can assist in mobilizing the practitioner's motivation to accomplish those goals. Ten minutes of imagery can reduce blood pressure, lower cholesterol and glucose levels in the blood, and heighten short-term immune cell activity. It can considerably reduce blood loss during surgery and morphine use after it. It lessens headaches and pain. It can increase skill at skiing, skating, tennis, writing, acting and singing; it accelerates weight loss and reduces anxiety; and it has been shown, again and again, to reduce the aversive effects of chemotherapy, especially nausea, depression and fatigue.

Affirmations and visualization techniques are frequently used by athletes, often without their explicit knowledge. An athlete may run a course, practice a high jump, or pitch a ball in his or her mind over and over and over again. The practice of imagery has also been advocated by writers and speakers in the human potential movement such as Dale Carnegie, Robert Schuller, and Steven Covey. Dr. Charles Garfield has done extensive research on peak performers, both in athletics and in business. He became interested in peak performance in his work with the NASA program, during which he observed astronaut training that included rehearsing every aspect of the space mission on Earth again and again in a simulated environment. His study of peak performers concluded that almost all world-class athletes and other peak performers are visualizers. They see, feel, and experience an activity before actually performing it.

The practice of guided imagery holds great potential for persons with ADD/ADHD. Current uses of therapeutic imagery usually involve 20- to 25-minute sessions that begin with relaxation exercises to center and focus the mind. The practitioner then teaches skills to address problem-solving, conflict resolution, goal-setting, or the most effective use of personal strengths and resources.

During a session of guided imagery, clients may focus on a predetermined image designed to help him or her control a particular symptom (active imagery), or they may allow the mind to produce images that offer insight into a particular problem (receptive imagery). By accessing their emotions, clients gain an awareness of how their emotions impact their physical and emotional health and their daily functioning. Clients remain fully aware of the practitioner's suggestions, and can be engaged in an active dialogue at all times during the session. The client may be asked to close his or her eyes and allow the mind to present a picture representing his or her problem. The client may then be guided in an imaginary dialogue with this image to explore and reveal its meaning and relevance to the problem or issue.

The resulting images can provide information not only about the problem, but also about the client's beliefs, expectations, fears, and potential resources and solutions. The practitioner works to make the person become more aware of his or her own thoughts, feelings, and emotional and physiological responses. Ultimately, this allows the client to gain control of how he or she feels and functions in previously difficult situations.

For children in particular, guided imagery can be an effective means of exploring and cultivating a more positive state of mind, assisting in developing an ability to focus, reducing stress, activating the child's imagination, and potentially enhancing creativity in oral expression and art.

Refer to Appendix A and F for key information resources for professionals and consumers and Appendix E for product descriptions and sources. Online, check out www.bahironline.com and www.agespublications.com, both part of the growing health information community at www.800line.com.

27
Tales to Empower™ Teachers, Parents and ADD/Hyperactive Children and Adults

Marla Hauer, B.A., B. Ed.

Excerpted with permission of the publisher,
from the Tools that Empower™ series.

*"A teacher affects eternity; he or she can never tell
where his or her influence stops."*
— Henry Adams

A foundation of logic for the story *The Nightmare,* a parable for teachers by Marla Hauer, can be found in *Scattered Minds,* the national bestseller about attention deficit disorder (ADD) by Gabor Mate, M.D., published by Vintage Canada Edition, 2000. Mate is a physician, psychotherapist and writer. Chapter 23, *Trusting the Child, Trusting Oneself: ADD in the Classroom,* is short and concise. Many of Mate's guidelines for teachers are implicit in *The Nightmare.*

This story is intended to inspire teachers to see the best in themselves as well as in their students. We must see the special needs student in a positive light, as a challenge to our professional and personal growth. Labels, like "ADD," can be a starting point for greater understanding and a willingness to try different strategies.

As teachers, we need to become children ourselves at times, and seek humor and fun as often as we possibly can in our day-to-day teaching. In doing so, we begin to integrate creative problem solving into our teaching strategies and approaches. When current methods aren't working, we must be ready to see the world through the eyes of the student with special needs. In doing so, we empower ourselves as teachers—for the student's success as well as ours.

Here are two samples from her forthcoming book: Empower! Tools for educators and parents to empower children and adults: from the Tools that Empower™ series (AGES Publications, 2002, ISBN 1-886508-31-3)

– Marla Hauer, B.A., B. Ed.

Interactive illustrations for classroom or home use, appearing in **Empower!** Tools for Educators and Parents to Empower Children and Adults (AGES Publications, 2002, ISBN 1-886508-31-3), from the Tools that Empower™ series, are not shown in this book.

Miss Delia: Dr. Royal, please, could you help me. I haven't had a good night sleep since the school year began. I keep having the same nightmare that wakes me up in the middle of the night.

As soon as I enter the classroom, Dillon, one of my students, throws an open deck of cards towards the front of the classroom where I'm standing and shouts out, "Miss Delia, want to play fifty-two pick up?" The cards are strewn all over the classroom, the floor, the desk, even on other students' laps. All the students are in an uproar laughing and Dillon is running around the room throwing cards everywhere.

Dr. Royal: Tell me a little about this student Dillon.

Miss Delia: Well first of all, his name isn't really Dillon. His middle name is Dillon. One day a colleague who had had a particularly terrible teaching day because of his behavior, nicknamed him "Dillon the Villain." The other students aren't allowed to call him that of course, but they do call him sometimes by his middle name when they've had it with his behavior or are angry with him. Oh did I forget to mention? How could I forget! He's ADHD.

Dr. Royal: I see. What would you do if this recurring nightmare unfolded in the classroom in real life?

Miss Delia: I don't even want to think about it! I have my hands full as is. I have thirty-five other students to deal with, many of whom have special needs as well—emotional, academic, social, even physical problems. There's a curriculum to cover, a different one for each subject, and deadlines to meet. It seems as if the school year started last week. I'm just beginning to get to know the students, their strengths and weaknesses, and report cards are due in the office soon.

Dr. Royal: I see. So Dillon has just disrupted the class with his antics. What do you do?

Miss Delia: It doesn't matter what I do. *"On pousse et ca deroule,"* as Jean Anouilh wrote in *Antigone*. What happens next is inevitable. It's called classroom chaos!

Dr. Royal: Tonight before you go to sleep I'd like you to suggest to yourself that there is a successful resolution to the nightmare scenario about Dillon and you're going to dream about the next scene in the drama.

Miss Delia: Do I actually have to believe that there's a solution?

Dr. Royal: Absolutely!

Miss Delia: Do you believe that?

Dr. Royal: I have faith in you. You have to have faith in your own inner wisdom.

At the next session with Dr. Royal.

Miss Delia: Thank you Doctor for your advice. You were right! I did find a solution in my dream, but now I have another problem. Dillon's behavior is getting worse and more frequent. Don't bother telling me to consult with the resource staff, the parents, or the school psychologist. They don't have the answer! The only thing that works is medication and his parents don't believe in using drugs!

Dr. Royal: Tell me about the solution in your dream.

Miss Delia: You won't believe this. It's not the next scene I dreamt about. It's the scene before the nightmare.

I enter the classroom and it's me who has the deck of cards in my hands. I tell the class that we're changing our class groupings for this month, only this time we're going to select groupings using the deck of cards. "It's an activity where everyone gets to move around the classroom and play fifty two pick up!" At this point Dillon is jumping out of his seat and shouting "Yes! Yes!" I thank him in front of the class for being the inspiration for this new card activity I've invented. Then I remind him he's allowed to be part of the activity only if he behaves while I explain the game. There is immediate silence in the class. Dillon is now the perfect student. I briefly explain the game and tell the students that they are responsible for helping each other to answer any questions about the process, with the help of the written version that I intend to hand out right after the oral instructions are delivered. I challenge them to figure out how we can use this game to learn about "probability" in math. I explain that I'll be busy recording their individual ideas about 'probability' which they are to present as a group to the rest of the class.

Dr. Royal: Do you have the details of the math activity worked out?

Miss Delia: I do!

Dr. Royal: This time I'd like you to suggest to yourself that you'll dream about the precise card that Dillon picks up.

At the next session:

Miss Delia: You're not going to believe this Dr. Royal. I not only dreamt about Dillon's card, but I was unexpectedly thrust into the game myself as the next scene in the dream unfolded.

        The students are grouping themselves according to the nine suits, the thirty-six cards I've tossed randomly around the room. It's the perfect active lesson, until Dillon's group can't find the fourth card in the suit. Instead it seems I had accidentally replaced the fourth ace with the joker card. Dillon of course had the joker card! He told me with his charming smile and exuberance: "Miss Delia, this problem isn't written in your instructions, so could you please help me?" I indeed had the missing ace of diamonds. The group insisted I'm now part of their group. Did our group ever have a lot to say about probability! Talk about probability. What are the odds your name is "Royal" and mine is "Delia?"

Dr. Royal: We can't explain all the synchronicities in life but perhaps the dream has another layer of meaning. It doesn't matter what cards you're dealt. There's a royal hand hidden that you may consciously attempt to access. You never know what magnificent surprises are there for you when you open the door. You don't need me now. You've opened that door.

Ordering information at end of this chapter.

"To teach is to touch a life for eternity."
— **Ken Vegotsky**

The children's story "Leap," by Marla Hauer, includes the themes of isolation, fear and emotional pain. In the concluding chapter of *Scattered Minds* (Vintage Canada Edition, 2000) these feelings are addressed. On page 320, Mate states, "Healing is not an event, not a single act. It occurs by a process; it is in the process itself. A person with ADD does start off with a sense of isolation. It is good to realize that many other people have had the same experience, are having the same experience."

This story may be used as a tool to help children understand that upheaval and change are part of life. A change of schools, a different class placement, or relocation can be seen as opportunities for new friends, interests and growth. By focusing on one's assets and goals the child may begin to see that he/she has the power to create the future that he/she chooses. Taking risks, an optimistic attitude and having faith in oneself are a key to success.

– Marla Hauer, B.A., B. Ed.

Interactive illustrations for classroom or home use, appearing in *Empower!* Tools for Educators and Parents to Empower Children and Adults (AGES Publications, 2002, ISBN 1-886508-31-3), from the Tools that Empower™ series, are not shown in this book.

Rocky and Mittens were very unusual twin frogs. Mittens was ginger colored with a white underside and white finger tips. He loved to eat so much that you had to gobble down your minnows if you wanted any at all whenever he was around! But he was the most gentle frog in the colony. He never complained and because he had the sweetest croak that sounded more like a purr, he was nicknamed "Purr." Rocky had black and white patches all over, and was nicknamed "Moo," which was a strange name for a frog that rarely croaked at all.

Free-Ella was a bright green frog with yellow streaks. It was only recently that she acquired these yellow streaks. She had just discovered how to extract color from the floating yellow flowers that surrounded the lily pad homes in the pond. For now she was the only frog with yellow streaks. Moo, Purr and Free-Ella were the brightest bundle of fun in the colony. They played together all day long. Some of the older frogs had to wear sunglasses to shield their eyes from the bright colors that flashed before their eyes whenever they were around. But they didn't mind, not one bit, because all the younger frogs complimented them on their "cool shades." These older folk developed a special croaking code to alert the others whenever these three were coming. The code was "F-L-A-S-H."

One day the peaceful pond was awakened to the loud roar of a jet ski. All alone in the middle of the pond, where no frog ventured, there was the FLASH trio, Free-Ella, Moo and Purr. Expert surfers one and all, they could not maintain their balance in the face of these tidal waves. Moo and Purr fell off their lily pads. Free-Ella remembered her lifesaving classes and managed to hold fast by lying flat on her belly and curling her toes and fingers around the edges of the lily pad. This was the wildest ride she'd ever had!

When the tidal waves subsided she looked around for her best friends. They were nowhere to be seen. In fact her home colony was nowhere in sight either! She knew her friends were expert swimmers and were safe, but she was afraid she would never see them again. She was all alone on a distant shore. Her only consolation was that she could fall asleep to the sound of the waterfall nearby. She was in no mood however, to try out this new waterfall ride without her friends. Her yellow streaks were gone and her skin turned from bright to pale green. Even if they spotted her would they recognize her now? For many long days Free-Ella cried and cried.

One morning a black and red flash appeared before her eyes when she awoke. Free-Ella rubbed her watery eyes and blinked. It disappeared and reappeared immediately.

A black and red spotted frog with a huge grin appeared on a lily pad.

"Ribbit. Hello. My name is Dayrya. What's yours?"

"I'm Free-Ella and I was afraid I'd be here alone forever." At that she burst into sobs. Suddenly embarrassed, Free-Ella asked how Dayrya got there.

"Well, I was surfing with my friend Shawna on the pond when a great tidal wave hit. It was the most exciting ride I was ever on! So here I am!"

"What about your friend?" asked Free-Ella.

"I don't know when I'll be seeing her again, but I know she's safe somewhere."

Confused, Free-Ella asked: "I don't understand why you're not upset like me. You've been all alone and lost in the pond!"

"Whenever I'd start to feel lonely or afraid, I'd look into the pond and see myself in the mirror. My reflection kept me company. After a while I started talking to my reflection and said, 'I know one day soon you'll show up, and if it's not you then some frog I've never met who is just as wonderful.' I decided it would be a leap frog expert just like me so we could play leap frog all day long."

Free-Ella took a flying leap—the farthest she'd ever dared—to join her new friend Dayrya on her lily pad.

If ever you see a bright green frog with yellow streaks playing leap frog on a lonely shore with a black and red spotted frog, listen carefully and you may hear them say, "Dayrya-come on down this way!"

To order your copy of **Empower!** Tools for Educators and Parents to Empower Children and Adults (AGES Publications™, 2002, ISBN 1-886508-31-3), from the Tools that Empower™ series, see the back of this book. Quantity discounted case-lot and corporate sponsored orders are available for schools and educators. Please enquire at telephone number at the back of this book.

Section Five

The Pharmaceutical Drugs

"I'll do the very best I know how, the very best I can do and I mean to keep doing so until the end. If the end brings me out all right, what is said against me won't amount to anything. If the end brings me out all wrong, ten angels swearing I was right will make no difference."

– Abe Lincoln

28

Are Drugs the Solution?
Why We Medicate.
How Drugs are Determined as
Being Safe or Unsafe by the FDA.

One of the most difficult decisions we faced was whether or not to reveal as much as possible, in an easily digestible form, the information published in the book the majority of American and Canadian health-care professionals rely on: the *Physicians' Desk Reference®*. Another resource used was the Royal Pharmaceutical Society's reference for health-care professionals, *Martindale: The Extra Pharmacopoeia*. We asked ourselves whether offering this information was in the best interest of children and adults. Should vital information be left solely in the hands of doctors and pharmacists?

There are a host of reasons for which drugs may be the best option at a given time. Sometimes, drug intervention is the only choice for stabilizing an individual who may become violent and inflict harm on him- or herself or others. In addition, the training given to our physicians determines their use of medicine—specifically "allopathic" medicine—in crisis intervention/management. This training is different from the expanding field of alternative, or what is now being called "complementary" medicine, which usually tries to deal with the underlying cause of a problem so that the body's wisdom to heal itself can be allowed to work at its highest capacity.

Pharmaceutical drugs generally mask symptoms and give a patient the time needed to find solutions. Rarely are they the best long-term approach for dealing with most health conditions. It is our belief that an informed consumer is the best care-giver and patient. Therefore, in addition to examining complementary options, it is wise to be aware of the possible consequences of the pharmaceutical drugs so often prescribed.

A few things happened which prompted us to offer this information. Parents repeatedly reported that they perceived their doctors were offering them insufficient information. Could this be because doctors and psychiatrists themselves are not fully aware of the potential affects of the drugs they were prescribing? Harriet Lerner, Ph. D., author of *The Dance of Deception*, makes the point that the old models of medical professionals, a model that includes withholding information "in the patient's best interest," is no longer appropriate or acceptable in our society. The transition from the old style of withholding information to one requiring disclosure has been brought about more by the fear of being sued or investigated than the idea of empowering those who are involved in the treatment process.

The system still does not hold those medical professionals and pharmaceutical companies in positions of power and trust accountable for giving partial information or outright misinformation. When it comes to communicating with consumers, there are no set guidelines. Communicating in a simple, easily-understandable way to consumers ought to be required. Only public demands for such legislation will create environments in which politicians and bureaucrats put the public's right to know before the interests of the medical-pharmaceutical-industrial complex. Decoding the information is ultimately the responsibility of the patient or, in the case of children, the caregiver.

When you go to a pharmacy and buy a medication, such as an antihistamine, what you see on the label and information insert is filled with multi-syllabic names and words. The average person has no clue about their meaning. This is one way drug companies protect themselves. The companies offer information, but in a way that is not fully understood by most people.

Thomas Moore, Pulitzer prize-winning investigative reporter and now a senior fellow in full-time research on health policy issues at George Washington University Medical Center, documents some drug companies' misdeeds in his book *Prescription for Disaster: The hidden dangers in your medicine cabinet*. He writes, " Enthusiasts for drug treatment claim hyperactivity in children is a "biochemical imbalance," apparently corrected by Ritalin. While such speculation may be plausible, researchers cannot identify which chemicals are involved or find the abnormal levels in the afflicted children. The chemical theory has not been established by scientific evidence."

In the *Physicians' Desk Reference®*, the drug company sums it up this way, "The specific (cause) is unknown." They also state, "The mode of action in man is not completely understood. Ritalin presumably activates the brain stem arousal system and cortex." What that means is the drug is given to children, even though the chemical effects are uncertain. So the child is being given a substance for a condition that is not precisely defined and whose cause is not known. In essence, the child or adult is a part of a massive experiment, and only if a major or minor side effect results from the drug will the information possibly be reported in a future edition of the *Physicians' Desk Reference®*.

A significant number of reactions to drugs are not being reported because the doctors do not recognize them for what they are. Sometimes the doctor cannot be bothered with the necessary paperwork. Making a submission is tantamount to declaring culpability.

Drugs are usually not tested on children or teenagers prior to their release to the public. In addition, drug companies may even recommend that a drug not be prescribed for children or adults with certain conditions, or in cases where people are taking other drugs. In any case, the power to prescribe or not to prescribe is left in the hands of doctors.

Once a drug is authorized for a specific use by the Food and Drug Administration or Canadian Health Protection and Promotion Branch, doctors or psychiatrists may choose to use the drug for conditions other than what it was originally tested and approved for. Patients unwittingly become a part of a massive legislated system that makes them subjects in an experiment. We suggest you refer to Bupropion, in the next chapter, to discover the degree to which new drugs are actually scientifically tested in order to meet the FDA approval requirements.

The multiple uses of a drug may come about because a side effect becomes the focus of a new use for the drug. Such is the case with Bupropion, which can cause an increase in sex-drive. In May 2000, the Associated Press reported on a study of women with extremely low sex drive who were given the drug not for depression, as it is commonly prescribed, but to test its impact on their very low libidos. Of the 51 women in the study who had been diagnosed with "hypoactive sexual desire disorder," 15 responded favorably to Bupropion. Their sexual interest increased from one episode to an average of 2.3 such episodes measured over two week intervals. The study only lasted eight weeks.

Sometimes, patients insist on drugs, and if they cannot get them from one doctor, they will go to the next one. Then the doctor is faced with replacing that patient, which they may see as an economic loss. At other times, doctors want to help the patient, and drugs may be the only tool they are aware of.

Surprisingly, some complementary therapies and treatments may produce faster and more pronounced results than drugs do. Complementary therapies are generally safer and more beneficial in the long-term, since they are based on the idea of enabling the body to cure itself. You may be pleasantly surprised at the safe and effective choices you have when you empower yourself with this knowledge.

Unfortunately, that is only a small part of the story. We recommend you read this book and become more informed. Your life, or the life of your child, teenager or loved one, may be the price you pay if you choose not to know. Ignorance is not bliss when it can destroy one's quality of life.

In many cases, pharmacies now distribute information sheets about the prescriptions they fill. Unfortunately, these sheets often do not give the full story, or even a sufficiently comprehensive base of information. Thus, users of these prescriptions are not as informed as they could be or should be.

Even doctors themselves many not be fully informed about all the side effects that may accompany the drugs they prescribe. By unintentionally omitting facts, they may mislead you. Such was the reported case of a doctor in British Columbia, Canada, who told the mother of a child being prescribed Ritalin that "Ritalin is no more dangerous than your child having candy." This is not the case. Comments such as this lead to his medical practice being put under the magnifying glass of the British Columbia Medical Association.

The vast majority of pharmaceutical drugs cause damage to the liver and/or kidneys. Many drugs may cause addiction. Some over-the-counter drugs, like aspirin, can cause gastrointestinal bleeding, and some drugs used improperly can be fatal. Many have increased cancer or cardiac risks associated with them. Some are significantly toxic. For example, according to Thomas Moore, three popular antidepressants Prozac® (Fluoxetine), Zoloft® (Sertraline), and Paxil® (Paroxetine), are responsible for over two hundred different adverse reactions. Treatment with these drugs is usually discontinued in 15 percent of cases.

Based on government records and information available from numerous sources, Moore estimated that prescription drugs are responsible for 100,000 deaths a year. On the other hand, he states that drugs like insulin keep 500,000 people a year alive. "However, among the 3,200 drugs in the armamentarium of modern medicine, only a handful have benefits of similar simplicity and magnitude," Moore states in *Prescription for Disaster*. He goes on to say, "But even when a very small benefit is measured, (for a prescription drug), some well-trained doctors declare a drug "is effective" and they prescribe it widely, forgetting about how few people will actually be helped."

There are no simple answers to the question about what is best for everyone. What is evident is that some health-care providers are not well educated or trained in the areas of nutritional, vitamin and mineral therapies, or the host of other options available to you, the consumer. Some health-care providers instill fear or disempower the individuals in their care. Ethical considerations aside, it is our aim to empower you concerning the pharmaceutical-drugs being prescribed. It is our aim to provide you with information you can share with physicians, teachers, parents, loved ones, and anyone else involved in or affected by the afflictions currently known as attention deficit disorder (ADD) and attention deficit hyperactivity disorder (ADHD).

With these powerful tools at your disposal, self-health care becomes a viable and surprisingly easy and cost effective option in the majority of cases. Since drugs are used for children, teenagers and adults afflicted with ADD and/or hyperactivity, our own disclosure includes all age ranges, and as much information as is possible, given our space limitations. We refer you also to the *Physicians' Desk Reference®* and *Martindale: The Extra Pharmacopoeia,* at least one of which your doctor, pharmacist or library should have.

We recommend you consult with your physician with regard to any matters dealing with the health and well-being of you or your loved ones.

29
The Top Ten Drugs Used In The Treatment of ADD/Hyperactivity

Psycho-stimulants: Generic and (Brand) name(s)
- Amphetamines (Adderall)
- Dextroamphetamine Sulfate (Dexedrine, Dextrostat)
- Methylphenidate Hydrochloride (Ritalin, Ritalin SR (slow-release))
- Pemoline (Cylert)

Antidepressants: Generic and (Brand) name(s)
- Bupropion (Wellbutrin, Wellbutrin SR, Zyban)
- Desipramine (Norpramin) • Fluoxetine (Prozac)
- Imipramine (Tofranil, Tofranil-PM)
- Nortriptyline (Aventyl, Aventyl Pulvules, Pamelor)
- Paroxetine (Paxil) • A discontinued safe option, Deaner

At-A-Glance Quick Reference™ Interaction Chart
Drug Interaction, Nutrient Depletion and
Side Effects Reference Chart

It is essential to have knowledge of the many benefits and hazards of the powerful medications commonly used in the treatment of ADD/Hyper-activity in children and adults. We are providing you with these check lists so that you may make a truly informed decision about these modes of treatment.

The primary focus of this chapter is to give you information of a general nature about these drugs, their potential side effects, an understanding of drug interactions with other drugs and herbs as well as possible nutrient depletions. There is an At-a-Glance Quick Reference™ Interaction Chart at the end of the chapter.

The following guidelines are recommended Do's and Do Not's when treatment with drugs is being considered.

- **Do** consult with your doctor and pharmacist if you are planning to become or are pregnant, or are breast feeding.
- **Do** follow dosages instructions precisely unless instructed to do so differently by your doctor or pharmacist.
- **Do** talk to your doctor and pharmacist about all natural remedies, supplements, over-the-counter drugs and prescribed medications you are currently taking or recently have taken, and any other relevant factors, such as diet.
- **Do** talk to your doctor and pharmacist about allergic reactions and sensitivities to drugs or other substances, as well as illnesses and diseases you have experienced.
- **Do** listen to your body for signs of change due to the drug, noting positive and negative effects or no change.
- **Do** closely monitor your or your child's reactions to drugs. Use the check lists provided in this chapter to help you keep track of any side effects observed.
- **Do** call your doctor or pharmacist immediately if you suspect the occurence of a side effect due to the medication.
- **Do** consult with your doctor and pharmacist if you have any questions or concerns.
- **Do** call your local poison control center or go to the emergency room if you suspect an overdose from a drug, and take the prescription bottle with you.
- **Do** get psychological and educational support for the ADD/Hyperactive child or adult.
- **Do Not** take drugs unless under the care of a doctor.
- **Do Not** take drugs that are beyond their expiration date.
- **Do Not** assume that natural remedies or supplements are substitutes for medications your doctor prescribes.
- **Do** become and stay informed about any drug or supplement you or your child is taking.

Build a Library

We recommend that you build a library of reference books at home. The following is a list of some useful resources.

General Book Titles

Merriam Webster's Medical Dictionary, Merriam Webster, Springfield, Massachusetts.

The Pill Book: The Illustrated Guide to the Most Prescribed Drugs in the United States, Bantam Books, New York, New York.

The Merck Manual of Medical Information: Home Edition, Pocket Books, New York, New York.

The PDR® Pocket Guide to Prescription Drugs, Pocket Books (a division of Simon and Schuster), New York, New York. It is based on the *Physicians' Desk Reference®* published by Medical Economics, Montvale, New Jersey.

The People's Pharmacy®, Joe Graedon and Teresa Graedon, St. Martin's Paperbacks, New York, New York.

Other Books of Interest

Dangerous Drug Interactions, Joe Graedon and Teresa Graedon, St. Martin's Paperbacks, New York, New York.

Drug Induced Nutrient Depletion Handbook, Lexi-Comp, Hudson, Ohio.

The All-In-One Guide to™ Natural Remedies and Supplements, Elvis Ali, et al., AGES Publications™, Niagara Falls, New York.

There are many other excellent books and on-line resources available to you. Some of them are listed in the appendicies at the back of this book.

Notes:

Every reasonable effort has been made to give you clear and concise information. Errors and omissions can still occur. The rate at which information is becoming available makes it almost impossible for a definitive work on this subject to be fully covered within the context of this book.

In all matters regarding drugs—whether they be prescription or over-the-counter drugs—always consult with your doctor and pharmacist. They may refer you to the *Physicians' Desk Reference®,* their primary source of information.

The Drug Lists

The purpose of these lists is to inform you of the general nature of a drug and the reported possible side effects and possible interactions. If side effects or interactions occur, the check lists will help you keep track of them. Follow your doctor's directions.

Psycho-stimulants

Amphetamines
Brand Name: Adderall

Amphetamines are prescribed in the treatment of attention-deficit disorder with hyperactivity, and are also used for the treatment of narcolepsy (uncontrollable attacks of sleep).

Important facts about Amphetamines:

Amphetamines carry with them a high potential for abuse. Large doses over long periods of time can cause dependence and addiction. Take only as prescribed. Do not take it for a longer time or any other use than prescribed. Late evening doses can interfere with sleep.

What do you do if you miss a dose?

If you miss a dose when taking 1 dose a day and there are at least 6 hours before bedtime, take the dose when you remember. If you don't remember until the next day, don't take a double dose.

When taking more than 1 dose a day, and you remind yourself within an hour of the scheduled time, take the missed dose right away. If more than an hour, skip the dose and return to your regular schedule. Never take 2 doses at the same time.

Document experiences and side effects with Amphetamines

Document your experiences with this drug. For side effects use the check lists that follow. If you have any concerns, share the information with your doctor and pharmacist. The more complete your information, the easier it is for you and your health care professionals to decide on the best course of action. If you experience a side effect which is not listed below, please use the Reader Feedback Form in Appendix G.

Possible side effects from Amphetamines include, but are not limited to, the following:

- Changes in sex drive
- Constipation
- Depression
- Diarrhea
- Dizziness
- Dry mouth
- Headache
- Heightened feelings of well-being
- High blood pressure
- Hives
- Impotence
- Insomnia
- Mental turmoil
- Overstimulation
- Rapid or pounding heartbeat
- Reduced appetite
- Restlessness
- Stomach and intestinal problems
- Trembling
- Twitches
- Very offensive taste
- Weakened heart
- Weight loss
- Worsening of tics (including Tourette's syndrome)

This drug is not to be prescribed if you have any of the following:

- Glaucoma
- Heart disease
- Hardening of the arteries
- High blood pressure
- Overactive thyroid

Never take Amphetamines within 14 days of taking an MAO inhibitor, such as Nardil or Parnate. A potentially dangerous rise in blood pressure may occur.

A doctor does not prescribe Amphetamines if you ever reacted negatively to similar stimulant drugs. A doctor also avoids prescribing Amphetamines if you are agitated, or if you have a history of substance abuse.

Amphetamines may make tics and twitches worse. If the patient has this condition, and in particular, if the patient suffers from Tourette's syndrome, inform the doctor.

When prescribing it for attention-deficit disorder, the doctor does a comprehensive evaluation before prescribing Amphetamines. He or she will be particularly attentive to the severity of the symptoms, and the patient's age. If the condition is due to a temporary reaction to a stressful situation, Amphetamines are usually not used.

Currently, there has been no long-term experience with Amphetamine therapy in children. Amphetamine-based medications may stunt growth, so your doctor will monitor the child carefully.

Food and drug interactions that may occur when taking Amphetamines include, but are not limited to, the following:

Generic name [examples or brand name(s)]
- Acetazolamide (Dazamide, Diamox, Diamox Sequels)
- Antihistamines like Benadryl and Chlor-Trimeton
- Drugs known as MAO inhibitors, and the antidepressants Nardil and Parnate
- Drugs that increase the acidity of urine, like Uroquid-Acid No. 2
- Fruit juices
- Glutamic acid (an amino acid)
- High blood pressure drugs like Calan, Esimil, HydroDIURIL, Hytrin, Procardia, and Serpasil
- Lithium carbonate, Lithium citrate, (Eskalith, Lithobid, Lithonate, Lithotabs)
- Major tranquilizers such as Haldol and Thorazine
- Meperidine (Demerol)
- Methenamine (Urised)
- Norepinephrine (Levophed)

- Propoxyphene hydrochloride (Darvon)
- Seizure medications like Dilantin, Phenobarbital, Zarontin
- "Tricyclic" antidepressants like Elavil, Norpramin, Tofranil, Vivactil, etc.
- Vitamin C

Symptoms of Amphetamine overdose can include:

- ❏ Abdominal cramps
- ❏ Changes in one's blood pressure
- ❏ Coma
- ❏ Confusion
- ❏ Convulsions

- ❏ Diarrhea
- ❏ Exaggerated reflexes
- ❏ Extreme Aggresiveness
- ❏ Hallucinations
- ❏ Heartbeat irregularity
- ❏ High fever

- ❏ Muscle spasms
- ❏ Nausea
- ❏ Panic
- ❏ Rapid breathing
- ❏ Restlessness
- ❏ Tremors
- ❏ Vomiting

Dextroamphetamine — *Dextroamphetamine Sulfate*
Brand Names: Dexedrine and Dextrostat

Dextroamphetamine is a central-nervous-system stimulant drug available in tablet or sustained-release capsule. It is prescribed for attention deficit disorder with hyperactivity, and narcolepsy (uncontrollable attacks of sleep). It is also prescribed on a short-term basis to treat obesity.

Important facts about Dextroamphetamine:

Dextroamphetamine has high abuse potential. The stimulant effect may lead to a period of depression and fatigue once its effects wear off. Although the depression and fatigue can be relieved by taking another dose, this soon develops into a vicious cycle.

If you continually take Dextroamphetamine in amounts higher than recommended or over a long period of time, dependency is likely and you will suffer from withdrawal symptoms.

Take Dextroamphetamine exactly as prescribed. If it is prescribed in tablet form, take it exactly as prescribed. The sustained-release capsules can be taken once a day, as per your doctor's instructions.

Dextroamphetamine is not to be taken late in the day because it can interfere with sleep. If experiencing insomnia or an unwanted loss of appetite, notify your doctor; a lower dosage may be needed.

Doctors periodically take you off Dextroamphetamine to assess whether or not you should still take it.

Do not crush or chew the sustained-release form.

Do not increase the dosage, unless advised to by your doctor.

Do not use it to increase mental alertness or keep yourself awake.

What do you do if you miss a dose?

If you miss a dose when taking 1 dose a day and there are at least 6 hours before bedtime, take the dose when you remember. If you don't remember until the next day, don't take a double dose.

When taking more than 1 dose a day, and you remind yourself within an hour of the scheduled time, take the missed dose right away. If more than an hour, skip the dose and return to your regular schedule. Never take 2 doses at the same time.

Document experiences and side effects with Dextroamphetamine

Document your experiences with this drug. For side effects use the check lists that follow. If you have any concerns, share the information with your doctor and pharmacist. The more complete your information, the easier it is for you and your health care professionals to decide on the best course of action. If you experience a side effect which is not listed below, please use the Reader Feedback Form in Appendix G.

Possible side effects from Dextroamphetamine include, but are not limited to, the following:

- ❑ Appetite suppression
- ❑ Changes in sex drive
- ❑ Constipation
- ❑ Depression/melancholy
- ❑ Diarrhea
- ❑ Dizziness
- ❑ Dry mouth
- ❑ Excessive restlessness

- ❑ Headache
- ❑ Heart palpitations
- ❑ Heightened feelings of well-being
- ❑ High blood pressure
- ❑ Hives
- ❑ Impotence
- ❑ Overstimulation
- ❑ Rapid heartbeat

- ❑ Sleeplessness
- ❑ Stomach and intestinal problems
- ❑ Tremors
- ❑ Uncontrollable twitching or jerking
- ❑ Unpleasant taste in the mouth
- ❑ Weight loss

Effects of continual use of Dextroamphetamine may include:

- ❑ Extreme insomnia
- ❑ Extremely bad skin disease
- ❑ Hyperactivity

- ❑ Irritability
- ❑ Personality changes
- ❑ Schizophrenia-like behavior and thoughts

Not to be prescribed if you have a sensitivity to it or are allergic to it. If suffering from any of these conditions, this drug is not prescribed.

- • Cardiovascular disease
- • Emotional upset/agitation
- • Glaucoma
- • Hardening of the arteries

- • High blood pressure
- • Overactive thyroid gland
- • Substance abuse

Not to be taken within 14 days of taking a monoamine oxidase inhibitor (MAO inhibitor) like Nardil or Parnate. Dextroamphetamine and MAO inhibitor antidepressants may cause a potentially life-threatening rise in blood pressure.

An inactive ingredient in Dextroamphetamine (Dexedrine) is tartrazine (Yellow No. 5) which can cause a severe allergic reaction especially if you are allergic to aspirin. For more information on this sensitivity, see Section 2, Chapter 12.

This drug may impair judgment or coordination. Driving or operating dangerous machinery is not recommended until your reaction to the drug is known.

The drug may stunt a child's growth. Children should be closely monitored to ensure their growth is not stunted.

Possible food and drug interactions when taking this medication

If Dextroamphetamine is taken with certain foods or drugs, the effects of either could be increased, decreased, or altered. Check with your doctor before combining Dextroamphetamine with the following:

Drug and food interactions that may occur when taking Dextroamphetamine include, but are not limited to, the following:

- Acetazolamide (Diamox)
- Ammonium chloride
- Antidepressants
- Antihistamines such as Benadryl
- Blood pressure medications
- Chlorpromazine (Thorazine)
- Ethosuximide (Zarontin)
- Fruit juices
- Glutamic acid hydrochloride
- Guanethidine (Ismelin)
- Haloperidol (Haldol)
- Lithium carbonate (Lithonate)
- MAO-inhibitor antidepressants like Nardil and Parnate Propoxyphene (Darvon)
- Meperidine (Demerol)
- Methenamine (Urised)
- Norepinephrine (Levophed)
- Phenobarbital
- Phenytoin (Dilantin)
- Reserpine (Diupres)
- Sodium acid phosphate
- Sodium bicarbonate (baking soda)
- Thiazide diuretics such as Diuril
- Veratrum alkaloids (in some blood pressure drugs)
- Vitamin C (as ascorbic acid)

Dextroamphetamine overdose symptoms can include, but are not limited to, the following:

- Abdominal cramps
- Coma
- Confusion
- Convulsions
- Depression
- Diarrhea
- Extreme aggressiveness
- Fatigue
- Hallucinations
- High fever
- High blood pressure
- Hyper-reflexes
- Irregular heart rhythm
- Low blood pressure
- Nausea
- Panic
- Rapid breathing
- Restlessness
- Tremors
- Vomiting

Methylphenidate — *Methylphenidate Hydrochloride*
Brand Names: Ritalin®, Ritalin SR® (slow-release)

Methylphenidate is a central nervous system stimulant used in the treatment of attention deficit disorder. Methylphenidate is also occasionally used in adults to treat narcolepsy (uncontrollable attacks of sleep).

Important facts about Methylphenidate:

Methylphenidate used in excessive amounts over long periods of time can cause addiction. A tolerance to the drug is also a possibility, resulting in larger doses to evoke the initial effect. Never change the dosage except under your doctor's advice. Your doctor's supervision is required to withdraw from the drug.

Methylphenidate is available in standard and sustained-release formulations. Never crush or chew sustained-release formulations, always swallow whole.

Methylphenidate is usually taken 30 to 45 minutes before meals. When sleeping is a problem, give the child the last dose before 6 p.m.

Not usually recommended during pregnancy or breast-feeding. Consult with your doctor if planning to become pregnant.

What do you do if you miss a dose?

As soon as you remember, contact your doctor or pharmacist for instructions. The remaining doses for the day should be taken at regularly spaced intervals. Do not give or take 2 doses at the same time.

Document experiences and side effects with Methylphenidate

Document your experiences with this drug. For side effects use the check lists that follow. If you have any concerns, share the information with your doctor and pharmacist. The more complete your information, the easier it is for you and your health care professionals to decide on the best course of action. If you experience a side effect which is not listed below, please use the Reader Feedback Form in Appendix G.

Possible side effects from Methylphenidate may include, but are not limited to, the following:

- ❑ Abdominal pain
- ❑ Abnormally fast heartbeat
- ❑ Inability to fall or stay asleep
- ❑ Loss of appetite
- ❑ Nervousness
- ❑ Weight loss during long-term therapy

The doctor usually controls these side effects by reducing the dosage and omitting the afternoon or evening dose.

Less common side effects in children may include:

- ❑ Abdominal pain
- ❑ Appetite, loss of
- ❑ Blood pressure changes
- ❑ Blurred vision
- ❑ Changes in pulse rate
- ❑ Chest pain
- ❑ Dizziness
- ❑ Drowsiness
- ❑ Fever
- ❑ Fluttery or throbbing heartbeat (palpitations)
- ❑ Headache(s)
- ❑ Hives
- ❑ Irregular heartbeat
- ❑ Jerking
- ❑ Joint pain
- ❑ Nausea
- ❑ Purplish or reddish skin spots
- ❑ Rapid heartbeat
- ❑ Reddening of the skin
- ❑ Severe twitching (Tourette's syndrome)
- ❑ Skin inflammation and peeling
- ❑ Skin rash
- ❑ Unusual muscular movements
- ❑ Visual Disturbances
- ❑ Weight loss in the course of long-term treatment

Not to be prescribed for anyone experiencing agitation, anxiety or tension. It may aggravate these symptoms. Not to be taken by anyone with glaucoma, or anyone who suffers from repeated involuntary twitches (tics) or whose family has a history of severe and multiple tics (Tourette's syndrome).

Not used in children whose symptoms are due to stress or a psychiatric disorder.

Not used for the prevention or treatment of normal fatigue.

Not used for the treatment of severe depression.

Not used with children under 6 years of age—the safety and effectiveness have not been established for these children.

No information established regarding the safety and effectiveness of long-term treatment in children. Stunted growth has been observed with the long-term use of stimulants. Doctors will carefully monitor children taking this drug.

Blood pressure monitoring in anyone taking Methylphenidate is required, especially if one has high blood pressure.

Anyone with a seizure disorder should not be taking Methylphenidate. Inform your doctor of any problem in this regard.

Possible food and drug interactions may include, but are not limited to, the following:

Other drugs can increase, decrease, or alter the effects of Methylphenidate. Check with your doctor before combining Methylphenidate with any of the following:

- Antidepressant drugs like Anafranil, Tofranil and Norpramin
- Antiseizure drugs like Dilantin, Mysoline and phenobarbital
- Blood thinners like Coumadin
- Drugs that reestablish blood pressure like EpiPen
- Guanethidine (Ismelin)
- MAO inhibitors (drugs like the antidepressants Nardil and Parnate)
- Phenylbutazone

Methylphenidate overdose symptoms can include:

- ❑ Agitation
- ❑ Confusion
- ❑ Convulsions (possibly followed by coma)
- ❑ Delirium
- ❑ Dryness of mucous membranes
- ❑ Enlarged pupils in the eye
- ❑ Excessive feelings of elation
- ❑ Flushing
- ❑ Hallucinations
- ❑ Headache
- ❑ High blood pressure
- ❑ Rapid or irregular heartbeat
- ❑ Sweating
- ❑ Tremor(s)
- ❑ Twitching Muscle(s)
- ❑ Very high body temperature

Pemoline
Brand Name: Cylert®

Pemoline is used in the treatment of children with attention deficit disorder with hyperactivity.

Important facts about Pemoline:

Long-term use of Pemoline may affect children's growth. Doctors will carefully monitor children taking Pemoline for an extended period of time.

Pemoline is taken once a day, in the morning, unless otherwise prescribed by the doctor.

If you are sensitive or allergic to Pemoline, do not use it and inform your doctor.

What do you do if you miss a dose?

Take it immediately once you remember, check with your doctor or pharmacist to determine when you should return to the prescribed schedule. If you remember the next day, then skip the missed dose and return to the prescribed schedule. Never take 2 doses at the same time.

Document experiences and side effects with Pemoline

Document your experiences with this drug. For side effects use the check lists that follow. If you have any concerns, share the information with your doctor and pharmacist. The more complete your information, the easier it is for you and your health care professionals to decide on the best course of action. If you experience a side effect which is not listed below, please use the Reader Feedback Form in Appendix G.

A Common side effect from Pemoline is:

❑ Insomnia/sleeplessness

Less common side effects may include, but are not limited to, the following:

❑ Depression
❑ Dizziness
❑ Drowsiness
❑ Drug hypersensitivity
❑ Hallucinations
❑ Headache(s)
❑ Hepatitis and other liver problems
❑ Irritability

❑ Involuntary, fragmented movements
  ❑ of the face
  ❑ of the eyes
  ❑ of the lips
  ❑ of the tongue
  ❑ of the arms
  ❑ of the legs
❑ Loss of appetite
❑ Mild depression
❑ Nausea

❑ Rash
❑ Seizures
❑ Stomachache
❑ Suppressed growth
❑ Uncontrolled outbursts like grunts, shouts, and obscene language
❑ Weight loss
❑ Yellowing of eyes or skin

Rare side effects may include:

- A rare form of anemia with symptoms such as bleeding gums, bruising, chest pain, fatigue, headache, nosebleeds, and abnormal paleness.
- This drug should not be prescribed if your child has liver problems.
- Since dizziness is a possible side effect, your child should be told to be careful on stairs or when doing physical activities that require mental alertness.
- If your child has kidney problems, Pemoline use should be closely monitored.

Notes:

- No reports that Pemoline is physically addictive, but it is chemically similar to a class of pharmaceutical drugs that can be addictive. Take only as prescribed.
- Pemoline decreases the seizure threshold, so anticonvulsants may be needed.

Drug and food interactions that may occur when taking Pemoline include, but are not limited to, the following:

When taken with certain other drugs, the effects of either drug may cause an increase, decrease, or altered effect. Check with your doctor before combining Pemoline with:

- Seizure medications like Tegretol
- Other drugs that can act on the central nervous system like Ritalin

Note: The doctor may stop treatment with Pemoline to see if behavioral problems recur and if further treatment with Pemoline is still necessary.

Pemoline overdose symptoms can include:

- Agitation
- Coma
- Confusion
- Convulsions
- Delirium
- Dilated pupils
- Extreme feelings of well-being
- Flushing
- Hallucinations
- Headache(s)
- High blood pressure
- Higher heart rate
- Increased reflex reactions
- Restlessness
- Sweating
- Tremor(s)
- Uncontrolled muscle movements
- Very high temperature
- Vomiting

Antidepressants

Bupropion — *Bupropion Hydrochloride*
Brand names: Wellbutrin®, Wellbutrin SR® (slow release), Zyban

Bupropion's effectiveness and safety have not been determined for children under 13 years of age.

This relatively new drug acts as a powerful dopamine reuptake inhibitor. Dopamine is a chemical in the brain. Bupropion is part of the amino-ketone class of drugs, and is not related to other types of antidepressants. Its precise neuro-chemical mechanims are unknown, but it is believed to work by preventing dopamine levels in the brain from rising, as well as by preventing normal adrenalin reuptake. It tends to be somewhat stimulating, in contrast to tricyclic antidepressants, like Imipramine (Tofranil), Amitriptyline (Elavil) and others.

Bupropion is an excellent example of the extent to which double-blind clinical testing is required before FDA approval can be obtained. Three key studies were done with subjects receiving the drug up to 8 weeks, at different dosage levels. A total of 1,420 adult patients were involved in these studies.

The effectiveness of Bupropion for periods longer then 8 weeks has not been evaluated. The potential negative affects of long-term use (that is, use for longer than 8 weeks) is unknown. Its effects on children and teenagers were not studied. Doctors and psychiatrists are recommended to periodically reexamine this drug's long-term usefulness with each patient. Patients' liver and kidney functions should be periodically tested to prevent permanent damage from occurring to them.

Bupropion is mainly used to treat specific types of major depression, that is depressions that are continuous and impacting the patient's ability to function daily for at least 2 weeks or longer. Severely depressed moods of this extreme nature may manifest these symptoms: agitation, appetite problems, concentration problems, decreased or low sex drive (libido), feelings of guilt, feelings of worthlessness, lethargy, low energy levels, sleep disturbances, suicidal thoughts.

Bupropion may cause weight gain, or as is usually the case, weight loss. About 28 per cent of those taking this drug lose 5 or more pounds. If the depressed patient has already lost weight, or if additional weight loss may be detrimental to their health, this is probably not the antidepressant of choice.

Bupropion should be taken exactly as prescribed by your physician. It is usually prescribed in 3 equal doses, taken at equal time intervals during the day. Six hours is usually the minimum time recommended between doses. To minimize side effects, doctors may start at low dose levels, gradually increasing the amount.

This drug may hinder your ability to drive or operate dangerous machinery. Do not take part in any activities that require your full attention, especially if you are unsure about your abilities, until you are aware of how this drug affects you. If unsure, consult with your doctor beforehand.

Drinking alcoholic beverages is not recommended.

What do you do if you miss a dose?

As soon as you remember, take the missed dose, except when it is 4 hours or less before your next dose. Never double up a dose. Return to your regular time and dose schedule.

Document experiences and side effects with Bupropion

Document your experiences with this drug. For side effects use the check lists that follow. If you have any concerns, share the information with your doctor and pharmacist. The more complete your information, the easier it is for you and your health care professionals to decide on the best course of action. If you experience a side effect which is not listed below, please use the Reader Feedback Form in Appendix G.

Common possible side effects from Bupropion include:

- ❑ Seizure
- ❑ Agitation
- ❑ Constipation
- ❑ Disturbed sleeping patterns
- ❑ Dizziness
- ❑ Dry mouth
- ❑ Headache(s)
- ❑ Increased or higher amounts of sweat
- ❑ Nausea
- ❑ Vomiting
- ❑ Skin rash
- ❑ Tremor(s)

Additional common side effects from the slow-release formulation of Bupropion (Wellbutrin SR) include:

- ❑ Abdominal pain
- ❑ Anxiety
- ❑ Decrease or loss of appetite
- ❑ Rapid heartbeat (palpitations)
- ❑ Sore throat

Other less common side effects can include, but are not limited to, the following:

- ❑ Acne
- ❑ Bed-wetting
- ❑ Changes in hair color
- ❑ Chest pain
- ❑ Chills
- ❑ Confusion
- ❑ Dry skin
- ❑ Dulled or slow ejaculation
- ❑ Excessive calmness
- ❑ Extreme muscle stiffness
- ❑ Fatigue
- ❑ Fever
- ❑ Flu-like symptoms
- ❑ Hair loss
- ❑ Hives
- ❑ Impotence
- ❑ Incidents of overactivity
- ❑ Indigestion
- ❑ Itching
- ❑ Increased sex-drive (libido)
- ❑ Irritability or elation
- ❑ Irritation and inflammation of the gums
- ❑ Lack of coordination and clumsiness
- ❑ Menstrual disorders
- ❑ Painful ejaculation
- ❑ Painful erections
- ❑ Palpitations
- ❑ Problems breathing
- ❑ Problems functioning sexually
- ❑ Rapid irregular heartbeat
- ❑ Retention of fluids
- ❑ Stevens-Johnson syndrome (blisters in the mouth and eyes)
- ❑ Suicidal thoughts
- ❑ Thirst problems
- ❑ Tinnitus (ringing in the ears)
- ❑ Toothache
- ❑ Total or almost total loss of movement
- ❑ Unbalanced moods
- ❑ Urinary problems
- ❑ Vision becomes blurred
- ❑ Weight gain
- ❑ Weight loss

Bupropion should not be prescribed if you are allergic or sensitive to it, or if you have ever had or currently have an eating disorder. People with a history of bulimia or anorexia nervosa appear to be more likely to have bupropion-related seizures.

You should also not take Bupropion if you currently suffer from any seizure disorders, if you have experienced seizures in the past, or if you have ever had brain damage.

Warning: Dosage levels that are too high can cause seizures. A single dose of Bupropion should not be more then 150 milligrams. Do not

take Bupropion with antipsychotics (powerful tranquilizers such as phe-
nothiazines or butyrophenones), certain antidepressants (such as MAO
inhibitors) and other medications, as they might increase the likelihood
of seizures.

Drug and food interactions that may occur when taking Bupropion include, but are not limited to, the following:

Never combine a monoamine oxidase inhibitor (MAO inhibitor) with
Bupropion. Other drugs can significantly decrease, increase, or alter the
effects of Bupropion. Never drink alcohol when taking Bupropion; the interaction between the two may increase your chances of seizures. It is critical
you check with your doctor and pharmacist before combining bupropion
and any drugs including the following:

Generic name [examples or brand name(s)]
- Amitriptyline hydrochloride (Elavil)
- Carbamazepine (Atretol, Epitol, Tegretol, Tegretol XR)
- Chlorpromazine (Thorazine) a major tranquilizer
- Cimetidine (Tagamet, Tagamet HB)
- Imipramine hydrochloride (Tofranil)
- Levodopa (Larodopa)
- Major tranquilizers like Chlorpromazine and Thioridazine
  hydrochloride
- MAO inhibitor antidepressants (such as Nardil and Parnate)
- Other antidepressants (like Tofranil and Elavil)
- Phenytoin sodium (Dilantin)
- Phenobarbital a barbiturate (Luminal)
- Theophylline (Theo-Dur)
- Thioridazine hydrochloride (Mellaril) a major tranquilizer

Bupropion overdose symptoms can include:

❑ A fast heartbeat   ❑ Loss of consciousness
❑ Hallucinations   ❑ Seizures
❑ Heart failure

Bupropion slow-release formulation overdose symptoms can include:

❑ Abnormal drowsiness   ❑ Extreme nervousness   ❑ Vision Problems
❑ Confusion   ❑ Nausea   ❑ Vomiting
❑ Dizziness -   ❑ Seizures
  lightheadedness

When combined with other drugs these symptoms may occur:

❑ Coma
❑ Extremely tight muscles
❑ Fever

❑ Greatly diminished
responsiveness
❑ Problems breathing

Desipramine — *Desipramine hydrochloride*
Brand Names: Norpramin®

Desipramine is used to treat depression. It is a tricyclic antidepressant believed to affect neurotransmitters, the brain's natural chemical messengers. It is sometimes prescribed to treat attention deficit disorders and bulimia, and is also used as an aid in cocaine withdrawal programs.

Desipramine's safety and effectiveness have not been proved for children.

Important facts about Desipramine:

When taken with a monoamine oxidase inhibitor (MAO inhibitor) antidepressant such as Nardil or Parnate, serious and fatal reactions have occurred. Discontinue using an MAO inhibitor antidepressant for at least 14 days before starting treatment with Desipramine. It is critical that your doctor and pharmacist know all the drugs and supplements being taken by the patient.

Follow prescription directions exactly. Desipramine may be taken with or without food. Never take Desipramine with alcohol. It may take up to 21 days for signs of improvement to begin.

What do you do if you miss a dose?

If taking a few doses each day, take the one you forgot when you remember, and consult with your doctor or pharmacist before taking the remaining day's doses at equally spaced periods. When instructed to take 1 dose a day at bedtime, and you forgot to, do not take the dose you missed in the morning. Never double up your dose, unless instructed to by your doctor.

Document experiences and side effects with Desipramine

Document your experiences with this drug. For side effects use the check lists that follow. If you have any concerns, share the information with your doctor and pharmacist. The more complete your information, the easier it is for you and your health care professionals to decide on the best course of action. If you experience a side effect which is not listed below, please use the Reader Feedback Form in Appendix G.

Possible side effects of Desipramine include, but are not limited to, the following:

- ❏ Abdominal cramps
- ❏ Agitation
- ❏ Anxiety
- ❏ Black, blue, or red spots on skin
- ❏ Black tongue
- ❏ Blockages of the intestines
- ❏ Blurred vision
- ❏ Breast enlargement in females
  - ❏ Development of breasts in males
- ❏ Confusion
- ❏ Constipation
- ❏ Coordination difficulties
- ❏ Decreased sex drive
- ❏ Delayed urination
- ❏ Delusions
- ❏ Diarrhea
- ❏ Difficulty urinating
- ❏ Dilated pupils
- ❏ Disorientation
- ❏ Dizziness
- ❏ Drowsiness
- ❏ Dry mouth
- ❏ Ejaculatory pain
- ❏ Excessive flow of milk
  - ❏ Spontaneous flow of milk

- ❏ Fatigue
- ❏ Fever
- ❏ Flushing
- ❏ Fluid retention - especially in tongue or face
- ❏ Frequent urination
- ❏ Hallucinations
- ❏ Hair loss
- ❏ Headache
- ❏ Heart attack
  - ❏ Irregularities in your heartbeat
- ❏ Hepatitis
- ❏ High blood pressure
- ❏ High blood sugar
- ❏ Hives
- ❏ Impotence
- ❏ Increased sex drive
- ❏ Inflammation of the mouth
- ❏ Insomnia
- ❏ Irregular heartbeat
- ❏ Itching skin
- ❏ Lightheadedness (particularly when rising from lying down)
- ❏ Loss of appetite
- ❏ Low blood pressure
- ❏ Low blood sugar
- ❏ Mild elation
- ❏ Nausea
- ❏ Nightmares

- ❏ Odd taste in mouth
- ❏ Palpitations
- ❏ Purple spots on skin
- ❏ Rapid heartbeat
- ❏ Restlessness
- ❏ Seizures
- ❏ Sensitivity to light
- ❏ Skin rash
- ❏ Sore throat
- ❏ Stomach upset or pain
- ❏ Stroke
- ❏ Sweating
- ❏ Swollen glands
- ❏ Tendency to fall
- ❏ Testicles swelling
- ❏ Tingling and/or numbness in feet and hands
- ❏ Tinnitus (ringing in the ears)
- ❏ Tremors
- ❏ Urinating at night
- ❏ Vision problems
- ❏ Vomiting
- ❏ Weakness
- ❏ Weight gain
- ❏ Weight loss
- ❏ Worsening of condition
- ❏ Yellowed skin and whites of eyes.

Important warnings about Desipramine

This drug should not be prescribed if you are hypersensitive to it or recovering from a recent heart attack. Check with your doctor.

Inform your doctor if you have
- • Difficulty urinating
- • Glaucoma (increased pressure in the eye)
- • Heart disease
- • Seizure disorder
- • Thyroid disease.

If you suddenly stop taking Desipramine, headaches, nausea, and uneasiness can result. Always speak to your doctor before you discontinue taking Desipramine, and follow their directions exactly.

Inform your doctor if you develop a sore throat and fever while taking Desipramine. Blood tests may be needed.

This drug may hinder your ability to drive a vehicle or operate machinery. Do not take part in any activities requiring your full attention, especially if you are not sure about your abilities.

Light sensitivity may occur when taking Desipramine. Too much exposure to sunlight may cause itching, rash, redness, sunburn. Stay out of direct sunlight or wear protective clothes as much as possible while taking Desipramine.

When having elective surgery, doctors usually take you off Desipramine as soon as possible before surgery.

Potentially serious effects, such as extreme drowsiness, may result from combining Desipramine with other depressants, alcohol, narcotic painkillers, sleeping drugs or tranquilizers.

Warning: This or any drug taken in excess may cause serious problems. Death can result from an overdose of Desipramine. There are indications that children are more susceptible to overdosing on Desipramine then adults. Immediately seek medical attention if you suspect an overdose.

Drug and food interactions that may occur, but are not limited to the following, when taking Desipramine.

Check with your doctor and pharmacist before combining desipramine and any of the following drugs:

Generic name (examples or brand name(s))
- Charcoal tablets
- Cimetidine (Tagamet®)
- Drugs for breathing, like Proventil
- Estrogen
- Fluoxetine (Prozac®)
- Guanethidine (Ismelin®)
- Muscle relaxants, such as Bentyl
- Oral contraceptives
- Paroxetine (Paxil®)
- Sedatives or hypnotics, like Halcion and Valium
- Sertraline (Zoloft®)
- Smoking
- Thyroid medications, for example Synthroid

Desipramine overdose symptoms can include, but are not limited to, the following:

- Agitation
- Coma
- Confusion
- Convulsions
- Coordination problems due to overactive reflexes
- Difficulties concentrating

- Dilated/enlarged pupils
- Drowsiness
- Hallucinations
- Heart failure
- Heart rate irregularities
- High fever
- Low body temperature

- Stupor
- Very low blood pressure
- Very stiff muscles
- Vomiting

Fluoxetine — *Fluoxetine hydrochloride*

Brand name: Prozac®

Mainly used to treat depression that is continuous and impacting one's ability to function daily. It works by enhancing the operation of serotonin, a chemical in the brain. It is believed to work by adjusting the brain's neurotransmitters, its natural chemical messengers, by modifying the brain's response to them.

Depressions of this extreme nature may manifest these symptoms:

- appetite changes
- coordination problems
- decreased sex drive
- feelings of worthlessness

- feelings of guilt
- increased fatigue
- sluggish thinking
- thoughts of suicide

Fluoxetine is also used to treat obsessive-compulsive disorder. An obsession is a preoccupation with a thought that doesn't go away. A compulsion is the need to do something again and again to achieve relief from anxiety.

Fluoxetine is also used to treat eating disorders and obesity.

Fluoxetine's effectiveness and safety have not been proved for children.

It is very important that you inform your doctor of all your medical conditions, before starting treatment with this drug.

Important facts about Fluoxetine:

When taken with a monoamine oxidase inhibitor (MAO inhibitor) antidepressant, serious and fatal reactions have occurred. Discontinue using Fluoxetine for at least 5 weeks before starting treatment with an MAO inhibitor antidepressant. Discontinue using an MAO inhibitor for at least 14 days before starting treatment with Fluoxetine. Extreme caution is required if you have been treated with high doses of Fluoxetine for a long period of time. It is critical that the doctor and pharmacist know all the prescription drugs, nonprescription drugs, and supplements being taken by the patient, before starting treatment with Fluoxetine.

Follow prescription directions exactly as prescribed.

Fluoxetine is typically taken once or twice a day and must be taken regularly to become effective. Get into a routine of taking the medication at the same time of day, for example, when you perform a specific daily activity. This helps ensure consistency of treatment, which is critical for successful results with Fluoxetine

What do you do if you miss a dose?

As soon as you remember, take the missed dose. If many hours have passed, do not take the dose. Do not double up a dose. Call your doctor or pharmacist if you are not sure what to do.

Document experiences and side effects with Fluoxetine

Document your experiences with this drug. For side effects use the check lists that follow. If you have any concerns, share the information with your doctor and pharmacist. The more complete your information, the easier it is for you and your health care professionals to decide on the best course of action. If you experience a side effect which is not listed below, please use the Reader Feedback Form in Appendix G.

Possible common side effects can include:

- ❏ Agitation
- ❏ Abnormal dreams
- ❏ Abnormal thoughts
- ❏ Allergic response
- ❏ Anxiety
- ❏ Appetite increases
- ❏ Bronchitis
- ❏ Chills
- ❏ Cough
- ❏ Diarrhea
- ❏ Dizziness
- ❏ Drowsiness
- ❏ Dry mouth
- ❏ Eye (vision) problems

- ❏ Fatigue
- ❏ Frequent urination
- ❏ Hay fever
- ❏ Headache
- ❏ Intestinal disorders
- ❏ Indigestion
- ❏ Inflamed sinuses
- ❏ Itching
- ❏ Lack of appetite
- ❏ Lightheadedness
- ❏ Loss of appetite
- ❏ Loss of weight
- ❏ Nasal inflammation
- ❏ Nausea

- ❏ Nervousness
- ❏ Not being able to fall or stay asleep
- ❏ Pain in the chest
- ❏ Pain in the joints
- ❏ Pain in limbs
- ❏ Pain in the muscles
- ❏ Sore throat
- ❏ Stomach disorders
- ❏ Sweating
- ❏ Symptoms of flu
- ❏ Tremor(s)
- ❏ Weakness
- ❏ Yawning

Other less common side effects can include, but are not limited to, the following:

- ❏ Abnormal stride
- ❏ Acne
- ❏ Amnesia
- ❏ Apathy
- ❏ Arthritis

- ❏ Hallucinations
- ❏ Haphazard stoppage of menstrual flow
- ❏ Heartbeat irregularities
- ❏ Heartbeat palpitations

- ❏ Pain in the ear(s)
- ❏ Pain in the eye
- ❏ Pain in the neck
- ❏ Pain in the pelvis
- ❏ Paranoid responses

- Asthma
- Bleeding excessively
- Breast cysts
- Breathing fast
- Chills combined with fever
- Confusion
- Conjunctivitis
- Convulsions
- Dark and tarry stools
- Difficulty swallowing
- Dilated pupils
- Ejaculatory abnormalities
- Esophageal inflammation
- Eyesight disturbances
- Extreme feeling of well-being
- Extreme sensitivity to light
- Fast heartbeat
- Feelings of being hung over
- Fever
- Fluid retention
- Gas
- Gums become inflamed
- Hiccups
- High blood pressure
- Hives
- Hostility
- Infection
- Inflammation of the mouth
- Inflammation of the skin
- Illogical ideas
- Involuntary movement
- Jaw pain
- Lack of movement coordination
- Loss of hair
- Low blood pressure
- Low blood pressure when standing up
- Low blood sugar
- Migraine headache(s)
- Muscle coordination problems
- Muscle spasms
- Neck stiffness
- Nosebleed
- Ovarian problems
- Pain in bones
- Pain in breasts
- Pneumonia
- Problems with teeth
- Rash(s) on the skin
- Reduced sex drive
- Severe chest pain
- Short term loss of consciousness
- Skin dryness
- Spots on the skin
- Stomach lining inflammation
- Swelling of the face due to fluid retention
- Taste sensations change
- Thirst
- Throwing up
- Tinnitus (ringing in the ears)
- Tongue becomes inflamed
- Twitching
- Uneasy feeling of bodily discomfort
- Urinary problems
- Vaginal inflammation
- Vertigo
- Weight gain

Extremely infrequent side effects include, but are not limited to, the following:

- Abdomen enlargement
- Accumulation of fluid and swelling in the head
- Area around the mouth has a tingling sensation
- Behavior becomes antisocial
- Bleeding eye(s)
- Bleeding muscle(s)
- Blood in urine
- Blood sugar rises
- Breast milk production in females
- Breathing stops temporarily
- Eyes and eyelids inflamed
- Excessive bleeding of the uterus
- Excessive coarse hair growth on chest, face, etc.
- Excessive vaginal bleeding
- Fallopian tubes inflamed
- Fluid buildup in larynx
- Fluid buildup in lungs
- Gallbladder inflamed
- Gallstones
- Glaucoma
- Purplish spots on the skin
- Rashes
- Reddish spots on the skin
- Reduced body temperature
- Reduced reflexes
- Rheumatoid arthritis
- Seborrhea
- Severe muscle tension
- Sexual intercourse becomes painful for women
- Shingles

- ❏ Cataracts
- ❏ Colitis
- ❏ Coma
- ❏ Deafness
- ❏ Dehydration
- ❏ Diarrhea that is bloody
- ❏ Difficulties controlling bowel movements
- ❏ Discoloration and swelling of tongue
- ❏ Diseased bone(s)
- ❏ Double vision
- ❏ Duodenal ulcer
- ❏ Enlarged breast(s)
- ❏ Enlargement of the thyroid gland
- ❏ Eyelids drooping

- ❏ Gout
- ❏ Heart attack
- ❏ Heart rate slows down
- ❏ Hepatitis
- ❏ Hysteria
- ❏ Increased activity of thyroid gland
- ❏ Increased salivation
- ❏ Inflamed muscle(s)
- ❏ Kidney problems
- ❏ Liver enlargement
- ❏ Loss of taste
- ❏ Lung(s) inflamed
- ❏ Menstrual problems
- ❏ Miscarriage
- ❏ Muscle convulsions
- ❏ Psoriasis

- ❏ Skin discoloration
- ❏ Skin disorders
- ❏ Skin inflammation
- ❏ Small intestine inflammation
- ❏ Sores in the mouth
- ❏ Speech is slurred
- ❏ Spitting blood
- ❏ Stomach ulcer(s)
- ❏ Stupor
- ❏ Suicidal thoughts
- ❏ Testes inflamed
- ❏ Tissue below the skin inflamed
- ❏ Urinary tract problems
- ❏ Vomiting blood
- ❏ Yellowing of the skin and eyes

This drug should not be used if you have ever had an allergic reaction or are sensitive to Fluoxetine or similar drugs like Paxil and Zoloft. If you experience any side effects, inform your doctor immediately.

This drug should not be used while taking a monoamine oxidase inhibitor (MAO inhibitor) antidepressant. Serious and fatal reactions have occurred. Refer to "Important facts about Fluoxetine" at the beginning of this section on Fluoxetine.

If you are recovering from a heart attack or have kidney disease, liver disease or diabetes, you should not be taking fluoxetine, unless your doctor tells you to.

If you have had seizures, you must tell your doctor before starting treatment with Fluoxetine.

Fluoxetine can make you less alert and may cause drowsiness. It may hinder your ability to drive or operate machinery. Do not do any hazardous activities that need your full attention—wait until you know how it affects you.

You may faint or feel faint upon rising from a sitting or lying position, or feel light-headed or dizzy when taking Fluoxetine. Inform your doctor immediately if getting up slowly is not helpful or the problem persists.

Immediately stop using Fluoxetine if hives or a skin rash develop during the course of treatment with this drug and contact your doctor right away.

Fluoxetine's effectiveness and safety have not been proved for children.

Drug and food interactions that may occur when taking Fluoxetine include, but are not limited to, the following:

It is extremely dangerous to combine Fluoxetine with a monoamine oxidase inhibitor (MAO inhibitor), or with alcohol.

Some other drugs can significantly decrease, increase, or alter the effects of Fluoxetine. Check with your doctor and pharmacist before combining fluoxetine with any drug, especially the following drugs:

Generic name (examples or brand name(s))
- Amitriptyline hydrochloride (Elavil) and other similar antidepressants
- Brain function impairing drugs such as Xanax
- Carbamazepine (Atretol, Epitol, Tegretol-XR)
- Diazepam (Valium)
- Digitoxin (Crystodigin)
- Flecainide acetate (Tambocor)
- Lithium carbonate (Eskalith, Lithobid, Lithotabs)
- Lithium citrate (Cibalith-S)
- Phenytoin sodium (Dilantin)
- Tryptophan, an amino acid
- Vinblastine (Velban)
- Warfarin sodium (Coumadin) and other blood thinning substances

Fluoxetine overdose symptoms can include:

❑ Agitation	❑ Irritability	❑ Restlessness
❑ Anxiety	❑ Nausea	❑ Vomiting

News flash:

What outsells Prozac (Fluoxetine),
one of North America's top selling antidepressants,
by 20 to 1 in Europe?

According to the highly respected investigative TV show "60 Minutes," St. John's wort (Hypericum perforatum), is used by psychiatrists and other health care practitioners throughout Europe, more than any other antidepressant. It is a perennial with regular flowers that bloom during the summer months. It contains many active ingredients including pseudohypericin, hypericin, xanthrones and flavonoids.

Xanthrones and hypericin contain monoamine oxidase (MAO) inhibitors that slow the breakdown of neurotransmitters, norepinephrine and serotonin, in the brain. Too much serotonin makes people obsessive and anxious, while too little is thought to be a major cause of depression.

Clinical trials with hypericin extract showed improvement in alleviating the stressful results of depressive symptoms such as anxiety, apathy, insomnia, and depression. Add to that the wound healing and anti-inflammatory properties that current research into flavonoids is showing, and the possible anti-viral properties of hypericin and pseudohypericin, and you have a powerful healing plant.

One of the greatest benefits of St. John's wort is that it appears to have none of the side-effects of pharmaceutical drugs. (See Chapter 18, Herbs and Botanical Approaches to ADD/ADHD)

(Excerpted from *Natural Remedies and Supplements: The All-in-One Guide to*™, AGES Publications. Ordering information at the back of this book.)

Imipramine — *Imipramine hydrochloride*
Brand names: Tofranil®, Tofranil-PM®

Imipramine is a tricyclic antidepressant believed to affect neurotransmitters, the brain's natural chemical messengers. This drug can be used in combination with behavioral therapies for the treatment of bed-wetting in children aged 6 years or older. It is sometimes prescribed to treat attention deficit disorder, bulimia, obsessive-compulsive disorder (OCD) and panic disorder.

Important facts about Imipramine:

When taken with Monoamine oxidase (MAO) inhibitor antidepressant, serious and fatal reactions have occurred. Discontinue using an MAO inhibitor antidepressant for at least 14 days before starting treatment with Imipramine. It is critical that your doctor and pharmacist know all the drugs and supplements being taken by the patient.

Follow prescription directions exactly. Imipramine may be taken with or without food. Never take Imipramine with alcohol.

It may take 7 to 21 days for signs of improvement to begin.

What do you do if you miss a dose?

When instructed to take 1 dose at bedtime each day and you forget to take the dose, speak to your doctor before taking it in the morning, since there is the possibility of side effects. When taking 2 or more doses each day, take the missed dose when you remember, unless it is almost time for you to take your next one, in which case you skip the dose you missed. Then go back to your established schedule. Never take 2 doses at once.

Document experiences and side effects with Imipramine

Document your experiences with this drug. For side effects use the check lists that follow. If you have any concerns, share the information with your doctor and pharmacist. The more complete your information, the easier it is for you and your health care professionals to decide on the best course of action. If you experience a side effect which is not listed below, please use the Reader Feedback Form in Appendix G.

Possible side effects from Imipramine include, but are not limited to, the following:

- ❑ Abdominal cramps
- ❑ Agitation
- ❑ Anxiety
- ❑ Appetite - loss of
- ❑ Black tongue
- ❑ Blood problems
- ❑ Blurred vision
- ❑ Breasts swelling
  - ❑ development of breast in males
- ❑ Collapse
- ❑ Confusion
- ❑ Congestive heart failure
- ❑ Constipation
- ❑ Convulsions
- ❑ Coordination problems
- ❑ Cough
- ❑ Delusions
- ❑ Diarrhea
- ❑ Dilated pupils
- ❑ Disorientation
- ❑ Dizziness
- ❑ Drowsiness
- ❑ Dry mouth
- ❑ Emotional instability
- ❑ Episodes of elation
- ❑ Episodes of irritability
- ❑ Excessive flow of milk
  - ❑ spontaneous flow of milk
- ❑ Fainting
- ❑ Fatigue
- ❑ Feeling pins and needles in feet and hands
- ❑ Fever
- ❑ Fluid retention or swelling (especially in tongue or face)
- ❑ Flushing
- ❑ Frequent urination
  - ❑ difficulty urinating
  - ❑ delayed urination
- ❑ Hair loss
- ❑ Hallucinations
- ❑ Headache
- ❑ Heart attack
- ❑ Heart failure
- ❑ High blood pressure
- ❑ High blood sugar
  - ❑ Low blood sugar
- ❑ High pressure of fluid in the eyes
- ❑ Hives
- ❑ Impotence
  - ❑ decreased sex drive
  - ❑ increased sex drive
- ❑ Inflammation of the mouth
- ❑ Insomnia
- ❑ Intestinal blockage
- ❑ Irregular heartbeat
- ❑ Itching skin
- ❑ Light sensitivity
- ❑ Lightheadedness (particularly when rising from lying down)
- ❑ Muscle spasms
- ❑ Nausea
- ❑ Nightmares
- ❑ Palpitations
- ❑ Problems with vision
- ❑ Purple spots on skin
- ❑ Rapid heartbeat
- ❑ Reddish-brown spots on skin
- ❑ Restlessness
- ❑ Seizures
- ❑ Skin rash
- ❑ Sore throat
- ❑ Sores - bleeding
- ❑ Stomachache
- ❑ Stroke
- ❑ Sweating
- ❑ Swollen glands
- ❑ Tendency to fall
- ❑ Testicles swelling
- ❑ Tingling and/or numbness in feet and hands
- ❑ Tinnitus (ringing in the ears)
- ❑ Tremor(s)
- ❑ Unusual taste in mouth
- ❑ Vomiting
- ❑ Weakness
- ❑ Weight gain
- ❑ Weight loss
- ❑ Yellowed skin
- ❑ Yellowed whites of eyes

Important warnings about Imipramine include cautions if you have ever suffered or are suffering from:

- Narrow-angle glaucoma (increased pressure in the eye)
- Difficulty urinating
- Seizures
- Heart disease
- Kidney disease
- Liver disease
- Thyroid disease

If taking thyroid medication proceed with caution.

This drug may hinder your ability to drive or operate machinery. Do not take part in any activities requiring your full attention, especially if you are not sure about your abilities.

Light sensitivity may occur when taking Imipramine. Stay out of sunlight as much as possible while taking Imipramine.

When having elective surgery, doctors take you off Imipramine.

Additional warnings

Potentially serious effects, such as extreme drowsiness, may result from combining Imipramine with other mental depressants or alcohol.

When switching from Prozac to Imipramine, you must follow your doctor's directions. Usually this means a 5 week wait to allow the Prozac to clear your system before starting treatment with Imipramine.

Warning: This or any drug taken in excess may cause serious problems. Death can result from an overdose of Imipramine. There are indications that children are more susceptible to overdosing on Imipramine then adults. Immediately seek medical attention if you suspect an overdose.

Drug and food interactions that may occur when taking Imipramine include, but are not limited to, the following:

Never combine a monoamine oxidase inhibitor (MAO inhibitor) with Imipramine. Some other drugs can significantly decrease, increase, or alter the effects of Imipramine. Check with your doctor and pharmacist before combining imipramine and any drug, especially the following drugs:

Generic name (examples or brand name(s))
- Albuterol (Proventil, Ventolin)
- Antidepressants that affect serotonin, including Paxil, Prozac, and Zoloft
- Barbiturates, for example Nembutal and Seconal
- Blood pressure medications, like Catapres and Ismelin
- Carbamazepine (Tegretol)
- Cimetidine (Tagamet)
- Decongestants like Sudafed

- Drugs that control spasms, like Cogentin
- Epinephrine (EpiPen)
- Flecainide (Tambocor)
- Major tranquilizers, like Mellaril and Thorazine
- Methylphenidate (Ritalin and Ritalin SR)
- Narcotic painkillers, like Percocet
- Norepinephrine
- Other antidepressants, like Elavil
- Phenytoin (Dilantin)
- Propafenone (Rythmol)
- Quinidine (Quinaglute)
- Thyroid medications, like Synthroid
- Tranquilizers and sleep aids, for example Halcion, Valium and Xanax.

Imipramine overdose symptoms may include:

- ❑ Agitation
- ❑ Bluish skin
- ❑ Breathing difficulties
- ❑ Coma
- ❑ Convulsions
- ❑ Dilated pupils
- ❑ Drowsiness
- ❑ Heart failure
- ❑ High fever
- ❑ Involuntary writhing
- ❑ Involuntary jerky movements
- ❑ Irregular heartbeat
- ❑ Low blood pressure
- ❑ Overactive reflexes
- ❑ Problems with coordination
- ❑ Rapid heartbeat
- ❑ Restlessness
- ❑ Shock
- ❑ Stupor
- ❑ Sweating
- ❑ Very stiff muscles
- ❑ Vomiting

Nortriptyline — *Nortriptyline hydrochloride*
Brand Names: Aventyl, Aventyl Pulvules or Pamelor®

Nortriptyline is mainly used to treat depression. It is a tricyclic antidepressant, which is believed to affect neurotransmitters, the brain's natural chemical messengers, by modifying the brain's reaction to them.

Nortriptyline is also prescribed to treat attention deficit hyperactivity disorder in children, bed-wetting, chronic cases of hives, and premenstrual depression.

Two key points about Nortriptyline are that it has to be taken consistently to be effective, and it can take many weeks before your mood begins to improve. Even if it does not appear to be working, you should never skip a dose.

Nortriptyline's safety and effectiveness have not been established for children.

What do you do if you miss a dose?

As soon as you remember, take your prescribed dose. If in doubt, consult with your doctor. If you are almost due to take another dose, skip the missed dose and go back to your regular timetable. When taken as a single dose at bedtime and you forget to take it, do not take it when you awaken, as undesirable side effects may occur. Do not take two doses at the same time.

Document experiences and side effects with Nortriptyline

Document your experiences with this drug. For side effects use the check lists that follow. If you have any concerns, share the information with your doctor and pharmacist. The more complete your information, the easier it is for you and your health care professionals to decide on the best course of action. If you experience a side effect which is not listed below, please use the Reader Feedback Form in Appendix G.

Possible side effects include, but are not limited to, the following:

- Abdominal cramps
- Agitation
- Anxiety
- Black tongue
- Bleeding sores
- Blood disorders
- Breasts swelling
  - Development of breast in males
- Confusion
- Constant urination
- Constipation
- Decreased sex drive
- Delusions
- Diarrhea
- Dilated pupils
- Disorientation
- Dizziness
- Drowsiness
- Dry mouth
- Excessive flow of milk
  - Spontaneous flow of milk
- Excessive night time urination
- Fatigue
- Feeling pins and needles in legs and arms
- Fever
- Fluid retention
- Fluttery heartbeat
- Food tastes strange
- Hair loss
- Hallucinations
- Headache
- Heart attack
- High blood pressure
- High blood sugar
- Hives
- Impotence
- Increased sex drive
- Inflammation of the mouth
- Insomnia
- Intestinal blockage
- Irregular heartbeat
- Itching skin
- Lack of coordination
- Loss of appetite
- Low blood pressure
- Low blood sugar
- Nausea
- Nightmares
- Numbness
- Obscured vision
- Odd tastes in mouth
- Panic attacks
- Perspiration
- Problems urinating
- Problems with vision
- Purple spots on skin
- Rapid heartbeat
- Reddish skin spots
- Restlessness
- Seizures
- Sensitivity to light
- Skin rash
- Stroke
- Swollen glands
- Swollen testicles
- Tingling
- Tinnitus (ringing in the ears)
- Tremors
- Upset stomach
- Vomiting
- Weakness
- Weight gain
- Weight loss
- Yellowed skin and whites of eyes.

Important warnings about Nortriptyline

After long term use of Nortriptyline, a rapid decrease or sudden withdrawal from it may cause nausea, headaches or bodily discomfort, none of which indicates addiction.

This drug should not be prescribed if you ever had an allergic reaction, or if you are sensitive to Nortriptyline or similar drugs. If you experience any side effects, inform your doctor immediately.

Do not take Nortriptyline if you are taking any monoamine oxidase inhibitor (inhibitor) antidepressants. Wait at least 14 days after taking an MAO inhibitor antidepressant before starting treatment with Nortriptyline. MAO inhibitors combined with Nortriptyline may cause convulsions, fever and can even be lethal.

If you are taking another type of antidepressant drug or recovering from a heart attack, only take Nortriptyline under your doctor's directions and supervision.

Nortriptyline can make you less alert and may cause drowsiness. It may hinder your ability to drive a vehicle or operate machinery. Do not do any hazardous activities that need your full attention, especially if you are not sure about your abilities—wait until you know how it affects you.

Caution is recommended when taking Nortriptyline if your medical history includes any of the following:

- Chronic eye conditions, such as glaucoma
- Diabetes
- Difficulty urinating
- Heart disease
- High blood pressure
- Overactive thyroid or taking a thyroid drug
- Seizures

Always talk with your doctor about any medical problems you have experienced prior to taking Nortriptyline. This is critical, particularly if you are undergoing treatment for manic depression, schizophrenia or any other severe mental condition.

Light sensitivity may occur when taking Nortriptyline. Too much exposure to sunlight may cause itching, rash, redness, or sunburn. Stay out of direct sunlight, use a sun block and wear protective clothes as much as possible while taking Nortriptyline .

Anesthetics, muscle relaxants, and other drugs used during diagnostic testing, surgery, and dental treatments can negatively interact with Nortriptyline. It is critical you inform your doctor, before any of these procedures.

Combining Nortriptyline and MAO inhibitors can be lethal.

Nortriptyline increases the affects of alcohol on the body. Drinking alcohol is prohibited when taking Nortriptyline.

Possible side effects can occur with and are not necessarily limited to just the following drugs:

- Bentyl to control spasms, and other drugs in this class.
- Catapres a blood pressure medication, and others in this class.
- Coumadin (Warfarin) a blood thinner, and others in this class.
- Desyrel an antidepressants, and others in this class.
- Dexedrine a stimulant, and others in this class.
- Dextroamphetamine a stimulant, and others in this class.
- Diabinese (Chlorpropamide)
- Diupres (Reserpine)
- Donnatal to control spasms, and others in this class.
- Esimil a blood pressure medication, and others in this class.
- Larodopa (Levodopa)
- Proventil an airway-opening drug, and others in this class.
- Mellaril a major tranquilizer, and others in this class.
- Paxil an antidepressant that affects serotonin, also known as selective serotonin reuptake inhibitors (SSRI), and others in this class.
- Prozac an antidepressant that affects serotonin, also known as selective serotonin reuptake inhibitors (SSRI), and others in this class.
- Quinidex (Quinidine)
- Rythmol for heart irregularities, and others in this class.
- Tagamet (Cimetidine)
- Tambocor for heart irregularities, and others in this class.
- Thorazine a major tranquilizer, and others in this class.
- Thyroid medication like Synthroid
- Ventolin an airway-opening drug, and others in this class.
- Wellbutrin an antidepressants, and others in this class.
- Zoloft an antidepressant that affects serotonin, also known as selective serotonin reuptake inhibitor (SSRI), and others in this class.

Nortriptyline overdose symptoms can include:

- Agitation
- Body temperature that is low
- Coma
- Concentration that is poor
- Confusion
- Convulsions
- Drowsiness
- Fever that is extremely high
- Hallucinations
- Heartbeat irregularities
- Heart failure (congestive)
- Lethargy
- Liquid in the lungs
- Low blood pressure that is severe
- Pupils that are dilated
- Reflexes that are excessive
- Restlessness
- Shock
- Tight muscles
- Vomiting

Warning: Antidepressants like this can cause death if an overdose occurs. If you have the least concern about an overdose, immediately seek medical help.

Paroxetine — *Paroxetine hydrochloride*
Brand Name: Paxil®

Paroxetine is used in the treatment of severe depression, a state of being where one's ability to function is reduced, and may manifest these symptoms:

- Consistent low moods
- Decreased libido (sex drive)
- Disturbed sleep patterns
- Feelings of guilt
- Feelings of worthlessness
- Increase or decrease in appetite
- Lack of interest in activities
- Lack of interest in people
- Problems concentrating
- Slow thinking

Important facts about Paroxetine:

It may take 1 to 4 weeks after beginning treatment to see improvement. Continue taking Paroxetine as per your doctor's instructions.

Take exactly as prescribed. Your doctor should be made aware of any prescriptions or over-the-counter drugs you plan to or are taking. Unfavorable interactions may occur.

Do not drink alcohol when taking Paroxetine.

What do you do if you miss a dose?

Do not take the forgotten dose. Resume your regular schedule with the next dose. Never take a double dose. Consult with your doctor if in doubt.

Document experiences and side effects with Paroxetine

Document your experiences with this drug. For side effects use the check lists that follow. If you have any concerns, share the information with your doctor and pharmacist. The more complete your information, the easier it is for you and your health care professionals to decide on the best course of action. If you experience a side effect which is not listed below, please use the Reader Feedback Form in Appendix G.

Possible side effects from Paroxetine may include:

- ❑ Constipation
- ❑ Diarrhea
- ❑ Drowsiness
- ❑ Dry mouth
- ❑ Easily excited or irritated
- ❑ Ejaculatory problems
- ❑ Gas (flatulence)
- ❑ Loss of appetite
- ❑ Nausea
- ❑ Problems sleeping
- ❑ Problems with sex drive
- ❑ Sweating
- ❑ Tremor(s)
- ❑ Vertigo (dizziness)
- ❑ Weakness

Less common side effects may include, but are not limited to, the following:

- ❑ Anxiety
- ❑ Burning or tingling sensation
- ❑ Changing taste sensations
- ❑ Dazed feeling
- ❑ Euphoria (feeling high)
- ❑ Increased appetite
- ❑ Migraine
- ❑ Muscle tenderness or weakness
- ❑ Pounding heartbeat
- ❑ Skin rash
- ❑ Tightness in throat
- ❑ Twitching
- ❑ Upset stomach
- ❑ Urinary problems
- ❑ Vision problems (blurring)
- ❑ Vomiting
- ❑ Weight gain
- ❑ Yawning

Not prescribed if you are also taking an MAO inhibitor antidepressant. At least 14 days must pass between ceasing treatment with an MAO inhibitor and starting treatment with Paroxetine. People with a history of manic disorders should be very cautious when being treated with Paroxetine.

Those with a history of seizures, should inform their doctor, and stop using the drug if seizures occur, as per your doctor's advice.

Metabolism or blood circulation diseases or conditions should be made known to your doctor. Caution must be exercised as Paroxetine can affect such conditions.

Impaired judgment, thinking, or motor skills can occur. Hazardous activities, driving and operating dangerous machinery are not recommended if one is not fully mentally alert.

Possible food and drug interactions that may occur, but are not limited to, the following:

Do not drink alcohol.

Increased, decreased, or altered effects may be experienced. Check with your doctor before taking any of the following with Paroxetine:

- Antidepressants
- Cimetidine
- Diazepam
- Digoxin
- Flecainide
- L-Tryptophan
- Lithium
- Phenobarbital
- Phenytoin
- Procyclidine
- Propafenone
- Propranolol
- Quinidine
- Thioridazine
- Tryptophan
- Warfarin

Symptoms of Paroxetine overdose may include:

- ❑ Agitation
- ❑ Drowsiness
- ❑ Hallucinations
- ❑ Involuntary muscle movements
- ❑ Nausea
- ❑ Rapid hearbeat
- ❑ Vomiting

Deaner

Deaner, an effective drug for dealing with ADD and hyperactivity, is principally made up of essential fatty acids. FDA requirements would have necessitated studies estimated to cost $10,000,000 at the time. The manufacturer was only doing a $1,000,000 of volume a year. They choose to discontinue producing the drug.

Fortunately, the drug's principal ingredient, DMAE, is available. To find out more about DMAE and other essential fats, refer to Chapter 17, Essential Fatty Acids: Fats That Heal The ADD/Hyperactive Brain.

At-A-Glance Quick Reference™ Interaction Chart
Drug Interaction, Nutrient Depletion and Side Effects Reference Chart

Trade Name • Generic Name	Type of Drug	Interaction With Other Drugs	Interaction With Herbs	Possible Nutrient Depletion	Side Effects
Adderall • amphetamine	CNS stimulant (sympathomimetic)	All antidepressants	Caffeine or ephedrine containing plants	None known	Appetite supression, insomnia, arrythmias
Comments:	Clinical trials show twice the effectiveness of Ritalin.				
Dexedrine • dextroamphetamine	CNS stimulant (sympathomimetic)	All antidepressants	Caffeine or ephedrine containing plants	None known	Appetite supression, cardiac valve abnormalities
Comments:	May impair ability to operate machinery.				
Ritalin insomnia, • methylphenidate	CNS stimulant	MAO inhibitors, some antihypertensives	Caffeine or ephedrine containing plants	None known	Suppresses appetite, headache, stomachache. Can cause dependency
Comments:	Don't use with Tourette's syndrome, seizures, glaucoma. Monitor liver functioning.				
Cylert • pemoline	CNS stimulant	Nasal decongestants (Benadryl)	Caffeine or ephedrine containing plants	None known	Can cause acute liver failure
Comments:	Signing a patient consent form is often necessary.				
Wellbutrin • bupropion	Catecholaminergic antidepressant	MAO inhibitors, any drug containing bupropion (Zyban), insulin, steroids, oral hypoglycemics	None known	None known	Dry mouth, appetite loss, skin rash, ringing in the ears
Comments:	This is a relatively new drug with possibly unpredictable side effects.				

At-A-Glance Quick Reference™ Interaction Chart
Drug Interaction, Nutrient Depletion and Side Effects Reference Chart

Trade Name • Generic Name	Type of Drug	Interaction With Other Drugs	Interaction With Herbs	Possible Nutrient Depletion	Side Effects
Pertofane • desipramine	Tricyclic antidepressant	Anticonvulsants (Carbamazepine), nasal decongestants, MAO inhibitors	St. John's Wort	CoQ10, Vitamin B_2	Dry mouth, dizziness, headache
Comments: Don't use with alcohol.					
Prozac • fluoxetine	SSRI antidepressant (Selective Serotonin Reuptake Inhibitor)	Tricyclic antidepressant	St. John's Wort	CoQ10, Vitamin B_2, melatonin	Hypomania, sleep disorders, sleep disturbance, GI tract disturbance
Comments: To be used with caution in patients with diabetes or seizures.					
Tofranil, Janimine • imipramine	Tricyclic antidepressant	Anticonvulsants (Carbamazepine), nasal decongestants, MAO inhibitors	St. John's Wort	CoQ10, Vitamin B_2	Hypertensive crisis, abdominal cramps, inhibits p450 liver enzymes, dry mouth
Comments: Giving 10 mg per day each of vitamins B_1, B_2, and B_6 to elderly, depressed persons already on tricyclic antidepressants improved their depression and ability to think more than placebo did.					
Pamelor • nortriptyline	Tricyclic antidepressant, antipsychotic	Anticonvulsants (Carbamazepine), nasal decongestants, MAO inhibitors	St. John's Wort	CoQ10, Vitamin B_2	Hypertensive crisis, inhibits p450 liver enzymes
Comments: Avoid prolonged sunlight exposure.					
Paxil • paroxetine	SSRI antidepressant (Selective Serotonin Reuptake Inhibitor)	MAO inhibitors or other SSRIs	St. John's Wort	CoQ10, melatonin S, Vitamin B_2	Inhibits p450 liver enzymes, nausea, dizziness, dry mouth, somnolence
Comments: Malaise and general, body aches frequently reported.					

At-A-Glance Quick Reference™ Interaction Chart
Drug Interaction, Nutrient Depletion and Side Effects Reference Chart

Trade Name • Generic Name	Type of Drug	Interaction With Other Drugs	Interaction With Herbs	Possible Nutrient Depletion	Side Effects
Zoloft • sertraline	SSRI antidepressant (Selective Serotonin Reuptake Inhibitor)	Nonsedating antihistamins, carbamazepine, tricyclic antidepressants	St. John's Wort	CoQ10, Vitamin B$_2$, melatonin	Anxiety, appetite loss, drowsiness, dizziness

Comments: Discontinue slowly, as withdrawal symptoms may occur.

NOTES:

- Two commonly used types of antidepressants, SSRIs (Selective Serotonin Reuptake Inhibitors) and MAO (Monoamine oxidase) inhibitors, both have increased serotonin concentration in some brain areas as a result of their action. Serotonin is a neurotransmitter made from the amino acid tryptophan, and serotonin deficiency leads to depression, insomnia, etc. MAO inhibitors will indirectly increase production of serotonin, whereas SSRIs will slow down the degradation of serotonin.

- Tricyclic antidepressants affect the levels of two other important 'mood' neurotransmitters: dopamine and norepinephrine.

- Sometimes the drugs for ADHD are given in single or multiple doses during the day, and sometimes in a sustained release form. Because some of the reviewed medications can cause dependency, caution is advised with following the prescribed dosage and discontinuing the medication carefully and gradually.

- The psychostimulant drugs mentioned in this chapter in fact have a CALMING effect on ADHD children, as shown by clinical trials.

- Depletion of vitamin B$_2$ may cause cracks at the corners of the mouth, inflammation of mucous membranes, soreness and burning of the lips, mouth and the tongue. Possible burning and itching of the eyes, itchy and scaly skin, possible depression and hysteria with long term depletion.

- Depletion of coenzyme Q10 (CoQ10) may cause hypertension, congestive heart failure, angina, stroke, arrhythmia, lack of energy, gingivitis, and general weakness of the immune system.

Section Six

In Closing

The Law And Your Rights

How To Use This Book

"Visioning is going to the end, to get back to the beginning."
– Ken Vegotsky, *The Ultimate Power*

The Law and Your Rights

The American and Canadian systems of laws and rights, when con-trasted, reveal vast differences in accessibility, but neither system guarantees solutions. Americans have rights along with remedies, but those remedies sometimes come at such a prohibitive cost that the rights are of little value. Canadians have rights without remedies, which in the case of learning disabled and other such persons makes those rights a mockery.

The American system understands the inherent weakness of creating laws or rights and at the same time enshrining them in bureaucratic ways that make them tools for those who wish to manipulate, control and disenfranchise those who most need the protection. To that end, they have of necessity created counterbalancing mechanisms to enable as many as possible to access those rights, seek remedies, and be compensated or rewarded for their efforts.

It is a falsehood to believe that any system or individual is protected under the law, especially if the person cannot find, access and effectively use the law to seek and receive justice. This is what "rights without remedies" means. It is the primary method of control the Canadian political system and bureaucracy uses to give an illusion of democracy. It isn't totally negative, but is the type of thing that eventually becomes the seed that causes a sore to fester and infect a society, and that may lead to violence.

America enfranchises and enshrines those rights in an all-inclusive way, in an attempt to achieve openness and fairness. Canada attempts to do the same thing, yet in reality struggles with this concept since it is contrary to its system of government which is ostensibly democratic, yet at the same time the most secretive of Western democracies.

The McCarthy era is an excellent example. In America, it was show-cased and became the primary form of entertainment for the masses at that time. In Canada, a secret war was waged against those believed to be Communists. However, there was no media coverage. It wasn't until the end of the 20th century, upon release of secret documents, that the Canadian

government's past came to light. Even then, little was revealed. Countless
thousands, whose lives were economically and emotionally shattered, suffered in silence, not knowing they had been targeted or why. Their stories
are generally still unknown.

The importance of examining both
systems in terms of their respective legal
rights and remedies serves a few purposes.
One is to understand that you have rights,
but that these rights are only valuable if
they are accessible and can be exercised. A
second is to give you the knowledge to
understand them and the ability to access
groups or government bodies that exist to
implement, protect or offer due process to
individuals dealing with ADD, hyperactivity or any form of disability. A third is to
empower you so you may ask your govern-
ments to improve upon what is. The law
and its application are constantly undergoing change. In addition to federal laws and
bureaucracies, there exist state, provincial,
municipal, school board, ombudsmen,
child protection, handicapped and other
regulatory bodies, which have different sets of rules and methods of accessing them. If you are unsure, call them and ask who handles the type of situation you are experiencing.

> "The basic difference in the
> American and Canadian
> political systems is summed
> up by how citizens and
> elected federal officials
> connect with each other. In
> America, the elected federal
> politicians can send mail to
> their constituents at no
> charge. In Canada, citizens
> send their mail to their
> elected federal politicians at
> no charge."
>
> Professor Ann Gertler
> Director of a
> Pugwash Group

We end on a rather curious note—one which may surprise you.

Over one hundred lawyers, government agencies, groups and individuals involved in promoting or protecting the rights of the disabled—and
unfortunately ADD and hyperactive children and adults fall into that general
category at this time—were contacted. Initially, some responded positively,
then upon reflection declined this opportunity to contribute to this book.
Often they cited the reasons outlined above, and sometimes they did not feel
they could do the topic justice.

We have chosen to draw this to your attention and refer you to
Appendix A at the back of this book listing Civil Rights offices and advocacy
groups throughout the United States, and those we could discover in
Canada.

We challenge you to take an active role in advocating for the learning
disabled, and all disabled. A society is best measured by how well it takes
care of its weakest of members. To that end, we ask you to get involved
today, if not for the sake of a loved one, then for the sake of our society and
our world as a whole. You can make a difference.

How to Use This Book

A Plan For Successfully Dealing With ADD and Hyperactivity

Work with a physician, naturopath or naturally orientated health care provider, or use this as a self-health care road map. Individual decisions are based upon many criteria: costs, parental, social, and psychological skills and support systems, single- or two-parent household, emotional state, educational resources, time constraints, expectations of the time it will take to deal with the problem. There are even more consideration; the list of possibilities is endless, based on your preferences.

Our preferences are based on the following criteria:

- That which is least intrusive should be done first.
- That which causes the healing response to occur within the child or adult with ADD, hyperactivity or any learning disability, is preferable over that which just masks the symptoms.
- That which results in long-term healing and does the least amount of harm to the child or adult, is always best.

Finally, whatever works for you and your ADD, hyperactive child or adult and whatever you feel most comfortable with, is the best choice you can make now. There is no one "right" answer, since people are not like "one size fits all" pieces of clothing. The fit must be just right for each individual involved in the process.

If drugs are currently being used on the ADD, hyperactive or learning disabled child or adult, then consult with your physician prior to doing anything, as drugs can have many side effects when other variables are changed, and these side effects can be harmful to those using them. The child or adult may have to be weaned off the drugs before changing the treatment plan.

Use the resources and reference sections in the back of the book to access those people, groups, information, products or whatever it is you have determined you need.

Finally, we need your help. We want to hear from you and the health-care professional you work with in your mutually beneficial quest for health and healing. Please photocopy the "Reader Feedback Form" in Appendix G and the "Health-Care Feed Back Form" in Appendix H, and mail them back to us, at one of the addresses in the About the authors Appendix I. The forms are also available online at the AGES Publications™ web site www.800line.com/ages/.

Our books are *Living Books*™ which means in future editions, as important pertinent or relevant information becomes available, we publish it. We have one goal in mind, and until that goal is achieved, we will try our best to keep you informed, as in the words of Bahir Ben Ken, from *The Prophet Revisited*, "So all may be healed."

Step 1 — Realization and Awareness

If the ADD/hyperactive child or adult is taking drugs, consult with your physician prior to making any changes to his or her medication(s), or any major lifestyle changes.

Refer to Section 5, "The Pharmaceutical Drugs," paying particular attention to the side effects section for the drug or drugs being taken. Use the check boxes for the side effects that maybe manifesting themselves. Keeping good records is vital for you so you can explain your situation to the health care providers you work with.

Refer to and share the information with your health care provider in the treatment plan or plans you choose from Section 1.

To decrease the amount of a drug being used, refer to Chapter 7, "Acupressure: The Use of Acupressure Beads In The Treatment of ADHD."

Step 2 — Discovery

Discover what the underlying cause or causes of the problem may be, and the treatment protocols. The order you choose to take, is up to you. Start with the approach you feel most comfortable with. Work your way through the list, until you discover the cause or causes of the problem.

Some may choose the self-health care route and start with diet. Some may prefer to work with their doctor, naturopath, or other health care professional. As long as you achieve the results you want, that is what is important.

The order is up to you. Just begin.

Notes:

1. To reduce the levels of medications being taken, refer to Chapter 7, Acupressure: The Use of Acupressure Beads In The Treatment of ADHD.
2. For specific conditions, such as yeast or asthma, refer to the index to find out where they are mentioned in this book.
3. If you do not understand a term, refer to Appendix B, Glossary of Terms.
4. To access products, refer to Appendix E, Product Descriptions and Sources.

Step 3 — Natural Health and Healing Options

Lifestyle Choices

Emotional Rebalancing Choices

Food and Nutrient Deficiency Choices

- Chapter 11   The Feingold Program: Diet
- Chapter 17   Essential Fatty Acids: Fats that Heal the ADD/Hyperactive Brain
- Chapter 13   The Secret World of Flavor Enhancers: MSG and Aspartame, The deadly duo
- Chapter 14   The Problems With Soft Drinks
- Chapter 15   Sugar - Friend or Foe!?
- Chapter 16   Water: A Source of Problems and Solutions
- Chapter 19   Amino Acids and Proteins

Note: A test for nutrient deficiencies is described in Chapter 4, Environmental Factors: Organic Acids and Hyperactivity.

Psychological, Behavioral and Home/School Environment Choices

- Chapter 26   The Healing Power of Sound: Music and Guided Imagery
- Chapter 16   Water: A Source of Problems and Solutions
- Chapter 14   The Problems With Soft Drinks
- Chapter 21   Bach Flower Remedies
- Chapter 27   Tales to Empower™ Teachers, Parents and ADD/Hyperactive Children and Adults
- Chapter 24   Neurofeedback for ADD/Hyperactivity
- Chapter 25   Mediation of Cognitive Competencies for Students in Need: The Fuerstein Method

Step 4 — Inspiration

Discover the power of inspiration. When ever you are frustrated, or feel you are at the end of your rope, read one or all of the following to yourself. Put a copy in your purse, wallet, on the refrigerator, in your bedroom, wherever you can access it quickly.

Serenity Prayer

God grant me the strength to accept the things I cannot change, courage to change the things I can, and the wisdom to know the difference.

The Daily Prayer — Patience Strong

Grant me the strength to do the tasks that every hour demands.
Give me hope and faith, a happy heart and willing hands.
Be thou close to me, O Lord, and hear me when I call.
Light a star above my path when twilight shadows fall.
Help me to accept whatever comes with every day.
And if I should meet with trials and troubles, this I pray...
Lead me by the quiet waters of tranquility
—where my soul may find its comfort and its peace in Thee.

Soliloquy of Devotion

"When I fail, or mess up, no matter what it is or who was involved, I am 100% responsible for the outcome. When I succeed, I am only 1% responsible, the other 99% is you, the people and the Unseen Hand. Some would say luck, God, Jesus Christ, Hashem, Mohammed, but I know it is the One, and it matters naught, for I am thankful for whatever comes my way, whether it be sunshine, or a cloudy day. That I may learn from all that happens to and for me, that is a gift. For each and every day, hour, minute, second, moment that passes is a treasure. Fragile, rare and everlasting... ever blossoming. As my life enfolds before me, my past reveals itself in a thousand silent moments, resonating in this moment, for this is the only moment... this is the only moment. Thank you, Unseen Hand."

– Bahir Ben Ken, from *The Prophet Revisited* by Ken Vegotsky

Step 5 — Stay Informed

Keep an open heart and mind. Be patient. Accept the fact that what may work for one individual, may not work for another.

- Chapter 3   A Refreshing Overview of Some Natural and Complementary Choices
- Chapter 28 Are Drugs the Solution?
- Chapter 29 The Pharmaceutical Drugs
- Chapter 30 The Law and Your Rights
- Use the appendices in the back of this book

and Finally...

...Never Give Up!!!

As this journey began, so shall it end,
in the words of the man whose vision lead to the creation of
The All-in-One Guide to™ *Add and Hyperactivity:*

"The healer is your inner physician,
guided by the power of the One, manifested in Love."

— Bahir Ben Ken, from *The Prophet Revisited*

**May love, peace, prosperity and
health be you and yours for eternity.**

To life!

Appendix A
Key Information Resources for Professionals and Consumers

Note: Due to changes in area codes, we apologize for any difficulty this may cause in trying to connect with a group or association. If a number is not working, please call the telephone operator, and verify if the area code has changed.

Appendix A-1 — Key Health Care Resources

For health care professionals and consumers, use these resources to get scientific and other studies related to natural remedies mentioned in this book. For additional information or references check the listing of books in the bibliography. Information exists, and it is up to you and your health care provider to arrange a mutually beneficial relationship, in your quest for optimal health.

The National Center for Complimentary and Alternative Medicine

Underwritten by the American federal government, it is located in Silver Springs, Maryland. Initially it was given a 25 million dollar budget to handle grants for researchers into the safety and effectiveness of alternative medicine. They offer professionals and consumers health related information through their

Toll free telephone: 1 (800) 644-6226.
Internet home page: altmed.od.nih.gov

Medical and alternative health information services that charge fees

They tell you what you what to know about a treatment and/or a product based on the studies and information available. They take the time to explain to you what the information means. This empowers you, so you can present it to your health care provider, or your health care provider can access it for your benefit. Two excellent ones are:

Health Resources in Conway, Arkansas.

Toll free telephone: 1 (800) 949-0090

Institute for Health and Healing Library

They offer an information service through the Plaintree Health Resources Center, 2040 Western Street, San Francisco, California

Telephone: (415) 923-3681
Fax: (415) 673-2629

Medical reference books used while researching this book

The books listed below offer extensive information and with generally well referenced materials from studies:

The Physicians Desk Reference: Can be found in resource and medical libraries, at pharmacies, doctors offices. Updated annually. It is the American and Canadian pharmacological reference book.

Martindale: The Extra Pharmacopeia. It is the United Kingdom's pharmacological and herb reference book. The herbs are well referenced and very conservatively dealt with. Superior supporting documentation compared to its North American equivalent, which is clearly slanted to pharmacological drugs only. In the U.S.A. and Canada, you can access it at most university medical libraries.

German Commission E Monographs: Translated into English, it is the German medical professions herb reference book. The detailed information gives health care providers the recognized uses of herbs and other substances as supported by scientific studies. Available for $189 through The Herb Research Foundation

Toll free telephone: 1 (800) 307-6267 or (303) 449-2265

Herbal Medicine Information

For herbal medicine information you can write to these two organizations and/or subscribe to *Herbalgram,* a top notch magazine that they jointly publish, which reviews the most recent botanical medicine developments.

The American Botanical Council   The Herb Research Foundation
PO Box 201660   1007 Pearl Street, Suite 200
Austin TX 78720   Boulder CO 80302

Herbalgram subscription toll free telephone number: 1 (800) 748-2617 or (303) 449-2265.

Appendix A-2 – Complementary Medicine Groups

This section lists Complementary Medicine Groups which may offer information, educational standards and/or referal services.

To be considered for a listing in future publications or to update your entry, organizations should mail information and media kits to AGES Publications™, 1623 Military Road, PMB 203-AH, Niagara Falls, NY, 14304-1745. Groups or organizations may insert a link on the AGES web-site at http://www.800line.com/ages/.

> **Note:** This is NOT a solicitation for manuscripts. Refer to manuscript submission guidelines on our web site. Our publishing schedule is filled for the foreseeable future.

Acupuncture

American Academy of Medical Acupuncture (AAMA) – This academy trains M.D.'s and D.O.'s in acupuncture. Write to AAMA for a local referral or go online for a list of practitioners.

5820 Wilshire Blvd Suite 500   Phone: 800-521-2262
Los Angeles CA 90036   Web site: www.medicalacupuncture.org

Acupuncture and Chinese Medicine

Acupuncture and Oriental Medicine Alliance – On the web sites, access over 10,000 practitioner whose accreditations are verified, plus information about training, including a list of schools of acupuncture and Oriental medicine. Some are practitioners of Chinese herbal medicine. For a small fee, they will send you a guide with legal information about acupuncture and Oriental medicine.

14637 Starr Rd SE   Phone: 253-851-6896 Fax: 253-851-6883
Olalla WA 98359   Web site: www.acuall.org
                                       www.acupuncturealliance.org

National Certification Commission for Acupuncture and Oriental Medicine (NCCAOM) – National certification program for acupuncturists, Oriental bodywork therapists and Chinese herbologists, which is required for licensing in every state (and the District of Columbia) except California and Nevada, which have their own exams. A practitioner directory is available by mail ($3 per state; $22 for the complete directory) or on the commission's web site which also includes certification criteria.

11 Canal Center Plaza Suite 300   Phone: 703-548-9004
Alexandria VA 22314   Web site: www.nccaom.org

Aromatherapy — see Massage, Bodywork, and Aromatherapy

Ayurveda — These groups offer referrals to their graduate practitioners:

American Institute of Vedic Studies
PO Box 8357   Phone: 505-983-9385
Santa Fe NM 87504-8357   Web site: www.vedanet.com

O.M.D. – Directed by prominent Ayurvedic physician and author David Frawley, O.M.D. offers programs in Vedic and yogic knowledge as well as the broader field of Hindu studies. Facilities located throughout the United States.

Ayurveda Holistic Center of New York – Their Web site shows their certification and Ph.D. programs. It offers an Ayurveda encyclopedia, a dosha self-test, online consultations and more.

82-A Bayville Ave   Phone: 516-628-8200
Bayville NY 11709   Web site: www.ayurvedahc.com

The Ayurvedic Institute – Program directed by Ayurvedic physician and author Dr. Vasant Lad, M.A.Sc., a former professor of medicine at the Pune University College of Ayurvedic Medicine in Pune, India, and medical director of their Ayurvedic hospital. They teache the traditional therapy of the East Indian Ayurveda, including acupressure massage, herbs, nutrition, panchakarma cleansing, Sanskrit, yoga, and Jyotish - Vedic astrology.

PO Box 23445   Phone: 505-291-9698
Albuquerque NM 87192-1445   Web site: www.ayurveda.com

College of Maharishi Vedic Medicine – They offer a B.A. in Maharishi Vedic medicine and a Ph.D. in physiology with specialization in Maharishi Vedic medicine. Ayurveda is included in the programs.

Maharishi Univ. of Management   Phone: 800-369-6480 or 515-472-1110
Fairfield, IA 52557   Web site: www.mum.edu

Raj Maharishi Ayurveda Health Center – Offers in-depth Ayurvedic treatments, consultations, and list of practitioners. Also sells Ayurvedic herbs and other products. The Web site offers you a health evaluation from a trained practitioner.

1734 Jasmine Ave   Phone: 800-248-9050
Fairfield, IA 52556   Web site: www.theraj.com

Biofeedback

Association for Applied Psychophysiology and Biofeedback (AAPB) – This association has more than 2,000 members who teach and conduct research in biofeedback. The Web site tells what problems biofeedback can help. A "how to find a practitioner" section of the site is under construction.

10200 W 44th Ave Suite 310   Phone:
Wheat Ridge CO 80033   Web site: www.aapb.org

Biofeedback Certification Institute of America (BCIA) – Only institute in the world for certification of biofeedback therapists. For a list of certified biofeedback therapists in your area, send a business-size, self-addressed, stamped envelope, or visit the Web site.

10200 W 44th Ave Suite 310   Phone: 303-422-8439
Wheat Ridge CO 80033   Web site: www.bcia.org

Bodywork — see Massage, Bodywork, and Aromatherapy

Chiropractic and Osteopathic Manipulation

American Academy of Osteopathy (AAO) – The professional group for all doctors of osteopathy (D.O.'s). Many M.D.'s are among the more than 4,000 members. Send $5 and a business-size, self-addressed, stamped envelope with your request for a list of members.

3500 DePanw Blvd Suite 1080   Phone: 317-879-1881
Indianapolis IN 46268-1136   Web site: www.aao.medguide.net

American Chiropractic Association Largest chiropractic organization in the United States, has chapters in every state. Call or visit online to find a chiropractor near you.

1701 Clarendon Blvd   Phone: 800-986-4636
Arlington VA 22209   Web site: www.amerchiro.org

American Osteopamic Association (AOA) – On the phone or on the Web, AOA can refer you to an osteopath in your area.

142 E Ontario St   Phone: 800-621-1773, ext. 8252
Chicago IL 60611   Web site: www.aoa-net.org

Association for Network Chiropractic – To find a practitioner, go to the Web site.

444 N Main St   Phone: 303-678-8101
Longmont CO 80501   Web site: www.networkchiropractic.org

Federation of Straight Chiropractors – They define straight chiropractic as contributing to health through the correction of vertebral subluxation. To find a practitioner, go to the Web site.

642 Broad St   Phone: 800-521-9856
Clifton NJ 07013   Web site: www.straightchiropractic.com

International Chiropractors Association – This is the oldest chiropractic organization. Call or visit the Web site for help in locating a practitioner in your area.

1110 N Glebe Rd Suite 1000   Phone: 800-423-4690
Arlington VA 22201   Web site: www.chiropractic.org

World Chiropractic Alliance Web site supplies information for the public as well as for doctors and students of chiropractic.Administered by a practicing chiropractor, not by an organization.

2950 N Dobson Rd Suite 1   Phone: 800-347-1011
Chandler AZ 85224   Web site: www.chiropage.com

Complementary and Holistic Therapies: *General*

Alternative Medicine Yellow Pages – A publication listing over 16,000 practitioners of complementary therapies throughout the U.S.A., including many M.D.'s and D.O.'s. Visit the Web page to search the yellow pages directory online.

Future Medicine Publishing   Phone: 800-333-4325
1640 Tlburon Blvd   Web site: www.alternativemedicine.com
Tlburon CA 94920

American Holistic Health Association (AHHA) – It is a national clearinghouse of information about complementary therapies and practitioners. Web site has a directory of holistic practitioners, resource lists and self-help articles.

PO Box 17400   Phone: 714-779-6152
Anaheim CA 92817   Web site: www.aKha.org

Upledger Institute

Florida   Phone: 800-233-5880 (USA and Canada)
                                       Phone: 561-622-4706 Fax: 561-627-9231
                                       Web site: www.upledger.com

International Alliance of Health-Care Practitioners – a web site listing complementary health practitioners such as craniosacral therapist.

                                       Web site: www.iahp.com

American Holistic Medical Association (AMMA) – Web site offers a practitioner directory, or you can send $10 for the association's list of practitioners. Also offers guidelines for choosing a holistic practitioner.

6728 Old McLean Village Dr   Phone: 703-556-9728
McLean VA 22101   Web site: www.holisticmedicine.org

Diet Therapy

Regardless of the diet you want to consider—low-fat, elimination, Feingold Diet, vegetarian—the American Board of Nutrition and the American Dietetic Association can provide referrals in any locality, or contact the associations directly.

American Board of Nutrition (ABN) – Publishes a free directory of certified nutritionists. Write or visit the Web site.

Univ. of Alabama - Birmingham   Phone: 205-975-8788
1675 University Blvd WEBB 234   Web site: www.uab.edu/nusc/abn.htm
Birmingham AL 35294-3360

American Dietetic Association (ADA) – To find a registered dietitian (R.D.) near you, call or search their Web site. They also are gateway to related sites including associations, consumer education sources, food service organizations, government sites, and other dietetic groups. To ask an R.D. nutritionrelated questions, dial 900-225-5267; the call costs $1.95 for the first minute, $0.95 per minute thereafter.

216 W Jackson Blvd Suite 800   Phone: 800-366-1655
Chicago IL 60606   Web site: www.eatright.org

Elimination Diets – Some M.D.'s may recommend an elimination diet for allergy tracking and treatment. Naturopaths have training in elimination diet therapies. For ways to find a naturopath refer to *Naturopathy*.

Feingold Association of the United States (FAUS) –

PO Box 6550   Phone: 800-321-3287 or 703-768-3287
Alexandria Virginia 22306   Fax: 703-768-3619
                                    Web site: win/wp.faus/articles
                                              www.feingold.org

Exercise & Walking

American Council on Exercise (ACE) – ACE can provide a registry of certified professionals to help you find a personal trainer, a group fitness instructor, or a lifestyle and weight management consultant.

5820 Oberlin Dr   Phone: 800-825-3636
San Diego CA 92121   Web site: www acefitness.org

Creative Walking Inc. – Trains educators and corporate and health care specialists to support walking programs in corporations, schools, and health care facilities. Write for information.

PO Box 50296   Phone: 800-762-9255
Clayton MO 63105

Prevention Walking Club – Walking club with over 15,000 members. A bimonthly newsletter, walkers' conventions, and other benefits. On the web page, a walking expert answers questions about the best walking shoes, weight loss programs, and ways to find fitness buddies.

33 E. Minor St   Phone: 800-666-1216
Emmaus PA 18098   Web site: www.healthyideas.com/walking/

Functional Medicine

Institute for Functional Medicine – For parents, adults and care-givers who would like a referral to a trained practitioner in Functional Medicine, contact the Institute or check their web site.

c/o HealthComm International Inc.   Phone: 253-851-3943
PO Box 1729   Web site: www.fxmed.com
Gig Harbor, WA 98335

Healthcare providers wanting to obtain further training in the emerging field of Functional Medicine are encouraged to research the educational resources available.

The Institute for Functional Medicine offers comprehensive full-credit courses, such as *Applying Functional Medicine in Clinical Practice,* as well as pertinent published material and audiovisual programs. *Functional Medicine Update,* their monthly audio program, is produced by Dr. Jeffrey Bland, Ph.D., and used by thousands of subscribers around the world.

The Institute's fully accredited continuing medical education Inter-national Symposium on Functional Medicine is an annual scientific conference attended by more then 1000 professionals, featuring some of the world's top scientists and clinicians. For more information about Functional Medicine and healing the hyperactive brain, you can access the web site www.PureLiving.com.

Herbal Therapy

American Herbalist Guild (AHG) – Professional member's to qualify for certification complete 4 years of formal training and hands-on experience in herbal therapy. They must be recommended by three professional members, and show competence in working with medicinal herbs and clients. Contact the guild or go on-line for referrals to its 100 professional members. For a copy of the AHG Directory of Herbal Education Prograrns, write to AHG; the training programs listed can give you referrals to their graduates.

PO Box 70   Phone: 435-722-8434
Roosevelt UT 84066   Web site: www.healthy.com/herbalists/

Holistic Therapies
— see Complementary and Holistic Therapies: General

Homeopathy

American Board of Homeotherapeutics – They certify M.D.'s and D.O.'s who practice homeopathy. See **National Center for Homeopathy** for practitioner directory information.

801 N Fairfax #306   Phone: 703-548-7790
Alexandria VA 22314   Web site:

Council for Homeopathic Certification – Practitioners trained and certified by them complete an examination process and agree to practice according to their code of ethics. The Web site lists certified practitioners.

1199 Sanchez St   Phone: 415-789-7677
San Francisco CA 94146   Web site: www.healthy.net/othersites/
                                              homeopathiccouncil/

Homeopathic Academy of Naturopathic Physicians (HANP) – Certifies naturopathic homeopaths, sets educational standards of practice, and offers referrals.

12132 SE Foster Pl   Phone: 503-761-3298
Portland OR 97266   Web site: www.healthy.net/HANP/

Homeopathic Educational Services – Call or write for a cat
books and medicines. Offers a practitioner directory by mail
2124 Kittredge St   Phone: 510-649-029
Berkeley CA 94704   Web site: www.homeopathic.com

National Center for Homeopathy – Nonprofit organization promotes homeopathy,
a training program and study groups, and publishes a monthly magazine,
Homeopathy Today. Send $10 or visit the Web site for a state-by-state list of prac-
ticing homeopaths. Note: Practitioners have paid a fee to be listed in the directory.
801 N Fairfax #306   Phone: 703-548-7790
Alexandria, VA 22314   Web site: www.homeopathic.com

North American Society of Homeopaths (NASH) – Site has a directory of registered homeopaths and the NASH journal and newsletter.
81122 Pike St Suite 1122   Phone: 206-720-7000
Seattle WA 98122   Web site: www.homeopathy.org

Massage, Bodywork, and Aromatherapy

American Massage Therapy Association – Provides phone and e-mail referrals to
certified massage therapists and schools in the U.S.A..
820 Davis St Suite 100   Phone: 847-864-0123
Evanston IL 60201   Web site: www.amtamassage.org

Associated Bodywork and Massage Professionals – Provides referrals to members
in the U.S.A. Go to their Web site to find a qualified practitioner.
28677 Buffalo Park Rd   Phone: 800-458-2267 or 303-674-8478
Evergreen CO 80439-7347   Web site: www.aLmp.com

American Society of the Alexander Technique (AmSAT) – Call or visit the Web site
for help in finding a qualified teacher of this bodywork technique.
401 E Market St Suite 17   Phone: 800-473-0620
Charlottesville, VA 22902   Web site: www.alexandertech.org

Aston-Patterning Center – Aston-Patterning is an integrated system of movement
education, bodywork, and ergonomics. Web site can help you find a practitioner.
PO Box 3568   Phone: 775-831-8228
Incline Village NV 89450   Web site: www.aston-patterning.com

Bonnie Prudden Myotherapy Pain Erasure – Myotherapy is a method of relaxing
muscle spasms, alleviating pain by using "trigger-point" pressure, and improving circulation. Call or visit on-line to locate a therapist near you.
PO Box 65240   Phone: 800-221-4634 or 520-529-3979
Tucson AZ 85728-5240   Web site: www.bonnieprudden.com

enkrais Guild of North America – Go to the Web site to read about this method awareness through movement and to find a practitioner.

3611 SW Hood Ave Suite 100   Phone: 800-775-2118
Portland OR 97201   Web site: www.feldenkrais.com

Hellerwork International, LLC. – Go to the Web site to find articles, testimonials, training information, and list of practitioners.

406 Berry St   Phone: 800-392-3900
Mt Shasta CA 96067   Web site: www.hellerwork.com

Rolf Institute – Through deep manipulatiors. Rolfer's balance the body and facilitate increased levels of efficiency and ease. Provides a free directory of certified practitioners. Web site helps you find a practitioner.

205 Canyon Blvd   Phone: 800-530-8875
Boulder CO 80302   Web site: www.rolf.org

Trager Institute – A psychophysical approach focusing on integration and Mentastics movement education. Web site helps locate practitioners.

21 Locust St   Phone: 415-388-2688
Mill Valley CA 94941-2806   Web site: www.trager.com

Meditation and Visualization

Academy for Guided Imagery (AGI) – The academy trains health professionals in using guided imagery in healing. For more information, send a stamped, self-addressed envelope. Web site locates a practitioner by city, zip code, area code, or state or province.

PO Box 2070   Phone: 800-726-2070
Mill Valley CA 94942   Web site: www.healthy.net/agi/

American Society of Clinical Hypnosis – For a practitioner list, send a stamped, self-addressed envelope.

33 W Grand Ave Suite 40Z   Phone:
Chicago IL 60610   Web site:

Society for Clinical and Experimental Hypnosis (SCEH) – A professional organization that can refer you to member hypnotherapists. Members include psychiatrists, psychologists, nurses, and other professionals dedicated to the use of hypnosis in a clinical setting. Write or visit their Web site for information.

2201 Hacder Rd Suite 1   Phone: 509-332-7555
Pullman WA 99163   Web site: www.sunsite.utk.edu/lJCEH/
                                       scehmain.htm

Music and Art Therapies

American Art Therapy Association, Inc. – For information packet about art therapy, send check or money order for $6 U.S. with a written request. Call for referrals to therapists or state organizations.

1202 Allanson Rd   Phone: 888-290-0878
Mundelein IL 60060-3808   Web site: www.arttherapy.org

American Music Therapy Association, Inc. – Provides printed and online referrals for training programs and therapists.

8455 Colesville Rd Suite 1000   Phone: 301-589-3300
Silver Spring MD 20910   Web site: www.musictherapy.org

Naturopathy

Association of Naturopathic Physicians (AANP) – AANP is open to practitioners who have completed training at any of the four schools offering the curriculum. Approximately 1,500 naturopaths are members. AANP offers a membership directory for a fee. For a practitioner referral, call the association or visit online.

601 Valley St Suite 105   Phone: 206-298-0125
Seattle WA 98109   Web site: www.naturopathic.org

Bastyr University – Leading American school of naturopathic medicine. Also offers training in Ayurvedic and other naturally oriented healing systems. Also has a student teaching clinic for the college.

14500 Juanita Dr NE   Phone: 425-823-1300
Kenmore WA 98028-4966   Web site: www.bastyr.edu

Canadian College of Naturopathic Medicine – Founded in 1978, the college offers a four-year full-time professional program in naturopathic medicine as well as continuing education programs. Graduates receive a Doctor of Naturopathic Medicine (N.D.) diploma. Enrollment has grown nine times since 1991, and public demand has steadily followed suit. The college is home to the Robert Schad Naturopathic Clinic, where students train under the direction of licensed naturopathic doctors. In Canada, naturopathic doctors are regulated under provincial statue in British Columbia, Saskatchewan, Manitoba and Ontario. Legislation is imminent in Alberta and Nova Scotia.

1255 Sheppard Ave E   Phone: 416-498-1255
Toronto ON M2K 1E2   Web site: www.ccnm.edu

Robert Schad Naturopathic Clinic   Phone: 416-498-9763

Canadian Naturopathic Association (CNA) – Write or go online to get information about naturopathic medicine and for referrals to naturopathic doctors or physicians in Canada.

1255 Sheppard Ave E   Phone: 416-496-8633
Toronto ON M2K 1E2   Phone: 877-628-7284 (toll-free in Canada)
                                          Web site: www.naturopathicassoc.ca

Homeopathic Academy of Naturopathic Physicians (HANP) – Certifies qualified naturopathic physicians in classical homeopathy. For a directory of naturopaths who specialize in homeopathy, call or visit the Web site.

12132 SE Foster Pl	Phone: 503-761-3298
Portland OR 97266	Web site: www.healthy.net/HANP/

National College of Naturopathic Medicine – They also have a student teaching clinic for the college.

049 SW Porter	Phone: 503-499-4343
Portland OR 97201	Web site: www.ncnm.edu

South West College of Naturopathic Medicine

2140 E Broadway Rd	Phone: 480-858-9100
Tempe Arizona 85282	Web site:

University of Bridgeport

60 Lafayette St	Phone: 203-576-4109
Bridgeport CT 06601	Web site: E-mail: natmed@bridgeport.edu

New Science of Functional Medicine — see Functional Medicine

Other Resources

Emmett E. Miller Source Cassettes – Basic relaxation tapes and other programs, such as *Smoke No More, The Sleep Tape, Imagine Yourself Slim,* and *Positive Images for People With Cancer.*

PO Box 6028	Phone: 800-528-2737
Auburn CA 95604	Web site: www.drmiller.com

Mind/Body Medical Institute – Herbert Benson, M.D., author of *The Relaxation Response,* offers a series of relaxation audiotapes. Request a free catalog by mail or order online.

110 Francis St Suite 1-A	Phone:
Boston MA 02215	Web site: mindbody.harvard.edu

Relaxation Response Institute – Eli Bay, Canada's leading expert. Relation training sessions, video and audiotape programs.

Toronto, ON	Phone: 416-932-2784

Stress Reduction Tapes – Jon Kabat-Zinn, Ph.D., of the Center for Mindfulness in Medicine, Health Care, and Society, produced a series of meditation audiotapes. Order books and tapes by mail or online.

PO Box 547	Phone:
Lexington, MA 02420	Web site: www.mindfulnesstapes.com

Vegetarianism

Vegetarian Resource Group – A nonprofit group, the Vegetarian Resource Group publishes Vegetarian Journal, books on vegetarianism, cookbooks, and pamphlets. Go to the Web site for recipes, journal articles, a list of alternatives to dairy and eggs, also vegetarian travel information.

PO Box 1463   Phone: 410-366-8343
Baltimore MD 21203   Web site: www.vrg.org

Toronto Vegetarian Association – Extensive library resource center, with books, videos, audiotapes, and fact sheets.

2300 Yonge St Suite 1101   Phone: 416-544-9800
PO Box 2307   Web site:
Toronto ON M4P 1E4

Social Support — see Appendix F Support Groups

Tai Chi and Qigong

Tai Chi for Health Living Arts – A 2-hour color video featuring Terry Dunn teaches a form of tai chi. For a catalog of tai chi, yoga, and massage products, including CDs and cassettes, visit online.

2434 Main St   Phone: 310-399-3700
Santa Monica CA 90405   Web site: www.livingarts.com

Wayfarer Publications – For a catalog of hundreds of products dealing with tai chi, qigong, and the martial arts, write, call, or visit their Web site.

PO Box 26156   Phone: 800-888-9119
Los Angeles CA 90026   Web site: www.tai-chi.com

Vitamin and Mineral Supplementation

See **Diet Therapy** for information about the **American Board of Nutrition** (ABN) and **American Dietetic Association** (ADA), organizations that can refer you to a registered dietitian. AGES Publications™ publishes books such as *The All-in-One Guide to*™ *Natural Remedies and Supplements* and *The All-in-One Guide to*™ *Tea Tree Oil*, dealing with health problems from A to Z. More complete information is in the back of this book. To order AGES Publications™ titles, call the order desk at 888-545-0053, or go to www.800line.com/ages/ for on-line services.

Yoga

Over 50 listings for yoga organizations appear on the American Yoga Association Web site. Some are administered by a city or university; others are one-person organizations. Ask a friend, neighbor, coworker, or health practitioner for a referral to a practitioner near you.

American Yoga Association (AYA) – Offers a list of books, tapes, and general tips including guidelines for choosing a yoga instructor. Send a business' size, self-addressed, stamped envelope for information. They do not provide a practitioner list or referrals. Visit online to see their catalog. They recommend *The American Yoga Association Wellness Book: Complementary Therapy for Common Conditions* by Alice Christensen.

PO Box 19986   Phone: 941-927-4977
Sarasota FL 34276   Web site: members.aol.com/amyogaassn

Appendix A-3 – Civil Rights Offices

Address correspondence to: Office for Civil Rights
(add the address for your area) U.S. Department of Education

Boston Office
Connecticut, Maine, Massachusetts, New Hampshire, Rhode Island, Vermont

J.W. McCormack Post Office &   Phone: 617-223-9662
Courthouse Room 701   TDD: 617-223-9695
Boston MA 02109

New York Office
New Jersey, New York, Puerto Rico, Virgin Islands

75 Park Place 14th Fl   Phone: 212-637-6466
New York NY 10007   TDD: 212-637-0478

Philadelphia Office
Delaware, Kentucky, Maryland, Pennsylvania, West Virginia

Wanamaler Bldg Suite 515   Phone: 215-656-8541
100 Penn Square E   TDD: 215-656-8604
Philadelphia PA 19107

Atlanta Office
Alabama, Florida, Georgia, South Carolina, Tennessee

61 Forsyth St SW Suite 19T70   Phone: 404-562-6350
Atlanta GA 30303   TDD: 404-331-7236

District of Columbia Office
North Carolina, Virginia, Washington, DC

1100 Pennsylvania Ave NW Rm 316	Phone: 202-208-2545
PO Box 14620	TDD: 202-208-7741
Washington DC 20044-4620	

Chicago Office
llinois, Indiana, Minnesota, Wisconsin

111 N Canal St Suite 1053	Phone: 312-886-8434
Chicago IL 60606	TDD: 312-353-2540

Dallas Office
Arkansas, Louisiana, Mississippi, Oklahoma, Texas

1999 Bryan St Suite 2600	Phone: 214-880-2459
Dallas TX 75201	TDD: 214-880-2456

Cleveland Office
Michigan, Ohio

Bank One Center Rm 750	Phone: 216-522-4970
600 Superior Ave E	TDD: 216-522-4944
Cleveland OH 44114	

Kansas City Office
Iowa, Kansas, Missouri, Nebraska, North Dakota, South Dakota

10220 N Executive Hills Blvd 8th Fl	Phone: 816-880-4200
Kansas City MO 64153	TDD: 816-891-0582

Denver Office
Arizona, Colorado, Montana, New Mexico, Utah, Wyoming

Federal Bldg Suite 310	Phone: 303-844-5695
1244 Speer Blvd	TDD: 303-844-3417
Denver CO 80204	

San Francisco Office
California

Old Federal Bldg	Phone: 415-556-4275
50 United Nations Plaza, Rm 239	TDD: 415-437-7783
San Francisco CA 94102	

Seattle Office
Alaska, Hawaii, Idaho, Nevada, Oregon, Washington, American Samoa, Guam, Trust Territory of the Pacific Islands

915 Second Avenue Rm 3310	Phone: 206-220-7900
Seattle WA 98174	TDD: 206-220-7907

Appendix B
Glossary of Terms

– A –

Abscess - an infection of a sebaceous gland. This results in an inflammation of the skin and localized painful swelling.

Absorption - the process by which a substance passes into the bloodstream.

Acupressure - a point-massaging technique that can be both relaxing and energizing. Applying pressure to energy meridians is thought to rebalance energy forces that have been compromised by illness, stress, or an unhealthy lifestyle.

Acupressure Bead - an acupressure device applied to the surface of the ear that stimulates "Qi" energy. (See Qi)

Acid - a sour substance that is usually water-soluble. Has a pH reading of less then 7.

ADD/ADHD - a condition in which the individual is unable to maintain a focused state of attention, or manage his or her impulses and behavior. It occurs in approximately 3-5% of school-age children, and in 1-2% of adults.

Adderall - an amphetamine drug used to treat Attention-Deficit Hyperactivity Disorder and Narcolepsy.

Addiction - a state of dependence on a drug characterized by uncontrolled drug-seeking behavior, growing tolerance for the effects of the drugs being taken, and symptoms of withdrawal when the drug is withheld.

Adrenals - glands above the kidneys that manufacture adrenaline, DHEA, and other vital substances that affect the quality of life.

Adverse Effect - an unexpected harmful response to a drug or herbal preparation. There are three types of adverse reaction: those due to an allergy to the drug, those caused by an individual's physical constitution, and those brought on by toxic effects of the drug.

Adverse Reaction - see Adverse Effect

Alcohol - a pungent, colorless liquid, forming esters in reaction with organic acids, sometimes used as a solvent when extracting essential oils or as a carrier base for essential oils.

Allergy - a condition that arises when the immune system reacts to environmental stimuli or certain foods.

Allergy, drug - an abnormal drug response that arises in individuals who produce antibodies that react to foreign substances-in this case, a drug. The individual who has a history of hay fever, asthma or eczema is more likely to develop drug allergies. Allergic reactions to drugs may take many forms: skin eruptions, fever, swollen glands, difficulty breathing, etc.

Alterative - agents that gradually and favorably alter the body's condition.

Alzheimer's disease - a degenerative disease of the central nervous system, usually exhibiting premature mental deterioration.

Amenorrhea - a condition occurring after the onset of menstruation in which there is an abnormal absence of the menstrual cycle.

Amino acids - the organic components from which proteins are made.

Analgesic - pain-relieving substances that do not affect consciousness.

Anthelmintic - stimulating herbs or substances that work against parasitic worms that may be in the digestive system.

Antibiotic - a substance that can inhibit the growth of microorganisms and that is capable of destroying or weakening bacteria.

Anti-catarrhal - herbs and substances that eliminate or counteract mucous formation.

Anticoagulant - a substance that prevents or delays blood clotting.

Anti-depressant - an agent or substance used to treat depression.

Anti-fungal - a substance that battles or is antagonistic to fungi.

Antigen - any substance normally not present in the body that stimulates an immune response.

Antihistamine - a drug or substance that counteracts or blocks the physiological action of histamine.

Anti-inflammatory - helps the body to combat the inflammation manifested by redness, pain, heat and swelling in the body.

Anthelmintic - a substance that works against worm infestations.

Antilithic - herbs and substances that help remove or prevent the formation of gravel or stones in the urinary tract.

Anti-microbial - substances used to rid the body or surface of the skin of microorganisms.

Anti-neoplastic - herbs or substances that have the precise action of inhibiting and fighting the development of tumors.

Antioxidant - an agent or material that inhibits oxidation and thereby prevents rancidity of fats or oils, or the deterioration of other substances caused by the oxidative process.

Antipyretic - reducing, removing, or preventing fever.

Anti-rheumatic - herbs and substances that have a reputation for prevention, relief and/or curing rheumatic problems.

Antiseptic - substances that counteract or prevent the growth of disease-causing germs and infections.

Anti-spasmodic - herbal remedies and substances that rapidly relax nervous tension causing colic or sudden involuntary digestive contractions.

Antiviral - a substance that checks the growth of a virus by weakening or abolishing its action.

Aromatherapy - the use of essential oils derived from plants for healing purposes.

Aromatic - the oils of aromatic herbs that are able to penetrate muscles and increase circulation.

Aromatic baths - baths in which oils are used for cosmetic or healing purposes.

Arthritis - an inflammation and/or pain in a joint or joints. Symptoms include swelling, redness of the skin, and impaired motion. Two types of arthritis are osteoarthritis, which is caused by the wear and tear of cartilage of the joints, especially those that are weight-bearing, and rheumatoid arthritis, which is a degenerative joint disease that can be crippling.

Aspartame - a substance made up of amino acids, the building blocks of protein. It is about 200 times sweeter than sugar, and is used in over 100 different types of products. It is regarded by many naturally-oriented health practitioners as one of the most dangerous food additives on the market.

Astringent - a substance that contracts blood vessels and body tissues, reducing blood flow. Also, a substance having a biting or harsh quality.

Autism - a disorder beginning in early childhood, characterized by extreme self-absorption, language disturbances, inability to form personal relationships, and a pattern of repetitive body movements.

Auto immune - the immune response of an organism against any of its own cells or tissues.

Auto-suggestion - a process that can be used to directly program the unconscious mind with positive affirmations and ideas. It can be used to reduce stress, accomplish desired tasks and goals, and eliminate unwanted behaviors and habits.

Ayurvedic medicine - a system based on the idea that health is a result of balance among emotional, physical and spiritual states. *Ayurveda* – the Sanskrit term for "science of life and longevity."

– B –

Bach Flower Remedies - a homeopathic healing system founded by Dr. Edward Bach, based on the principle that a negative state of mind must be replaced with the opposite virtue in order to regain the inner harmony needed to heal. Using plants and trees, he created a revolutionary therapeutic system that is safe, natural and gentle. Through observation, he classified 38 negative states of mind common to most people. He discovered the corresponding flower from plants or trees for each state of mind, from which substances could be derived to alleviate specific negative moods. There are hundreds of other homeopathic flower remedies.

Bactericide - an agent that kills germs or bacteria.

Base oil - the main, essential or principal ingredient acting as the vehicle for an essential oil. It is usually used for therapeutic purposes, such as aromatherapy. It is best to use high quality, cold-pressed, light vegetable oils.

Bioavailability - the rate and degree to which a substance is absorbed by the body or is available at the site of the physiological activity.

Biofeedback - a form of relaxation therapy in which heart rate, skin conductivity, and muscle tension are recorded and displayed on a computer screen or used to activate electrical signals. Through this feedback, patients can learn how to monitor, respond to, and control bodily functions and tension levels.

Bioflavonoids - biologically active flavonoids, usually sourced from lemon and orange rinds. It maintains blood-vessel walls as well as providing other health benefits. Also known as vitamin P complex.

Bitter - an herb that aids digestion and promotes appetite.

Blood purifiers - a substance which rids the blood of impurities, such as heavy metals, toxic substances, yeast, etc.

Boil - a boil is technically called a "furuncle." It is caused by an infection of a sebaceous gland. This results in an inflammation of the skin and localized painful swelling.

Botanical Medicine - a theory and practice of treatment that utilizes herb-based remedies.

Bupropion - an antidepressant that is used for patients who do not tolerate or experience benefits from other antidepressants. It causes seizures in 4 out of 1000 patients.

– C –

Calmative - any agent or substance that reduces an individual's level of excitement or agitation and promotes a state of sedation.

Candida albicans - also know as moniliasis or candidiasis, it can take many forms. Candida albicans is a fungus that causes a yeast-like fungal infection. It thrives in the warm moist parts of the body such as the mouth (candidiasis), penis (balanitis), vagina (thrush), and beneath the breasts and between folds of the buttock (diaper rash). Each condition manifests itself in a slightly different way, but all are caused by the Candida albicans fungi.

Carcinogen - a cancer-causing substance or event.

Carrier oil - see Base oil.

Carminative - substances, usually herbs and spices, taken to relieve gas and griping.

Carotene - the yellow-orange pigment from plants that becomes vitamin A in the body.

Catalyst - a substance that causes change, usually increasing the rate of a chemical reaction. The catalyst remains unchanged at the end of the reaction.

Catarrh - an inflammation of a mucous membrane, especially one chronically affecting the nose and air passages.

Cathartic - substances that have a laxative effect.

Chelation - the use of an agent to bind with a mineral so that it is more easily absorbed by the body. The chelating agent is reputed to be able to eliminate heavy metals in the body, and to hasten the cure of a number of diseases.

Chi - see "Qi"

Chicken pox - an acute, highly contagious viral disease, especially during childhood. It is caused by the herpes zoster virus, the same one responsible for shingles. It is characterized by skin eruptions of itchy spots that blister, then turn to crusts. Also called Shingles or Zona.

Chinese Medicine - a system of diagnosis and treatment that is rooted in ancient Chinese philosophy and utilizes techniques such as acupuncture, auricular therapy, acupuncture, and herbal medicine.

Cholagogue - promotes the flow and evacuation of the bile into the small intestine.

Cholestatic - a failure or checking of bile flow.

Coenzyme - the nonprotein component that produces the active part of an enzyme system.

Cold-pressed - mechanical method used to extract oil by crushing the whole plant or part of the plant, without using heat. The oil is then filtered. This produces "virgin" oil.

Cold sore - a viral infection brought on by the herpes simplex type one virus, causing inflammation to the skin—usually the lips, mouth and face. It is characterized by small blisters. Herpes simplex type one is highly infectious and can spread to other parts of the body.

Colitis - inflammation of the colon.

Colloidal - a description used to describe a substance made up of small insoluble, nondiffusible particles that remain suspended in a different type of medium, such as water, alcohol, et cetera.

Colon Hydrotherapy - a process in which warm water is introduced into the colon in order to loosen and flush out built-up waste matter. Colon hydrotherapy, along with a proper diet and herbal supplementation, is considered by most naturally-oriented health practitioners to be an essential part of any healing process, whether the condition be fatigue, skin problems, depression, or any other physical or emotional disorder.

Complementary Medicine - a broad range of therapies that fall outside the methods of treatment used by mainstream medicine. Complementary Medicine may include such treatments as acupressure, aromatherapy, chelation therapy, flower remedies, homeopathy, macrobiotics, and reflexology.

Compress - a folded cloth pad, often moist or medicated, that is applied to part of the body for healing, pressure, or to alter the temperature of a body part.

Conjunctivitis - an inflammation of the mucous membrane that covers the front of the eye and lines the inside of the eyelid.

Cylert - a central nervous system stimulant used to treat attention-deficit-disorder in children.

Cystitis - a bladder infection caused by bacteria. It results in an inflammation of the bladder.

– D –

Dandruff - a condition affecting the scalp. Overactive sebaceous gland secretions in the scalp cause the formation of scales that may itch and burn. It may be caused by poor diet, inadequate stimulation of the scalp, or poor blood circulation.

Decongestant - a medication or treatment that relieves congestion, especially in the nose.

Demulcent - substances that sooth and protect damaged tissue.

Dermatitis - an inflammation of the skin. Characteristics may include flaky skin, redness, itchiness, and rashes resulting in blisters, sores and scabs.

Desipramine - an antidepressant that is also used to treat attention deficit disorder in children over 6 years of age. It is also used to treat bulimia nervosa and the cravings and depression that accompany cocaine withdrawal.

Detoxification - a deliberate program of encouraging the body's elimination process and preventing the day-to-day buildup of toxins. This program includes drinking 8-10 glasses of pure water each day, taking baths and saunas, eating fresh, raw foods, using herbs, fiber, and supplements, fasting, stress management, and using enemas and colonic irrigation to flush toxins out of the colon.

Dexedrine - an amphetamine drug used to treat attention-deficit hyperactivity disorder and narcolepsy.

Diaphoretic - substances used to induce sweating.

Diffuser - an apparatus that spreads an essential oil throughout the air in a room.

Digestive - assists and aids in the process of digestion.

Distillation - a process of heating a mixture, using steam and high pressure to separate the components of the mixture, and condensing the resulting vapors to produce a concentrated purer essential oil.

Diuretic - a substance that increases the flow of urine.

Dysmenorrhea - a menstrual condition involving cramping pains that may be incapacitating.

– E –

Eczema - a skin disorder characterized by inflammation, itching, and scaling.

Emollient - a substance that, when applied to skin, soothes or softens it. Taken internally, it acts as a lubricant to the intestinal wall, and softens feces.

Endogenous - produced internally from the body.

Endogenous depression - a severe form of internally derived depression often characterized by insomnia, weight loss, and inability to experience pleasure.

Enteric coated - a pill treated so that it passes through the stomach unaltered and disintegrates in the intestines.

Enzyme - a complex protein substance that initiates chemical changes. Enzymes are vital for digestion and other processes in the body.

Essential Amino Acids - amino acids that the body cannot manufacture on its own and must be obtained through diet.

Essential Fatty Acids - like the essential amino acids, essential fatty acids must be taken in with food. The body needs three essential fatty acids to property metabolize fats. Children with ADD/ADHD may be deficient in essential fatty acids, and may be helped by taking supplements.

Expectorant - a medicine or agent that helps to bring up phlegm or mucous so it can be expelled from the respiratory tract.

Exogenous - produced outside of the system or body.

Extra-virgin - the highest grade of olive oil from the first pressing of the olives.

– F –

FDA - Food and Drug Administration.

Febrifuge - reducing, removing, or preventing fever.

Feingold Diet - a diet devised by pediatric allergist Benjamin Feingold, M.D., which eliminates salicylates, artificial colors, and artificial flavors, which Dr. Feingold asserted were the cause of hyperactivity in children.

Fever - an abnormally increased body temperature, which is a vital part of your body's defense mechanism.

Flatulence - passing gas through the anus. Usually due to improper or incomplete digestion of sugars.

Flu - an acute, contagious viral disease, characterized by inflammation of the respiratory tract, fever and muscular pain. It is also known as "influenza."

Fluoxetine - an antidepressant medication that works by affecting levels of the chemical serotonin in the brain.

Food Additives - substances added to foods during processing to prevent spoilage, or to enhance appearance, taste, texture, or nutritional value. In the United States, the U.S. Food and Drug Administration is responsible for testing and regulating food additives. Food additives are regarded by many complimentary and naturally-oriented health practitioners as potentially hazardous substances that may be responsible for a variety of allergic reactions, and for long-term physical and mental incapacitation in certain individuals.

Food Allergies - food allergies produce many symptoms in the skin, digestive, and respiratory systems. Some common symptoms of food-allergic reactions are flushing, hives, itching, swelling, nausea, abdominal pain, coughing, and sneezing. The most common allergy-producing foods in adults are shellfish, milk, fish, eggs, and peanuts, a legume that is one of the main causes of anaphylactic reactions. In complimentary and alternative health circles, food allergies are considered responsible for an enormous variety of conditions, such as migraine headaches, colitis, depression, fatigue, skin eruptions, and memory, behavioral and emotional problems.

Free radical - an atom that has at least one electron missing. Electrons are negatively charged components of an atom. The missing electron(s) create an unstable atom, which seeks a component to complete it. This causes a chemical reaction to occur in which other molecules or atoms attracted to the free radical atom are easily able to bond with it. The process can cause a lot of damage to the body.

Functional Medicine - an approach to patient care that does not rely on a single treatment or procedure to address a medical condition, but rather, takes a complex, multi-faceted approach and considers biochemical, physiological, environmental and psychological factors that may be impacting upon the patient.

Fungal infections of the skin - fungal organisms are found on all healthy skin of humans, cats and dogs. Fungal infections occur when the natural balance is disturbed. In humans, opportunistic infections can arise especially in those with weakened immune systems.

Fungicidal - a substance that checks the growth of fungi, molds or spores.

– G –

Gastritis - inflammation of the mucous membrane of the stomach.

Gingivitis - a build up of bacterial plaque that causes the gums to swell, redden and bleed easily.

GLA - Gamma-linolenic acid produced from linoleic acid in the body. It is an Omega-6 fatty acid.

Glucose - the form in which carbohydrates are usually assimilated by animals; the blood sugar.

Glycemic Index - a list of carbohydrates that includes a number indicating how each carbohydrate effects blood glucose. Those carbohydrates with a high glycemic index cause a greater rise in blood sugar. Those foods with a low glycemic index cause a low rise in blood sugar.

Guided Imagery - a technique that focuses the imagination and directs it toward picturing a desired sequence of events.

– H –

HDL - high-density lipoprotein, the "good" cholesterol, that transports cholesterol and fats through the blood system.

Hemolytic anemia - red blood cells dying at a faster rate than that of replacement by the body.

Hemorrhoid - a painful swelling of a vein in the region of the anus or rectum, often with bleeding. It is a varicose vein. Also known as "Piles."

Hemostatic - an agent that shortens the clotting time of blood.

Hepatic - a substance that tones, strengthens and stimulates the secretive functions of the liver.

Herbs - a plant or plant parts prized for their savory or medicinal qualities.

Hives - an allergic skin condition or hypersensitive reaction characterized by itching, burning and the formation of smooth patches.

Holistic Medicine - a medical philosophy that sees disease as a manifestation of many elements: physical, mental, emotional, and even spiritual. All aspects of the person's life are taken into consideration by the holistic health-care professional. Holistic care also supports the idea that the individual is responsible for his or her own well-being.

Homeopathy - founded by Samuel Hahnemann, a therapeutic system based on the principle that "like heals like" in which diseases are treated with remedies having a minute amount of the disease-causing agent. This elicits symptoms similar to the disease, thereby calling forth the body's own healing response.

Hops - a natural sedative that helps to calm nerves and reduce stress and anxiety. It is also an effective remedy for sleeplessness.

Hormone - a product of living cells in the endocrine organs, transported by body fluids and producing a specific effect by activating receptive cells remote from the point of origin.

HPB - Health Protection Branch (Canada's FDA).

Hypercalcemia - excessive amounts of calcium accumulation in the blood.

Hypervitaminosis - a state resulting from ingesting an excessive amount of a vitamin(s).

Hypoglycemic - a state brought about by abnormally low blood sugar levels.

Hypouremic - lowers uric acid levels in the blood.

Hypovitaminosis - a deficiency disease due to a lack of vitamins in the diet.

Hypoxia - below normal oxygen levels.

– I –

Imipramine - an antidepressant drug that is also used to treat bed-wetting in children over 5 years of age.

Immune System - a network of organs, tissues, blood cells and body chemicals that provide protection against invasion by disease-producing organisms.

Influenza - commonly known as flu, it is an acute, contagious viral disease, characterized by inflammation of the respiratory tract, fever and muscular pain.

Inner-Ear/Cerebellar-Vestibular Theory - a theory about the origins of dyslexia originated by Dr. Harold Levinson. He has found significant evidence to support the idea that dyslexia is a disorder involving the part of the brain known as the cerebellum, which is closely linked with the inner ear.

Insulin - the hormone involved in the metabolism of sugar in the body. It is secreted by the pancreas.

– K - L –

Kava Kava - an herbal sedative that relaxes the body and reduces anxiety and stress.

Laxative - a substance that loosens the bowels and relieves constipation. Results in a moderate evacuative effect.

LDL - low-density lipoprotein. The component that when oxidized causes cholesterol deposits along arterial walls.

Leg ulcer - an open sore on the leg that discharges pus.

Legumes - plants having seeds that grow in pods, such as beans or seeds.

Leucorrhoea - an inflammation of the vagina that is caused by an excessive amount of bacteria or fungi. Often there is a thick yellow or white discharge accompanied by severe itching to the vagina.

Linoleic acid - a polyunsaturated fat that is a component of lecithin. It is a key member of the Omega-6 family. Vital for life, linoleic acid can only be obtained from foods. Also known as vitamin F.

Lipid - organic compounds consisting of fats or fatty substances.

Lipoprotein - a transporter of fatty substances, characterized by weight (e.g., low-density, high-density, et cetera)

Lipotropic - inhibits excessive or abnormal accumulation of fat in the liver.

– M –

MAO Inhibitors - a class of antidepressant drugs. Monoamine oxidase is a complex enzyme system.

Megavitamin therapy - the use of large doses of vitamins to treat illness.

Mercury - one of the most toxic substances known to humankind. It is present in almost all conventional dental fillings.

Metabolize - the physical and chemical reactions in living cells through which energy is provided for critical processes and activities and new material is assimilated.

Mineral - essential nutrients required for the body to function properly.

MSG - Monosodium Glutamate. It is derived from the processing of products containing glutamic acid, one of the 22 amino acids. This amino acid can be found in the protein naturally occurring in seaweed, vegetables, and the gluten in grain. There have been numerous reports of adverse reactions to MSG ranging from headaches and dizziness to depression and fatigue.

Music Therapy - a discipline in which music is applied to the treatment a variety of diseases and disabilities, both physical and emotional. Music therapists often work in psychiatric facilities, schools, and nursing homes. They may also work in private practice.

– N –

Naturopathy - a system of treatment of disease that uses natural agents (e.g., water, vitamins, minerals, air, herbs, homeopathy, nutrition, et cetera) and physical methods (e.g. acupressure, acupuncture, manipulation, et cetera) along with underlying principles such as doing the patient no harm, using the body's natural wisdom to heal itself, disease prevention, and maintaining optimal health.

Neurofeedback - a form of biofeedback combined with a process that uses technology to provide users with information about bodily responses to various stimuli. This information, or "feedback," helps patients learn to use their minds to develop more control over their brain functioning.

Nutraceuticals - substances from natural sources that can positively affect one's health. These unusual healing products are not herbs, minerals or vitamins. In the proper dosage and concentration, they may stimulate and support the body's healing process. It is their wide range of effectiveness and safety that offers benefits for a variety of health conditions. Properly used, they can eliminate the need for prescribed drugs and help patients to avoid the potential side effects prescription drugs can cause.

Nervine - substances used to ease anxiety and stress, as well as nourish the nerves.

Nortriptyline - an antidepressant drug that elevates mood by raising the level of neurotransmitters in the brain.

– O –

Oat Straw - a nerve tonic used in the treatment of insomnia and depression.

Omega-3 - a part of an essential fatty acid group, usually deficient in modern diets. External food sources supply the body's needs. Alpha-linolenic acid is the main Omega-3 fatty acid.

Omega-6 - a part of an essential fatty acid group, usually abundant in modern diets. External food sources supply the body's needs. Linolenic acid is the main Omega-6 fatty acid.

Organic - a class of foods grown and produced without synthetic chemicals and pesticides.

– P –

Parasites - organisms that live in and on other organisms and live off the host organism. It has been estimated that a large percentage of North Americans have at least one type of parasite living in their bodies.

Paronychia - a fungal infection that affects toenails and fingernails. Cuticles become painful and red, with a small discharge. Skin below nails becomes discolored.

Passion Flower - a medicinal herb used in the treatment of nervousness and insomnia. It is also employed as a sedative for anxiety and insomnia.

Paxil - a type of antidepressant drug that affects levels of serotonin in the brain. It is also used to treat obsessive-compulsive disorders, panic disorders, and social anxiety.

Phenylketonuria - an inherited inability to oxidize a metabolic product of phenylalanine.

Phytochemicals - the medicinal qualities of plant life, such as the vitamins, minerals, and thousands of healing substances in the herbs and foods we eat. Some of these remedies have been passed down through the ages, while others are recent discoveries.

Polyunsaturated fats - vegetable-sourced highly non-saturated fats that may lower blood cholesterol levels.

Prickly heat - a skin eruption caused by inflammation of the sweat glands.

Probiotics - the introduction of bacteria into the digestive tract which bring the intestinal flora back to an optimal state of balance, help boost the immune system, and encourage the breakdown of poisons in the colon.

Protein - one of three types of energy foods. Nearly all proteins are composed of 20 amino acids.

Psoriasis - a chronic skin disease characterized by scaly, reddish patches and itching. The inflammation sometimes shows up as silvery scales that appear on elbows, knees, scalp and torso. It is not contagious. The cause is unknown.

Purgative - a substance which promotes increased contractions and dilations of the alimentary canal.

– Q - R –

Qi - in Chinese medicine, the concept of Chi or energy is central. The Chinese believe that Chi flows through the body in 14 channels or meridians. Pervades all things.

Rash - an eruption of spots on the skin.

RDA - Recommended Dietary Allowance. Established by the National Academy of Sciences, National Research Council, and the Food and Nutrition Board.

Reflexology - a system of foot massage based on the idea that the feet and hands mirror the entire body, and that massaging pressure points on specific reflex points will affect the corresponding body parts and internal organs.

RDI - Recommended Daily Intake. It is the recommended nutrient intake levels, regardless of age, sex, weight, lifestyle, et cetera, and is based on the Recommended Dietary Allowance. On food labels it appears as the Percent of Daily Value (%/DV).

Ritalin - a central nervous system stimulant used to treat attention-deficit-disorder.

RNA - abbreviation used for ribonucleic acid.

– S –

Saint John's wort - a very popular and widely-used herb. Its main area of function is the nervous system. St. John's wort contains hypericin, a natural compound that helps support the nervous system. It is useful for the treatment of stress and depression.

Saturated fatty acids - typically solid at room temperature. Predominately found in animal food sources. Saturated fatty acids tend to raise blood cholesterol levels.

Sedative - a substance that calms and/or quiets nervous excitement.

Shingles - the non-technical term used for the herpes zoster virus, the same one responsible for chicken pox.

Sinusitis - an inflammation of the sinuses. The mucous membranes that line the cavities above, behind, and to each side of the nose become swelled.

Sitz bath - a therapeutic bath in which only the hips and buttocks are immersed.

Stimulant - enliven and/or quicken the physiological functioning of the body.

Stye - a small inflamed swelling on the rim of an eyelid.

Sublingual - under the tongue.

Sugar - a carbohydrate that occurs naturally in every fruit and vegetable. It is the major product of photosynthesis, the process by which plants transform the sun's energy into food.

Synergistic - the result of a combination of two or more substances in which the end product is greater than the individual components.

Synthetic - artificially produced or manufactured.

Systemic - affecting the body generally. Able to spread through the whole body.

– T –

Tachycardia - relatively rapid heart rate due to physiological or pathological conditions.

T Cells - the white blood cells produced in the thymus. T cells protect the body against viruses, bacteria, and cancer-causing substances. At the same time, they control the manufacture of B cells, the antibody producers. T cells also control the unwanted manufacturing of potentially harmful T cells.

Thyroid - a gland that produces a hormone called thyroxine which controls the body's rate of metabolism.

Tincture - an herbal extract usually composed of a mixture of water and alcohol.

Tocopherols - the group of substances that make vitamin E. They are derived from vacuum distillation of edible vegetable oils.

Tonic - herbs that enliven or strengthen either specific organs or the whole body.

Toxin - any poison produced by living or dead animals, plants or organisms.

Trans-fatty acids - artificially created fatty acids produced by the process of hydrogenation. They are unsaturated, yet act like saturated fats. They extend the shelf-life of processed foods and are very unhealthy.

– U - Z –

Ulcers - open sores on the skin or mucous membrane.

Unsaturated fatty acids - found mainly in vegetable, nut, and seed fats. Usually liquid at room temperature.

Vaporization - to change something into a steam suspension (vapor) or mist for dispersion through the air. It can be done by heating, spraying, or evaporating an essential oil.

Wholistic - see Holistic

Yeast - a naturally-occurring fungus present in the body's mucus membranes, e.g. mouth, nose, vagina, skin, and digestive tract. In a healthy body, it is kept in balance by "friendly" bacteria. It is harmless unless illness or dietary imbalance cause it to overgrow.

Appendix C
Conventional American Fluid
Measurements and
Their Standard International
Equivalents

Fluid Measurements

1 tsp	=	1/3 tbsp	=	1/6 oz	=	4.9 ml
3 tsp	=	1 tbsp	=	1/2 oz	=	14.8 ml
2 tbsp	=	1 oz	=	29.6 ml	=	.0296 l
1 c	=	16 tbsp	=	8 oz	=	236.6 ml
1 l	=	1.0567 qt =		33.814 oz	=	4.2268 c
1 l	=	1000 ml	=	2.113 pt		

Essential oils are measured in drops, due to their high concentration.

20 drops = 1/30 oz = 1 ml

tsp – teaspoon	tbsp – tablespoon	c – cup	pt – pint
oz – fluid ounce	qt – liquid quart	ml – milliliter	l – liter

International System of Units for
Liquid and Dry Weights of Mass

IU — International Unit
an agreed to standard of measurement for supplements

1 gm	=	1,000 mg	=	0.03527 oz
1 mg	=	1,000 mcg	=	0.00003527 oz

gm - gram   mg - milligram   mcg - micrograms   oz - ounce

Appendix D
Bibliography

Chapter 1
Thirty-Five Years and 35,000 Patients Later

Harold N. Levinson, M.D., – Groundbacking work on ADD/ADHD and Related Learning and Anxiety Disorders – Their Inner-Ear/Cerebellar-Vestibular Origins, Understanding, and Treatment

A. Pertinent References

Total Concentration (Evans, 1990)

Smart But Feeling Dumb (Warner, 1984, Revised 1994)

The Discovery of Cerebellar-Vestibular Syndromes and Therapies - A Solution to the Riddle Dyslexia (Springer-Verlag, 1980; Stonebridge, Revised 2000)

B. Recent Independently Validating References

Attentional activation of the cerebellum independent of motor involvement. From Science, March 28, 1997: Magnetic resonance imaging was used to demonstrate that the cerebellum is involved in diverse cognitive and noncognitive neurobehavioral systems, with attention and motor systems each activating distinct cerebellar regions. (G. Allen, et al., San Diego State University, Joint Doctoral Program in Clinical Psychology, San Diego)

Cerebellum in attention-deficit hyperactivity disorder: a morphometric MRI study. From Neurology, April, 1998: Clinical, neuroanatomic, and functional brain-imaging studies suggest a role for the cerebellum in cognitive functions, including attention. It was found that a cerebello-thalamo-prefrontal circuit dysfunction may contribute to deficits encountered in ADHD. (P. C. Berquin, et al., CHU Hopital Nord, Service de Pediatrie 1, Amiens, France)

The human cerebro-cerebellar-system: its computing, cognitive, and language skills. From Behavioral Brain Research, Vol. 44, 1991: Results of a study suggested that the cerebellum contributes to the learning of cognitive and language skills, as well as its acknowledged traditional role in motor functions. (Henrietta Leiner et al., Channing House, Palo Alto, CA and Robert S. Dow Neurological Sciences Institute, Portland, OR)

Abnormal visual-vestibular interaction and smooth pursuit tracking in psychosis: Implications for cerebellar involvement. From Journal of Psychiatry and Neuroscience, March 1991: Findings suggest that cerebellar dysfunction may contribute to irregularities in smooth pursuit tracking and fixation suppression found in psychotic patients. (P. M. Cooper, et al., School of Psychology, University of Ottawa, Ontario)

Cerebellum implicated in sensory acquisition and discrimination rather than motor control. From Science, April 26, 1996: Magnetic resonance imaging suggests that the cerebellum may be active during motor, perceptual, and cognitive performance. (J. H. Gao, et al., University of Texas Health Science Center, Research Imaging Center, Medical School, San Antonio)

Cerebellar size and cognition: correlations with IQ, verbal memory and motor dexterity. From Neuropsychiatry, Neuropsychology and Behavioral Neurology, January, 1997: Results indicate that the cerebellum contributes to cognition as well as volume significantly correlated with the ability to retain already encoded information – verbal and fine motor skills. (S. Paradiso, et al., University of Iowa College of Medicine, Department of Psychiatry, Iowa City)

The cerebellar cognitive affective syndrome. From Brain, April, 1998: In a neuroimaging study of patients with cerebellar diseases, researchers found impairments of verbal fluency, abstract reasoning and working memory; spatial cognition; inappropriate personality and behavior; and language deficits such as agrammatism and dysprosodia. (J. D. Schmahmann, et al., Department of Neurology, Massachusetts General Hospital, Boston)

Does the cerebellum contribute to cognitive aspects of speech production? A functional magnetic resonance imaging (fMRI) study in humans. From Neuroscience Letters, May 15, 1998: Positron emission tomography studies suggest a contribution of the lateral aspects of the right cerebellar hemisphere to higher-level (cognitive) aspects of speech production. (H. Ackermann, et al., University of Tubigen, Department of Neurology, Germany)

Dysfunctional cortico-cerebellar circuits cause "cognitive dysmetria" in schizophrenia. From Neuroreport, June 1, 1998: Studies made point to a dysfunctional cortico-cerebellar circuit leading to poorly coordinated mental activity ("cognitive dysmetria"), which could explain the broad range of schizophrenic symptoms. (A. K. Wiser, et al., University of Iowa, College of medicine, Mental Health Clinical Research Center, Iowa City)

Metabolic abnormalities in developmental dyslexia detected by 1H magnetic resonance spectroscopy. From The Lancet, June 20, 1998: Using proton magnetic resonance spectroscopy, this study led to the conclusion that the cerebellum is involved in dyslexia. (Caroline Rae, Ph.D., et al., University of Sydney, Australia and University of Oxford, UK)

Association of abnormal cerebellar activation with motor learning difficulties in dyslexic adults. From The Lancet, May 15, 1999: A study found lower brain activation in dyslexic adults undertaking tasks known normally to involve cerebellar activation. (R. I. Nicolson, Ph.D., et al., University of Sheffield, the MRC Cyclotron Unit at Hammersmith Hospital and the Institute of Neurology, UK)

Physiological and behavioral effects of an antivertigo antihistamine in adults. From Perceptual and Motor Skills, Vol. 88, 1999: A study found physiological support for the use of an antimotion sickness antihistamine to improve cognitive-related performance with obvious implications in treating learning-disordered children. (J. L. Lauter, Ph.D., et al., University of Oklahoma Health Sciences Center, OK)

Cerebellar Deficiency Model of Dyslexia Upheld. From Clinical Psychiatry News, January 2000: A study showed that dyslexic adults failed to learn an associative type of eye blink conditioning learning that is controlled by the cerebellum. (Joan M. Coffin, Ph.D., King's College, PA)

Rational dosages of nutrients have a prolonged effect on learning disabilities. From Alternative Therapeutic Health Medicine, May 2000: A study on the effects of certain nutrients on children with learning disabilities showed significant academic and behavioral improvements within a few weeks of treatment with nutrient supplements. (R. M. Carlton, et al., Stonybrook University Medical School, New York)

The role of the cerebellum in cognition and behavior: a selective review. From Journal of Neuropsychiatry and Clinical Neuroscience, Spring 2000: A study on the role of the cerebellum in cognition and behavior, highlighted cognitive deficits and personality changes associated with cerebellar disease. (M. Rapoport, et al., Dept. of Psychiatry, Sunnybrook Health Sciences Centre, University of Toronto, Canada)

Chapter 2
Healing the Hyperactive Brain Through the New Science of Functional Medicine

For the extensive list of references Michael R. Lyon, M.D., B.Sc. used to create this chapter, we refer you to his bestselling book, *Healing the Hyperactive Brain; Through the New Science of Functional Medicine.* Michael R. Lyon, M.D., Focused Publishing, 1999 (596 pages).

In addition for parents, adults and care-givers who would like a referral to a trained practitioner in Functional Medicine, contact the Institute for Functional Medicine c/o HealthComm International Inc., P.O. Box 1729, Gig Harbor, Washington, 98335. Tel: (253) 851-3943 or through their web site: www.fxmed.com

Those healthcare providers who would like to obtain further training in the emerging field of Functional Medicine are encouraged to explore the educational resources available through the Institute for Functional Medicine in Gig Harbor, WA. (www.fxmed.com). This organization offers comprehensive full-credit courses such as "Applying Functional Medicine in Clinical Practice" as well as pertinent published material and audiovisual programs. *"Functional Medicine Update"* is a monthly audio program produced by Dr. Jeffrey Bland, Ph.D. which is heard by thousands of subscribers from around the world. As well, the fully (continuing medical education) accredited International Symposium on Functional Medicine is an annual scientific conference attended by well over 1000 professionals and features some of the world's most sought after scientists and clinicians. For more information about Functional Medicine and healing the hyperactive brain, you can access www.PureLiving.com

Dr. Michael Lyon M.D, the author of this chapter may be accessed through his E-mail: Drlyon@island.net. For more information about Michael R. Lyon, M.D., B.Sc., please refer to Appendix I, About the Authors.

Chapter 3
A Refreshing Overview of
Some Natural and Complementary Choices

Ali, Elvis and Pam Floener, David Garshowitz, George Grant, Gordon Ko, Dorothy Marshall, Alvin Petal, Ken Vegotsky, *The All-in-One Guide to™ Natural Remedies and Supplements.* AGES Publications™, Niagara Falls, NY, 2000

Refer to general references, immediately following the annotated chapters, in the bibliography.

Chapter 4
Environmental Factors: Organic Acids and Hyperactivity

1. Lord, R., and J. Bralley, *Organics in urine: Assessment of gut dysbiosis, nutrient deficiencies and toxemia.* Nutr Pers, 20(4), 25-31, 1997.

2. Bralley, J., and R. Lord, *Urinary organic acids profiling.* In *Textbook of Natural Medicine,* P. A. Murray, Ed., Churchill Livingstone, Edinburgh, 1998, pp. 229-237.

3. al Aqeel, A., et al., *A new patient with alpha-ketoglutaric aciduria and progressive extrapyramidal tract disease.* Brain Dev, 16. 33-7, 1994.

4. Greenamyre, J. T., M. Garcia-Osuna and J. G. Greene, *The endogenous cofactors, thioctic acid and dihydrolipoic acid, are neuroprotective against NMDA and malonic acid lesions of striatum.* Neurosci Lett, 171(1-2), 17-20, 1994.

5. Poucheret, P., et al., *Vanadium and diabetes.* (In Process Citation), Mol Cell Biochem, 188(1-2), 73-80, 1998.

6. Thompson, R., *The value of blood pyruvate determinations in the diagnosis of thiamine deficiency.* In *Thiamine deficiency: Biochemical lesions and their clinical significance,* G. Wolstenholme, Ed., Churchill, London, 1967.

7. Boitier, E., et al., *A case of mitochondrial encephalomyopathy associated with a muscle coenzyme Q10 deficiency.* J Neurol Sci, 156(1). 41-6, 1998.

8. Duez, P., A. Kumps and Y. Mardens, *GC-MS profilng of urinary organic acids reviewuated as a quantitative method.* Clin Chem, 42(10), 1609-1615, 1996.

9. McGregor, N. R., et al., *Preliminary determination of a molecular basis of chronic fatigue syndrome.* Biochem Mol Med, 57(2), 73-80, 1996.

10. Croal, B. L., et al., *Transient 5-oxoprolinuria (pyroglutamic aciduria) with systemic acidosis in an adult receiving antibiotic therapy.* Clin Chem, 44(2), 336-40, 1998.

11. Alfieri, A. B. and L. X. Cubeddu, *Effects of inhibition of serotonin synthesis on 5-hydroxyindoleacetic acid excretion in healthy subjects.* J Clinical Pharmacology, 34, 153-157, 1994.

12. Naito, E., et al., *Thiamine-responsive lactic acidaemia: role of pyruvate dehy-drogenase complex.* Eur J Pediatr, 157(8), 648-52, 1998.

13. Norman, E. J., *Urinary methylmalonic acid to detect vitamin B_{12} deficiency* [letter]. Jama, 273(18), 1420, 1995.

14. Soda, H., et al., *Prenatal diagnosis and therapy for a patient with vitamin B_{12} responsive methylmalonic acidaemia.* J Inherit Metab Dis, 18(3), 295-8, 1995.

15. Toyoshima, S., et al., *Excretion from rats of ketone bodies and methylmalonic acid in urine resulting from dietary vitamin B_{12} deficiency.* Biosci Biotechnol Biochem, 59(8), 1598-9, 1995.

16. Toyoshima, S., et al., *Accumulation of methylmalonic acid caused by vitamin B_{12} deficiency disrupts normal cellular metabolism in rat liver.* Br J Nutr, 75(6), 929-38, 1996.

17. Norman, E. J. and J. A. Morrison, *Screening elderly populations for cobalamin (vitamin B_{12}) deficiency using the urinary methylmalonic acid assay by gas chromatography mass spectrometry* [see comments]. Am J Med, 94(6), 589-94, 1993.

18. Mock, N., et al., *Increased urinary excretion of 3-hydroxyisovaleric acid and decreased urinary excretion of biotin are sensitive early indicators of decreased biotin status in experimental biotin deficiency.* Am J Clin Nutr, 65, 951-8, 1997.

19. Folkers, K., et al., *Lovastatin decreases coenzyme Q levels in humans.* Proc Natl Acad Sci USA, 87(22), 8931-4, 1990.

20. Feller, A. G. and D. Rudman, *Role of carnitine in human nutrition.* J Nutr, 118(5), 541-547, 1988.

21. Persaud, C., T. Forrester and A. A. Jackson, *Urinary excretion of 5-L-oxopro-line (pyroglutamic acid) is increased during recovery from severe childhood malnutrition and responds to supplemental glycine.* J Nutr, 126(11), 2823-30, 1996.

22. Jackson, A. A., et al., *Urinary excretion of 5-oxoproline (pyroglutamic aciduria) as an index of glycine insufficiency in normal man.* Br J Nutr, 58(2), 207-14, 1987.

23. Amsel, L. P. and G. Levy, *Drug biotransformation interactions in man. II. A pharmacokinetic study of the simultaneous conjugation of benzoic and salicylic acids with glycine.* J Pharm Sci, 58(3), 321-6, 1969.

24. Nowaczyk, M. J., et al., *Ethylmalonic and methylsuccinic aciduria in ethyl-malonic encephalopathy arise from abnormal isoleucine metabolism.* Metabolism, 47(7), 836-9, 1998.

25. Van der Heiden C, W. E., D. Ketting, M. Duran and K. Wadman, *Gas chro-matographic analysis of urinary tyrosine and phenylalanine metabolites in patients with gastrointestinal disorders.* Clinical Chimia Acta, 34, 289-296, 1971.

26. Eaton, K. K., et al., *Abnormal gut fermation: Laboratory studies reveal defi-ciency of B vitamins, zinc, and magnesium.* Journal of Nutritional Biochemistry, 4, 635-638, 1993.

27. Bralley, J. A., and R. S. Lord, *Laboratory reviewuations in Molecular Medicine*. Nutrients, Toxicants and Cell Controls, Norcross, GA, IAMM, 2000.

Chapter 5
Parasites and Detoxification:
Important Aids in Self-Healing for ADD and Hyperactive Children and Adults

Refer to general references, immediately following the annotated chapters, in the bibliography.

Chapter 6
The Thyroid and Hyperactivity

Barnes, B. O., *Basal temperature versus basal metabolism*. J Am Med Assoc. 119:1072-1074, 1942.

Barnes, Broda O., M.D., and Lawrence Galton, *Hypothyroidism: The Unsuspected Illness*. Harper and Row, New York, NY, 1976.

Bunevicius, R., G. Kazanavicius, R. Zalinkevicius and A. J. Prange. *Effects of thyroxine as compared with throxine plus triiodothyronine in patients with hypothyroidism*. New Engl J Med. 340(6):424-429, 1999.

Cooke R. G., R. T. Joffe and A. T. Levitt. *T3 augmentation of antidepressant treatment in T4-replaced thyroid patients*. J Clin Psychiatry. 53:16-18, 1992.

Means, J. H., L. J. DeGroot and J. B. Stanbury. *The thyroid and its diseases*. McGraw Hill, New York, 1963.

Chapter 7
Acupressure:
The Use of Acupressure Beads in the Treatment of ADHD

This report is a preliminary anecdotal finding written by Michael O. Smith, M.D. For patient treatment and professional inquiries about the use of acupressure beads in the treatment of Attention Deficit Hyperactivity Disorder (ADHD) contact:

Lincoln Medical and Mental Health Center
Recovery Program Center
234 Eugenio Maria De Hostos Blvd.
Bronx NY 10451
Tel: (718) 993-310

Chapter 8
A Cure for Autism and the ADD/Hyperactivity Connection

Over 1,000 studies, around the world, substantiate the preliminary findings written about in this chapter. This following is a small sampling of those studies:

1. Whitaker, J. A., M. H. Dopson, L. H. Mattman and D. N. Reifsnyder, *Preliminary Study of Transfer Factor (TF) in Patients with Fibromyalgia (FM), Chronic Fatigue Syndrome (CFS), and Concomitant Lyme Borreliosis.* Presented at the XI International Congress on Transfer Factor. Monterrey Nuevo Leon, Mexico, March, 1999.

2. Whitaker, J. A., E. G. Font, M. H. Dopson and M. H. Mattman, *The New Great Imitator: Lyme Disease (LD).* Presented at Biotechnologia Habana, December, 1999.

3. Mattman, L. H., *Cell Wall Deficient Forms: Stealth Pathogens.* CRC Press, New York, 1993.

4. Lang, D. and J. Territo, *Coping With Lyme Disease.* Henry Holt and Company, New York, 1997.

5. Fudenberg, H. H., *Dialysable Lymphocyte Extract (DlyE) in Infantile Autism: A Pilot Study.* Biotherapy 9:143-147, 1996.

6. Fudenberg, H. H. and G. Pizza, *Transfer Factor 1993: New Frontiers.* In Jucker, E., Ed. *Progress in Drug Research.* Boston: Birkhauser Verlag Basel, 42:309-399, 1994.

7. Wakefield, Andrew J., *Testimony Before Congressional Oversight Committee On Autism And Immunisation.* September, 2000.

8. Fudenberg, H. H. and H. Fudenberg, *Transfer Factor: Past, Present, and Future.* Ann. Rev. Pharmacol. Toxicol. 29: 4756-516, 1989.

9. Fudenberg, H. H., M. Coleman, D. Rosenberger, H.I. Fudenberg and V. Singh, *Immunotherapy of Autistic Children.* Clin. Res. 37(2): 605a, April, 1989.

10. Singh, V. K. and H. H. Fudenberg, *Immunodiagnosis and Immunotherapy of Autistic Children.* Ann. NY Acad. Sci., 1988.

Chapter 9
Mercury Poisoning — A Cause of Learning Disabilities

Refer to the dental suppliers and other web sites, in the chapter. Extensive data and studies, regarding the dangers of mercury, can be accessed through regulatory and environmental agencies around the world.

Ali, Elvis, et. al., *The All-in-One Guide to™ Natural Remedies and Supplements,* pp. 135-136, AGES Publications™, Niagara Falls, NY, 2000.

Chapter 9
Chelation Therapy a Way to Deal With Mercury

Brecher, H. and A., *Forty Something Forever.* 1997.

Casdorph, R., and M. Walker, *Toxic metal syndrome.* 1995.

Chang, L. W., *Neurotoxic effects of mercury.* Environ. Res. 14: pp 329-373, 1977.

Huggins, H., *It's all in your head.* 1993.

Koller, L., *Immunosuppression produced by Lead, Cadmium and Mercury.* Am. J. Vet Res. 34:11 pp 1457-1458, 1973.

Lindquist, B., and H. Mornstad, *Effects of removing amalgam fillings from patients with diseases affecting the immune system.* Medical Science Research 24, 1996.

Magos, L., *Mercury-blood interaction and mercury uptake by the brain after vapor exposure.* Environ Res. 1:323-337, 1967.

Racz, W. J. and J. S. Vanderwater, *Perspectives on the central nervous system toxicity of methylmercury.* Can. J. Physiol & Pharm, 60: pp 1037-1045, 1982.

Siblerud, R. L., *The relationship between mercury from dental amalgam and cardiovascular system.* Sci Total Environ 99(1-2):23-35, Dec. 1, 1990.

Siblerud, R. L., *The relationship between mercury from dental amalgam and mental health.* Am J Psychother, 43(4):575-587, Oct. 1989.

Siblerud, R. L., and E. Kienholz, *Evidence that mercury from silver dental fillings may be an etiological factor in multiple sclerosis.* Sci Total Environ 142(3):191-205, Mar 15, 1994.

Traktenberg, I. M., *Chronic Effects of Mercury on organisms.* U.S. DHEW Publication No. (NIH) 74-473, pp 49-50.

Wolff, M., *Mercury toxicity from dental amalgam.* Neurotoxicology (4) pp 203, 1983.

Workshop on Mercury American College of Advancement of Medicine (ACAM), 1999.

Chapter 10
Chinese Medicine

Bensky, D. and A. Gamble, *Chinese Herbal Medicine*, Materia Medica, Eastland Press Inc., 1986.

Campbell, A. and R. S. MacDonald, *Natural Health Handbook*, Chartwell Books Inc., New Jersey, 1984.

First International Chinese Medicine and Acupuncture Academic Convention, C.M.A.A.C., 1986.

Lam, Dr. David, Lecture notes O.C.N.M., 1985.

Lewith, George, *Acupuncture, It's Place in Western Medical Science,* Thorsons Publishers Ltd., Wellingborough, Northamptonshire 1982.

Lucas, Richard, *Secrets of the Chinese Hebalists*, Parker Publishing Co., Inc., New York, 1987.

Marcus, Dr. Paul, *Acupuncture*, Thorsons Publishers Inc., 1985.

Wollerton, H. and McLean Co., *Acupuncture Energy in Health and Disease, A Practical Guide for Advanced Students,* Thorsons Publishers Ltd., Wellingborough, Northamptonshire, 1983.

Chapter 12
Food and Hidden Additives

Little Monsters, the television video show by the London British Broadcasting Corporation (1992) is video documentation of the *Great Saint Ormand Street Hospital Study: Hyperactivity and the Role of Food in Children,* by the Great Saint Ormand Street Hospital, London. The video also documents similar behavioral changes in children convicted of crimes, who were put on a special diet. *Why Can't My Child Behave* by Jane Hersey, Pear Tree Press, is available through the Feingold Association. In the USA, call toll free: 1 (800) 321-3287, Overseas call (703) 768-3287 or fax (703) 768-3619.

1. Blaylock, Russell L, M.D., web site: www.aspartamekills.com/blayartl.html

2. Leading Edge International Research Group, glutamate web site: www.trufax.org/research/f34.html

3. Rhodes, Richard, *Deadly Feasts.* Simon and Schuster, New York, NY, 1998.

4. Schwartz, George R., *In Bad Taste: The MSG Syndrome.* Health Press, 1988.

5. The Glutamate Association web site: www.msgfacts.com/

Chapter 13
The Secret World of Flavor Enhancers:
MSG and Aspartame — The Deadly Duo

Blaylock, Russell L., M.D., web site: www.aspartamekills.com/blayartl.html

Glutamate Association, web site: www.msgfacts.com/

Kaplan, H. K., et al., *Behavioral effects of dietary sucrose in disturbed children.* AM J Psychiatry. 143(7):944-945, 1986.

Kreusi, M. J. P., et al., *Effects of sugar and aspartame on aggression and activity in children.* AM J Psychiatry. 144(11): 1487-90. 1987.

Leading Edge International Research Group, glutamate web site: www.trufax.org/research/f34.html

Schwartz, George R., *In Bad Taste: The MSG Syndrome,* Health Press, 1988.

Whitney, Eleanor Noss, & Sharon Rady Rolfes, *Understanding Nutrition,* 7th ed., West Publishing Company, St. Paul, MN, 1996.

Williams, Sue Rodwell, *Nutrition and Diet Therapy,* 8th ed., Mosby-Year Book, St. Louis, MO, 1997.

Zimmerman, Marcia, *The A.D.D. Nutrition Solution,* Henry Holt and Company, New York, NY, 1999.

Chapter 14
The Problems With Soft Drinks

Ali, Elvis, et al., *The All-in-One Guide to™ Natural Remedies and Supplements,* AGES Publications™, Niagara Falls, NY, 2000.

Alleman, Gayle, M.S., R.D., *Save Your Child from the Fat Epidemic: 7 Steps Every Parents Can Take to Ensure Healthy, Fit Children for Life*, Prima Publishing, Rocklin, CA, 1999.

Anderson, Jean, and Barbara Deskins, *The Nutrition Bible*, William Morrow and Company, Inc., New York, 1995.

Kaplan, H. K., et al., *Behavioral effects of dietary sucrose in disturbed children.* AM J Psychiatry. 143(7):944-945, 1986.

Kreusi, M. J. P., et al., *Effects of sugar and aspartame on aggression and activity in children.* AM J Psychiatry. 144(11):1487-90, 1987.

Whitney, Eleanor Noss, and Sharon Rady Rolfes, *Understanding Nutrition*, 7th ed., West Publishing Company, St. Paul, MN, 1996.

Williams, Sue Rodwell, *Nutrition and Diet Therapy*, 8th ed., Mosby-Year Book, St. Louis, MO, 1997.

Zimmerman, Marcia, *The A.D.D. Nutrition Solution*, Henry Holt and Company, New York, NY, 1999.

Chapter 15
Sugar - Friend or Foe!?

1. DeMarco, *Pre-exercise carbohydrate meals: application of glycemic index.* Med Sci Sports Exerc 31(1):164-70, 1999.

2. Foster-Powell & Miller, International tables of glycemic index. Am J Clin Nutr 62(4):871S-890S, 1995.

3. Jenkins, et al., *Glycemic index of foods: a physiological basis for carbohydrate exchange.* Am J Clin Nutr 34(3):362-6, 1981.

4. Liljeberg, et al., *Effect of the glycemic index and content of indigestible carbohydrates of cereal-based breakfast meals on glucose tolerance at lunch in healthy subjects.* Am J Clin Nutr 69(4):647-55, 1999.

5. Ludwig, et al., *High glycemic index foods, overeating, and obesity.* Pediatrics 103(3):E26-32, 1999.

6. Morris & Zemel, *Glycemic index, cardiovascular disease, and obesity.* Nutr Rev 57(9 Pt 1):273-6, 1999.

7. Salmeron, et al., *Dietary fiber, glycemic load, and risk of NIDDM in men.* Diabetes Care 20(4):545-50, 1997.

8. Salmeron, et al., *Dietary fiber, glycemic load, and risk of non-insulin-dependent diabetes mellitus in women.* JAMA 277(6):472-7, 1997.

9. Thomas, et al., *Carbohydrate feeding before exercise: effect of glycemic index.* Int J Sports Med 12(2):180-6, 1991.

10. Trout & Behall, *Prediction of glycemic index among high-sugar, low-starch foods.* Int J Food Sci Nutr 50(2):135-44, 1999.

11. Stockhorst U., H. J. Steingruber and W. A. Scherbaum, *Classically conditioned responses following repeated insulin and glucose administration in humans.* Behav Brain Res. Jun 1:110(1-2):143-59, 2000.

12. Teff, K. L., J. Devine and K. Engelman, *Sweet taste: effect on cephalic phase insulin release in men.* Physiol Behav. Jun:57(6):1089-95, 1995.

13. Abdallah, L., M. Chabert and J. Louis-Sylvestre, *Cephalic phase responses to sweet taste.* Am J Clin Nutr. Mar:65(3):737-43, 1997 .

Chapter 16
Water:
A Source of Problems and Solutions

Ali, Elvis, et al., *The All-in-One Guide to™ Natural Remedies and Supplements.* excerpted, AGES Publications™, Niagara Falls, NY, 2000.

Whitney, Eleanor Noss, and Sharon Rady Rolfes, *Understanding Nutrition.* 7th ed., West Publishing Company, St. Paul, MN, 1996.

Williams, Sue Rodwell, *Nutrition and Diet Therapy.* 8th ed., Mosby-Year Book, St. Louis, MO, 1997.

Zimmerman, Marcia, *The A.D.D. Nutrition Solution.* Henry Holt and Company, New York, NY, 1999.

Chapter 17
Essential Fatty Acids

1. Koletzko, B., and A. Sinclair, *LC-PUFAs in diets for infants: Choices for recommending and regulating bodies and for manufacturers of dietary products.* Lipids, 34:215-20, 1999.

2. Birch, E. E., et al., *A randomized controlled trial of early dietary supply of LC-PUFAs and mental development in term infants.* Dev Med Child Neurol 42:174-181, 2000.

3. Horrobin, D. F., *Gamma Linolenic Acid: An Intermediate in Essential Fatty Acid Metabolism with Potential as an Ethical Pharmaceutical and as a Food.* Rev. Contemp Pharmacother 1:1-45, 1990.

4. Erasmus, Udo, *Fats that Heal Fats that Kill*, Alive Books, Burnaby, B.C., 1986.

5. Manku, M. S., et al., *Reduced levels of prostaglandin precursors in the blood of atopic patients: defective delta-6-desaturase function as a biochemical basis for atopy.* Prostaglandins Leuko Med 9:615-628, 1982.

6. Horrobin, D. F., and H. A. Carmichael, *Essential fatty acids in relation to diabetes.* In Horrobin D. F., Ed., *Treatment of Diabetic Neuropathy: A new Approach.* Churchill Livingstone, U.K., pp. 21-39, 1992.

7. Horrobin, D. F., and M. S. Manku, *Premenstrual syndrome and premenstrual breast pain (cyclical mastalgia): disorders of essential fatty acid (EFA) metabolism.* Prostaglabdins Leukot Essent Fatty Acids Reviews 37:255-261, 1989.

8. Brush, M. G., et al., *Abnormal essential fatty acid levels in plasma of women with premenstrual syndrome.* Am Obstet Gynecol 10:363-366, 1984.

9. Cunnane, S. C., et al., *Essential fatty acid and lipid profiles in plasma and erthrocytes in patients with multiple sclerosis.* Am J Clin Nutr 50:801-906, 1989.

10. Navarro, E., et al., *Abnormal fatty acid pattern in rheumatoid arthritis. A rationale for treatment with marine and botanical lipids.* J Rheumatol 27:298-303, 2000.

11. Stevens, L., et al., *Essential fatty acid metabolism in boys with attention-deficit hyperactivity disorder.* Am J Clin Nutr 62(4):761-768, 1995.

12. Burgess, J. R., et al., *Long-chain polyunsaturated fatty acids in children with attention deficit hyperactivity disorder.* Am J Clin Nutr 71:327-330, 2000.

13. Stordy, B., *Dyslexia, attention deficit hyperactivity disorder, dyspraxia - do fatty acids help?* Dyslexia Review 9(2):1-4, 1997.

14. Colquhoun, I., and S. Bunday, *A lack of essential fatty acids as a possible cause of hyperactivity in children.* Med Hypotheses 7:673-679, 1981.

15. Stevens, L., et al., *Omega-3 fatty acids in boys with behavior, learning and health problems.* Physiol Behav 59(4-5):915-920, 1996.

16. Clandinin, M. T., et al., *Assessment of the efficacious dose of arachidonic and docosahexaenoic acids in preterm infant formulas:fatty acid composition of erthrocyte membrane lipids.* Pediatric Research 42(6):819-825, 1997.

17. Stordy, B., *Benefit of docosahexaenoic acid supplements to dark adaptation in dyslexics.* Lancet 346(8971):385, 1995.

18. Richardson, A., et al., *Abnormal cerebral phospholipid metabolism in dyslexia indicated by phosphorus-31 magnetic resonance spectroscopy.* NMR in Biomedicine 10:309-314, 1997.

19. Richardson, A., et al., *Is developmental dyslexia a fatty acid deficiency syndrome?* Proceedings of the Nutrition Society, 1998.

20. Brenner, R. R., *Nutritional and hormonal factors influencing desaturation.* Prog Lipid Res 20:41-47, 1981.

21. Crawford, M., *The role of essential fatty acids in neural development: Implications for perinatal nutrition.* Am J Nutr 57:703S-710S, 1993.

22. Stordy. J. B., *Feeding the Brain From Conception to Maturity.* ADD News 2(2):14&23, 1999.

23. Stordy. J. B., *Feeding the Brain From Conception to Maturity.* An educational audiotape Copyright © Efamol Canada (1998) Limited, NS, Canada, 1999.

24. Holman, R. T., et al., *Deficiency of essential fatty acids and membrane fluidity during pregnancy and lactation.* Proc Natl Acad Sci 88:4835-4839, 1991.

25. Sattar, N., et al., *Essential fatty acids in relation to pregnancy complications and fetal development.* British Journal of Obstetrics and Gynaecology 105:1248-1255, 1998.

26. Neuringer, M., *Infant vision and retinal function in studies of dietary long-chain polyunsaturated fatty acids: methods, results, and implications.* Am J Clin Nutr 71(suppl):256S-67S, 2000.

27. Bakker, E. C., et al., *Early nutrition, essential fatty acid status and visual acuity of term infants at 7 months of age.* European Journal of Clinical Nutrition 53:872-879, 1999.

28. Willatts, P., et al., *Effect of long chain polyunsaturated fatty acids in infant formula on problem solving at 10 months of age.* Lancet 352(9129):688-691, 1998.

29. Willatts, P., et al., *Influence of long chain polyunsaturated fatty acids on infant cognitive function.* Lipids 33(10):973-980, 1998.

30. Lutz, M., *Diet as a determinant of central nervous system development: role of essential fatty acids.* Arch Layinoam Nutr 48(1):29-34, 1998.

31. Uany, R., and D.R. Hoffman, *Essential fat requirements of preterm infants.* Am J Clin Nutr 71(suppl):245S-50S, 2000.

32. Gibson, R. A., and M. Makrides, *n-3 polyunsaturated fatty acid requirements of term infants.* Am J Clin Nutr 71(suppl):251 S-5S, 2000.

33. Makrides, M., et al., *Is dietary docosahexaenoic acid essential for term infants?* Lipids 31(1):115-9, 1996.

34. Gazella, K. A., *Essential fatty acids and learning disorders.* Int J of Integrative Med 1(4):27-33, 1999.

35. Makrides, M., et al., *A randomized trail of different ratios of LA & ALA in the diet of term infants: effects on visual function and growth.* Amer J Clin Nutr 71:120-9, 2000.

36. Cunnane, S. C., et al., *Breast-fed infants achieve a higher rate of brain and whole body DHA accumulation than formula-fed infants not consuming dietary DHA.* Lipids 35:105-11, 2000.

37. Gerster, H., *Can adults adequately convert ALA to EPA and DHA?* Int J Vitam Nutr Res 68(3):159-73, 1998.

38. Birch, E. E., et al., *Breast-feeding and optimal visual development.* J Pediatr Ophthalmol Strbis Mus pp. 30-33, 1993.

Chapter 18
Herbs:
Botanical Approaches to ADD/ADHD

Blumenthal, M., *The commission E monographs.* American Botanical Council, Austin, TX, 1998.

Blumenthal, M., *Drug-herb interactions.* In Chandler, F., *Herbs: everyday guide for health professionals.* Canadian Pharmacists Association, Canadian Medical Association, Ottawa, ON.

Chandler, F., et al., *Herbs: everyday guide for health professionals.* Canadian Pharmacists Association, Canadian Medical Association, Ottawa, ON, 2000.

Ellingwood, E., and J. U. Lloyd, *American materia medica, therapeutics and pharmacognosy.* Reprinted, Eclectic Medical Publications, Sandy, OR, 1983.

Felter, H. W., and J. U. Lloyd, *King's American dispensatory.* 2 vols, Reprinted, Eclectic Medical Publications, Sandy, OR, 1983.

Mills, S., and K. Bone, *Principles and practice of phytotherapy.* Churchill Livingstone, Edinburgh, Scotland, 2000.

Saunders, P. S., and F. A. Wolfe, *The Complete Idiots guide to herbal remedies for Canadians.* Alpha Books, Toronto, ON, 2000.

Saunders, P. R., *North American herbal traditions.* In Chandler, F., et al., *Herbs: everyday guide for health professionals.* Canadian Pharmacists Association, Canadian Medical Association, Ottawa, ON, 2000.

Weiss, R. F., *Herbal medicine.* translated from 6th German ed., Beaconsfield Publishers Ltd., Beaconsfield, UK, 1988.

Chapter 19
Amino Acids and Proteins — A team effort

Ali, Elvis, et al., *The All-in-One Guide to™ Natural Remedies and Supplements*, Excerpted, AGES Publications™, Niagara Falls, NY, 2000.

Chapter 20
Homeopathy and Cell Salts

Refer to general references immediately following the annotated chapters in the bibliography.

Chapter 21
Bach Flower Remedies

Ball, Stefan, *Principles of Bach Flower Remedies.* Thorsons HarperCollins Publishers, Hammersmith, London, 1999.

Ball, Stefan, *The Bach Remedies Workbook.* and *Teach Yourself Bach Flower Remedies.*

Chapter 22
The Benefits of Exercise for
ADD and Hyperactive Children and Adults

Refer to general references immediately following the annotated chapters in the bibliography.

Chapter 23
The Benefits of Swimming for
ADD and Hyperactive Children and Adults

Refer to general references immediately following the annotated chapters in the bibliography.

Chapter 24
Neurofeedback for ADD/Hyperactivity

Barkley, R. A., *Attention deficit hyperactivity disorder: A handbook for diagnosis and treatment*. Guilford Press, NY, 1990.

Brown, Bordon, Wyne & Shieser, *Methylphenidate and Cognitive therapy with ADD children: A methodological reconsideration*. Journal of Abnormal Child Psychology 14:481-497, 1986.

Cheng, Pui-wan, *Metacognition and giftedness: The state of the relationship*. Gifted Child Quarterly Vol. 37:3 Summer:105-112, 1993.

Etevenon, P., *Applications and Perspectives of EEG cartography*. In Duffy, F. H., Ed., *Topographic mapping of brain electrical activity*. pp. 113-141, Butterworth, Boston, MA, 1986.

Fein, G., D. Gain, J. Johnstone, C. Yingling, M. Marcus, and M. Kiersch, *EEG power spectra in normal and dyslexic children*. Electroencephalography and Clinical Neurophysiology 55:399-405, 1983.

Gray, Susan S., *Ideas in practice: Metacognition and mathematical problem solving*. Journal of Developmental Education Vol. 14, 3:24-28, 1991.

Greenberg, L., *An objective measure of methylphenidate response: Clinical use of the MCA*. Psychopharmacology Bulletin 23:279-282, 1987.

Hartmann, Thom, *Attention Deficit Disorder: A Different Perception*. ISBN 1-88733-156-4, Underwood Press, CA, 1993.

IVA, Intermediate Visual and Auditory Continuous Performance Test, available through BrainTrain, 727 Twin Ridge Lane, Richmond, VA, 23235.

Janzen, T., and G. Fitzsimmons, *Differences in Baseline EEG Measures for ADD and Normally Achieving Preadolescent Males*. Biofeedback and Self Regulation Vol. 20, No. 1, 1995.

Landers, D. M., S. J. Petruzzello, W. Salazar, D. J. Crews, K. A. Kubitz, T. L. Gannon and M. Han, *The influence of electrocortical biofeedback on performance in pre-elite archers*. Medicine and Science in Sports and Exercise 23:(1):123-128, 1991.

Linden, M., T. Habib and V. Radojevic, *A controlled study of EEG biofeedback effects on cognitive and behavioral measures with attention-deficit disorder and learning disabled children*. Biofeedback and Self-Reguation Vol. 21 1:35-49, 1996.

Lubar, J. F., *Discourse on the development of EEG diagnostics and biofeedback treatment for attention deficit/hyperactivity disorders*. Biofeedback and Self-Regulation 16:202-225, 1991.

Lubar, J. F., M. O. Swartwood, J. N. Swartwood, and P. O'Donnell, *Evaluation of the effectiveness of EEG neurofeedback training for ADHD in a clinical setting as measured by changes in T.O.V.A. scores, behavioral ratings, and WISC-R performance*. Biofeedback and Self Regulation Vol. 20, No. 1, 83-99, 1995.

Lubar, J. F., *Neocortical dynamics: Implications for understanding the role of neurofeedback and related techniques for the enhancement of attention.* Applied Psychophysiology and Biofeedback, 22:(2), 1997.

Mann, C. A., J. F. Lubar, A. W. Zimmerman, C. A. Miller and R. A. Muenchen, *Quantitative analysis of EEG in boys with attention-deficit-hyperactivity disorder: Controlled study with clinical implications.* Pediatric Neurology 8:(1):30-36, 1992.

Monastra, Vincent J., et al., *Assessing Attention Deficit Hyperactivity Disorder via Quantitative Electroencephalography: An Initial Validation Study.* Neuropsychology Vol. 13, No. 3, pp. 424-433, 1999.

Palincsar, A. S., and D. A. Brown, *Enhancing instructional time through attention to metacognition.* Journal of Learning Disabilities Vol. 20:(2):66-75, 1987.

Robbins, Jim, *A Symphony in the Brain.* Atlantic Monthly Press, New York, 2000.

Rossiter, T. R., and T. J. LaVaque, *A Comparison of EEG Biofeedbaclk and Psychostimulants in Treating Attention Deficit Hyperactivity Disorders.* Journal of Neurotherapy Summer:48-59, 1995.

Safer, Daniel J., *Increased methylphenidate usage for Attention Deficit Disorder in the 1990's.* Pediatrics 98:(6):1084-1088, December 1996.

Sears, W., and L. Thompson, *The A.D.D. Book, New Understandings, New Approaches to Parenting Your Child.* Little Brown and Company. New York, NY, 1998.

Sterman, M. B., *Basic Concepts and Clinical Findings in the Treatment of Seizure Disorders with EEG Operant Conditioning.* Clinical Electroencephalography Vol. 31, No. 1, 2000.

Swanson, J. M., K. McBurnett, T. Wigal, L. J. Pfiffner, L. Williams, D. L. Christian, L. Tamm, E. Willcutt, K. Crowley, W. Clevenger, N. Khouam, C. Woo, F. M. Crinella and T. M. Fisher, *The Effect of Stimulant Medication on Children with Attention Deficit Disorder: A "Review of Reviews".* Exceptional Children, 60:(2):154-162, 1993.

Tansey, M., *Wechsler (WISC-R) changes following treatment of learning disabilities via EEG biofeedback training in a private setting.* Australian Journal of Psychology 43:147-153, 1991.

Thompson, L., and M. Thompson, *Neurofeedback Combined with Training in Metacognitive Strategies: Effectiveness in Students with ADD.* Applied Psychophysiology and Biofeedback Vol. 23, No. 4, 1998.

Thompson, L., and M. Thompson, *Exceptional Results with Exceptional Children.* Proceedings of the Society for the Study of Neuronal Regulation, Scotsdale, AZ, 1995.

TOVA, Test of Variables of Attention. available from Universal Attention Disorders Inc., 4281 Katella Ave. #215, Los Alamitos, CA, 90720.

Zametkin, A. J., T. E. Nordahl, M. Gross, A. C. King, W. E. Semple, J. H. Rumsey, S. Hamburger and R. M. Cohen, *Cerebral glucose metabolism in adults with hyperactivity of childhood onset.* New England Journal of Medicine 323:(20):1361-1366, 1990.

Chapter 25
Mediation of Cognitive Competencies

1. Long, Madeleine, and Meir Ben-Hur, *Informing Learning Through the Clinical Interview*. Arithmetic Teacher, pp. 44-47, February 1991.
2. Vygotsky, Lev, *Mind in Society*. Harvard University Press, Cambridge, MA, 1978.
3. Feuerstein, Reuven, Rafi Feuerstein and Yaron Schur, *Process as Content in Education of Exceptional Children*. In Arthur L. Costa and Rosemarie M. Liebmann, Eds., *Supporting the Spirit of Learning: When Process Is Content*. Corwin Press, Thousand Oaks, CA, 1997.
4. American Association for the Advance of Science, *Project 2061: The Nature of Mathematics, Grades 3-5*. Oxford University Press, New York, 1993.

Chapter 26
The Healing Power of Sound:
Music and Guided Imagery

Heller, G., and A. Solomon, *Historical Research in Music Therapy: a Bibliography*. University of Kansas, Dept. of Art and Education and Music Therapy, Lawrence, KS, 1992.

Le Mie, Katherine, *Chant: The Origins, Form, Practice, and Healing Power of Gregorian Chant*. Bell Tower Books, 1995.

Ostrander, Sheila, and Lynn Schroeder, *Superlearning 2000*. Island Books, 1997.

Rauscher, Frances, et. al., *Listening to Mozart Enhances Spatial-Temporal Reasoning: Toward a Neurophysiological Basis*. Neuroscience Letters 184, 1995.

Shaw, Gordon, *Keeping Mozart in Mind*. Academic Press, San Diego, CA, 2000.

Steiner, Rudolf, *The Inner Nature of Music and the Experience of Tone: A Series of Seven Lectures from 1906-1923*. Anthroposophic Press, Spring Valley, NY, 1983.

Tame, David, *The Secret Power of Music*. Turnstone Press, Wellingborough, Northamptonshire, 1984.

Tomatis, Alfred, *The Conscious Ear: My Life of Transformation through Listening*. Station Hill Press, Barrytown, NY, 1991.

Children's Imaginations Help to Eliminate Migraine Headaches. KidSource web site: www.kidsource.com/kidsource/content/news/headaches.5.27.html

The Mozart Effect web site: www.mozarteffect.com

Chapter 27
Tales to Empower™ Teachers, Parents and
ADD/Hyperactive Children and Adults

Mate, Gabor, *Scattered Minds*, Vintage Canada Edition, Toronto, ON, 2000.

Chapter 28
Are Drugs the Solution?

Graedon, Joseph, and Teresa Graedon, *Dangerous Drug Interactions.* St. Martin's
Press, New York, 1999.

Moore, Thomas, *Prescription for Disaster.* Simon & Shuster, New York, 1999.

Physician's Desk Reference. Medical Economics Company, Montvale, NJ, 1999.

Wilens, Timothy, *Straight Talk About Psychiatric Medications for Kids,* Guilford
Press, New York, 1999.

Chapter 29
The Top Ten Drugs Used in The Treatment of ADD/Hyperactivity

Graedon, Joseph, and Teresa Graedon, *Dangerous Drug Interactions.* St. Martin's
Press, New York, 1999.

Moore, Thomas, *Prescription for Disaster.* Simon & Shuster, New York, 1999.

Martindale: The Extra Pharmacopeia, 31st ed., James Reynolds, Editor, Royal
Pharmaceutical Society, London, England, 1992.

Pelton, Ross, et al., *Drug-Induced Nutrient Depletion Handbook.* Lexi-Comp Inc.
Houston, TX, 1999.

Physician's Desk Reference. Medical Economics Company, Montvale, NJ, 1999.

Silverman, Harold, et al., *The Pill Book.* 9th ed., Bantam Books, New York, NY,
2000.

Trace Elements in Human Nutrition and Health. World Health Organization,
Geneva, 1996.

Wilens, Timothy, *Straight Talk About Psychiatric Medications for Kids.* Guilford
Press, New York, 1999.

Bibliography — General

Ali, Elvis, Pam Floener, David Garshowitz, George Grant, Gordon Ko, Dorothy
Marshall, Alvin Petal and Ken Vegotsky, *The All-in-One Guide to™ Natural
Remedies and Supplements.* AGES Publications™, Niagara Falls, NY, 2000.

Ali, Elvis, George Grant, Selim Nakla, Don Patel and Ken Vegotsky, *The Tea Tree
Oil Bible*, AGES Publications™, Niagara Falls, NY, 1999.

Ambau, G. T., *The Importance of Good Nutrition, Herbs & Phytochemicals.* Falcon
Press International, Mountain View, CA, 1997.

American Psychiatric Association, *Diagnostic and Statistical Manual of Mental
Disorders,* 4th ed., American Psychiatric Association, Washington, DC, 1994.

Anderson, Jean, and Barbara Deskins, *The Nutrition Bible,* William Morrow and
Company, Inc., New York, 1995.

Ball, Stefan, *Principles of Bach Flower Remedies.* Thorsons HarperCollins
Publishers, Hammersmith, London, 1999.

Barkley, Russell, *Taking Charge of ADHD*. Guilford Press, New York, 1995.

Barkley, Russell, and Christine Benton, *Your Defiant Children: 8 Steps to Better Behavior,* Guilford Press, New York, NY, 1998.

Berkow, Robert, et al., *The Merck Manual of Medical Information,* Simon & Shuster, New York, 1999.

Branden, Nathaniel, *The Power of Self-Esteem*. Health Communications, Deerfield, FL, 1992.

Butler, Kathleen A., *It's All in Your Mind: A Student s Guide to Learning Style*. The Learner's Dimension, Columbia, CT, 1988.

Carper, Jean, *Food Your Miracle Medicine*. HarperCollins Publishers, New York, 1998.

Carper, Jean, *Miracle Cures*. HaperCollins Publishers, New York, 1997.

Carroll, Lee, and Jan Tober, *The Indigo Children: the new kids have arrived*. Hay House, Carlsbad, CA, 1999.

Colgan, Michael, *Hormonal Health*. Apple Publishing, Vancouver, BC, Canada, 1996.

Copeland, Edna, and Valerie Love, *Attention Without Tension: A Teacher's Handbook on Attention Disorders (ADHD and ADD)*. Speciality Press, Plantation, FL, 1995.

Cummings, Stephen, and Dana Ulman, *Everybody's Guide to Homeopathic Medicines*. Jeremy P. Tarcher/Perigee Books, New York, 1991.

Cytryn, Leon, and Donald McKnew, *Growing Up Sad: Childhood Depression and its Treatment*. W. W. Norton & Company, New York, 1996.

DePorter, Bobbi, *Quantum Learning*. Dell Publishing, New York, 1992.

Dryden, Gordon, and Jeannette Vos, *The Learning Revolution*. Jalmar Press, Torrance, 1994.

Feingold, Ben F., *Why Your Child is Hyperactive*. Random House, New York, NY, 1975.

Flick, Grad, *ADD/ADHD Behavior-Change Resource Kit*. The Center for Applied Research in Education, West Nyack, NY, Random House, New York, 1998.

Fredericks, Carlton, and Herman Goodman, *Low Blood Sugar and You*. Berkley Books, New York, 1987.

Garrison, Robert H., and Elizabeth Somer, *The Nutrition Desk Reference*. 3rd ed., Keats Publishing, Inc., New Canaan, CT, 1995.

Glasser, William, *Schools Without Failure*. Harper and Row, New York, 1969.

Gray, John, *Men are From Mars, Women Are From Venus*, HarperCollins, New York, 1992.

German Commission E Monographs. English Translation, American Botanical Council, Austin, TX, 1998.

Graedon, Joseph, and Teresa Graedon, *Dangerous Drug Interactions*. St. Martin's Press, New York, 1999.

Greene, Ross W., *The Explosive Child: A New Approach for Understanding and Parenting Easily Frustrated, Chronically Inflexible Children.* HarperCollins, New York, 1998.

Hallowell, Edward, and John Ratey, *Driven to Distraction.* Simon & Shuster, New York, 1994.

Hampton, Aubrey, *Natural Organic Hair and Skin Care.* Organica Press, Tampa, FL, 1987.

Hersey, Jane, *Why Can't My Child Behave.* Pear Tree Press, Alexandria, VA, 1999.

Jeffers, Susan, *Feel the Fear... and Beyond: Mastering Techniques for Doing it Anyway.* Random House, New York, 1998.

Keefe, J. W., *Learning Style Theory and Practice.* NASSP, Reston, VA, 1987.

Lambert-Lagace, Louise, and Michelle Laflamme, *Good Fat Bad Fat.* Stoddart Publishing Co., Toronto, ON, Canada, 1995.

Lerner, Harriet, *The Dance of Deception.* HaperCollins, New York, 1993.

Levinson, Harold N., *Smart but Feeling Dumb.* Warner Books, New York, 1994.

Levinson, Harold N., *Total Concentration: How to Understand Attention Deficit Disorders with Treatment Guidelines for You and Your Doctor.* M. Evans and Company, New York, 1992.

Martindale: The Extra Pharmacopeia. 31st ed., James Reynolds, Editor, Royal Pharmaceutical Society, London, England, 1992.

Moore, Thomas, *Prescription for Disaster.* Simon & Shuster, New York, 1999.

Murray, Michael, and Joseph Pizzorno, *Encyclopedia of Natural Medicine.* 2nd ed., Prima Publishing, Rocklin, CA, 1998.

Ostrander, Sheila, and Lynn Schroeder, *Super-Learning.* Dell, New York, 1982.

Pelton, Ross, et al., *Drug-Induced Nutrient Depletion Handbook.* Lexi-Comp Inc. Houston, TX, 1999.

Physician's Desk Reference. Medical Economics Company, Montvale, NJ, 1999.

Presseisen, Barbara, Ed., *Teaching for Intelligence: A Collection of Articles.* pp 305-318, Skylight Training and Publishing Inc., Arlington Heights, IL, 1999.

Rea, William, *Chemical Sensitivity.* Vol. 1-4, Boca Raton, FL, 1997.

Reichenberg-Ullman, Judyth, and Robert Ullman, *Ritalin Free Kids.* Prima Publishing, Rocklin, CA, 1996.

Rief, Sandra, *How to Reach and Teach ADD/ADHD Children.* The Center for Applied Research in Education, West Nyack, NY, 1993.

Rief, Sandra, *The ADD/ADHD Checklist.* Prentice Hall, Pasramus, NJ, 1998.

Rona, Zoltan, *Childhood Illness and the Allergy Connection.* Prima Publishing, Rocklin, CA, 1997.

Silverman Harold, et al., *The Pill Book.* 9th ed., Bantam Books, New York, NY, 2000.

Silvernail, D., *Teaching Styles as Related to Student Achievement: What Research Says to the Teacher.* National Education Association, Washington D.C., 1979.

Sims, Pamela, *Awakening Brilliance*. Bayhampton Publications, Atlanta, GA, 1997.

Tobias, Cynthia, *The Way We Learn*. Focus on the Family, Colorado Springs, CO, 1994.

Trace Elements in Human Nutrition and Health. World Health Organization, Geneva, 1996.

Vegotsky, Ken, *The Ultimate Power: Lessons from a Near-Death Experience/How to Unlock Your Mind-Body-Soul Potential*. AGES Publications™, Niagara Falls, NY, 1995.

Wilens, Timothy, *Straight Talk About Psychiatric Medications for Kids*. Guilford Press, New York, 1999.

Whitney, Eleanor Noss, and Sharon Rady Rolfes, *Understanding Nutrition*. 7th ed., West Publishing Company, St. Paul, MN, 1996.

Williams, Sue Rodwell, *Nutrition and Diet Therapy*. 8th ed., Mosby-Year Book, St. Louis, MO, 1997.

Zimmerman, Marcia, *The A.D.D. Nutrition Solution*. Henry Holt and Company, New York, 1999.

Appendix E
Product Descriptions and
Sources

Products to Address Autism or A.D.D

Refer to Chapter 8, A Cure for Autism, to see if the the underlying cause of autism is the one the autistic child or adult has, and to determine if these are the appropriate products for them.

There are 3 products that are required to be taken in succession, and in conjunction with Beta-1,3-D glucan

\# 1) Immunfactor™ 1, including Beta-1,3-D glucan

\# 2) Immunfactor™ 4, including Beta-1,3-D glucan

\# 3) Immunfactor™ 8, including Beta-1,3-D glucan

"Beta-1,3-D glucan is now an improved and more highly purified with removal of fatty acids. This was done to increase purity, palatability, synergy and quality of product."

Recommended dosage: Each immunfactor product is to be taken for 3 months in succession, one capsule per day in conjunction with Beta-1,3-D glucan, one in morning and one capsule in evening. Recommended dosages may vary, according to the constitution of the autistic child or adult.

For more detail information check the web site:
www.bahironline.com

To order these products, call toll free 1 (866) 297-8218

Knowledge Products

Refer to Chapter 5, Parasites and Detoxification, to see why it is noted that "If the body is full of toxins, the best nutrition and supplements cannot be fully utilized. Thus, relying solely on the use of nutritional supplements with the hope of bridging the gap between what our bodies need and what may be missing is not sufficient for bringing about a better state of health."

30 Day Paraway Cleanse

A specially formulated program of herbs traditionally used for parasite and candida.

A timed administration to maximize the antifungal properties and deworming benefits of Artemisia/Wormwood, Cloves, Black Walnut Tincture... to tonify the body.

Uri-Harmony — A kidney/bladder cleanser and tonifier.

Hepatica/Liver Harmony
— A formulation of herbs to detoxify and strengthen the liver.

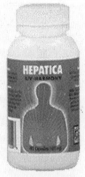

30 Day Fabulax Bowel Cleanse

A comprehensive internal cleansing and balancing program that promotes regularity, removes candida.

Contains Fabulax Fiber, a combination of intestinal fibers, and Fabulax Cleanser, herbs known for their laxative properties.

Circu Balance — Provides cleansing nutritive elements for the skin and for the proper functioning of the circulatory and lymphatic systems.

Lion's Heart — Balances cardiovascular system, cholesterol, normalizes blood pressure.

Brain Booster — supports mental clarity, improves memory functions, aids in longevity.

Painfree Oil — powerful deep penetrating oil that relieves headache, stiffness in joints, tendons, ligaments and muscles.

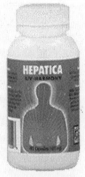

To order any of these products, call the Order Desk at 1 (866) 270-7486.
For more detail on product line, check our web site: www.bahironline.com

Entrox® — The potent, patented, multi-EFA!

Refer to Chapter 17, Essential Fatty Acids: Fats that Heal the ADD/ Hyperactive Brain, to find out more about why essential fatty acids are required "for our bodies to function properly," and Chapter 19, Amino Acids and Proteins: Keeping the Body's Systems in Balance, to see why "naturally occurring amino acids are used by the body to create the proteins necessary for optimal functioning."

Entrox® is a palatable, digestible soft gel pill (patent pending enteric coating) that contains a patent dose of the essential fatty acids, Omega 3, Omega 6 and Omega 9, phytochemicals and amino acids that come from a plant oil named, "Zi Su," the primary ingredient in Entrox. Entrox's formulation, as a soft gel cap with enteric coating, reduces the oxidation of EFAs, thereby eliminating rancidity, unpleasant aftertaste and indigestion. Entrox is excellent for people who do not wish to use fish source based EFAs. As well, according to Carolwood Corporation, (manufacturers of Lignisul MSM) gram for gram entrox contains more alpha-linolenic acid (Omega 6) than flax seed oil.

For more detail check our web site: www.bahironline.com

The Music of Hennie Bekker

Refer to Chapter 17, **The Healing Power of Sound:** Music and Guided Imagery, for more on why "music is used both as a mental stimulant and as a means for inducing feelings of relaxation."

Hennie Bekker is an award-winning, multi platinum selling musician and composer whose eclectic career spans decades, continents, generations and genres. Best known for his New Age sound on the Solitudes, Kaleidoscope, Tranquility and Tapestries series collections, he is truly a creative force.

"I know that you will probably never see this email, but I hope that you might. Your music is "beyond" mere words. I could listen to it for hours and hours. I wish that I could find a store here in Victoria that carried "ALL" of your music. I would buy the lot, if I had a chance."
— Robert Gibson

His excellence in composition of ambient melodies complemented Dan Gibson's nature sounds to create the many gold, platinum, double platinum and triple platinum albums in the Solitudes series. Bekker went on to arrange, compose and produce a solo series of soothing, meditative, nature-inspired works. In the Kaleidoscope and Tranquility series, he applied his signature style to original songs and familiar classics, capturing the essence of a mood, memory or season. His renowned African Tapestries series is "an expedition of World music interwoven…"

Solitudes — A series of over 20 CD-ROMs

Explore nature with music... Solitudes presents a relaxing and thought provoking sound experience... Caresses the body and soul with waves of soothing sound to provide luxurious comfort and revitalization...

...and even more to experience.

BREAKING THROUGH THE MIST

Hennie Bekker, a master of musical technology, blends, stretches, layers and enhances his core sounds. As a prolific professional, he is constantly creating, expanding, exploring and recording auditory portraits that captivate a wide audience. Bekker's artistry continues to inspire.

Reverie

Tranquility, Kaleidoscope, Tapestries, Horizons, and other series

Beautiful melodies colored with light percussion and nature sounds... Gentle fibers of sound weave through your consciousness... to relax and rejuvenate...

...a world of sound interwoven.

"Hi, my name is James Osu and I am writing this letter to let you know that I bought the CD of Temba. I must sincerely say that it is the best music that I have ever listened to in my 29 years of existence.

The synchronization of the music is so captivating and emotional that it brings tears of joy into my eyes. The sound effects are so real that I can actually imagine myself in the forest-like setting. You could never begin to imagine how much happiness and serenity this wonderful creation has brought me.

I wish you long life, and a blessed musical career so you can give us more master-pieces. You are one of a kind. I wonder if you have concerts, and if you do I would give the world just to hear your music live. Stay blessed." — James Osu

Awakenings

For more detail check our web site: www.bahironline.com

To order these CDs call the order desk 1 (866) 689-4962

Appendix F
Support Groups for Educators and Parents

United States and Canada:

This section lists many parent and educational organizations which offer information and help on specific educational issues and social support groups. If a regional office is not listed, contact the national office for your local chapter.

To be considered for a listing in future publications or to update your entry, organizations should mail information and media kits to AGES Publications™, 1623 Military Road, PMB 203-AH, Niagara Falls, NY, 14304-1745. Groups or organizations may insert a link at www.800line.com/ages/ on the AGES web-site.

Note: This is NOT a solicitation for manuscripts. Refer to manuscript submission guidelines on our web site. Our publishing schedule is filled for the foreseeable future.

United States Associations — by category

DROPOUT PREVENTION

Aspira Association, Inc., National Office,
1112-16th Street, NW, Suite 340,
Washington, DC 20036
(202) 835-3600

Big Brothers/Big Sisters of America,
230 North 13th Street,
Philadelphia, PA 19107
(215) 567-7000

Boys and Girls Clubs of America,
1230 West Peachtree Street NW,
Atlanta, GA 30309
(404) 815-5700 or (800) 854-CLUB

Cities in School, Inc.,
1199 North Fairfax, Suite 300,
Alexandria, VA 22314-1963
(703) 519-8999

Girls Incorporated,
30 East 33rd Street,
New York, NY 10016
(212) 689-3700

National Dropout Prevention Center,
Clemson University, 205 Martin Street,
Clemson, SC 29634-5111
(803) 656-2599 or (800) 443-6392

EDUCATIONAL ASSOCIATIONS

American Assoc. of School Administrators,
1801 North Monroe Street,
Arlington, VA 22209
(703) 528-0700

American Forum for Global Education,
120 Wall Street, Suite 2600,
New York, NY 10005
(212) 742-8232

American Indian Institute, College of
Continuing Education, U. of Oklahoma,
555 Constitution, Suite 237,
Norman, OK 73072-7820
(405) 325-4127 or (800) 522-0772

American School Counselor Association
801 North Fairfax Street, Suite 310
Alexandria, VA 22314
(703) 683-2722

Appalachia Educational Laboratory, Inc.
P.O. Box 1348 - 1031 Quarrier Street
Charleston, WV 25325
(304) 347-0400 or (800) 624-9120

Associates for Renewal in Education, Inc.
45 P Street NW
Washington, DC 20001
(202) 483-9424

Assoc. for Community Based Education
1805 Florida Avenue NW
Washington, DC 20009
(202) 462-6333

Association for Experiential Education
2885 Aurora Avenue, Suite 28
Boulder, CO 80303-2252
(303) 440-8844

Center for Educational Renewal,
313 Miller Hall, Box 353600,
University of Washington,
Seattle, WA 98195-3600
(206) 543-6230

Center for Research on the Education of
Students Placed at Risk
Holy Cross Hall, Room 427
2900 Van Ness Street NW
Washington, DC 20008
(202) 806-8484

Center for School Change, Humphrey
Institute of Public Affairs, University of
Minnesota, 301 19th Avenue S
Minneapolis, MN 55455
(612) 626-1834

Center for Social Organization of Schools
Johns Hopkins University
3505 North Charles Street
Baltimore, MD 21218
(410) 516-8800

Center for the Study of Small/Rural
Schools, University of Oklahoma
555 East Constitution Street, #213
Norman, OK 73072-7820
(405) 325-1450 or (800) 522-0772

Center on Families, Schools, Communities
and Children's Learning
Boston University, School of Education
605 Commonwealth Avenue
Boston, MA 02215
(617) 353-3309

Coalition of Essential Schools,
Brown University, PO Box 1969,
Providence, RI 02912
(401) 863-3384

Consortium for School Networking
1555 Connecticut Avenue NW, Suite 200
Washington, DC 20036
(202) 466-6296

Creative Education Foundation,
1050 Union Road, Suite 4,
Buffalo, NY 14224
(716) 675-3181

Enthusiasm for Learning Foundation
PO Box 40291
Portland, OR 97240-0291
(800) 353-5270

Far West Laboratory for Educational
Research and Development
730 Harrison Street
San Francisco, CA 94107-1242
(415) 565-3000

National Black Child Development Institute
1023 15th Street NW, Suite 600
Washington, DC 20005
(202) 387-1281

National Catholic Educational Association
1077 30th Street NW, Suite 100
Washington, DC 20007-3852
(202) 337-6232

National Center for Children in Poverty
Columbia University, 154 Haven Avenue
New York, NY 10032
(212) 927-8793

National Center, Education in Inner Cities
Temple University, 933 Ritter Hall Annex
13th Street and Cecil B. Moore Avenue
Philadelphia, PA 19122
(215) 204-3001

National Coalition of Title 1/Chapter 1
Parents, Edmonds School Bldg.
9th and D Streets NE, Rm. 201
Washington, DC 20002
(202) 547-9286

National Education Association
1201 16th Street NW
Washington, DC 20036
(202) 833-4000

National Head Start Association
1651 Prince Street
Alexandria, VA 22314
(703) 739-0875

National Research Center on Student
Learning, University of Pittsburgh Learning
Research and Development Center
3939 O'Hara Street
Pittsburgh, PA 15260
(412) 624-2881

Southern Early Childhood Association
PO Box 56130
Little Rock, AR 72215-6130
(501) 663-0353 or (800) 305-7322

Southwest Educational Development
Laboratory, 211 East 7th Street
Austin, TX 78701
(512) 476-6861

Wave, Inc.
501 School Street SW, Suite 600
Washington, DC 20024
(202) 484-0103 or (800) 274-2005

EDUCATIONAL INFORMATION

Educational Information and Resource
Center Research Department
606 Delsea Drive
Sewell, NJ 08080
(609) 582-7000

Eric Clearinghouse on Elementary and Early
Childhood Education
University of Illinois at Urbana-Champaign
805 W Pennsylvania Ave
Urbana, IL 61801-4897
(217) 333-1386 or (800) 583-4135

Eric Clearinghouse on Higher Education
The George Washington University
One Dupont Circle NW, Suite 630
Washington, DC 20036-1183
(202) 296-2597 or (800) 773-3742

Eric Clearinghouse on Rural Education and
Small Schools, Appalachia Educ. Laboratory
1031 Quarrier Street, PO Box 1348
Charleston, WV 25325-1348
(304) 347-0400 or (800) 624-9120

Eric Clearinghouse on Teaching and
Teacher Education, American Association of
Colleges for Teacher Education
One Dupont Circle NW, Suite 610
Washington, DC 20036-1186 (202) 293-
2450 or (800) 822-9229

Eric Clearinghouse on Urban Education
Columbia University Teachers College
Institute for Urban and Minority Education
Main Hall, Room 303, P.O. Box 40
New York, NY 10027-9998
(212) 678-3433 or (800) 601-4868

LaBriola National American Indian Data
Center University Libraries
Arizona State University, PO Box 871006
Tempe, AZ 85287-1006
(602) 965-6490

HOME SCHOOLING

Alliance for Parental Involvement in Educ.
29 Kinderhook Street
Chatham, NY 12037
(518) 392-6900

National Center for Home Educ.
PO Box 125
Paeonian Springs, VA 22129
(540) 338-7600

National Coalition of Alternative
Community Schools, PO Box 15036
Sante Fe, NM 87506
(505) 474-4312

National Homeschool Association
PO Box 157290
Cincinnati, OH 45215-7290

Parents as Teachers National Center, Inc.
10176 Corporate Square Drive, Suite 230
St. Louis, MO 63132
(314) 432-4330

PARENT ASSOCIATIONS

Children's Defense Fund
25 E Street NW
Washington, DC 20001
(202) 628-8787

Family Resource Coalition
200 S Michigan Avenue, 16th Floor
Chicago, IL 60604-2404
(312) 341-0900

Feingold Association of the United States
(FAUS) P.O. Box 6550,
Alexandria, Virginia 22306
(800) 321-3287 or (703) 768-3287

Int. Institute for Secular Humanistic
Judaism, 28611 W Twelve Mile Rd
Farmington Hills, MI 48334
(810) 477-9014

National Association of Hebrew
Day School PTAS, 160 Broadway
New York, NY 10038
(212) 227-1000

National Community Education Association
3929 Old Lee Highway, Suite 91-A
Fairfax, VA 22030
(703) 359-8973

National Family Partnership
11159-B South Towne Square,
St. Louis, MO 63123
(314) 845-1933

National Lutheran Parent-Teacher League
(NLPTL), 3290 South Tower Road
Aurora, CO 80013
(303) 766-7116

National PTA
National Congress of Parents and Teachers
330 North Wabash Avenue, Suite 2100
Chicago, IL 60611
(312) 670-6782 or (800) 312-6782

National Urban League
500 East 62nd Street
New York, NY 10021
(212) 310-9212

Parent Advocacy Coalition for Educational
Rights, Inc., 4826 Chicago Avenue South
Minneapolis, MN 55417-1055
(612) 827-2966 or (800) 53-PACER

Parent Educational Advocacy Training
Center, 10340 Democracy Lane, Suite 206
Fairfax, VA 22030
(703) 691-7826 or (800) 869-6782

Parents League of New York
115 East 82nd Street
New York, NY 10028
(212) 737-7385

Parent Network
6236 Utah Avenue NW
Washington, DC 20015
(202) 363-0835

Technical Assistance to Parent Programs
Project 95, Berkeley Square, Suite 104
Boston, MA 02116
(617) 482-2915

United Parents and Teachers Association of
Jewish Schools, 426 West 58th Street
New York, NY 10019
(212) 245-8200

SPECIAL EDUCATION ASSOCIATIONS
(Disabilities and Gifted)

American Association for Gifted Children
Talent Identification Program, Duke Univ.
1121 West Main Street, Suite 100
Durham, NC 27701
(919) 683-1400

American Assoc. on Mental Retardation
444 North Capitol Street NW, Suite 846
Washington, DC 20001-1512
(202) 387-1968 or (800) 424-3688

Association for Gifted and Talented
Students, Louisiana State University,
Baton Rouge, LA 70809
(318) 738-5459

Center for Innovations in Special Education,
Parkade Center, Suite 152
601 Business Loop 70
West Columbia, MO 65211
(314) 884-7275 or (800) 976-CISE

Center on Human Policy
805 South Crouse Avenue
Syracuse, NY 13244-2280
(315) 443-3851

Council for Exceptional Children,
Learning Disabilities,
1920 Association Drive,
Reston, VA 22091-1589
(703) 620-3660

Has divisions for: Children with
Behavioral Disorders, Early Childhood,
Mental Retardation and Developmental
Disabilities, Visual Handicaps, Gifted

Council for Learning Disabilities
PO Box 40303
Overland Park, KS 66204
(913) 492-8755

Disability Rights Education and Defense
Fund, Inc., 2212 Sixth Street,
Berkeley, CA 94710
(510) 644-2555 or (800) 466-4232

Eric Clearinghouse on Disabilities and
Gifted Education, Council for Exceptional
Children, 1920 Association Drive,
Reston, VA 22091-1589
(703) 620-2521 or (800) 328-0272

Federation for Children with Special Needs
95 Berkeley Street, Suite 104
Boston, MA 02116
(617) 482-2915 or (800) 331-0688

Learning Disabilities Association of America
4156 Library Road
Pittsburgh, PA 15234
(412) 341-1515

National Association for Children
PO Box 1088
Ogden, Utah 84402
(801) 621-8606 - Fax: (801) 621-8389
Internet: www.NACD.org

National Association for Gifted Children
1707 L Street NW, Suite 550
Washington, DC 20036
(202) 785-4268

National Assoc. for Visually Handicapped
22 W 21st Street
New York, NY 10010
(212) 889-3141

National Association of Private Schools for
Exceptional Children
1522 K Street NW, Suite 1032
Washington, DC 20005
(202) 408-3338

National Center for Learning Disabilities
381 Park Avenue S, Suite 1420
New York, NY 15016
(212) 545-7510

National Information Center for Children
and Youth with Disabilities, P.O. Box 1492
Washington, DC 20013
(202) 884-8200 or (800) 695-0285

The National Research Center on the Gifted
and Talented, University of Connecticut
362 Fairfield Road, U-7
Storrs, CT 06269-2007
(203) 486-4676

The Orton Dyslexia Society
Chester Bldg, 8600 LaSalle Rd, Suite 382
Baltimore, MD 21286-2044
(410) 296-0232

Western Regional Resource Center
University of Oregon
Eugene, OR 97403-1268
(541) 346-5641

SUBSTANCE ABUSE

American Council for Drug Education
164 W 74th Street,
New York, NY 10021
(212) 758-8060 or (800) 488-DRUG

American Council on Alcoholism, Inc.
2522 Paul Street
Baltimore, MD 21218
(410) 889-0100 or (800) 527-5344

Character Education Institute
8918 Tesoro Drive, Suite 575,
San Antonio, TX 78217-6253
(210) 829-1727 or (800) 284-0499

Drug Information & Strategy Clearinghouse
P.O. Box 6424,
Rockville, MD 20850
(800) 578-3472

National Association of Substance Abuse
Trainers and Educators, Inc.
1521 Hillary Street
New Orleans, LA 70118
(504) 286-5000

National Clearinghouse for Alcohol and
Drug Informahon
PO Box 2345
Rockville, MD 20847-2345
(301) 468-2600 or (800) 729-6686

National Families in Action,
2296 Henderson Mill Road, Suite 300
Atlanta, GA 30345
(770) 934-6364

National Federation Target Program
P.O. Box 20626, 11724 NW Plaza Circle,
Kansas City, MO 64195
(816) 464-5400

Office of National Drug Control Policy and
Crime Clearinghouse
1600 Research Blvd
Rockville, MD 20850
(800) 666-3332

Pennsylvania Substance Abuse and Health
Informahon Center
Keystone University Research Corporation
652 West 17th Street
Erie, PA 16502
(814) 459-0245 or (800) 582-7746

Safer Society Foundation
PO Box 340
Brandon, VT 05733-0340
(802) 247-3132

Southwest Regional Center, University of
Oklahoma, College of Continuing Educ.
555 Constitubon Avenue
Norman, OK 73037-0005
(800) 234-7972

VIOLENCE IN EDUCATION

Grace Contrino Abrams Peace Education
Foundation, 1900 Biscayne Boulevard
Miami, FL 33132
(305) 576-5075 or (800) 749-8838

Juvenile Justice Clearinghouse
Box 6000
Rockville, MD 20850
(800) 638-8736

National Center for the Study of Corporal
Punishment and Alternatives
Temple University, Ritter Hall Annex 253
Philadelphia, PA 19122
(215) 204-6091

National School Safety Center
4165 Thousand Oaks Blvd, Suite 290
Westlake Village, CA 91362
(805) 373-9977

Parents and Teachers Against Violence in
Education, PO Box 1033
Alamo, CA 94507-7033
(510) 831-1661

Canadian Associations — by Province

Alberta

Alberta Home and School Association
11010 142nd Street, Suite 607
Edmonton, AB T5N 2R1
(403) 454-9867

Calgary Association for Effective Education
of the Learning Disabled
Site 2, S.S. 3, PO Box 103,
Calgary, AB T3C 3N9
(403) 686-6444

Calgary Society for Students with Learning
Difficulties, 3930 20th Street SW
Calgary, AB T3C 3N9
(403) 686-6444

Learning Disabilities Association Of Alberta,
11343 61st Avenue NW, #145
Edmonton, AB T6H 1M3
(403) 448-0360

British Columbia

Delta Association for Handicapped Children
3800 72nd Street, #3
Delta, BC V4K 1M2
(604) 946-6622

Learning Disabilities Association of British
Columbia, 15463 104th Avenue, #203
Surrey, BC V3R lN9
(604) 588-6322

Native Education Center
285 E 5th Avenue
Vancouver, BC V5T 1H2
(604) 873-3761

Surrey Association for Early Childhood
Education, 6225B 136th Street
Surrey, BC V3X 1H3
(604) 597-3200

Manitoba

Learning Disabilities Association of
Manitoba, 60 Maryland Street, 2nd Floor
Winnipeg, MB R3G 1K7
(204) 774-1821

New Brunswick

Learning Disabilities Association of New
Brunswick, 138 Neill Street,
Fredericton, NB E3A 2Z6
(506) 459-5521

Newfoundland
Learning Disabilities Association of
Newfoundland and Labrador
PO Box 26036
St. John's, NF A1B 3T1
(709) 754-3665

Nova Scotia
Learning Disabilities Association of Nova
Scotia, 55 Ochterloney Street
Dartmouth, NS B2Y 1C3
(902) 464-9751

Northwest Territories & Inuavik
Learning Disabilities Association of the
Northwest Territories, P.O. Box 242
Yellowknife, NT X1A 2N2
(403) 873-6378

Ontario
Association of Early Childhood Educators,
40 Orchard View Blvd, Suite 217
Toronto, ON M4R lB9
(416) 487-3157

Association of Parent Support Groups of
Ontario, Box 27581, Yorkdale Postal Outlet
Toronto, ON M6A 3B6
(416) 221-1999

Big Brothers of Canada
5230 South Service Road
Burlington, ON L7L 5K2
(905) 639-0461

Boys and Girls Clubs of Canada
7030 Woodbine Avenue
Unionville, ON L3R 6G2
(905) 477-7272

Canadian Alliance of Home Schoolers
272 Hwy 5, R.R. #1
St. George, ON NOE 1N0
(519) 448-4001

Canadian Association for Co-op Education
55 Eglinton Avenue E, Suite 805
Toronto, ON M4P 1G8
(416) 483-3311

Canadian Education Association
252 Bloor Street W, Suite 8-200
Toronto, ON M5S 1V5
(416) 924-7721

Coalition for Education Reform
3266 Yonge Street, Suite 1720
Toronto, ON M4N 3P6
(905) 477-5397

Head Injury Association
45 Sheppard Avenue E, Suite 419
Toronto, ON M2N 5W9
(416) 222-1911

International Institute for Secular
Humanistic Judaism, 260 Henderson Ave
Thornhill, ON L3T 2M2
(905) 731-7066

Learning Disabilides Association of Canada
323 Chapel Street, Suite 200
Ottawa, ON K1N 7Z2
(613) 238-5721

Learning Disabilities Association of Ontario
124 Merton Street, 3rd Floor
Toronto, ON M4S 2Z2
(416) 487-4106

Ontario Association for Bright Children
2 Bloor Street W, Suite 100-156
Toronto, ON M4W 2G7
(416) 925-6136

Ontario Federation of Home and School
Associations, 252 Bloor Street W
Toronto, ON M5S 1V6
(416) 924-7491

Organization for Quality Education
170 University Avenue W, Suite 12-218
Waterloo, ON N2L 3E9
(905) 477-5397

Prince Edward Island
Learning Disabilities Association of P.E.I.
PO Box 1081, Station Main
Charlottetown, PE C1A 7M4
(902) 892-9664

Quebec
Quebec Learning Disabilities Association
284 Notre Dame Street W, Suite 300
Montreal, QC H2Y 1T7
(514) 847-1324

Saskatchewan
Learning Disabilities Association of
Saskatchewan
610 S Clarence Avenue, Suite 213
Saskatoon, SK S7H 2E2
(306) 652-4114

International Associations

Association for Childhood Education International
11501 Georgia Avenue, Suite 315
Wheaton, MD 20902
(301) 942-2443 or (800) 423-3563

The Global Alliance for Transforming Education (GATE), PO Box 21
Grafton, VT 05146
(802) 843-2382

International Alliance for Learning
PO Box 1298
Cardiff, CA 92007
(619) 722-0348 or (800) 426-2989

"Just Say No" International
2101 Webster Street, Suite 1300
Oakland, CA 94612
(510) 451-6666 or (800) 258-2766

Association of International Educators (NAFSA)
1875 Connecticut Avenue NW, Suite 1000
Washington, DC 20009-5728
(202) 462-4811

World Council for Gifted and Talented Children
University of Toronto, Faculty of Education
371 Bloor Street W
Toronto, ON M5S 2R7
(416) 978-8029

Parent Support Group Associations

National Associations

CHADD
(Children with Attention Deficit Disorders)
499 NW 70th Avenue, Suite 109
Plantation, FL 33317
(305) 587-3700

> Supported and funded indirectly through contributions from a pharmaceutical company.

ADDA
(Attention Deficit Disorders Association)
19262 Jamboree Boulevard
Irvine, CA 92715
(800) 487-2282

ADDA Group
8091 S. Ireland Way
Aurora, CO 80016

Learning Disabiliffes Associaffon (LDA)
4156 Library Road
Pittsburgh, PA 15234
(412) 341-1515

Tourette Syndrome Associaffon (TSA)
40 Bell Blvd, Suite 42
Bayside, NY 11361
(718) 224-2999

Canadian Association

Foundattion for Attentional Disorders
57 Pinecrest Road
Toronto, Ontario M6P 3G6
(416) 769-7979

Social Support and Information Groups

American Self-Help Clearinghouse
St. Clare's Health Services
25 Pocono Road
Denville, NJ 07834-2995
(973) 625-3037
www.selfhelpgroups.org

Puts callers in touch with any of hundred's of national and international self-help groups. Also refers to clearinghouses in other states. (Call between 9 A.M. and 5 PM., weekdays only.) Visit the Web site to link to related consumer resources, referral services, support groups.

Life Innovations, Inc.
PO Box 190
Minneapolis, MN 55440
(800) 331-1661
www.lifeinnovation.com

Formerly called Premarital Personal and Relationship Evaluation (PREPARE), this organization provides referrals to a counselor near you. Call or visit the Web site. (Note that "innovation" is singular in the Web address.) Provides premarital counseling and marriage enrichment using its PREPARE/ENRICH program.

National Institute of Relationship
Enhancement (RE)
4400 East-West Hwy., Suite 28
Bethesda, MD 20814-4501
(800) 432-6454
www.nire.org

Provides information about weekend workshops. Web site describes institute's couples weekends and provides information about couples, family, child, and stepfamily counseling as well as marriage preparation and enrichment.

Practical Application of Intimate
Relationship Skills (PAIRS)
318 Indian Trace, Suite 158
Weston, FL 33326-2996
(888) PAIRS-4U (888-724-7748), ext. 110
www.pairs.com

Offers workshops worldwide for individuals and couples in any stage of a relationship as well as for students from elementary through high school.

Prevention and Relationship Enhancement
Program, Inc. (PREP)
PO Box 102530
Denver, CO 80250-2530
(800) 366-0166 or (303) 759-9931
ext. 932
www.PREPinc.com

They will mail you information about weekend workshops for couples. Web site features a couple's quiz.

Appendix G
Reader Feedback Form

Your comments are very important to us. They help us improve on future editions of this and other books in our series of *Living Books™* to better inform and serve your needs and the needs of others. Your comments help others help themselves.

If you have access to the Internet, the easiest way for you to provide your feedback is through our on-line forms. There is one At-A-Glance Quick Reference™ Feedback Form for each of our information products.

The At-A-Glance Quick Reference™ Feedback Form for *The All-In-One Guide to™ ADD & Hyperactivity* can be accessed on-line from our home page at http://www.800line.com/ages/ and each of the book's information pages. It is quick and easy to use. On-line forms also allow for a little more comment space than the following printed form, save you the postage and give you the option of submitting your personal contact information over a secure server.

The At-A-Glance Quick Reference™ Feedback Form may differ from the printed form on the following page because it, too, evolves as a result of your feedback.

If you do not have access to the Internet, you may copy the feedback form and mail your comments to:

	for the convenience of Canadians
AGES Publications™	AGES Publications™
ADD Book Comments	ADD Book Comments
1623 Military Road, PMB 203	1054-2 Centre St., PMB 153
Niagara Falls NY 14304-1745	Thornhill, ON, L4J 8E5

...so that all may be healed.

<u>Reader Feedback — ADD & Hyperactivity</u>

Was the book easy to use?	❏ No	❏ Yes
Did the information meet your expectations?	❏ No	❏ Yes
Did you discover information that helped you?	❏ No	❏ Yes
Was your physician receptive to the information you shared with him or her?	❏ No	❏ Yes
Did the ADD/Hyperactive child or adult benefit from this book?	❏ No	❏ Yes

What has been most helpful?

_____

_____

_____

Did the resource and product sections help you?	❏ No	❏ Yes
Do you want more information about products?	❏ No	❏ Yes

Would you like to know about anything that was not covered in this book?

_____

_____

_____

Is there anything else you'd like to tell us?

_____

_____

_____

May we use your comments on our website and in future   ❏ No   ❏ Yes
information products?
     If yes, please sign here _____

If you want to be added to our mailing list, please fill in the following (please print):

Name: _____

Address: _____

_____

City: _____ State/Prov: _____ Zip/Post Code: _____

E-Mail: _____

Due to the volume of mail and Internet traffic we receive, it is not possible to respond to your comments. We will use them to improve on future editions of this and other books in the series. You will be helping others help themselves.

Thank you... **for taking the time to share your feedback.**

Appendix H
Professional Health-Care
Provider Feedback Form

Your comments are very important to us. They help us improve on future editions of this and other books in our series of *Living Books*™ to better inform and serve your needs and the needs of others. Your comments help others help themselves.

If you have access to the Internet, the easiest way for you to provide your feedback is through our on-line forms. There is one At-A-Glance Quick Reference Quick Reference™ Feedback Form for each of our information products.

The At-A-Glance Quick Reference™ Feedback Form for *The All-In-One Guide to*™ *ADD & Hyperactivity* can be accessed on-line from our home page at http://www.800line.com/ages/ and each of the book's information pages. It is quick and easy to use. On-line forms also allow for a little more comment space than the following printed form, save you the postage and give you the option of submitting your personal contact information over a secure server. The At-A-Glance Quick Reference™ Feedback Form may differ from the printed form on the following page because it, too, evolves as a result of your feedback.

If you do not have access to the Internet, you may copy the feedback form and mail your comments to:

for the convenience of Canadians

AGES Publications™
ADD Book Comments
1623 Military Road, PMB 203
Niagara Falls NY 14304-1745

AGES Publications™
ADD Book Comments
1054-2 Centre St., PMB 153
Thornhill, ON, L4J 8E5

...so that all may be healed.

Professional Health-Care Provider Feedback — ADD & Hyperactivity

Was the book easy to use?	❑ No ❑ Yes
Did the information meet your expectations?	❑ No ❑ Yes
Did you discover information that helped you?	❑ No ❑ Yes
Did the information help you and your patient develop a treatment plan?	❑ No ❑ Yes
Did the information help your patient understand the treatment plan?	❑ No ❑ Yes

What has been most helpful? _____

_____

_____

Did the resource and product sections help you?	❑ No ❑ Yes
Do you want more information about products?	❑ No ❑ Yes

Would you like to know about anything that was not covered in this book?

_____

_____

_____

Is there anything else you'd like to tell us?

_____

_____

_____

May we use your comments on our website and in future information products?   ❑ No ❑ Yes

    If yes, please sign here _____

If you want to be added to our mailing list, please fill in the following (please print):

Name: _____

Address: _____

_____

City: _____ State/Prov: _____ Zip/Post Code: _____

E-Mail: _____

Due to the volume of mail and Internet traffic we receive, it is not possible to respond to your comments. We will use them to improve on future editions of this and other books in the series. You will be helping others help themselves.

Thank you... **for taking the time to share your feedback.**

Appendix I
About The Authors

To Write to the Authors

If you wish to write the authors, please write in care of AGES Publications™, and we will forward your request. Both the authors and publisher appreciate hearing from you and learning of the benefits and enjoyment you received from this book. AGES Publications™ cannot guarantee that every letter written can be answered by the authors, but all will be forwarded.

AGES Publications™
Attn: (Insert Co-Author's Name)
1623 Military Road, PMB 203-ADD
Niagara Falls NY 14304-1745

Please enclose a self-addressed, stamped envelope for reply, and $3.00 to cover costs.

for the convenience of Canadians
AGES Publications™
Attn: (Insert Co-Author's Name)
1054-2 Centre St., PMB 153-ADD
Thornhill, ON, L4J 8E5

Please enclose a self-addressed, stamped envelope for reply, and $4.00 to cover costs.

If outside the U.S.A. or Canada, enclose international postal reply coupon with a self-addressed envelop and $3.00 U.S. to cover costs.

The Author's...

Dr. Elvis Ali, B.Sc., N.D., Dipl. Ac., M.R.N.

...is a licensed Naturopathic Doctor and a Registered Nutritional Consultant, R.N.C.. He graduated with a B.Sc. in Biology in 1979, and became one of Canada's first full time registered undergraduates in the field of Naturopathic Medicine. He received a Doctorate in Naturopathic Medicine in 1987 from the Canadian College of Naturopathic Medicine, one of only five accredited schools offering a four year full time program in Naturopathic Medicine in the U.S.A. and Canada. Elvis has been in private practice for over 12 years specializing in Chinese Medicine, Nutrition and Sports Medicine.

"My mission is to educate the public and be a spokesperson for complementary health and wellness options and continued research in the field of herbal remedies, bringing safe and non-intrusive options into the public domain," says Dr. Ali. He has written numerous articles on nutrition, stress and alternative healing options.

One of Canada's premier natural remedy and supplement companies, Swiss Herbal Remedies, retains Dr. Ali as their resident Naturopath with ongoing responsibility for product research and development. He is currently involved in making seminar presentations throughout the U.S.A. and Canada, in addition to numerous media appearances on radio and TV, as his commitment to increase the health and wellness of every man, woman and child in the U.S.A. and Canada.

He is married and the father of two children.

To arrange a keynote, seminar and/or workshop presentation by Dr. Ali, send e-mail to ages@800line.com or write to AGES Publications™, Attention: Dr. Ali at the address noted on page 377.

Stefan Ball

...has been associated with the Bach Centre since 1990. As a co-Principal of the Dr Edward Bach Foundation, he teaches the Bach Flower remedies at practitioner level, and has written several books on the Bach Flower remedies, including *Principles of Bach Flower Remedies, The Bach Remedies Workbook,* and *Teach Yourself Bach Flower Remedies.* Web site: http://www.bachcentre.com/

Kyle Brownell

...is a 4th year Honors student in Physical Education, and has been a Lifeguard and Swim Instructor for the past 6 years. He contributed the section on the benefits of swimming for ADD and hyperactive children and adults.

Minter H. Chip Dopson, B.Sc.

...holds a B.Sc. degree in Organic Chemistry from University of Georgia. Chip lectures to fellow scientists, physicians and lay public all over the world on the development and use of Transfer Factor (TF). Chip is frequently interviewed on radio and TV. *Alternative Medicine* Magazine has featured Chip and Michelle's work with a focus on immune potentiating nutritionals.

He is President of Chisolm Biological Laboratory (CBL). Established in 1976 with his wife Michelle DiMaria, who also holds a B.Sc. degree, CBL has been involved in TF research and development for more than 20 years, producing quality immune potentiating nutritionals. Their line of TF products is marketed under the brand name ImmunFactor™. ImmunFactor™ formulae have been developed to support the immune response for a variety of organisms.

Physicians and other health care professionals use ImmunFactor™ formulae in patients suffering with HIV, EBV, CMV, hepatitis, herpes, candida, chronic fatigue, fibromyalgia, autism and Lyme disease. In addition to managing the day-to-day operation of Chisolm Biological Laboratory, Chip also consults on the production of Transfer Factors with companies in Europe and the US.

Pam Floener, P.T., R.M.A., C.N.C., CT.

...is a Registered Medical Assistant, Certified Nutritional Counselor and Chelation Technician. She graduated from Tampa College as a Physician's Technician in 1975. Pam lectures, trains and provides consulting services to physicians, dentists and pharmacists in specialized laboratory testing, oral nutritional and IV therapies. She owned a laboratory testing service in Atlanta, Georgia, for 8 years .She has worked with all medical specialties in traditional and alternative medicine in the U.S., Canada and Europe.

Pam is the President of Preventhium International, Inc., which produces a dl-methionine based nutritional product. Pam is also the US and Canadian representative for Heyltex in Houston, Texas, a division of Heyl Pharm. Fabrik in Berlin, Germany, manufacturer of DMPS, an antidote to toxic metal poisoning.

She is a member of the American Registry of Medical Assistants, American Association of Nutritional Consultants, National Association of Compounding Pharmacists, Viet Nam Veterans of America and International Academy of Oral Medicine and Toxicology where she serves as vice-chair of the Anti-toxic Program committee. Her principal area of interest is heavy metal toxicity. Her motto is, "I've seen the science—ban mercury now."

To contact Pam, e-mail to Preventhium@mindspring.com, health.preventhium @mindspring.com or write to Preventhium International, Inc., 5885 Cumming Hwy 108-291, Sugar Hill, Georgia, 30518.

S. David Garshowitz, B.Sc. Phm., F.A.C.A.

...graduated from the University of Toronto Faculty of Pharmacy in 1955, majoring in drug manufacturing and hospital pharmacy administration. He is the President of San Pharmacy Limited, operating York Downs Pharmacy, 3910 Bathurst Street, Toronto, Ontario, 1 (800) 564-5020, and San Total Health Pharmacy, 5954 High-way 7 East, Markham, Ontario, 1 (888) 993-3666.

Garshowitz's pharmacies specialize in the compounding of sterile injectable medications, natural hormone replacement therapy, preparation of allopathic medications—integrating mainstream and complementary medicine (supplementation, enzymes, homeopathic remedies, et cetera). These pharmacies act as information centers to the community and to health practitioners concerning drug/drug, drug/herb, and herb/herb interactions.

Garshowitz is a member of the following professional pharmaceutical organizations: Professional Compounding Centers of America, Fellow American College of Apothecaries, American Nutraceuticals Association, American Academy of Antiaging Medicine, Ontario College of Pharmacists, Ontario Pharmaceutical Association, Canadian Pharmaceutical Association, Drug Information and Research Center, Metro Toronto Pharmacists Association, and the Rho Pi Phi International Pharmaceutical Fraternity.

Naomi Gold

...is completing a Ph.D. dissertation on the relationship between psychology and religious belief. She is also widely read in "alternative," non-traditional philosophies of education, and maintains an active interest in contemporary religious movements, eastern religions, and the phenomenon of "New Age" spirituality.

Dr. George Grant, M.Sc., M.Ed., Ed.D., C. Chem.

...is a multi-talented scientist who pioneered the research on Beta Endorphins, anti-cancer drugs, Lactobacilus viridescens model system to investigate microbial greening, HPLC analysis of B vitamins, GC-MS drug identification of potential drugs for prostate cancer, indoor air quality problems as related to Tight Building Syndrome and his well known research on Stress Management and Wellness.

He is listed in the International Who's Who of Professionals. Dr.Grant holds two patents on Modified Atmosphere Packaging (MAP) and Liposomal Weight Management spray.

He is the author of several published research articles, book reviews, conference presentations, and hundreds of public speaking engagements across North America. Dr. Grant is an active member of five professional organizations in the U.S.A. and Canada. He is a licensed Analytical Chemist, Certified Industrial Hygienist, Food/Nutrition Scientist, College Professor and Consultant for several international firms. He is married and a father of two boys.

Dr. Grant is known nationally and internationally as a wellness coach. He makes presentations in the U.S.A. and Canada. To contact Dr. Grant via E-mail: drgeorgegrant@hotmail.com or write c/o AGES Publications/Ellipsis address on page 377.

Marla Hauer, B.A., B. Ed.

...is an elementary school teacher in Ontario, Canada, since 1979. She has qualifications in Special Education and French. Marla has written children's stories, educational French plays, and screen play treatments.Her first collection of parable's for children is to be published in 2002.

Marla makes presentation to educators/teachers and parent groups.

To arrange a seminar and/or workshop presentation by Marla, contact her via e-mail at marlahauer@hotmail.com or write c/o AGES Publications, address on page 377.

Jane Hersey

...has worked with chemically-sensitive children for 25 years. Using the findings of pediatrician/allergist Ben Feingold, M.D., she first helped her family and went on to volunteer in the parent support group called the Feingold Association. She worked closely with Dr. Feingold until his death in 1982, and served the Association in many capacities: first vice-president, president, executive director, and editor of the Association's newsletter, *Pure Facts*. She is currently the national director. Hersey has testified before the National Institutes of Health and has represented the Association on radio and television.

Jane can be contacted at the Feingold Association of the U.S.A., in Alexandria, VA by calling (703) 768-3287 or 1 (800) 321-3287, or through the web site http://www.ADHDdiet.com/.

Fred Hui, M.D.

...is an examiner and the past president of the Acupuncture Foundation of Canada. He graduated as an M.D. from the University of Toronto, and is a lecturer at its faculty of Medicine. Dr. Hui's practice idealized the beauty of the integration of Eastern and Western medicine, complimentary and allopathic medicine. He possesses tremendous in-depth knowledge on Chelation therapy, natural hormone replacement therapies, Western, Chinese and Herbal medicine, Acupuncture and various Injection Therapies.

Dr. Hui is a highly respected medical practitioner in the treatment of heart and circulatory problems, mercury and other heavy metal toxicities, neuralgic and musculoskeletal pain, chronic tiredness and other "challenging" problems. His patients described him as "ethical, keen, conscientious, caring and resourceful."

He is well known as a newspaper columnist, radio host, much sought after lecturer and keynote speaker. His numerous national TV and media appearances earned him the reputation as an "eloquent, dynamic, smiling and knowledgeable teacher and scholar."

To read the numerous articles written by the media and his patients about Dr. Hui, please visit the Web Site at www.drhui.com.

To contact Dr. Hui, send your e-mail to ages@800line.com or write AGES Publications™, Attention Dr. Hui at the address on page 377.

Harold N. Levinson, M.D.

...is a world-renowned psychiatrist and neurologist. Dr. Levinson began his pioneering research on dyslexia 35 years ago within the New York City Board of Education. Previously Clinical Associate Professor of Psychiatry at NYU Medical Center, Dr. Levinson is currently Clinical/Research Director of the Levinson Medical Center for Learning Disabilities—now active in New York, England, and Hong Kong.

He has written eight books and many scientific papers dealing with the cerebellar-vestibular (inner-ear) origins and treatments of dyslexia and related learning, attention deficit and anxiety or phobic disorders. His groundbreaking research has been reviewed by such popular media as The New York Times, Science, Time, and Smithsonian, as well as by national and even international radio and TV.

Dr. Levinson's best selling books include:
- *Feeling Smarter and Smarter* (Stonebridge, in press 2001)
- *The Discovery of Cerebellar-Vestibular Syndromes and Therapies – A Solution to the Riddle – Dyslexia* (Stonebridge, 2000, a reprinting of the 1980 publication)
- *Smart But Feeling Dumb* (Warner, 1984; revised 1994)
- *A Scientific Watergate – Dyslexia* (Stonebridge, 1994)
- *Turning Around the Upside-Down Kids* (Evans, 1992)
- *The Upside-Down Kids* (Evans, 1991)
- *Total Concentration* (Evans, 1990)
- *Phobia Free* (Evans 1986)
- *A Solution to the Riddle – Dyslexia* (Springer-Verlag, 1980)

To obtain invaluable insights into Dr. Levinson's clinically based research as well as world-wide media responses, and most important, the dramatic improvement of his many and diverse patients, visit his web site at www.dyslexiaonline.com

Dr. Richard Lord, Ph.D.

...received his PhD in biochemistry from the University of Texas in 1970 with subsequent postdoctoral fellowships at the Clayton Foundation Biochemical Institute, the University of Arizona and the National Institutes of Health. He taught biochemistry and nutrition for 10 years at Life University, where he was instrumental in the initiation and design of a Bachelor of Science degree program in Clinical Nutrition. Since joining MetaMetrix in 1989, he has been actively involved in laboratory method development, clinical research, lecturing, authoring books and papers and consulting with health professionals regarding the application of nutritional metabolic assays to patient care.

Dr. Lord has received numerous awards including the following:

- Clayton Foundation Post-Doctoral Fellowship, Univ. of Texas, 1970.
- National Institutes of Health Post-Doctoral Fellowship, 1971.
- Clinical Laboratory Director License, 1976.
- Director of Research, S. Acad. Clin. Nutr., 1980-1984.
- National Board of Chiropractic Examiners Test Selection Committee, 1982-86.
- Editorial Board Member, Today's Chiropractic, 1985-89.
- Georgia Nutrition Council, Member, 1988
- The Magic Foundation for Children's Growth, Outstanding Medical Service Award, 1996

Dr. Lord has been instrumental in the development of the following laboratory methods:

- Trace elements in blood, urine, and hair by ICP/MS, ICP/OA, GFAA and Hg/Cold Vapor.
- Fatty acids in erythrocytes and plasma by GC/MS.
- Organic acids in urine by GC/MS.
- Amino acids in plasma and urine by HPLC.
- IgG4 90-well plate reader data transform automation.
- COBAS FARA/MIRA data acquisition and user interface.

Dr. Lord's has been published in numerous professional publications and made numerous presentations to professional groups in the U.S.A.

To contact Dr. Richard Lord, email Metametrix Clinical Laboratory in Norcross, Georgia at info@metametrix.com.

Michael Lyon, M.D.

...is a physician and medical researcher, and is the Director of Research and Education at the Oceanside Functional Medicine Research Institute on Vancouver Island, Canada.

He earned degrees in biology and medicine at the University of Calgary and he then successfully completed three years of accredited post graduate residency training in Oklahoma, Texas, Kansas and British Columbia. Following this, he served for four years as an Olympic Team physician as well as the head of a National Sport Science Committee for a division of Sport Canada.

He has lectured extensively in the fields of preventive and sports medicine and he received a national award for teaching by the Society for Teachers in Family

Medicine. His current research efforts are directed toward developing new, non-pharmacologic strategies for the treatment of attention deficit hyperactivity disorder.

Dr. Lyon is the author of *Healing the Hyperactive Brain; Through the New Science of Functional Medicine.*

To discover more information about Functional Medicine, visit Dr. Michael Lyon's web site at: www.oceansidemedicine.ca

Additional web sites on Functional Medicine include www.PureLiving.com and www.fxmed.com.

To contact Dr. Lyon send your e-mail to Drlyon@island.net

By mail write c/o AGES Publications, Attention Dr. M. Lyon at the address on page 377.

Dorothy Marshall, Ph.d., N.D., N.H.C.

...is the Chief Executive Officer of the International Academy of Natural Health Sciences and the International Academy of Massage (www.intlacademy.com), as well as, the Resident Practitioner at the Natural Health Clinic, all in Ottawa, Ontario, Canada. She is also the founder of the Reflexology Association of Canada.

Dorothy is an internationally respected lecturer, educator and practitioner. Recipient of the Star of Asia and the coveted Dag Hammarskjold awards. She has dedicated over 30 years to improving the health of individuals, through her philosophy of "educating the patient towards self participation and responsibility for their own health care."

Correspondence address: International Academy of Natural Health Sciences, 2605 Carling Ave., Ottawa, Ontario, Canada K2B 6V3 or send your email to iamnhs@intlacademy.com.

To discover more information about Dorothy Marshall's educational facility visit their web site www.intlacademy.com

Nancy L. Morse, B.Sc. [Hons], CNPA

...began her career in medical research in 1982 at the Efamol Research Institute in Kentville, Nova Scotia, where she was involved in developing nutritional and pharmaceutical products based on fatty acids. She was appointed Deputy Laboratory Director in 1993, and promoted to Vice President and Corporate Director in 1994. She is co-author of more than 25 publications in peer-reviewed biochemical and medical journals. She has also been an invited speaker at universities, taught courses and workshops throughout North America and has been a guest on radio and television talk shows.

Nancy is a Governor for the Atlantic Provinces Economic Council (APEC) and has been since 1994. She was appointed to the Board of Directors of *BioNova*, the Nova Scotia Life Sciences Industry Association in 1995, and has been the Vice President since 1997. In 1999, Nancy was awarded an entry in the distinguished publication, *Chatelaines Who's Who of Canadian Women*.

Nancy is currently the Scientific Advisor for Efamol Canada (1998) Limited (Nutricia) and is a certified Natural Products Advisor through the Canadian Health Food Association and the Canadian College of Naturopathic Medicine.

Selim Nakla, M.D.

...is a medical graduate from the oldest university in the world, Alexandria University, Egypt. He has been published in the American Journal of Obstetrics, Gynecology and Neunatology. For the past fourteen years he has been practicing a blend of traditional and holistic medicine. His primary focus is holistic medicine, including modalities such as physiotherapy, rehabilitation medicine, and acupuncture.

Dr. Nakla presentations currently focus on nutrition and alternative medicine. His primary focus is helping people help themselves, using as non-intrusive a style as possible, for their health and wellbeing. He has presented in the U.S.A., Canada, Italy and Egypt.

Selim is a member of the American Academy of Anti-aging, SPA Canada Associations, and Canadian Complementary Medical Association.

He is the President of the Medical Resource Group, an internet company listed on the Nasdaq. Selim was the doctor for the year 2000 World Champion Canadian Pankration team, the oldest form of competitive wrestling, and continues in that position as their doctor for the 2004 Olympic Games being held in Athens, Greece.

To access the the Medical Resource Group visit their web site: Wellnessinfonet.com. To contact Dr. Nakla, email him at: sn@wellnessinfonet.com

Aleks Radojcic, Dr. Ac., R.N.C.P.

...is of a doctor of acupuncture and registered nutritional consultant practitioner (Dr. Ac., R.N.C.P.). He is a formulator and president of Knowledge Products and founder of the Holistic Clinic for Health and Harmony in Toronto, Ontario, Canada. He is a:

Professional Member of Nutrition Consulting Organization of Canada.
Bonafide Member, Canadian Academy of Chinese Traditional Health Sciences.
Member of Consumers Health Organization of Canada.
Professional Member of Canadian Health Food Association.

Dr. Aleks Radojcic has studied various methods of holistic healing since 1976. Some of his well known teachers included: Bernard Jehnsen D.C., N.D., John Ray D.C., N.D., George Lewith M.D., D.Ac., Prof. Anton Jayasuria, M.D., D.Ac., Master Choa Kok Sui and others. For about 10 years, Aleks Radojcic was a member of Natural Hygiene Association following the teachings of Dr. Shelton.

Over the years, Dr. Aleks Radojcic has given lectures at the Whole Life Expo, CHFA Expos, Lectures on iridology, nutrition, whole body cleansing methods and pranic energy healing. He has written articles for Vitality Quebec, Alive magazine, and Knowledge Products, and is in process of completing a book entitled *Knowledge of Complete Healing*.

In his clinic, Aleks uses the leading edge body stress testing instrument— B.E.S.T. (Biomeridian), a testing tool with ability to screen individual patient's needs from thousands of homeopathic, herbal and dietary supplements.

Aleks Radojcic holistic approach to health is carried through his teachings and preventive herbal cleansing formulae.

To discover more information about Knowledge Products herbal cleansing formulae for parasite and detoxification products visit these web sites: www.800line.com or www.bahironline.com

Michael Rae

...is the technical writer for Advanced Orthomolecular Research, one of Canada's most advanced supplement lines. AOR was the first Canadian company to make such potent orthomolecules as SAMe, Tocotrienols, and Pantethine, as well as Prostaphil defined pollen extract, available to Canadians. For more information, access their website: www.holisticinternational.com.

Dr. Paul Richard Saunders, Ph.D., N.D., D.H.A.N.P., C.C.H.
Chair, Materia Medica Canadian College of Naturopathic Medicine

...is Chair of Materia Medica (Botanical and Homeopathic Medicines), Professor of Clinical Medicine and has a private practice in Dundas. After completing undergraduate premedical training, a master of science and a year in seminary he earned a Ph.D. in plant ecology from Duke University and taught for over a decade at Clemson University and Washington State University. Still interested in medicine, he took a sabbatical, attended and graduated from Ontario (now Canadian) College of Naturopathic Medicine with an N.D., and did additional training and residency at National College of Naturopathic Medicine, Portland, Oregon, and served as their interim Research Director. Paul completed his board examinations and was awarded a Diplomate from the Homeopathic Academy of Naturopathic Physicians (D.H.A.N.P.) and Certified Classical Homeopath (C.C.H.) from the American Council on Homeopathic Certification in 1993.

He completed his board examinations in chelation therapy with the Great Lakes Academy of Clinical Medicine in 1998. In 2000, he assumed the position of Editor, The Canadian Journal of Herbalism.

In 1994, he was honored as the Ontario Naturopathic Doctor of the Year for his contributions to student clinical education. In 1996, he was appointed to the Advisory Committee on Management, Therapeutic Products Division, and in 1999, to the Transition Team for the Office of Natural Health Products, Health Protection Branch, Ottawa, Canada.

In 1998, he received the President's Award from the Canadian Naturopathic Association for his advancement of naturopathic medicine internationally. His teaching responsibilities have included botanical and homeopathic medicine, differential diagnosis, physical and clinical diagnosis, laboratory diagnosis, history and philosophy and parenteral therapy.

Paul has been published in numerous magazine, books and professional associations. He frequently lectures on naturopathic medicine, which can be arranged through the Communications and Marketing Department of the college.

To access more information about Naturopathic Medicine visit the colleges web site at www.ccnm.edu or call the college in Toronto, Canada at (416) 498-1255.

Laurie Simmons, H.D., D.H.M.S.,

...is a homeopathic doctor in Toronto, Canada. She received her training in homeopathy and medical sciences from the Homeopathic College of Canada. In addition to her private practice in Toronto, she speaks regularly on homeopathy and has made several television appearances promoting the natural health care of children. She is an executive director of The Ontario Homeopathic Association and is currently writing a book on children's health.

Dr. Michael O. Smith, M.D.

...works at the Lincoln Hospital Recovery Center Bronx, New York. His contribution is about the use of acupressure beads, called "ear magnet seeds" in Chinese, in the treatment of ADHD.

For patient treatment and professional inquiries about the use of acupressure beads in the treatment of Attention Deficit Hyperactivity Disorder (ADHD), contact:

Lincoln Medical and Mental Health Center
Recovery Program Center
234 Eugenio Maria De Hostos Blvd.,
Bronx, New York, 10451
Tel: (718) 993-3100

Daniel Tamin, B.Sc., (Biology/Kinesiology)

...works as a personal trainer and health consultant. Areas of interest include; benefits of strength training for older adults and persons with special disabilities, cardiac rehabilitation, sports nutrition, weight gain/loss ergogenic aids, endocrinology/intracrinolgy and pharmacology.

Can be contacted at biofit@hotmail.com

Dr. Lynda Thompson, Ph.D.

...is the Executive Director of the ADD Centre in Toronto, Canada. Her doctorate is in Applied Psychology (University of Toronto). Prior to graduate studies, she left Canada to take a position teaching high school in Europe. Her Ph.D. thesis dealt with self esteem in hyperactive children treated with methylphenidate (Ritalin). That research was conducted at the Neuropsychology Research Unit at the Hospital for Sick Children in Toronto, Canada in the mid 1970s.

Since that time, Lynda has worked in clinical psychology, in school psychology, and as the owner/director of learning centers. Since 1993, she has been the Executive Director of the ADD Center.

She holds certification in EEG Biofeedback from the Biofeedback Certification Institute of America (BCIA), is on the Executive Committee of the BCIA and is the former Chair of the Education Committee of the Association for Applied Psychophysiology and Biofeedback.

Together with Dr. William Sears, one of America's most trusted pediatricians. She has co-authored the *A.D.D. Book: New Understandings, New Approaches to Parenting Your Child,* and is a contributor to this book.

To access information about the ADD Centre visit their web site: www.addcentre.com

Ken Vegotsky, B.Sc.

...is the project coordinator. He is a professional speaker, author and entrepreneur who has given keynote addresses and seminars in the U.S.A. and Canada. He has been featured in print, radio and TV in the U.S.A., Canada, Australia, New Zealand, United Kingdom and a host of other countries.

"Ken is the Victor Frankl of our day," noted Dottie Walters, President, Walters Speakers Bureau International, and author of *Speak & Grow Rich.*

Mark Victor Hansen, New York Times #1 bestselling co-author of the *Chicken Soup for the Soul* series, says Ken's work is, ***"Brilliant and illuminating."***

"In recognition of being seen as a model of courage and hope for others, who demonstrates to all of us the nobility of the human spirit," begins the Clarke Foundation nomination of Ken for a *Courage to Come Back Award*. These awards were originated by the St. Francis Health Foundation of Pittsburgh, Pennsylvania.

Ken has served on the boards of NACPAC (affiliate of the American Chronic Pain Association), a community information service and a half-way home for mentally challenged people in transition. After numerous inspirational speeches, he was encouraged by listeners to tell his story.

In his National Bestseller, *The Ultimate Power,* Ken shares his captivating first-person account of his near-death experience, garnished with proven keys for unlocking your personal power.

He is the author of the soon to be released *The Prophet Revisited*. Michael Murray, N.D., author of international bestselling *The Encyclopedia of Natural Medisine,* writes *"The Prophet Revisited is inspirational and uplifting. Powerful messages delivered in a gentle yet thought provoking way. Sprinkled with humor, which will enrich your life. A spiritual classic destined to become a bestseller that will stand the test of time. Read it and tell everyone you know to do the same."*

"A true reflection of Kahlil Gibran's The Prophet. You will treasure this beautiful book for now and for always. I loved it. A masterpiece!" writes Hennie Bekker, multi-platinum award winning composer/producer of the "Tranquility", "Kaleidoscopes", "Solitudes" and "African Tapestries" series.

Discover *How to Make Love With Life!*™ and you'll feel embraced by caring and compassion as you share Ken's thought provoking, life affirming powerful message and moving experiences.

Contact Ken Vegotsky via E-mail through: ages@800line.com or write AGES Publications, Attention Ken Vegotsky at the address on page 377.

For presentations by Ken, contact Speakers Unlimited, Box 27225, Columbus, Ohio, 43227, Tel: 614-864-3703, Fax: 614-864-3876, *or* Masterpiece Corporation Speakers and Trainers Bureau™, One Babington Court, Islington, Ontario, Canada M9A 1J7, Tel: 416-239-6300, Fax: 416-232-9343

Index

Glucose, 44, 66, 140–143, 171–172, 176,
180, 251.
Glutamic acid, 45, 134, 136, 171,
178–180, 184, 272, 275.
Glutamine, 45, 70, 169, 171, **178–180**.
Glycemic Index, 140–143.
Glycerin, 121, 166, 182.
Glycine, 47, 67–68, 169, 171, **176**, 178,
180, 186, 188.
Gotu Kola, 163.
Graci, Sam, 120.
Grant, George, **168**.
Great Ormand Street Hospital Study, 116.
Green, Elmer, 227.
–also see Biofeedback Research Society
Guaranteed potency, 166.
Guided Imagery, **244**, 248, 250–253.

— H —

Haldol, 272, 275.
Hampton, Aubrey, 120.
Hartmann, Thom, 223.
Hauer, Marla, **254–255**, 258.
Hazardous waste, 92, 131.
Health Canada, 92, 132.
Health Protection Branch, 120, 131, 134.
Health Protection and Promotion Branch,
265.
Herbalist, 162–165.
Herbs, –see Avena sativa, Centalla asiatica,
Gelsemium sempervirens, German
chamomile, Gotu Kola, Hops,
Humulus lupulus, Hypericum perfora-
tum, Kava Kava, Lactuca virosa,
Matricaria chamomilla, Oat straw,
Passilfora incarnata, Passion flower,
Piper methysticum, St. John's wort,
Valerian, Valeriana officinalis, Wild let-
tuce, Yellow jasmine.
Hersey, Jane, **107**.
High blood pressure, –see Side effect.
Histidine, 171, **181**.
Holistic, 32, 72, 75, 98, 208.
Homeopathy, 72, 171, **193–195**, 203.
Homeostasis, 99, 145, 151.
Hops, 104, 164.
Hormone, 74, 78–79, 120, 135, 152, 155,
170–172, 178–179, 182, 184, 188.
HPB, –see Health Protection Branch.

HPPB, –see Health Protection and
Promotion Branch.
Hsien-t'ien chi, 99.
Hui, Dr. Fred, **91**, 95, **168**.
Humulus lupulus, 162.
HydroDIURIL, 272.
Hypericum perforatum, 164, 291.
–also see St. John's wort.
Hypoactive sexual desire disorder, 265.
Hytrin, 272.

— I —

Imipramine, –see Drug Treatment.
Impulsive, 24, 30, 35, 198, 200, 212, 219,
222, 225, 234, 238.
Infection, 37, 64, 72, 74, 76–77, 79,
84–89, 99, 114, 139, 146, 157, 163,
179, 182, 187, 206, 202, 289.
Infusion, 96, 166.
Inner-Ear, **21–23**, 26–29, 32.
–also see Cerebellar-Vestibular dysfunction
Insomnia, 30, 102, 104, 163–165, 195,
204, 212, 271, 273, 279, 285,
292–293, 296, 302, 304.
Insulin, 66, 126, 143–144, 172, 176, 179,
184, 187, 266, 302.
Isolation, 258.
Isoleucine, 168, 171, **181–182**, 189.

— J —

Jensen, Dr. Bernard, 55, 58, 72–73, 75.

— K —

Kamiya, Dr. Joe, 229.
Kava Kava, 165.
Ken, Bahir Ben, 310, 313–314.
Koletzko, Dr., 152.
Kosher, 131–132.
Ku chi, 99.

— L —

Lactuca virosa, 164.
LDL, –see Cholesterol –LDL.
Leap (story), 258.
Legumes, 142–144.
Leucine, 168, 171, 180, **182**, 189.

-blood pressure low, 276, 285, 289, 295–296, 298.
-blood pressure low when standing up, 289.
-blood sugar high, 285, 293, 296.
-blood sugar low, 285, 289, 293, 296.
-blood sugar rises, 289.
-bluish skin, 295.
-blurred vision, 277, 282, 285, 293, 300.
-bone disease, 290.
-breast cysts, 289.
-breast(s) enlarged, 285, 290, 293, 296.
-breast milk production in females, 289.
-breathing fast, 273, 276, 289.
-breathing stops temporarily, 289.
-bronchitis, 288.
-burning or tingling sensation, 300.
-cataracts, 290.
-changes in pulse rate, 277.
-chest pain severe, 277, 279, 282, 288–289.
-chills, 282, 288, 289.
-colitis, 290.
-collapse, 293.
-coma, 273, 276, 280, 284, 287, 290, 295, 298.
-confusion, 273, 276, 278, 280, 282–283, 285, 287, 289, 293, 296, 298.
-congestive heart failure, 293.
-conjunctivitis, 289.
-constipation, 271, 274, 282, 285, 293, 296, 299.
-convulsion, 273, 276, 278, 280, 287, 289–290, 293, 295, 298.
-coordination problems, 275, 282, 285, 289, 293, 296.
-cough, 288, 293.
-dazed feeling, 300.
-deafness, 290.
-dehydration, 290.
-delirium, 278, 280.
-delusions, 285, 293, 296.
-depression, 271, 274, 276, 279, 303, 304.
-diarrhea, 271–274, 276, 285, 288, 290, 293, 296, 299.
-diarrhea that is bloody, 290.
-difficulties concentrating, 287, 298–299.
-difficulties controlling bowel movements, 290.

-disorientation, 285, 293, 296.
-dizziness, 271, 274, 277, 279, 282–283, 285, 288, 293, 296, 299, 303–304.
-double vision, 290.
-drowsiness, 277, 279, 283, 285, 286–288, 290, 293–300, 304.
-drug hypersensitivity, 279.
-dry mouth, 271, 274, 282, 285, 288, 293, 296, 299, 302–303.
-dryness of mucous membranes, 278, 304.
-duodenal ulcer, 290.
-ejaculatory abnormalities, 282, 285, 289, 299.
-emotional instability, 293.
-exaggerated reflexes, 273, 280, 287, 295, 298.
-excessive calmness, 282.
-excessive flow of milk, 285, 293, 296.
-extreme Aggresiveness, 273, 276.
-eyelids drooping, 290.
-eyes and eyelids inflamed, 289.
-eyes yellowing of, 279, 285, 290, 293, 296.
-esophageal inflammation, 289.
-excessive coarse hair growth, 289.
-extreme feeling of well-being, 271, 274, 280, 289, 300.
-extreme sensitivity to light, 285–286, 289, 293–294, 296–297.
-eyesight disturbances, 289.
-fainting, 290, 293.
-fallopian tubes inflamed, 289.
-fatigue, 276, 279, 282, 285, 288, 293, 296.
-fever, 273, 276–277, 282, 284–287, 289, 293, 295–298.
-flushing, 278, 280, 285, 293.
-frequent urination, 285, 288, 293, 296.
-flu symptoms of, 282, 288.
-fluid retention, 285, 289, 293, 296.
-gallbladder inflamed, 289.
-gallstones, 289.
-gas (flatulence), 289, 299.
-glaucoma, 289.
-gout, 290.
-gums inflamed, 282, 289.
-hair loss of, 282, 285, 289, 293, 296.
-hallucinations, 273, 276, 278–280, 283, 285, 287–288, 293, 296, 298, 300.
-hay fever, 288.

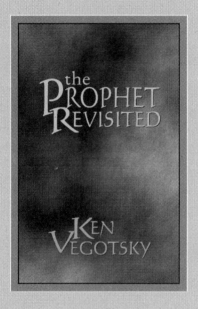

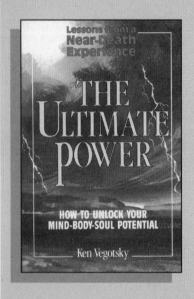

AGES Publications™ Order Form

	Qty	Price	Total
the All-In-One Guide to™ ADD & Hyperactivity		$12.95	
the All-In-One Guide to™ Natural Remedies and Supplements		$9.95	
the All-In-One Guide to™ Tea Tree Oil		$7.95	
The Prophet Revisited - Hardcover book		$15.00	
The Prophet Revisited - CD Gift Set		$29.95	
The Ultimate Power		$9.95	
••• Round-Up ••• *By E-Mail* A Summary of the Best in Health Newsletters from Around the World™		$18.97	
••• Round-Up ••• *By Postal Service*		$36.97	

($5.00 for 1st + $0.50 for each additional item)	Shipping	
	Total	

E-Mail _____

Name _____

Address _____

_____

City _____ ZIP _____

Phone _____

Please make certified check/money order payable to and send to
Adi, Gaia, Esalen Publications Inc.
1623 Military Rd. PMB 203-AD, Niagara Falls, NY 14304-1745

VISA ❏   MasterCard ❏   American Express ❏

Card #: _____ Exp. Date: _____

Signature: _____

North America – Order Toll Free 1 888 545-0053

Order or request information On-Line
www.agespublications.com

Trade and Bulk order enquiries welcomed